A HISTORY OF COMMUNICATIONS

A History of Communications advances a new theory of media that explains the origins and impact of different forms of communication – speech, writing, print, electronic devices, and the Internet – on human history in the long term. New types of media are "pulled" into widespread use by broad historical trends, and, once in widespread use, these media "push" social institutions and beliefs in predictable directions. This view allows us to see for the first time what is truly new about the Internet, what is not, and where it is taking us.

Marshall T. Poe, Associate Professor of History at the University of Iowa, is the author or editor of several books, including *A People Born to Slavery: Russia in Early Modern European Ethnography* (2000), *The Russian Elite in the Seventeenth Century* (2004), and *The Russian Moment in World History* (2006). He is the co-founder and editor of *Kritika: Explorations in Russian and Eurasian History* and founder and host of "New Books in History" (http://newbooksinhistory.com), as well as a former writer and editor for *The Atlantic Monthly*. Professor Poe has been a Fellow at the Institute for Advanced Study (Princeton University), the Harriman Institute (Columbia University), and the Kennan Institute (Washington, DC).

A HISTORY OF COMMUNICATIONS

Media and Society from the
Evolution of Speech to the Internet

MARSHALL T. POE

University of Iowa

 CAMBRIDGE
UNIVERSITY PRESS

CAMBRIDGE UNIVERSITY PRESS
Cambridge, New York, Melbourne, Madrid, Cape Town, Singapore,
São Paulo, Delhi, Dubai, Tokyo, Mexico City

Cambridge University Press
32 Avenue of the Americas, New York, NY 10013-2473, USA

www.cambridge.org
Information on this title: www.cambridge.org/9780521179447

First published 2011

Printed in the United States of America

A catalog record for this publication is available from the British Library.

Library of Congress Cataloging in Publication data
Poe, Marshall.
A history of communications : media and society from the evolution of speech
to the Internet / Marshall T. Poe.
p. cm.
Includes bibliographical references and index.
ISBN 978-1-107-00435-1 (hardback) – ISBN 978-0-521-17944-7 (pbk.)
1. Communication – Social aspects.   2. Digital media – Social aspects.   I. Title.
HM1206.P64   2010
302.209 – dc22   2010031501

ISBN 978-1-107-00435-1 Hardback
ISBN 978-0-521-17944-7 Paperback

CONTENTS

TABLES AND CHARTS

TABLES

CHARTS

vii

PREFACE

I suppose it would be fair to say that I began writing this book in 1989, when I had the good fortune of working for Professor Albert Lord just before his death. Professor Lord, together with his colleague, Professor Milman Parry, had, many decades earlier, revolutionized Classical scholarship by proposing that "Homer" was not a writer, but an oral tradition. In a series of landmark studies, Professors Lord and Parry showed that the traces of oral composition – in this case, singing – could be seen in the texts of the *Iliad* and the *Odyssey*. Honestly, it was all lost on me. I was just there to keep Professor Lord's office uncluttered and sort his mail. Since his office was already uncluttered and he sorted his own mail, I was often left with free time. I used it to look through Professor Lord's library. In it, I found several books devoted to the study of the media and their effects by Marshall McLuhan, Jack Goody, and others. Having nothing better to do except work on my dissertation, I read them and was rather taken away. These early communications theorists made all kinds of fascinating claims about the impact of the media on, well, everything. I didn't know whether they were right or not, but I decided I could use their sexy ideas to make my own pedestrian research seem "theoretically informed," which, to that point, it was not. The result was a series of articles that, thankfully, have passed from obscurity into still deeper obscurity.

Thereafter, I thought nothing of the media until, by another lucky stroke, I landed a job in it at *The Atlantic Monthly* in 2002. I was part of a small team that the owner of the magazine, David Bradley, had given the humble task of preparing the storied magazine for the twenty-first century. You will not be surprised to learn that the thing principally on our minds was the Internet and the question principally on our lips was "What will it do?" I was immediately reminded of my lazy days in Professor Lord's well-kept office and the reading I had done there. Upon quick review, I concluded that the early media theorists had left me – or rather us – singularly unprepared to understand the Internet. What wisdom did they have to impart about, say, the birth and explosion of Wikipedia? None that I could see. More recent media theorists proposed that the Internet was incomprehensible by the lights of older theories because it was new. They said that we had never seen anything like the Internet in world history, that it "broke all the rules." I suspected that these theorists didn't know very much about world history or the supposedly shattered rules. With this in mind, I began to try to understand the Internet historically; not as something brand new, but as the most recent iteration of something very old – the appearance of a new medium. It had, after all, happened before. First we spoke. Then we wrote. Then we printed. Then we listened to the radio and watched TV. And now we surf the Internet. Each of these media was different from the others, but all of them were of a piece – tools that we used to send, receive, store, and retrieve messages. The Internet, it seemed to me, was not so much brand new as a variation on an ancient theme.

The book before you is the result of my attempt to discover the ways in which that theme has varied with successive media technologies. Whether I've hit the mark is for the reader to judge. My only hope is that Professor Lord would smile on my effort to understand something that was so close to his heart for so long.

ACKNOWLEDGMENTS

It has become customary in acknowledgments to provide a long list of people who contributed to the project at hand. Alas, I have no such list because I researched and wrote this book largely in solitude. Still, there are people to thank, people without whom this book would not exist. They include Craig Kennedy, who handed me a review of a book by Jack Goody about two decades ago; Matt Kay, who got me a job working for Albert Lord, also a long time ago; the "Ninjas" at *The Atlantic Monthly*, with whom I investigated the "new media" in the early 2000s; Scott Stossel, also of *The Atlantic Monthly*, who helped me write an article about Wikipedia in 2005; my agent, Bob Mecoy, who encouraged me to write a book about Wikipedia and who, when I spent several years not doing so, stuck with me; my colleagues in the history department at the University of Iowa, who patiently waited for a book that was "done" to be done; my editor at Cambridge University Press, Eric Crahan, who had outsized faith in this outsized project; and, most of all, my wife, intellectual companion, and mathematician extraordinaire, Julianna Tymoczko, who, were this a math article, would be credited as a co-author. This book is dedicated to her.

Marshall Poe
May 27, 2010
Iowa City

INTRODUCTION

MEDIA CAUSES AND MEDIA
EFFECTS

The premises with which we begin are not arbitrary ones, not dogmas, but real premises from which abstraction can only be made in the imagination. They are the real individuals, their activity and the material circumstances in which they live, both those which they find and those produced by their activity. These premises can thus be verified in a purely empirical way.

      – Karl Marx, *The German Ideology*, 1845[1]

In 1846, Karl Marx surveyed the philosophical scene in Germany. He was not happy with what he saw. The thinkers of his day, he complained, had mistaken speculative philosophy for hard science. They loved to play with ideas, but they never quite got around to testing them in the real world. The result was a thick bramble of vague concepts, imprecise notions, and fuzzy impressions that, while perhaps entertaining, never really added up to a concrete theory of anything. Marx thought these philosophers were doing their countrymen a disservice. Things were changing rapidly, and people needed to understand why. He therefore set about trying to explain these ongoing changes by means of a rigorous, empirically testable theory of history.

A similar situation obtains today in communications studies. The most influential thinkers in the field are, like the philosophers of Marx's day, a bit too fond of high-flown ideas and not fond enough of the solid facts. They propose theories that are at once hard to understand, difficult to test, and sometimes just plain wrong. These deficiencies are unfortunate because, as in Marx's era, things are changing rapidly. In the last quarter century, we have witnessed a rare event in human history: the birth of a new medium, the Internet. Although pundits tend to exaggerate its impact, it is certain that that impact is significant. The

Internet has changed the way we work, what we consume, how we play, whom we interact with, how we find things out, and myriad other details about the way we live. Yet we don't have a good way to understand where the Internet came from and what it is doing to us, so we are to some degree adrift.

This book is intended to help us find our way by means of two theories about the media in general and the Internet in particular. The first endeavors to explain why successive media – speech, writing, print, audiovisual devices, and the Internet – arose when and where they did. The second endeavors to explain what these media did and are doing to the way we organize ourselves and what we believe. In this introductory chapter, we will begin by discussing existing theories of media causes and effects, all of which, save one, are deficient. We will then turn to the single exception, the theory of media genesis and effects propounded by Harold Innis. Finally, building upon Innis's ideas, we will lay out the theories that form the backbone of this book.

MARSHALL McLUHAN

Any discussion of media theory must begin with Marshall McLuhan, if only because he coined its most famous expression – "the medium is the message." Everyone knows this cliché, everyone repeats it, but, alas, few agree on what it means or whether it's true. The same might be said of McLuhan's writings generally: they are widely known, they are widely read, yet they provoke as much head-scratching as comprehension. By all accounts, McLuhan was an adventurous, inventive, and imaginative thinker, but he didn't write very clearly. Here he is, for example, explaining "the medium is the message" in 1964.

In a culture like ours, long accustomed to splitting and dividing all things as a means of control, it is sometimes a bit of a shock to be reminded that, in operational and practical fact, the medium is the message. This is merely to say that the personal and social consequences of any medium – that is, of any extension of ourselves – result from the new scale that is introduced into our affairs by each extension of ourselves, or by any new technology.[2]

How should we understand this crucial passage? With a bit of effort, we can find the central hypothesis of all media studies – that media do *something* to us. Here McLuhan says they have "personal and social consequences," a promising start. You might think that the next sentence – or at least one nearby – would be something like "and those consequences are...," followed by a series of empirical claims. This medium does this, this medium does that, and this medium does the other thing. If you had such an expectation, you would be disappointed. Reading on, however, you would encounter random nuggets like "An abstract painting represents direct manifestation of creative thought processes as they might appear in computer design," and "Alexis de Tocqueville was the first to master the grammar of print and typography."[3] Yet, search as you might, you will find no clear, well-articulated theory linking specific causes – kinds of media – with specific effects – "personal and social consequences." Perhaps such a theory could be constructed out of carefully selected passages in McLuhan's oeuvre, but it would be a bit of a Frankenstein's monster – an unholy composite of parts never intended by their maker to be united in one being.

McLuhan, then, was not really a theorist in any straightforward, empirical sense. Nonetheless, we should recognize that he made a crucial contribution to media studies and therefore our project: he focused scholarly attention on the media themselves – talking, writing, printing, electronic signals – as opposed to the information the media convey. He separated the medium from the message and, in so doing, founded the central program of modern media studies, that which attempts to describe and explain the effects of media on the human mind and human groups. Nearly all researchers in media studies pursue some version of this program today. A number of reasonably coherent "schools," however, stand out: the Mentalist, the Marxist, and the Matrixist.

THE MENTALISTS, THE MARXISTS, AND THE MATRIXISTS

The Mentalists – Walter Ong, Eric Havelock, and Jack Goody being the best-known among them – are united in the conviction that media in general and literacy in particular make people think differently.[4] Learning to read and write, they propose, rewires the brain and enables new cognitive abilities. This was and remains a sensible, sexy hypothesis. We know that the brain undergoes radical changes during maturation, and as it does, new mental capacities emerge. Children can't talk and then they can. They can't reason and then they can. They can't do arithmetic and then they can. Learning to read and write – and by extension learning to use any other medium – must do something to our minds. It's true, it must. The difficulty is discovering just what that may be. If media are the cause, then what are the cognitive effects? The answer would seem to be simple enough: new modes of thought. But what are these "modes of thought"? How many are there? And what exactly differentiates them? The Mentalists often answer this question by positing dichotomies: "civilized" versus "savage" thought, "rational" versus "irrational" thought, "logical" versus "illogical" thought. These dualities are not very specific, but they do have the virtue of being real and therefore observable. Take the last of them, logical versus illogical. There is indeed something very specific called "logic"; it is used by the human mind to think; and it is unevenly distributed among humans – some people reason logically and some don't.

Logic, then, presents a clear test of the Mentalists' thesis that media change the way people think. If literacy causes logic, then the Mentalists are right; if not, they are wrong, at least as far as the impact of literacy is concerned. Careful anthropologists have run this test in the field and the results are definitive: there is no direct, causal relationship between learning to read and write and the cognitive capacity to think logically.[5] Teaching people to read and write has a significant impact on their ability to read and write, but not necessarily on their ability to reason. This result, of course, doesn't mean the Mentalists are incorrect on all counts. We may yet find ways in which media mold the mind. At present, however, we don't know of any.

While the Mentalists pursue the cognitive side of McLuhan's program, the Marxists and their modern followers, the Critical Theorists, investigate the macro-political side. The founders of this line of inquiry – Theodor Adorno, Max Horkheimer, Herbert Marcuse[6] – were practitioners of "media studies" *avant le lettre* and *avant* McLuhan. They were interested in a lot of different things, but one of their central concerns was to explain the persistence of capitalism long after Marx predicted it would collapse. Their disciples are still mining this vein.[7] The *marxisant* Critical Theorists are much less focused, though it would be fair to say that they are concerned with comprehending the way capitalist mass media engender and maintain various forms of illusion, alienation, and oppression.[8] The idea of a "Culture Industry" is central to the Marxists and Critical Theorists. Simply stated, the Culture Industry thesis holds that the late capitalist mass media turn people into obedient consumers, making them willing victims of exploitation, and thereby ensuring the survival of capitalism itself. In Marx's day, religion was the opiate of the masses; in our day, the Marxists and Critical Theorists claim, it's the mass media.

Like the Mentalists' literacy thesis, the Culture Industry thesis has the cardinal virtue of being testable. If we find that the presence of mass media hinders the development of socialist (or, generally, noncapitalist) institutions, then they are right; if not, they are wrong. Over the past half century this test has been run all over the world, and again the results are unmistakable: the presence of mass media has no discernable impact on the likelihood that a region will drift to the left. After World War II, Western Europe evolved a sort of free-market socialism; the United States did not. Since both had robust Culture Industries, we can conclude that the mass media had no determinative effect.[9] The Marxists and Critical Theorists are certainly correct that the media affect society. It's just that their theory is unable to describe or explain those effects.

The third school might be called "Postmodernist" or "Poststructuralist," but those tags are too broad. A more telegraphic tag would be the "Matrixist School," after the popular 1999 science fiction film *The Matrix*. The film portrays a universe comprised of a real part (the earth) and a computer-simulated part (the Matrix). Humans actually exist in the real part in life-support pods. They, however, don't know this. As far as they're concerned they live in a modern city circa 2000. But their city is only a very sophisticated representation. In short, the "residents" of the Matrix are brains in vats. The writings of Jean Baudrillard in some measure inspired the film.[10] In essence, Baudrillard argues that modern media have produced something like the Matrix.[11] Thanks to mass communications, Baudrillard says, we no longer live in a real world where representations refer to realities. Rather, we live in a media-created world where representations only refer to other representations. Of course, like the people in the fictional Matrix, we don't realize we are brains in vats. Thus, Baudrillard overturns McLuhan: the medium is no longer the message, but instead the technology that obscures all *real* messages.

It's hard to know what to make of Baudrillard's theory. It rests on a solid empirical foundation: people are sometimes fooled into thinking that representations are real. But, like the Marxists, the Matrixists seem to go too far.[12] Media are powerful, but they are not all-powerful. Most people have no difficulty distinguishing reality from representation, even when the latter is presented by fancy modern devices. Is there anyone who thinks that "Reality TV," for example, is reality in the full-blooded sense? Moreover, most people realize that the media can be used to trick them. Everyone knows not to "believe the hype" produced by the media. Hollywood is the "Dream Factory," not the "Reality Factory." The key question, empirically speaking, is this: How effective are different media *qua* media at deceiving people, or rather, at prompting them to confuse representation and reality? The Matrixists never pose this question, so they never answer it.

HAROLD INNIS

McLuhan pointed media studies in the right direction by telling us that media themselves – not the information they convey – do something to us, but he refused to be specific. The Mentalist, Marxist, and Matrix schools are specific, but their theories are empirically unsatisfying. If we desire a convincing theory of media effects, one that will explain the impact of media generally, then we will have to look elsewhere.

Fortunately, there is someplace promising to look, namely, to the neglected work of Harold Allen Innis. Innis was a peculiar figure.[13] He worked as an economic historian at the University of Toronto, where McLuhan was a student and later a professor. All of his early writings suggest a cast of mind that was profoundly different from McLuhan's. The titles of Innis's early monographs tell us much of the man: *A History of the Canadian Pacific Railroad* (1923), *Fur Trade in Canada: An Introduction to Canadian Economic History* (1930), *Cod Fisheries: The History of an International Economy* (1940).[14] These works were exercises in economic empiricism, not abstract engagements in high-flying theory. Believe it or not, they turned Innis into an academic celebrity. He was perhaps the most respected scholar in Canada in the prewar years, the celebrated founder of what is still known as the "Staples Theory" of Canadian economic development. In the early 1940s, Innis began – predictably enough – to study another staple of the Canadian economy, pulp and paper. This research, however, led him in a new and unforeseen direction.

Although all of Innis's writing had focused on Canadian economic history, he was an admirer of grand historical thinkers such as Oswald Spengler, Arnold Toynbee, Alfred Kroeber, and Pitrim Sorokin, all of whom had written well-received books charting the rise and fall of civilizations.[15] By a peculiar connection, pulp and paper gave Innis the opportunity to try his hand at this sort of universal narrative. In the 1930s, two Classics scholars, Milman Parry and Albert Lord, set about trying to prove, *horribile dictu*, that the works of beloved Homer were first sung by ancient, pre-literate bards and only much later written down.[16] To demonstrate this outrageous thesis, they needed to show that something of Homeric complexity, beauty, and length could be composed and vocalized by unlettered minstrels. So they traveled to the Balkans to record singers who, so it was said, still sang long heroic tales. Sing they did, and Parry and Lord rocked the world of Classical scholarship by demonstrating that "Homer" might have been an oral tradition rather than a great writer. The traces of what came to be known as "orality," they showed, were evident in the written versions of the *Iliad* and the *Odyssey*. The buzz about Parry and Lord's research could be heard in Classics departments all over the world, including that at the University of Toronto. Innis knew people there, and knew them well. Whether Professors Charles N. Cockrane or Edmund T. Owen introduced Innis to Parry and Lord's revolutionary work is not known, but they are credited by Innis himself with stimulating his "interest in the general problem" of communications history.[17]

Whatever the source, Innis realized that Parry and Lord's primary theoretical finding might be fruitfully extended: communications technologies might not only shape content, as orality had shaped the *Iliad* and *Odyssey*, but they might also mold the societies in which they were deployed. Over the next few years before his tragic death from cancer in 1952, Innis explored this hypothesis with respect to two questions: (1) How do new media arise? and (2) What do different media do?[18] His answers, we hope to show, were in the main correct.

WHY MEDIA ARISE

Innis proposed that new media were "pulled" into broad use by rising demand, not driven by rising supply. Demand comes first and supply follows. This theory has been validated by scholars studying the more general process of technical innovation, adoption, and dissemination.[19] Thanks to their work, we know what might be called the "rules" governing the discovery of a new tool, its initial use, and its spread through a population. As we will see, new media follow these rules rather exactly.

Rule 1: Groups of tinkerers discover new technologies. How are new technologies conceived? We sometimes say that protean geniuses – your da Vincis, Edisons, and Oppenheimers – come up with them, but that's wrong. These folks were smart and creative, but they had a lot of help.[20] Others were on the "trail of discovery," and some were quite close to the end when *the* discovery was made. Alas, we forget about them in our haste to create idols. We also sometimes say that "necessity is the mother of invention," but that's wrong too. Clearly, something impels people to create, but we know it's not necessity.[21] For the first 170,000 years of human existence we lived under dire necessity – thirst, hunger, disease – yet we invented almost nothing. Alas, we seem to have forgotten that as well. What the record shows is that groups of interested people – tinkerers – almost always stand behind the discovery of new technologies. Tinkerers do not work alone, and they do not work because they must. They work together with others on problems that may or may not be "objectively" important.

Rule 2: Tinkerers can only discover the technologies in their technome. We like to talk about technological "leaps," moments at which we jump from now into the future. This is a flattering metaphor, but it's inaccurate. Like evolutionary change, technological change is almost always incremental. Darwin said *natura non facit saltum*; we should say *technologia non facit saltum*. Indeed, the parallel is quite close. One of the principles of biological evolution is that the potential of a species to evolve new traits is constrained by its genome, that is, the set of genes it has available. It might be evolutionarily advantageous for your progeny to have wings, but it's simply not possible given the genes *Homo sapiens* has to work with. The same principle holds for technological progress: the potential of tinkerers to invent new technologies is constrained by their "technome," that is, the set of technologies (in the broad sense) available to them. Leonardo and his colleagues probably would have been pretty excited about building an A-bomb, but the technome they were tinkering with didn't have the technologies needed for them to conceive, let alone build one. As in all things, you can only do what you can do.

Rule 3: Technological supply does not produce technological demand. We generally say that new technologies are invented because people find them useful. That, however, is not quite right. If it were, then we wouldn't find that the supply of useful tools almost always outstrips demand for useful

8

tools. For most of our history we've had what amounts to excess technical capacity: we can build more tools than we can use. The reason is that tinkerers do not always – or even very often before modern times – produce new technologies because they think anyone will use them. They know that if you build it, sometimes they will come and sometimes they won't. But they build it anyway, creating the aforementioned excess capacity.

Rule 4: Technological demand, if unfocused, does not produce technological supply. We generally say that new technologies enter mass use because a lot of people want them. That, however, isn't quite right either. If it were, then we would find that mass demand for useful tools always translates into mass supply, and it doesn't. That's because technological demand is often unfocused. For a whole variety of reasons, new tools generally cost more and are worth less when they first appear than once they have been adopted en masse.[22] This is another way of saying that the barrier to early adoption is higher than the barrier to late adoption. The problem is that the barrier to early adoption is often too high for individuals, even if there are a large number of them. Thus, for want of early adopters, the new tool never enters mass use.

Rule 5: Only organized interests can produce the demand necessary to "pull" a new technology into mass use. We live in an individualistic age and therefore think individuals make history. They don't – at least not technological history. Only what we will call "organized interests" can make technological history because only they can overcome the barriers to early adoption mentioned above. Individuals are too poor to accomplish this feat, and so are disorganized masses of individuals. Organized interests, however, can "get the ball rolling" because they are coordinated and have a common purpose. They can create, gather, and pool resources; compel their members and others to do their bidding; and focus their power on specific goals – such as engineering and adopting a new technology. Organized interests can take many forms and pursue many purposes. As a general rule, however, we can identify three main types: economic organizations (businesses, industries, classes), political organizations (functionaries, leaders, castes), and religious organizations (believers, priests, orders).[23] Almost whenever and everywhere we find complex society, we find these sorts of organizations. Clearly there is something essential about them, though just what it is extends far beyond our present concerns.

Rule 6: When it comes to technological adoption, organized interests are reactive and not proactive. We tend to think of organizations – outside ones like revolutionary political parties – as conservative: they generally don't fix things that aren't manifestly broken. That's exactly right as it concerns the history of technology. Historically speaking, organized interests have not adopted new tools in anticipation of some *future* change in conditions. Rather, they have adopted new tools in response to some *ongoing* change in conditions, particularly one that makes them unable to do something they want to do. When these conditions arise, organized interests begin to search for, engineer, and adopt new tools. More likely than not, those tools will already be available in prototypical form because of excess technical capacity (see Rule 3).

Rule 7: Organized interests are most likely to adopt new tools in response to fundamentally new economic conditions. We find it very easy to say that Marx was "wrong." But in fact he was right, at least about the long-term driver of technological development. There have been five fundamental shifts in the way humans make their livings: the Behavioral Revolution (40,000 BC), the Agricultural Revolution (10,000 BC), the Capitalist Revolution (AD 1200), the Industrial Revolution (AD 1760), and the Information Revolution (AD 1940). During each of these shifts, there was an upsurge in innovation, adoption, and dissemination of new tools. It's not hard to understand why: the old tools, while still useful, didn't work well under new conditions, so new tools had to be brought into play. By Rules 1, 2, and 3 we know that the prototypes of these tools were available because of excess capacity; by Rules 4, 5, and 6 we know that organized interests under pressure to adapt to new conditions engineered, adopted, and spread them.

Together these rules suggest the following "pull" theory of media adoption: "New Economic Conditions → Technical Insufficiency → Increased Demand from Organized Interests → New Media Technology." This theory, however, is not quite complete. As we hinted previously, there are two additional factors that affect the adoption process: the timing of adoption and the nature of the technology adopted. As to timing, there can be no doubt that the rate of adoption has been increasing rapidly for at least the last 40,000 years. To take a pertinent example, it took several thousand years for writing to go from idea to widely used implement; it took only several decades for the personal computer to do the same. The rate of adoption, therefore, is a function of time. As to the nature of the technology adopted, there can be no doubt that some tools are naturally more appealing than others. To take another pertinent example, it took more than four centuries following the introduction of the printing press for mass literacy to develop in Europe; it took only a few decades for television to become a staple of everyday life. Reading is hard and not much fun; watching is easy and fun. The rate of adoption, then, is also a clear function of natural ease-of-use and enjoyment.

Innis argued that the physical attributes of media "push" societies and ideas in new directions. This theory is largely correct, but needs expansion and refinement. We will re-formulate it as follows: "Medium Attributes → Network Attributes → Social Practices and Values." We will argue that media, networks, and cultures each have their own type-specific attributes and that these attributes are causally related one to the other. Let's describe each set of attributes and the relationships between them in turn.

Medium Attributes

Innis proposed a typology of medium attributes based on weight and durability. This classification has the virtue of simplicity, but it sacrifices too much in terms of depth. We need something more complete. In order to get it, we should put ourselves in the shoes of those who use media and ask what really matters to them. Most basically, a medium is a tool for sending, receiving, storing, and retrieving information. Given these fundamental uses, what attributes would make a medium really handy?

A handy medium would be inexpensive to obtain and easy to use. A medium you can't afford or don't know how to operate is a bad medium, or rather no medium at all as far as you're concerned. For most of us, television stations fall into this category – we can't afford them (only Rupert Murdoch can) and we don't have the technical know-how to operate them (only engineers do). A handy medium would be private, or at least have a private mode. A medium that identifies you and what you've communicated as soon as you use it has drawbacks, especially if you want to blow the whistle on some malefactor or subscribe to risqué magazines. Sometimes you *don't* want everyone to know your name or what you're reading. A handy medium would have high fidelity, meaning that the signal you want to send is the same as the signal received. Speech, for example, does not have high fidelity when it comes to visual perceptions. If you see a white swan and then say to someone,

"I saw a white swan," the person who hears you won't *see* a white swan. Rather, they will *hear* some words that indicate you saw a white swan. Photography has higher fidelity in this regard. If you see a white swan, take a picture of it, and then hand the snapshot to someone, they will *see* an image of the very same white swan you saw. A handy medium would convey information in high volumes. With information, more capacity – or, to use the obvious metaphor, "bandwidth" – is generally better than less. You don't really need to know *some* of what's going to be on the test, you need to know it all. Books are good for that. A handy medium would move data quickly. No one likes to wait. When you're stuck in Podunk and your wallet's been pilfered by street urchins, you want money wired, not sent by letter. A handy medium would store information for a long time. Sometimes the tax man comes calling. And when he does, you'd better hope that your tax records survived the basement flood last year. Finally, a handy medium would allow you to search, find, and retrieve stored information easily. Stored information that can't be found isn't really "stored" at all – it's lost and might as well not exist. Big libraries often have signs warning "a misshelved book is a lost book." Think about that the next time you decide to do the library a favor by putting a book back on the shelf yourself.

These considerations suggest the following media attributes are significant from the perspective of the user:

Accessibility: the availability of a medium itself.
Privacy: the covertness with which data can be transmitted in a medium.
Fidelity: the faithfulness with which data can be transmitted in a medium.
Volume: the quantity in which data can be transmitted in a medium.
Velocity: the speed with which data can be transmitted in a medium.
Range: the distance over which data can be transmitted in a medium.
Persistence: the duration over which data can be preserved in a medium.
Searchability: the efficiency with which data can be found in a medium.

We might well say that a really handy medium would possess all of these attributes and a nearly useless medium would possess none of them. That, however, would be a mistake. For in fact all media possess them to one degree or another. It's easy to see that speech has the attribute "accessibility" because virtually everyone has access to it. It's harder to understand that Chappe semaphore lines – series of towers with manually operated signaling devices atop them – *also* have the attribute "accessibility" given that almost no one has access to them. But they do: after all, someone has access to them when they were built. It's just that speech has a lot of accessibility and the Chappe semaphore line only has a little. Similarly, we might think that the way a medium scores on an attribute is fixed. Speech, we might say, will always score well on accessibility, while Chappe semaphore lines will always score poorly. That, however, would also be a mistake. Speech could be made very inaccessible, for example, by cutting out everyone's tongue. Similarly, Chappe semaphore lines could be made very accessible, for example, by building everyone their own semaphore tower. In principle, then, any medium can be made to score well or poorly on any attribute *given a sufficient outlay of resources*. The actual score of a medium on a particular attribute, then, is a function of cost. This insight enables us to recast our definition of attributes as follows:

Accessibility: the cost of getting and using a medium.
Privacy: the cost of hiding the identity of users and the content of messages in a medium.
Fidelity: the degree to which data in a medium are coded.
Volume: the cost of sending messages in a medium relative to size.
Velocity: the cost of sending messages in a medium relative to speed.
Range: the cost of sending messages in a medium relative to distance.
Persistence: the cost of storing messages in a medium relative to time.
Searchability: the cost of finding messages in a medium.

Where the cost is low, the score will be high; where the cost is high, the score will be low. The cost of acquiring and using speech is generally low, so it will be highly accessible. The cost of acquiring and using Chappe semaphore lines is generally high, so they will be relatively inaccessible.

Medium Attributes → Network Attributes

Innis proposed that media attributes directly affected what he called "civilizations," a vague and controversial term we would probably do best to avoid. In its place we will use "media networks." Media may or may not do a lot of things (that's what we are trying to find out), but there is no doubt that they directly and necessarily create networks. We know this because it is a purely definitional matter. By definition, all communications media allow people to communicate with one another. By definition, when people communicate through a particular medium, they become linked by that medium. And by definition, when they become linked by the medium, a media network appears. Thus, speaking creates speech networks, writing creates writing networks, printing creates print networks, electronic broadcast creates broadcast networks, and surfing (or any of the myriad things we do on networked computers) creates Internet networks. We sometimes forget that we create media networks when we use media. The media networks just seem to be there. Few of us think, when speaking to a friend, "I'm creating a speech network." But in fact we are, just as certainly as telephone linesmen create telephone networks when they string wire from pole to pole. Neither do we often reflect on the fact that media networks are finite. They seem to be everywhere. Few of us think, when speaking to our neighbor, "Lucky this person is on the speech network, or I wouldn't be able to talk to her." But we are lucky, because there are people who are not on the speech network (mutes, those who do not speak our language), just as surely as there are people who do not have telephones and therefore are not on the telephone network.

We can now formulate a simple hypothesis about what media do: *different kinds of media foster different kinds of media networks*. More formally, media with attributes A_1, B_1, and C_1 engender media networks with corresponding attributes A_2, B_2, and C_2. This hypothesis seems promising. Take one of the aforementioned medium attributes, range, that is, the distance a medium can carry a message without significant decay. According to our conception, media with different ranges should foster media networks with different attributes. Thus, unaided speech has a short range and therefore the effective networks built with it should be small. This seems correct. How many people are in your circle of friends, a typical speech network? Perhaps a few dozen. Television signals have a long reach and therefore the effective networks built with them should be large. Again, this seems right. How many people watch a major broadcast TV network? Millions. The correlation between spatial reach and network size we find in the instances of speech and TV should be true for media in general: media with short range create geographically concentrated networks, while media with long range create large, diffuse networks. As we will see, this is in fact the case.

Media, then, create media networks, and particular media attributes create particular network attributes. Since there are eight significant media attributes, there should be at least eight corresponding media network attributes. They are:

1. *Accessibility → Concentration.* Depending on the cost of getting and using a medium, the network it fosters will be more or less concentrated. Concentrated networks are those in which control of the medium rests in the hands of a relative few; diffuse networks are those in which control is dispersed throughout the network.

2. *Privacy → Segmentation.* Depending on the cost of hiding identities and the contents of messages in a medium, the network it engenders will be more or less segmented. Segmented networks are those in which senders, recipients, and the exchanged data can be hidden from others; connected networks are those in which the identities of senders and recipients and the data exchanged cannot be hidden.

3. *Fidelity → Iconicity.* Depending on the cost of sending messages relative to fidelity in a medium, the network it engenders will be more or less iconic. Iconic networks are those in which transmitted messages do not have to be laboriously decoded by the recipient (they are simply recognized); symbolic networks are those in which messages must be manually decoded.

4. *Volume → Constraint.* Depending on the cost of transmitting messages relative to size in a medium, its network will be more or less constrained. Unconstrained networks are those in which a large amount of data can be easily exchanged and there is excess capacity; constrained networks are those in which only small amounts of data can be exchanged and all available capacity has been used.

5. *Velocity → Dialogicity.* Depending on the cost of exchanging messages relative to speed in a medium, its network will be more or less dialogic. Dialogic networks are those in which multiple

parties can easily exchange messages quickly; monologic networks are those in which such exchange is difficult.

6. *Range* → *Extent*. Depending on the cost of transmitting messages relative to distance and reach (number of recipients) in a medium, its network will be more or less extensive. Extensive networks are those in which messages are exchanged over a large area or number of people; intensive networks are those in which messages are exchanged over a small area or number of people.

7. *Persistence* → *Addition*. Depending on the cost of preserving messages relative to time in a medium, its networks will be more or less additive. Additive networks are those in which messages accumulate; substitutive networks are those in which new messages replace old messages and therefore the amount of data is stable.

8. *Searchability* → *Mappedness*. Depending on the cost of finding messages in a medium, the network constructed with it will be more or less mapped. Mapped networks are those in which it is easy to search, find, and retrieve stored messages; unmapped networks are those in which it is not.

Medium Attributes → *Network Attributes* → *Social Practices and Values*

We have established "Medium Attributes → Network Attributes," a set of regularities that correlate eight properties of media with eight characteristics of media networks. Now we face a final challenge: we must determine if and how these medium attributes, through the device of network attributes, mold the way we live and what we believe. It's important to recognize that the entire media studies program as set out by McLuhan rises or falls on this step. Either the medium is the message – that is, media technologies in and of themselves shape human institutions and values – or they don't. That is what we will try to find out. Our hypothesis is this: *media networks engender certain social practices, and these social practices engender related values.*[24] There are two separate arguments here: "Media Networks → Social Practices" and "Social Practices → Values." Let's treat each in turn.

Among the most sensible things Marx ever wrote was this: "Men make their own history, but they do not make it of their own free will; they do not make it under circumstances chosen by themselves, but under circumstances directly found, given, and handed down from the past."[25] This is a powerful statement. Despite what we might vainly imagine, we are not free. Rather, we are constrained by "circumstances" we do not select, we do not create, and in many cases we cannot alter. They are of two types. The first circumstance is simply human nature, the set of evolutionarily programmed behaviors that distinguishes *Homo sapiens* as a species.[26] We call them by various names – "needs," "impulses," "reflexes," "urges," "hungers," "wants," "desires," "inclinations" – but in the end they are all the same: things we are driven to do because it is in our nature to do them. The second circumstance is environmental, the varied physical and social terrain upon which humans, driven by their natures, "make history." This terrain has many features, each of which constrains human action in different ways. Famously, Marx investigated one such feature, the "mode of production"; we are investigating another feature, the "media network." But the basic explanatory logic is the same. Two sets of "circumstances" – one biological and one historical – interact in such a way as to shape human action, which in turn leads to the generation of particular social practices. Humans need to do certain things. Different historical terrains – in our case media networks – either *facilitate* or *impede* the fulfillment of those needs. According to whether they do the one or the other, different social practices will emerge.

Marx also said something clever about the relationship between social practices and values. "Ruling ideas," he wrote, "are nothing more than the ideal expression of ruling material relationships, the ruling material relationships grasped as ideas."[27] What he's saying, *inter alia*, is that what we *actually* do in relation to others determines to a large extent what we think we *should* do. This is exactly the reverse of what most people think about the relationship between actions and values. We like to believe that we are, perhaps uniquely among animals, moral creatures: we can know what is right and what is wrong. We can know this, we say, because God has granted us a moral code (the religious version) or because we evolved a kind of innate moral sense (the secular version). In either case, we don't exactly decide what is right and wrong. Our values are "just there," an intrinsic part of the universe. When we act, we say we are guided by these transcendental values. The timeless "ought" shapes the temporal "is," or at least should. Marx – and he was hardly alone[28] – believed we have it backward: the earth-bound "is" molds the heavenly "ought." We don't do what we should do because it's right, we do what we should do because we've defined "should" in such a way that it justifies what we want to do and can do. This may seem awfully cynical, but there is no good reason to see it that way. All Marx is trying to say (and all we are trying to say) is that morality doesn't fall out of the sky or emerge directly from your genes, but rather results from a constant process whereby the "ought" – beliefs, morals, ethics, norms, values, principles, standards, ideals – is brought into line with the "is" – what we want to do, what we can do, and what we actually do in pursuit of our interests.

Now that we have established that human nature and media networks constitute the "circumstances" that shape social practices, and that particular social practices give rise to commensurate values, we are ready to complete the theory of what media do to us. We saw that any medium could be defined in terms of eight attributes. Then we saw that each of these attributes engendered a corresponding network attribute. Now we'll see how each network attribute tends to produce a corresponding set of social practices and values. In each of the following cases, we have "Media Attributes → Media Network Attributes → Social Practices + Values."

1. *Accessibility → Concentration → Hierarchicalization + Elitism.*
   The less accessible a medium, the more concentrated its network; the more concentrated a network, the more social practices realized in it will be hierarchicalized. The link between concentration and hierarchicalization is established by the innate human drive for power over others: if humans can easily monopolize a scarce resource – such as a medium – in order to use it as an instrument of domination, they will, and will establish corresponding social practices. Concentration facilitates monopolization. In concentrated media networks, therefore, we should see hierarchical social practices and an ideology – elitism – that legitimates them. Elitism is premised on the idea that some are superior to others. Conversely, the more accessible a medium, the more diffuse its network; the more diffuse a network, the more social practices realized in it will be equalized. Diffusion impedes monopolization. In diffuse media networks, therefore, we should see social

18

practices characterized by equality among group members and an ideology – egalitarianism – that affirms equality. Egalitarianism is rooted in the idea that no one is superior to anyone else.

2. *Privacy → Segmentation → Closure + Privatism.* The more private a medium, the more segmented its network; the more segmented a network, the more social practices realized in it will be closed. The link between segmentation and closure is established by the innate human desire to conceal: if humans can easily use a medium to remove certain activities from public gaze – to privatize them – they will, and will establish corresponding social practices. Segmentation facilitates hiding. In segmented networks, therefore, we should see multiple private social practices and an ideology – privatism – that justifies them. Privatism is premised on the idea that information need not be shared. In contrast, the less private a medium, the more connected its network; the more connected a network, the more social practices realized in it will be opened. Connection impedes hiding. In connected media networks, then, we would expect to see few if any private spaces and an ideology – publicism – that values transparency. Publicism is rooted in the idea that information should be shared.

3. *Fidelity → Iconicity → Sensualization + Realism.* The higher the fidelity of a medium, the more iconic its network; the more iconic a network, the more social practices realized in it will be sensualized. The link between iconicity and sensualization is established by the innate human desire for physical pleasure: if humans can conveniently use a medium to receive such pleasure, they will, and will create commensurate social practices. Iconicity facilitates physical pleasure-seeking. In iconic networks, therefore, we will witness many social practices that stimulate the senses by realistic depictions, especially of sound and sight, and an ideology – realism – that valorizes them. Realism is premised on the idea that the seen world is more enriching than the unseen world. In contrast, the lower the fidelity of a medium, the more symbolic its network; the more symbolic a network, the more social practices in and around it will be conceptualized. Conceptualization impedes sensuality. In symbolic media networks, then, we would expect to see abstracted social practices and an ideology – idealism – that

justifies them. Idealism is rooted in the idea that the unseen world is more enriching than the seen world.

4. *Volume → Constraint → Hedonization + Hedonism.* The higher the volume of a medium, the less constrained its network; the less constrained a network, the more social practices realized in it will be hedonized and value entertainment. The link between constraint and hedonization is established by the innate human desire for diversion: if humans can easily use a medium for the purposes of pleasant diversion, they will, and will establish matching social practices. Lack of constraint facilitates hedonistic use. In an unconstrained network, therefore, we should see abundant amusements and an ideology – hedonism – that justifies them. Hedonism is premised on the idea that the self develops through experience. In contrast, the lower the volume of a medium, the more constrained its network; the more constrained a network, the more social practices realized in it will be economized. Constraint impedes divertive use of the media. In constrained media networks we should see social practices in which self-denial is practiced and an ideology – asceticism – that makes self-denial a virtue. Asceticism is rooted in the idea that the self develops through restraint.

5. *Velocity → Dialogicity → Democratization + Deliberativism.* The faster a medium, the more dialogic its network; the more dialogic a network, the more social practices realized in it will be democratized. The link between dialogicity and democratization is established by the innate human desire to express one's self to others: if humans can easily use a medium to be heard by others, they will, and will create related social practices. Dialogicity facilitates expression. In dialogic networks, therefore, we would expect to see democratic social practices and an ideology – deliberativism – that validates them. Deliberativism is premised on the idea that everyone should speak for themselves. In contrast, the slower a medium, the more monologic its network; the more monologic a network, the more social practices realized in it will be centralized. Monologicity impedes expression. In monologic media networks, then, we should see centralized social practices and an ideology – dictatorism – that justifies them. Dictatorism is rooted in the idea that some should speak for others.

6. *Range → Extent → Diversification + Pluralism.* The longer the range of a medium, geographically and demographically, the more extensive its network; the more extensive a network, the more social practices realized in it will be diversified. The link between extent and diversification is established by innate human curiosity about the present and the desire to learn about and from it: if humans can use a medium to find out about unfamiliar people and things, they will, and will create social practices built on these interests. Extensiveness facilitates exploration of the present. In extensive media networks, therefore, we should see diversified social practices and an ideology – pluralism – that defends them. Pluralism is premised on the idea that there are many kinds of people and things. In contrast, the shorter the range of a medium, the more intensive its network; the more intensive a network, the more social practices in it will be simplified. Intensiveness impedes curiosity about the present. In intensive networks, then, we should see simplified social practices and an ideology – monism – that supports them. Monism is rooted in the idea that there is only one kind of person and thing.

7. *Persistence → Addition → Historicization + Temporalism.* The greater the persistence of a medium, the more additive its network; the more additive a network, the more social practices realized in it will be historicized. The link between persistence and historicization is constituted by innate human curiosity about the past and the desire to learn about and from it: if humans can use a medium to find out about the past, and particularly people of the past, they will, and will create social practices built on these interests. Addition facilitates exploration of the past. In an additive network, therefore, we should see historicized social practices and an ideology – temporalism – that supports them. Temporalism is premised on the idea that things change in time. In contrast, the less persistent a medium, the more substitutive its network; the more substitutive a network, the more social practices realized in it will be ritualized. Substitution impedes exploration of the past. In substitutive networks, then, we would expect to see ritualized social practices and an ideology – eternalism – that validates them. Eternalism is rooted in the idea that things have always been as they are.

8. *Searchability* → *Mapping* → *Amateurization* + *Individualism*. The more searchable a medium, the more mapped its network; the more mapped a network, the more social practices realized in it will be amateurized. The link between mapping and amateurization is established by the innate human need for autonomy, specifically to know for oneself: if humans can easily use a medium to find out what they need to know by themselves, they will, and will establish commensurate social practices. Mapping facilitates independent discovery. In a mapped network, therefore, we should see many "self-help" (in the generic sense) social practices and an ideology – individualism – that promotes self-reliance. Individualism is premised on the idea that everyone is autonomous. In contrast, the less searchable a medium, the less mapped its network; the less mapped a network, the more social practices realized in it will be professionalized. The lack of mapping impedes independent discovery. In unmapped media networks, then, we would expect to see professions and an ideology – collectivism – that validates them. Collectivism is rooted in the idea that everyone is dependent on others.

Bear in mind that the attributes listed in the table are *continuous*; they are presented here as extreme *dichotomies* simply for clarity's sake. For example, empirically speaking, particular media lie somewhere on the continuum between high and low accessibility, networks between diffuse and concentrated, social practices between equalized and hierarchicalized, and cultural values between egalitarian and elitist. It would be interesting to try to quantify or score media, their networks, and the social practices and values they engender. That task, however, goes far beyond our limited goal, which is simply to demonstrate that different media have predictable effects on social practices and values. Those effects may be – and in fact sometimes are – very subtle, but we hope to show that they are usually present. The entire "push" theory is summarized in Table 1.

If we are serious about understanding media, we need to formulate real theories – the kind that associate specific causes with specific effects, the kind that can be true or false on the evidence, the kind that allow

TABLE 1. *Push Theory of Media Effects*

Medium Attribute				Network Attribute	Human Need ←→ Network		Social Practices		Cultural Values
Accessibility	=	High	→	Diffused	Need for power	is impeded by network's diffusion	→	Equalized	→	Egalitarianism
		Low	→	Concentrated		is enabled by network's concentration	→	Hierarchicalized	→	Elitism
Privacy	=	High	→	Segmented	Need for secrecy	is enabled by network's segmentation	→	Closed	→	Privatism
		Low	→	Connected		is impeded by network's openness	→	Opened	→	Publicism
Fidelity	=	High	→	Iconic	Need for pleasure	is enabled by network's iconic-ness	→	Sensualized	→	Realism
		Low	→	Symbolic		is impeded by network's abstraction	→	Conceptualized	→	Idealism
Volume	=	High	→	Unconstrained	Need for diversion	is enabled by network's capacious-ness	→	Hedonized	→	Hedonism
		Low	→	Constrained		is impeded by network's constrained-ness	→	Economized	→	Asceticism

(continued)

23

TABLE I *(continued)*

Medium Attribute		Network Attribute		Human Need ← → Network			Social Practices		Cultural Values
Velocity	=	High → Dialogic	→	Need for expression	is enabled by network's dialogic-ness	→	Democratized	→	Deliberativism
		Low → Monologic			is impeded by network's monologic-ness	→	Centralized	→	Authoritarianism
Range	=	High → Extensive	→	Curiosity about the present	is enabled by network's extensive-ness	→	Diversified	→	Pluralism
		Low → Intensive			is impeded by network's intensive-ness	→	Simplified	→	Monism
Persistence	=	High → Additive	→	Curiosity about the past	is enabled by network's additive-ness	→	Historicized	→	Temporalism
		Low → Substitutive			is impeded by network's substitutive-ness	→	Ritualized	→	Eternalism
Searchability	=	High → Mapped	→	Need for autonomy	is enabled by network's mapped-ness	→	Amateurized	→	Individualism
		Low → Unmapped			is impeded by network's unmapped-ness	→	Professionalized	→	Collectivism

us to make predictions about what will happen if the theory is correct. I have laid out two such theories. The first tries to explain why certain media were adopted in certain times and places. The second attempts to explain what media do to the way we live and what we believe. Both make precise forecasts concerning what we should see in the historical record. In what follows, we will test the theories on five successive historical media: speech, writing, print, audiovisual media, and the Internet. If what we have said is true, then the theories will offer satisfying explanations as to why each medium spread and what each did.

I

HOMO LOQUENS

Humanity in the Age of Speech

Yes indeed, dear Phaedrus. But far more excellent [than writing], I think, is . . . the art of dialectic.[1]

    – Plato, *Phaedrus*, 276E

Most people know Plato as the world's first philosopher, but he was also the world's first media critic. Plato wanted to find the Truth, and he said that the only way to do it was using a method he called "dialectic." By this he meant reasoned discussion, a kind of debate in which real people present arguments and other real people affirm or refute them by means of logic. He showed how one could use dialectic to arrive at the Truth in the dialogues for which he is justly famous. Plato, however, not only used his dialogues to demonstrate how to get to the Truth, but also to explain what the Truth was. And one of the Truths he pointed out was that some of his competitors were selling philosophical snake oil. These were the rhetoricians, professional speechwriters in the ancient Hellenic world. They were charlatans, Plato complained, and not really interested in the Truth at all. Rather, their only aim was to teach politicians to flatter their constituents, to feed what Plato pejoratively called the "Great Beast" of public opinion. Instead of showing statesmen the light, the rhetoricians transformed them into pastry chefs who served up sweets according to vulgar tastes without thought as to whether they were healthy or not (*Gorgias*, 465A).[2] For Plato, you either discuss or deceive. Philosophers discussed, rhetoricians and those they trained deceived. There was no middle ground. It's little wonder that Plato banished rhetoric from the ideal city he described in *The Republic*. There was just no place for it.

Plato thought people were meant to talk *to* one another, not *at* one another. He was more right than he knew. As we'll see in this chapter, nature fashioned *Homo sapiens* into a creature both fantastically skilled in dialogic communication and driven to engage in it. We do not talk because we want to. We talk because we have to. In this sense, we are all natural-born Platonists – eager, tireless, unstoppable talkers. Talking is in our natures, so it is with talking that we should begin our history of media and their consequences.

WHY WE TALK

There is an important sense in which talking is not like later media: we did not invent it. Talking happened to us, just like the ability to grasp with our hands, walk on our legs, and stick out our tongues. This being so, any explanation of the rise of talking must be couched in terms of natural selection, and that means the origins of talking afford us no opportunity to test our "pull" theory of media origins. Its first trail must wait for writing, the first invented medium. For now, we need to talk about the evolution of talking.

Why did we, uniquely among all animals, evolve the ability to talk? The answer may seem obvious. We came to talk because it was to our evolutionary advantage to talk. And this is true. Those proto-humans who could talk produced more offspring than those who couldn't, and gradually the genetic capacity for talking spread throughout the species until everyone could talk. But this appeal to evolutionary advantage, as commonsensical as it may be, isn't very satisfying, primarily because it doesn't explain specifically *why* it was to our evolutionary advantage to talk. Evolutionary theorists are aware of this problem and they have advanced many theories regarding exactly what talking did for us, evolutionarily speaking.[3] They say we evolved talking because it enabled us to make better tools, or to share more information, or to exchange gossip, or impress members of the opposite sex. Some of these theories make good sense, but they all raise a troublesome question of their own: why don't other mammals in our branch of the tree of life talk?

In *A Treatise of Human Nature* (1739), the English philosopher David Hume proposed a fundamental principle of scientific reasoning: "the same cause always produces the same effect."[4] It's a good rule, and has stood the test of time. But apparently it doesn't apply to the evolution of talking, at least as laid down by some evolutionary theorists. According to them, the ancestors of humans began to talk because doing so helped them do X, Y, and Z, where X, Y, and Z improved their ability to reproduce, or "fitness." Following Hume's lead, then, if we were to find another ancestral species that would have benefited from X, Y, and Z – as proto-humans did – then we should expect its descendants to talk. As Hume said, like causes should produce like effect. The problem is that we know there were other primate species that definitely would have benefited from X, Y, and Z but did not evolve the ability to talk. For example, the ancestors of modern chimps, who were both much like proto-humans and lived in a similar environment, would have profited from the ability to make better tools, share more information, exchange gossip, and impress members of the opposite sex. Neither chimps nor any higher mammal, however, ever developed anything like human language. So here we have a like cause – the supposed general utility of speech – but a different effect – no talking.

The fact that humans can talk and chimps can't leads us to another, much more productive question: Why was it advantageous for humans to talk and not other species of higher mammals, proto-chimps in particular? The French scholar Jean-Louis Dessalles has given a novel and convincing answer. It can be summarized as follows.[5]

Many higher mammals, proto-humans among them, probably lived in small groups millions of years ago. The fact that they did (and most of their ancestors still do) presents an evolutionary puzzle: group living is a form of cooperation and, according to Darwin, animals are dyed-in-the-wool genetic egomaniacs. They are supposed to want to pass on *their* genes, and not to give a whit about those of strangers. It's hard to imagine, then, why any strictly self-interested organism would help another strictly self-interested organism, unless the two were genetically related. In that case, what appears to be altruistic isn't, because by helping your sister pass on her genes you are actually helping yourself pass on your genes because the two of you share genes.[6] This kind of passage-by-proxy is common in the animal kingdom. What's rarer is cooperation among genetically *unrelated* individuals. The reason is clear: cooperation is risky. To employ the obvious metaphor, say you and I agree to scratch each other's backs. If we can scratch at the same time, there is no problem as neither of us can really cheat. But if we go by turns, a sticky question arises: who's going to go first? How do I know you won't renege on the deal the minute I'm done scratching your back? I don't, so I'm not going to make the deal. Thus, cooperation never evolves. Evolutionarily speaking, one way to make cooperation spread in a species is to make cheating costly.[7] This obviously happened, because cooperation evolved. We aren't sure just how it occurred, but it probably had something to do with the development of reputations.[8] If you are able to remember that someone cheated you (a capacity that itself must be evolved), you are not likely to do business with her again: once bitten, twice shy. The same is true of others observing the cheater: once observed biting, twice avoided. Over time, the cheater will develop a bad reputation. Eventually, no one will cooperate with him, and so in effect his cheating is made very costly. His genes will decline in the population, as will the propensity to cheat. Since cheating always pays sometimes, however, it will never be extinguished completely.

Our ancestors, living in small groups, had overcome the initial barriers to low-level cooperation by the time our line hived off the proto-chimp line some six million years ago. The extent of their cooperative capacities, however, did not end there, for the proto-human group itself had internal collaborative structures.[9] Judging by modern chimp communities (and there is good reason to do this, as chimps are very evolutionarily conservative, that is, they haven't changed much in six million years), two of these subgroups were most important: the mother-child pair and the multi-male coalition. The former need not concern us, as its evolutionary logic is quite straightforwardly kin-selective: chimp mothers invest in their children in order to ensure their own genes are passed on to later generations. The multi-male coalition, however, is of greater interest.[10] It is a temporary alliance that forms to impose political dominance within the group and to protect group assets (females, territory) from interlopers. In a typical power grab, a small number of ambitious male chimps will form a raiding party and, using superior strength, violently subdue their enemies. The result is often a bloody mess, with the vanquished losing limbs and even lives. The victorious coalition will then rule the group until the alliance falls apart or another, stronger coalition comes along.

It's reasonably easy to see how the propensity to form multi-male coalitions would be selected for: those in the triumphant coalitions breed more than their competitors, so their coalition-forming genes are passed on and spread throughout the species. One might think that the opportunity to cheat would hinder the evolution of coalitions, but this isn't the case. Though the alliances are far from stable, there is little opportunity to cheat *effectively* as the contribution of members can be verified continuously. The exchange that goes on in the coalition is simultaneous, not serial. Everyone in the raiding party is murderously pummeling his competitors at the same time. They don't take whacks by turns. Thus, if one of the coalition members doesn't pull his weight, the others will notice immediately and the coalition will disintegrate with no great loss to the remaining members. In that sense, then, there really can't be any sustained cheating in a multi-male coalition – there can only be defection and dissolution.

From the coalition members' perspective, the real problem with alliances isn't cheating, but that of selecting the right allies. This choice is crucial, as it will largely determine how often you breed. But how do you know whom to team up with? Clearly, you want to pick allies with characteristics that are predictive of fighting and mating success. For chimps, this is some combination of size, strength, and, perhaps, loyalty (as evinced by grooming behavior). This propensity to go with the "big guy" when seeking allies would seem to be widespread among all higher mammals, humans included. If you recall (painful though it is), the schoolyard bully had a lot of "friends." The difficulty is that this criterion for selection loses its effectiveness as competing coalitions grow in size. A big guy can tip the balance in fighting between small groups, say ones with only two or three members. But a big guy is not going to make much of a difference in a struggle between large coalitions, particularly if outnumbered. In a contest between a large and a small coalition, the large coalition is usually going to win even if the small one has the big guy. Even the schoolyard bully and his sycophantic underlings couldn't take on *all* of you.

Thanks to the work of the evolutionary anthropologist Robin Dunbar, we have good reason to believe that shortly after the proto-human line split off from the proto-chimp line, the size of proto-human groups and the multi-male coalitions in them began to increase.[11] If you: (a) measure the brains of living primate species; (b) determine the size of the groups in which they typically live; and then (c) compare the two data sets, you get a positive correlation: as brain size increases, so does typical group size. It stands to reason that what is true of living primates was probably true of extinct apes, that is, as their brain size increased, so did their group size. Happily, we know quite a bit about the cranial capacity (a proxy for brain size) of our ancestors: *Australopithecus afarensis* had a cranial capacity of around 450 cc; *Homo habilis*, around 500 cc; *Homo erectus*, 1,250 cc; and *Homo sapiens*, 1,450 cc. Using the aforementioned brain-size/group-size formula, Australopithecines typically would have lived in groups of about 65 individuals. Moving forward in time, *Homo habilis* lived in groups of around 80 individuals; *Homo erectus* lived in groups of around 130 individuals; and early *Homo sapiens* lived in groups of 150 individuals. To put this in perspective, modern chimps have brains of about 400 cc and live in groups averaging about 50 individuals.

If it is correct that the size of proto-human groups and subgroups grew in this way, then it seems reasonable to infer that the chimp strategy for picking allies based on strength, size, and loyalty became unworkable for our ancestors. Male chimps still living in small bands could go on as they always had – and, in fact, still do – picking the big guy. But proto-humans looking for allies had to select another characteristic. Dessalles proposes that this criterion was the ability to communicate "relevance."[12] "Relevance" here means utterances that will profit a listener and thereby recommend the speaker as an ally. If you can regularly say "there's some food over there" and be right, then you have signaled to me that you can probably do me some good and therefore that I should select you as a partner. Being relevant helps you a lot: the more relevant you are, the more allies you will have; the more allies you have, the larger your coalition; the larger your coalition, the more likely it will be that it will dominate the band; the greater your coalition's dominance of the band, the greater your fecundity; the greater your fecundity, the faster your relevance-producing genes will be spread throughout the population. As individuals like you compete with one another to be relevant, the average level of relevance increases until, well, we all speak like humans.

Dessalles's argument rests on the theory of "costly signaling." It holds that fit individuals display their relative superiority by means of true signals that seem to tempt fate.[13] The peacock's tail is the classic example. A garish fan of plumage doesn't seem to do the peacock any good insofar as it exposes him to predators and makes escape difficult. But a big tail also says, "I'm so fit that it doesn't matter who

sees me or whether I can get away. Bring 'em on! Now let's mate."
If the ostentatious peacock succeeds in mating more often than his
competitors before he gets killed and eaten, then his rakish ornament
will have done its evolutionary work. Speech, Dessalles says, evolved in
the same way as the peacock's tail except the costly signal wasn't bright
feathers but relevant words. Speaking, then, is a kind of dangerous
showing off.

At first blush, this position doesn't seem very promising. In order
for costly signaling to drive natural selection, it must be costly. Outside
of places like courtrooms, words ordinarily aren't. Most conversations,
after all, seem to be of no consequence at all unless you are *really*
interested in, say, the weather. But, Dessalles points out, that's only
the way it seems. Speech *is* costly in that it exposes the speaker to the
judgment of listeners and that judgment strongly, if not immediately,
affects the speaker's fitness. Speaking shows listeners you have guts,
that you are willing to put your status on the line. And if you speak
well – that is, relevantly – it shows listeners that you might be a good
ally. Of course, speaking is risky: you could "put your foot in your
mouth" and lose status and, ultimately, fitness. But that's the price you
pay to play the relevance game. In this view, speech is not so much a
form of cooperation as a contest between speakers for the approbation
of listeners. You don't play the relevance game because you genuinely
want to help people, though you might tell yourself that and believe it.
You play because – whether you know it or not – there is something in
it for you, namely, status and fitness.

If Dessalles's theory that speech emerged from countless rounds of
the relevance game is correct, then we should find several things to
be true about the way we think and speak today. This is to say that
thinking and speaking should be optimized for competition in the game.
And here we come to what is perhaps the greatest strength of Dessalles's
theory, for he shows that this is precisely the case: the reasons we came
to speak *then* can be seen in the way we think and talk *now*.

Humans, Dessalles points out, are extraordinarily good at identify-
ing, remembering, and recalling anomalies. Cats are specially attuned
to sense movement. Bats are specially attuned to sense sound. Humans
are specially attuned to sense things that are out of the ordinary. Each
of us has in our heads a kind of probabilistic model of the world. As

we perceive new things, we unconsciously compare them to the model and update it. Only really unusual things are likely to come into our conscious minds, but they will do so reflexively. Completely ordinary things, like the fact that there is a red car on the road in front of us, are not even consciously registered. More unusual things, like the fact that the red car is swerving slightly, might draw our passing attention. But really strange things, like the fact that the swerving red car seems *to have no driver!* pop right into our minds. We can't help but think about them because they are so at odds with our model of the world. A car with no driver is relevant indeed. After all, it might just kill you.

Not only do we notice anomalies, but we often look for them and, when we find them, investigate them.[14] Humans, Dessalles notes, are naturally curious. If something "just doesn't fit" we will often try to figure it out, to make it consistent with our picture of the world. To return to the driverless car, it wouldn't be far outside the scope of normal human behavior for someone, having witnessed this oddity, to at least have the impulse to overtake the car to see what exactly was going on. In fact, not a few of us would act on this urge just to satisfy our inborn curiosity. From an evolutionary point of view, this is strange behavior. Why would someone risk her life just to find out why there is no driver in a nearby moving car? Yet people do this sort of thing all the time. Dessalles has a good explanation: we are gathering valuable information, information that can be used in the relevance game. Seeing a driverless car is a relevant fact, the foundation of what we usually call a "good story." But being able to explain why the car could continue on its way without a driver is even more relevant, and can serve as the ending to an even better story. Unconsciously, your mind calculates the risks and rewards. Should you overtake the car and get the facts or should you hang back and forgo their reward? You remember that "curiosity killed the cat," a relevant proverb indeed. But you let your curiosity get the better of you and you speed ahead for a peek. You see that it's really no mystery at all, it's only . . .

Naturally you want to know what it was, what explains the driverless car. You can't wait to find out. Neither, for that matter, can you wait to tell someone once you do. We like to think that speech is something under our conscious control. We speak when we want and we don't when we don't. But, as Dessalles shows, that just isn't so. When we come across a relevant fact, we automatically notice it and remember it. We may even be impelled to investigate it despite considerable danger. But the force of our mental compulsion to be relevant does not end there. Once we have a relevant fact in our possession, we cannot help but relate it to someone. The fact that humans will speak reflexively is widely known, but reflexive speaking is usually understood to be limited to physically or emotionally prompted outbursts. You say "Ouch!" when you are pricked by a needle. You say "Damn!" when you get upset. But if you think about it carefully, you'll see that sometimes you automatically blurt out entire sentences and even entire stories. Take the moment at which you saw that the red car had no driver. You might have unconsciously, though quite audibly, said, "Well I'll be damned. That car has no driver!" even though there was nobody there to hear you. This seemingly purposeless utterance, Dessalles would argue, is a reflex of what might be called your "relevance organ." To your brain, the fact of a driverless car was just *too* relevant not to put into words, even though no one would hear them but you. Now take yourself to the moment after you figured out why the car had no driver. You might think, "I can't wait to tell so-and-so." And when you are next in the presence of so-and-so, you unthinkingly and automatically launch into the story about the car with no driver, and how you risked your life to discover why it had no driver. You get pleasure from sharing your relevance.

We sometimes think that the basic purpose of speech is the exchange of information. You tell me this, and I'll tell you that, and we'll both be better off. There is something to this theory, but it's not a good description of what actually goes on in a typical conversation. According to Dessalles, conversations are not structured by quid pro quos. In fact, they are much more like performances in which a speaker presents something relevant for the entertainment and enlightenment of a listener. Imagine that you are telling the story of the driverless car to so-and-so. How does that person behave? She doesn't exchange information, rather she listens and probes. You do most of the talking, but occasionally she interrupts to make a remark or ask a question. She might say "really?" as if to cast doubt on what you've claimed, or she might say "that's interesting" as if to affirm that your story is believable. She might even say something like "Oh, I've seen tons of driverless cars.

So what?" in order to suggest that your story, though perhaps true, is not really relevant, as it matches her picture of the world rather exactly.

By Dessalles's lights, the listener behaves this way because she has been programmed by natural selection to carefully evaluate the truth and relevance of your utterances, to judge you as a potential ally. The ability to separate the conversational wheat from the chaff by means of meticulous interrogation clearly would have been selected for in the contest to appear relevant. Cheating is a real danger in the relevance game. The speaker is often reporting things that occurred in the past or in some distant locale. In the case of the car *sans* driver, the thing reported is both. The listener, therefore, cannot directly verify the truth of the speaker's claims. Speakers know this, so they will often "gin up" the relevance of what they report, and sometimes they will just lie. Advertisers take advantage of the first of these rhetorical strategies, and con men use the second. The only means a listener has to check the relevance and veracity of a speaker's report is to probe it while it is being related. In practice, this means testing it for logical consistency (the car can't be red *and* blue), testing it for empirical consistency (the car can't fly), testing it for relevance (a driverless car must be judged unusual). If, under examination, the speaker fails any of these tests, then his report will be dismissed and his status will fall. If he fails dramatically, then he will be judged mentally incompetent and a candidate for institutionalization of one sort or another. In conversation, you *must* be truthful and relevant. If you aren't, then you're worthless, criminal, or crazy.

A nose for anomalies, a penchant for problem solving, a compulsion to speak, an impulse to question – all of these things are echoes of the age-old competition to be more relevant than others, to improve our status in the eyes of others, to gain allies and, ultimately, to pass on our genes. The result of this struggle was man the talker, *Homo loquens*. The forces of natural selection programmed all primates to do several things – to eat, to sleep, to mate, to live with others. Every primate instinctively does these things and indeed finds pleasure in them. But only humans instinctively talk and find joy in talking. Why, then, do we talk? The answer has two parts. The first is this: evolutionarily speaking, we talk because we were the only primates who gained social status and therewith fitness by talking. The second is this: psychologically speaking, we talk because we must be heard.

WHAT TALKING DID

Talking was the first uniquely human medium, and – setting aside gesture – for more than 150,000 years it was the only medium we knew. There was no writing, no printing, no audiovisual media, and no Internet. If you wanted to convey complex meaning, the only way to do it was by talking to someone. According to our "push" theory of media effects, speech should have had a profound impact on early human social practices and values; it should have formed the basis of a distinct Talking Culture in the distinct Talking Era (180,000 BC to 3500 BC).

What evidence, primary and secondary, is available to test this theory? The primary evidence is very thin: early hunter-gatherers left remarkably little in the way of physical artifacts. One can learn something of ancient hunter-gatherers by studying their modern counterparts – a standard technique in the field – but these comparisons are problematic.[15] Given the lack of good primary data, one can only marvel that paleoanthropologists are able to say anything at all about the way early humans lived. What they can say tends to be general and not related to the impact of talking on living.[16] It would be helpful, then, if we had another source. Happily, we do: our daily observation of modern intimate groups like the family, circle of friends, and workplace. These groups share two characteristics that make them comparable to the early hunter-gatherer band: they are small and they do most of their business through face-to-face verbal communication. Naturally, the analogy is hardly exact: your office isn't the savannah and your co-workers aren't your relatives (if you're lucky). Nonetheless, it has the cardinal advantage of familiarity. Without any additional study, we already know by direct and daily observation how speech and memory shape our intimate groups; therefore, it shouldn't be very difficult to make inferences about how they affected early hunter-gatherer bands. We will use this technique, albeit cautiously, in all that follows.

Accessibility

Talk, as they say, is cheap. So is hearing, though we don't usually acknowledge it. The fact of the matter is that the vast majority of us are born with all the equipment we need to both send speech and receive it: a mouth, a pair of ears (though one will do), and a brain capable of encoding and decoding language. Setting aside the problem of non-native languages, you don't need to be formally taught to send and receive "your" auditory code using these on-board tools, so there are no initial training costs if you are healthy. Speech and hearing are not only easy to get, they are inexpensive to use. Once you begin speaking, the per-unit costs of production – encoding and transmitting messages – are low. You can easily produce 150 words a minute in your native language.[17] For the cost of a good night's sleep and a hearty breakfast, you can therefore speak 34,200 words if you begin at 9:00 AM and quit at noon. Receiving spoken messages – that is, hearing and decoding them – is also inexpensive. A native speaker can understand 250 words per minute with fair comprehension.[18] So, a well-rested and well-fed listener can take in all of your 34,200 words, though she will probably think you something of a bore. Speech and auditory comprehension are so easy that we are not really even conscious of the fact that we are using them. Moreover, speech and hearing are hard to take away, which is to say make them more expensive than they naturally are. Tyrants, mafias, and gangs try to muzzle people and prevent them from saying and hearing things all the time, both with credible threats of violence and violence itself. Sometimes force works, especially when taken to extremes. If your tongue has been cut out, then you will not speak. If your eardrums have been punctured, then you will not hear. And if you have been murdered, then, well, you are dead and can't do much at all. Yet such measures are often themselves dangerous: people, no matter how downtrodden, tend to get angry when they or their relatives are mutilated or murdered, and when people are angry they tend to lash out. Good tyrants know to avoid making their subjects too angry. For this reason, and especially in modern times, efforts to silence people and to prevent them from listening to banned speech have usually failed. The dictators of the former Soviet Union and East Germany, for example, created the most robust surveillance and censorship apparatus ever known, and they coupled it with a brutal speech code. If you said or heard the wrong thing in Moscow or East Berlin, you could do quite a bit of hard time, and your family would probably suffer as well. But people still talked and listened – in kitchens, in parks, and sometimes even to the Western press. They did this knowing that they might be caught, and knowing that they would "pay the price." But they couldn't help themselves. As we've already pointed out, talking – and listening, for that matter – only seem to be acts of pure will, when in actual practice they are often psychological reflexes. If you really have to say something, you'll probably say it. If someone says something of interest in earshot, you'll probably listen.

The fact that talking and listening are cheap and difficult to make expensive means that they comprise the most accessible medium ever known – speech. In terms of access, then, speech networks are *diffused*: almost everyone in the community possesses the means to send and receive messages using it. According to our theory, diffuse media networks will *equalize* social practices realized within and around them. Here "equalize" means to establish relations of rough parity among members. The reason is this: as a purely practical matter, diffuse networks make everyone equal as far as communication is concerned; thus, diffusion blocks the road to media monopolization and inequality.

This is true in intimate speech networks today. Groups such as the family, friendship circle, and workplace operate within a context of relative equality among members because they have no other way to get things done. Of course parents are still parents, the popular kid is still the popular kid, and the boss is still the boss. But as anyone who has held one of these so-called positions of authority will attest, the fact that everyone can chime in at almost any moment imposes practical limits on power. Even if you hold formal authority, you need to get along to be an effective leader. Members of the team must be respected; they will have their say, and everyone will be allowed to listen. Much the same must have been true in the early hunter-gatherer band. Unequal authority was exercised in all manner of social practices. Adults had more authority than children; men had more of it than women; Big Men had more of it than Little Men. Nonetheless, all (adult) members of the band were permitted to have their say and listen, primarily because no one could effectively stop them. The Big Man might try to stop someone from chiming in or hearing this or that, but such an attempt would entail significant risks. If a fight ensued, there was no telling who would get the better of whom. And even if the Big Man triumphed and his foe were silenced or denied the right to listen, his victory would probably be temporary, for his foe would live to talk another day. The Big Man could permanently quiet a loquacious critic or overly attentive listener by killing him or her, but that too would bring serious repercussions. In hunter-gather bands, murder was strongly discouraged: almost everyone was, after all, related to everyone else (if distantly) and no one was really expendable. From the perspective of the majority of band members, a murderous Big Man was not a very good Big Man, and should probably be removed – permanently.

In both the ancient hunter-gatherer band and our intimate speech communities today, the diffusion of speech shaped values. The fact that everyone was going to be able to speak and listen had to be accommodated ethically, and it was via a rough-hewn egalitarianism. In terms of communications, people were equal and therefore it was believed they *should be* equal, or at least relatively so. By this code, ancient Big Men were not allowed to act tyrannically and modern office managers are not allowed to muzzle anyone capriciously. Moreover, equal access to speech and hearing promoted the notion that property should be held in common, that goods and food in particular should be shared, and that everyone had a duty to take care of everyone else. This was probably more true among hunter-gatherers than it is in the modern family, circle of friends, or workplace. But even in these cases we believe that sharing and mutual aid are right and proper. Remember, if you bring something, you should bring enough for everyone.

Privacy

If we were in the business of shooting at people, we would probably want weapons that didn't give away our position. Guns with silencers and flash suppressors, for example, would enable us to attack them without them knowing where we were. That's good for us and bad for them. It's simple to imagine situations in which it would be advantageous for us to be able to talk or listen to them without "giving away our position," that is, our identities. Such a capacity would make whistleblowing and eavesdropping much easier. But, for good or ill, no one has really figured out how to bring off face-to-face anonymity. You have to be pretty good with masks, makeup, or false mustaches to fool anyone looking right at you, and most of us aren't. You might be well-practiced at disguising or even throwing your voice, but you aren't going to be able to disguise it for very long or to throw it very far. Then there's

lying about who you are. Grifters are good at this, but most of us reg-
ular folks aren't. Concealing your identity when speaking or listening
to someone is made that much more difficult by humankind's virtuosic
ability to remember faces and, to a lesser extent, voices.[19] You probably
don't remember your own driver's license number, even though you've
looked at it, repeated it out loud, and written it down many times.
But you only need to see, talk with, and listen to someone once to fix
his face and voice in your memory. And, of course, everyone remembers your face and voice as well, which means the minute they see
you or hear you speak, you're going to "give away your position." As
in the *Wizard of Oz*, so in face-to-face communications: the man behind
the curtain usually doesn't remain behind the curtain for long. That's
the nature of in-person talking and listening: it's public and there is no
getting around that fact. Naturally you can talk and listen to yourself,
but one wonders whether that's really conversing with someone in the
sense we mean. Besides, you might be seen or overheard. You can also
talk and listen to people in private, but isn't that just conversing in a
smaller public? And who's to say your confidants won't leak who you
are and what you said to a larger public? You could swear them to
secrecy, but just what is "secrecy"? Does that mean they can't tell their
wives or husbands? They don't think so. So they tell their spouses, who
are not sworn to secrecy, with predictable results. Your cover, if you
ever had it, is blown.

In sum, if you talk or listen to people face-to-face, they – and probably
a lot of others – are going to know who you are and what you said.
In-person conversation is intrinsically public. Media that are public will
necessarily engender networks that are *connected*, which is to say the
identities of those on the network as well as who communicated what to
whom will be widely known. Following our theory, connected networks
will *open* social practices. Here, "open" means making known who is
doing what with whom. The reason is this: you can't easily hide who
you are or what you are doing on a connected network – information
flows too freely.

This is apparent in our own tiny speech networks today. It is notoriously difficult to keep things secret in a family, circle of friends, or
workplace. "Word gets around" and there is little you can do about it.
So it was in early hunter-gatherer bands. It is difficult to imagine how
any of the band's major activities – political, economic, cultural – could

have been concealed from public view. They were all organized via face-to-face verbal interaction and were therefore difficult to hide. This is not to say that everything done was known to everyone. People had secrets, both individual and shared. If they didn't they wouldn't have been able to practice deception, which is essential to human nature and perhaps even to human well-being. Nor is it to say that early humans had no private life. There are certain social activities – having sex, giving birth – that nearly every human culture has hidden from public gaze. Doubtless the hunter-gatherers had a set of private activities as well. The point is that with no privatizable medium and thus no segmented network relations, the proportion of social practices that were pursued in public with full knowledge of all network members was necessarily greater than that in a context with privatizable media and segmented network relations. There was no place to hide.

The necessary public-ness of speech shaped values in early hunter-gatherer bands and continues to do so in small modern speech networks today. The fact that nothing could truly be private had to be accommodated ethically, and it was via publicism, the idea that information – and especially high-value information – should be shared. In the hunter-gatherer band the code implied that band members must speak openly and truthfully about things that affected the entire band, which, in this confined context, was virtually everything. In contrast, people who kept things to themselves, attempted to hide things from the group, or consistently lied to others would be condemned as selfish. In an all-talking environment, words were common property and had to be shared. Much the same is true in our intimate circles today: among family members, friends, and co-workers we believe we are obliged to share the truth where it concerns our common affairs. If you don't, you will be deemed "untrustworthy."

Fidelity

Speech is remarkable in that you can describe and transmit almost anything you sense with it. Imagine you have just returned from a relaxing nap in a field of daisies. You want to "paint the picture" (metaphorically speaking) to your friend. You *gazed* at a clear and blue sky. You *heard* the birds singing in the distance. You *smelled* spring flowers in the air. You *tasted* honeysuckle on your lips. You *felt* the breeze brushing your face. You may have sensed all these things, but the person to whom you describe them will sense none of them. She will not see the sky, hear the birds, smell the daisies, taste the honeysuckle, or feel the breeze. All she will sense – specifically, hear – is a flow of meaning-bearing sounds, spoken words built into spoken sentences like "The air smelled of spring flowers." She will understand you were dozing in a field of daisies, but will not sense anything like what you sensed. This is because speech represents data from all five senses (vision, sound, smell, taste, and feeling) through one encoded sensory channel (sound). Speech is a five-to-one code. As such, the only sense data that it can represent iconically is sound, and only those sounds within the range of the human vocal apparatus (that is, those that can be mimicked). Here, "iconically" means that the form of the representation – the sign – itself is determined by the form of the thing it's supposed to represent – the signified.[20] For example, a picture of a daisy is an icon of a daisy because it looks like the thing it signifies. Linguists sometimes call these "motivated signs" because their form is determined by the thing they signify – an iconic sign of a daisy *must* look like a daisy or it is not a sign of a daisy at all.[21] In contrast, the spoken word "daisy" is not an icon of a daisy because it looks nothing like a daisy. In fact, because it is a sound, it doesn't "look" like anything at all. Linguists call these "arbitrary signs" because there is no necessary relationship between the sign and the thing it signifies – the spoken word for a daisy could just as well be "toaster." When we encode sense data using arbitrary signs like spoken words, a lot of information is lost. The experience of a daisy is rich and full; the spoken word "daisy" does not reproduce that experience. We have a saying that nicely captures this phenomenon: "A picture's worth a thousand words."

Speech, then, is a low-fidelity medium. What comes in – rich sense data – is not what comes out – a one-channel code. It follows that speech networks will be *symbolic*. In order to get on them and use them, you will have to know the code. And the only thing you will be able to send and receive will be symbols, arbitrary signs that must be encoded and decoded. According to our theory, symbolic media networks should *conceptualize* social practices and values that emerge within them. Here, "conceptualized" means to make things observed into abstract ideas. The reason is this: if humans are compelled to use a mode of communication built on arbitrary signs, then they will begin to play with those signs and build systems of ideas out of them; speech forces humans to use arbitrary signs.

We can see the process of conceptualization in our small speech networks today. Naturally our family members, friends, and co-workers are unique individuals with whom we interact – and therefore directly sense – everyday. We *see* them and recognize that nobody *looks* like them. They are who they are and nobody else. But the minute we speak their names, we are engaged in the process of conceptualization. We say that proper names refer exclusively to unique individuals. But they almost never do. Something on the order of 15 million men around the world carry a variation of the given name "Mohammed" today.[22] Around 93 million Chinese bear the surname "Wang."[23] In 1990, there were approximately 50,000 men named "John Smith" in the United States.[24] An identifier such as "ID number 760399287654" can only refer to one concrete thing; an abstract category like "Mohammed" can refer to many things simultaneously. It follows that every spoken word we use and understand, aside from unique IDs and some onomatopoeic terms, is an abstraction defined by tacit or explicit convention. To speak is to abstract, to remove perception from its concrete time and place and put it in conceptual buckets. It could have been no different for our hunter-gatherer ancestors. They used general words to refer to different things: the word "man" could refer to *that* man or any other; the word "tree" to *that* tree or any other; the word "cloud" to *that* cloud or any other. For them as for us, the generality of words raised a vexing question: what is the epistemic status of words? They exist, but they are not entirely of this world: you cannot sense "man," "tree," and "cloud" in the same way you can *that* man, *that* tree, or *that* cloud. Plato drew a reasonable conclusion, so reasonable that he could not have been the first and was certainly not the last to draw it: words, he said, must come from some other "higher" world that we cannot sense, a world of perfect abstract forms. When we use words, then, we are interacting with that other, spiritual world – there was no way around it.

The unavoidable abstraction of speech molded mores in prehistory and, at least among some, continues to do so today in face-to-face speech groups. The fact that social practices had to be abstracted needed to be accommodated, and it was via idealism, the notion that the unseen world – the world of ideas and spirits – was somehow more important than the seen world. Since one used words to interact with the unseen world, they had to be treated very carefully. Thus, hunter-gatherers developed a code that governed how one could most effectively and safely use them. Some things had to be said in order to ensure that the unseen world remained favorably disposed to ours, for example, prayers, incantations, and spells. Some things could not be said because they would anger the residents of the unseen world, for example, curses, blasphemies, and profanities. Elders were duty-bound to teach novices the code and to make sure (or as sure as possible in an egalitarian community) that everyone observed it as closely as possible. Those who did so were deemed virtuous and would be rewarded; those who didn't were deemed wicked and would be punished. Though many people today have come to believe, *pace* Plato, that words do not signal the existence of a hidden sphere, many others do. Religious people still hold to the notion that some things must be said and others must not because words themselves are a kind of window to a higher sphere. And the echo of this ritual behavior and the belief that stands behind it can be seen even among non-religious people who observe a superstitious avoidance of certain words and phrases. You don't say "good luck" to someone about to go on stage because it's bad luck. Rather, you say "Break a leg!"

Volume

On March 24, 2007, one Jaysimha Ravirala began a public lecture titled "Personality Development Concepts" at the Federation of Andhra Pradesh Chambers of Commerce and Industry, Hyderabad, India. On March 29, Mr. Ravirala concluded his remarks. His 120-hour speech was the longest in history.[25] It was probably the most annoying as well. By all appearances, humans were not designed to send, receive, or exchange spoken messages comprising approximately 500,000 words and lasting five days. Actually, it's hard to say with any certainty what the maximum length of a *practical* spoken message is. It stands to reason that it should be a function of: (1) the number of words we can comfortably speak without getting a sore throat; and (2) the number of words we can comfortably comprehend without "zoning out." No one knows either of these numbers, so no calculation can be made.

That said, we can make a rough estimate based on the well-established practice of limiting lectures to about 50 minutes. The logic here is that if the 50-minute mark were significantly sub-optimal – if speakers were passing out and listeners were falling asleep – then it would have been changed at some point in the last several hundred years. It hasn't been. In 50 minutes, a fluent speaker can produce 7,500 words talking at an easy pace. If said lecturer is good, then she can hold the audience's attention for the duration but not much longer. That, then, is an approximation of the upper bound, the largest a spoken message can practically be. The lower bound is naturally one word. The vast majority of spoken messages don't fall in the middle, but rather are quite close to the lower bound. In a typical conversation, you say several sentences – tell a little story – and your interlocutor listens. Then you exchange roles. Pretty soon, you both get tired. The conversation stops. In short, most spoken messages are short. Now, the volume of information a medium can carry is not only determined by the rate at which senders can transmit data, but also by the number of people who receive – or can receive – the message. When you say ten words to one person, then you have communicated ten words. When you say ten words to two people, you have communicated two sets of ten words, or twenty words. In order to figure out what the capacity of speech is to transmit information, we need to know how many people you can talk to at once. We'll deal with this question in more detail in a later section (see "Range"), but the answer is approximately 800 without the aid of any special technology, like an amphitheater or a megaphone. The lower bound is usually considered one, but you can talk to yourself, which would make it functionally zero. The average, again, falls toward the lower bound: typically you speak with one or two people at a time.

All of this means that the practical capacity of human speech to transmit information is low. The messages we can conveniently send and receive are short, and our ability to communicate them to others is limited. Media with low capacity give rise to *constrained* networks, that is, networks in which the rate of data transmission between nodes is limited. According to our theory, constrained networks should *economize* social practices realized within and around them. Here "economize" means to promote spare, efficient use of resources. The reason is this: all things considered, constrained networks do not have the excess capacity necessary for the gathering and transmission of non-essential data; thus they are less likely to permit frivolous use. The network will be used primarily for necessary communications, and only secondarily for other sorts of activity.

This is the case in our small speech networks today. Since these networks can only accommodate comparatively light traffic, most of their capacity is taken up by essential tasks – maintenance of existing relationships, processing of routine business, and planning future activities. In speech networks, talking is a means of organization, a way to get things done, not generally a means of entertainment. That doesn't mean, of course, that it isn't also a way to have fun. Humans enjoy talking, and they will do it just for its own sake, particularly with familiars. Nonetheless, most of the talking we do is instrumental – we use it to make people do things like clean up the family room, order another round at the bar, or finish the big project. Very rarely do we organize events that are specifically focused on live verbal fun, for example, plays, poetry recitations, song fests or what have you. We have neither the time, nor does speech have the surplus bandwidth, necessary to allow us to do such things freely. It must have been the same among hunter-gatherers long ago. Like us, they needed to maintain relationships, to process routine business, and to plan future activities. Unlike us, all they had to do it with was speech, which, as we've said, doesn't really have high bandwidth. This constraint meant that they saw speech as a tool, and a reasonably expensive one at that. When they had excess capacity, they used speech for entertainment. But there wasn't much excess capacity. They understood that words had to be used sparingly, for there weren't that many of them.

The limited bandwidth of speech shaped values among hunter-gatherers and continues to do so today in intimate groups. The fact that speech had to be used sparingly needed to be accommodated, and it was via asceticism, the notion that the self develops through discipline. Thus, hunter-gatherers believed that words should be used in a certain way, that there was a code of proper speaking. Those who spoke well – were disciplined – were virtuous; those who spoke poorly – were undisciplined – were not. We can see echoes of speech-asceticism in the Classical World's love of rhetoric, Plato notwithstanding. Then a person was judged by how they spoke, which is to say how well they hewed to the code of proper speaking. We see a similar sort of thing among family, friends, and in the workplace today. We often judge our intimates by how they speak. Concision and eloquence are virtues; verbosity and coarseness are vices. Nobody likes the "big mouth" or the "foul mouth."

Velocity

Speech is fast. How much time elapses between the moment you intend to say something and the moment you say it, that is, between thought and expression? According to physiologists, your brain fires signals to your body at a pace of something on the order of 300 feet per second.[26] That's about as fast as a typical Formula 1 race car. If the distance from your brain's language-processing regions to your vocal apparatus is roughly six inches, then the typical lag between a really compelling thought like "Marry me!" and the utterance of the exclamation "Marry me!" is going to be about 1/600th of a second. Of course, you don't have to immediately say everything you think, and it's probably advisable that you don't. Once "Marry me!" emerges, we confront another question: How much time elapses between the moment you speak it and the moment your words reach your beloved? Physicists have proposed an answer. They say that words fly out of your mouth at 1,128 feet per second, depending on atmospheric conditions.[27] That's about the velocity of a typical rifle bullet. If your intended is three feet away (closer would be better), then your proposal will reach her in around 1/376th of a second. In much less than a blink of an eye (between one-tenth and three-tenths of a second),[28] you have gone from hanging out to getting hitched. Or not.

There is no doubt, then, that speech is a high-velocity medium. Combine speech's speed with its low cost (see "Accessibility"), and it's easy to see that the networks built with it will be thoroughly dialogic. If both senders and recipients can produce, dispatch, and comprehend messages in an instant, and it costs virtually nothing to do so, there is every reason to expect a rapid exchange of messages, that is, dialogue. According to our theory, dialogic networks should *democratize* the social practices that are realized in and around them. Here "democratize" means encouraging broadly deliberative and consensual decision making. The reason is this: if humans are given a low-cost opportunity to exchange opinions about any important matter, they usually will; dialogic networks afford them this opportunity.

Again, witness our small speech networks today. They are generally run – if not officially organized – along democratic lines. The family head, leader of the pack, or boss can make decisions by fiat, but he or she would be well advised not to do so. Best to discuss important issues until some rough consensus – or the face-saving appearance of consensus – is reached. Early human bands probably operated in the same way. There was no getting around the fact that members could and would discuss things of common interest – they could not be stopped, at least at a bearable cost. This meant that the easiest way to organize any collective activity was to deliberate to the point of consensus. Democratization did not mean that everything was discussed all the time. Indeed, much had already been decided and was enshrined in tradition. But even the social practice of tradition was democratized insofar as the status of something as "traditional" was always open to debate and likely to be debated. In such a context, negotiation was the way things were accomplished.

The velocity and therefore dialogicity of speech had a definite impact on the mores of hunter-gatherers and so it does today in small speech networks. The fact that everyone was able to engage in a rapid-fire back-and-forth needed to be accommodated, and it was via deliberativism, the idea that everyone should speak for themselves and that opinions should be equally weighted. There were justifiable exceptions: the Big Man would sometimes decide himself, and his words would generally have more weight than the Little Man's. But in most instances it was deemed proper that things be discussed by adult members of the band as a whole. Gods could dictate; men had to talk. Roughly the same tacit ethical code operates in our small groups today. As family members, friends, and co-workers, we generally agree that things should be discussed more or less democratically in the normal course of affairs. There are still justifiable exceptions: your superior sometimes "makes the call," meaning what she says matters more than what you say. Nonetheless, we hold that surveying opinion and working toward consensus is the right thing to do in most instances. If you think otherwise, you are quite likely to be called "bossy."

Range

It's true that voices carry, so you have to watch what you say. But in point of fact they don't carry very far, so you needn't be that careful. Imagine you are talking to a colleague in your workplace in a normal voice at a distance of three feet. You don't have to raise your voice and she doesn't have to strain to hear. Now imagine that you triple the distance between the two of you, making the gap nine feet. Because sound intensity decays quickly as it travels through the atmosphere, your six-foot retreat reduces the *objective* power of the sound reaching her by nine times.[29] But that doesn't mean she *perceives* your words as one-ninth as loud. If that were so, she couldn't really hear you, and clearly she can. In fact, from her perspective, your voice is roughly half as loud as it was at three feet. The reason changes in sound intensity are not matched one-to-one by changes in perceived loudness is evolutionary. In order to survive, our ancestors needed to register an enormous range of sonic signals, from very weak ones to very strong ones. To accommodate this range, natural selection designed the auditory system to compensate for huge swings in sonic power: the system steps-up soft signals to make them audible and steps-down powerful ones to make them safe. Thus, we can comfortably listen to a mosquito and a rock concert even though the sonic intensity of the former is one-billionth that of the latter. A band is louder than a buzzing insect, but it's not one billion times as loud. The practitioners of psycho-acoustics have devised a rule for relating movements in sound intensity and loudness: each 10-point shift in decibels changes loudness by a factor of two, that is, doubles it or halves it.[30] Doubling the distance between you and your colleague resulted in a reduction of 10 decibels in sound intensity from her perspective; hence the sound is half as loud. You are still audible and perhaps even understandable, but softer. Now imagine that you triple the distance once more, that is, move from nine feet away to 27 feet away. That reduces the strength of your signal by nine times again and results in a further 10-decibel drop. Again the loudness of your voice from your interlocutor's perspective is cut in half, making it one-quarter as audible as it was when you were three feet away. Since the ambient noise in a quiet office can easily exceed 40 decibels[31] – approximately the intensity with which your words strike your co-worker's ear – you can no longer be heard. It's time to raise your voice. Most healthy adults shout at about 80 decibels, though screams can break 115 decibels.[32] If you begin to shout at 80 decibels, your words will strike your co-worker's ear 27 feet way at about 60 decibels. So you are right back where you started, though you are annoying your colleagues and ruining your throat. But you are a glutton for punishment. You triple the distance between you and her again. You are 81 feet way (you've got a big office), your words strike her with a force of about 50 decibels, and are half as loud as they were when you were 27 feet away. She can hear you, and sort of make out what you are shouting. She shouts back that she wants you to stop yelling. But you proceed with your bizarre experiment and again triple the distance. Now you are 243 feet way from her (let's say you work in an airplane hangar), your words hit her at around 40 decibels, and are half as loud as they were when you were 81 feet away. Once again you've reached the point at which ambient noise has canceled your signal. She can't hear you, particularly over the sound of your boss threatening to fire you. Besides, your voice is shot.

Because the range of the human voice is short, so is its practical reach. Reach is the number of people within range of a message. The unaided voice is a broadcast medium, meaning its signal moves over an area like a radio wave rather than from point to point like a telephone line. The shape of the area covered by a voice is really conical in that it begins at a point of origin and expands along two axes. Think of a conical megaphone that goes on and on. To simplify matters, however, let's just say that the voice expands in all directions, that is, radiates. Let's also say that you can shout intelligibly at 50 feet. Given these two assumptions, your voice can potentially be heard by anyone standing not more than 50 feet away from you in any direction. Your physical reach, then, is a circle with an area of 7,854 square feet. This sounds like a lot, but it's not. The highest crowd density humans can sustain without injury is about two square feet per person, about what you experience in a very crowded elevator.[33] At that rate, subtracting your two square feet, your reach would theoretically be 3,926 people. But practically that level could never be obtained, first because crowds are noisy and second because it would not take long for the first fight to break out. A much more reasonable allotment of space would be 10 square feet per person, about what you experience in a "loose crowd."[34] Then your reach would be only 784 people. But even an audience of that size will be difficult to hold for long. Remember, you are yelling and they need to eat, drink, and use the facilities. It's no wonder that most speeches come in well under an hour.

Speech, then, is a short-range medium with small reach. It's just not effective beyond about 20 or 30 feet, the point at which you begin to have to shout to be understood. Cries, shrieks, and screams can be heard at greater distances – perhaps up to a half mile in the right conditions – but all you can say is "Arrrrrrgh!" and that's not much. Media with short range generally give rise to intensive networks. According to our theory, intensive networks should *simplify* social practices. Here, "simplify" means to make different things the same. The reason is this: people in focused networks are less likely to encounter unfamiliar people, things, and ideas. The world of the intensive network will not be completely uniform, but neither will it be as diverse as that engendered by an extensive network.

Social practices in modern speech networks are simplified in just this way. You tend to know the people you can and do talk to regularly. They are like you, or will probably become like you (or you like them) if you continue to interact with them. The boundaries of the "known" are surprisingly rigid: for reasons probably having to do with the natural human fear of strangers, you don't tend to talk to people you don't already know. Talking to strangers is hard work, and getting to know them is harder still. So most people avoid it and "stick to their own," at least as far as talking is concerned. Naturally you have many relationships outside the family, circle of friends, and workplace based on "weak ties." If you are an outgoing person, these weak relationships might be many, but for most people – especially if they live in an all-talking environment – they will be few and weak indeed. All this was probably the case for early humans living in hunter-gatherer bands. The members of the band talked to one another – people like themselves – and rarely encountered anyone who wasn't already known. When they met strangers, they probably feared them as they had had little experience dealing with people not like themselves. A long-range medium might have afforded them the opportunity to learn of people different from themselves. But they had none.

In both the hunter-gatherer band and the modern intimate circle, short range and limited reach shaped values. The fact that the known universe was small needed to be accommodated, and it was via monism, the notion that there is only one kind of person – yours – and one kind of thing – those around you. In that world, there was no "us" and "them": there was only "us." To be sure, hunter-gatherers encountered "different" people and things. But they did not recognize them as such. Rather, they either assimilated them to "us" or rejected their status as people or things, that is, classified them as "strangers." If determined to be the latter, then they could only be dangerous and should therefore be avoided. We see a similar sort of mentality in operation in our small speech groups. Our "us" – the family, circle of friends, co-workers – is strictly demarked from everything that is "non-us." Those who fall into the category of "non-us" are not "them" (a group known and different) but "strangers" (a group unknown and different). And everyone knows that you shouldn't talk to strangers.

Persistence

In general, the earth's atmosphere is a poor slate on which to record information. It's full of clouds, buffeted by winds, and periodically wiped clean by rain. The best anyone has ever come up with is sky-writing, which uses the air to suspend what are really just elaborate smoke signals. Truth be told, skywriting is good for advertisements but worthless for data storage. But even humble skywriting is superior to speech as a storage medium, for spoken words *instantly* "vanish into thin air." You say something and a moment later every external trace of it is gone. You can't see it, hear it, smell it, taste it, or touch it. All you can do is remember it. Alas, as a device for recording experience, memory has definite limits. First of all, memory is small. Short-term memory is especially tiny. According to one oft-cited study, it can grasp between five and nine elements and hold them for roughly 20 seconds.[35] Then said elements disappear, unless, that is, they make it into long-term memory. Most don't. Shifting things from short-term to long-term memory is hard work. Ask anyone cramming for an exam. We don't know the capacity of long-term memory, but it certainly has an upper bound. By one estimate, adult humans typically have on the order of 100 megabytes of *learned* data stored in their memories.[36] A typical CD holds 650 megabytes. Second, memory is low fidelity. Imagine you see a tree. Photons reflected from the tree strike the rods and cones in your eyes; your eyes send them to the brain as electrical impulses; your brain then stores them as neural networks. Seems simple, but it's not. In essence, the "tree" has been translated from photons to electrons and from electrons to neurons. Moreover, at each translation the amount of data in the photonic image has been radically reduced. It's as if you translated the original Russian version of *War and Peace* into English as "A big book about war by a Russian." A half million Russian words have been reduced to eight English words. Memory encodes and compresses everything in this way. It doesn't store pictures; it stores gists. Gists are remarkable. They are extraordinarily well addressed and can store any kind of sensation. That means you can easily call up the gist of the tree you saw, and it might well contain data about the way the tree looked, sounded, and smelled. The problem arises when you want to share your experience of the tree with someone. The only way you can do that is to translate the neural gist into speech. That definitely means another encoding and probably means more compression. Thus, a verbal description of a tree is at least three removes from the tree itself: photons to electrons (perception), electrons to neurons (memory), neurons to words (recall and speech). At each moment, the data are translated into a different medium and thinned out. It's no wonder that a poem has never been as lovely as a tree, for the word "tree" doesn't *sound* anything like a tree *looks*. Finally, memory is impermanent. From the moment we are born, we are constantly forgetting things. There's a common if confusing expression that goes "I've forgotten more than I ever knew." Whatever it means, it's certainly true that at an early age the sum of things most people have forgotten exceeds the things they have ever known at any given point in time. To say that the memory is like a sieve is to insult sieves.

So speech is not persistent. It neither remains floating around in the air nor firmly fixed in memory. Media that are not persistent should encourage the formation of *substitutive* networks, that is, ones in which new data supplant old data because the total amount of data that can be archived is severely constrained. According to our theory, substitutive networks should *ritualize* social practices realized within and around them. Here, "ritualize" means to use the *form* of expression to store content. The reason is this: people in substitutive networks have limited means to fix new content, and therefore must employ mnemonic devices such as rhyme, meter, rhythm, and behavioral routines to do so. Raw memory just won't do the job, and there is no way to record anything in an external medium because there are none. Therefore, the data are, so to say, inscribed in actions that can be easily repeated. The past exists as behavior in the present.

Evidence of ritualization is apparent in our speech networks today. The daily interactions of family members, friends, co-workers, and strangers are full of routines that preserve valuable information and thereby free up memory for more important stuff. Some of them must be acted out, as in the case of appropriate comportment: how to greet someone (handshaking, embraces, salutes), how to look at them (sometimes in the eye, sometimes not), how far to stand from them (close but not too close). Others are spoken, as in the case of clichés expressing regret ("Excuse me"), sorrow ("Bummer"), joy ("Great"), appreciation ("Thank you"), and so on. We never have to think when using these devices: we simply recognize the situation in which they are to be performed and perform them. We just don't have the memory capacity (or patience) to think of what to do or say every time we are in one of these stereotyped contexts, and we certainly don't have the time to record what we did or said in every such situation so we can look back on it and adjust it for the next interaction. Now imagine what it must have been like for early humans without any means of recording information outside their nearly zero-sum memories. They would have to capture everything of real value in some sort of ritual that could be more or less "automatically" performed. Not just the niceties of interpersonal relations, but *everything* – how to hunt, gather, cook, eat, clean, sew, travel, camp, marry, name the young, heal the sick, bury the dead, and worship the spirits. Some of this could be entrusted to raw memory. But memory faded, and the rememberers died. So all this vital information had to be preserved by incorporation in rituals.

The constraint of memory and the necessity of ritualization shaped the mores of hunter-gatherers and continues to do so in face-to-face speech communities. The fact that very little could be recorded needed to be accommodated, and it was via eternalism, the notion that things have always been basically as they are. In this world, time was not very linear. Of course there was a "before now," "now," and "after now." But there was no well-elaborated idea of a continuous, knowable past-present-future. Neither was time very cyclical. Naturally the same kinds of things happened over and over – the sun rose and set, the rains came and went, people were born and then died. But everyone knew that they really weren't the same things, because things changed. The important point is, however, that they didn't generally change very much, or rather that there was little evidence that they changed very much. This is why the rituals always worked, and why they had to be protected, preserved, and performed correctly. Life depended on it. People today seem to be much more practical, and many dismiss "empty ritual" as a waste of time. Nonetheless, our direct interactions with family members, friends, and co-workers are highly ritualized, and we hold fast to the notion that we should observe these rituals even if we don't call them such. Intimates who routinely violate the code of established, routinized comportment are thought of in harsh terms. They are "thoughtless," "insensitive," and "rude." Such people, we say, "just don't know how to act" and therefore are "difficult to deal with."

Searchability

As we just said, words appear (that is, are audible) and vanish very quickly. Alas, they leave virtually no trace in the primary propagating medium – the atmosphere – and only a slight and fleeting hint in secondary propagating media – for example, a vibrating window pane. Sound waves deflect, so if you are in the right acoustical environment – say, a canyon – then they might rapidly come back to you once or twice as echoes. Other than that, they are gone forever. The evanescence of speech is important because it means that speech – or rather the primary medium in which speech is propagated – does not store words and therefore cannot be searched. In an all-talking environment, your memory is the only storage device available (aside from rituals; see "Persistence") and thus the only one that can be searched. Fortunately, memory is very searchable for a number of reasons. First, searching memory is cheap and almost always possible. If you are healthy, it costs you virtually nothing to search your memory. Short of knocking you out, it's hard to prevent you from conducting a mental search. Second, you not only have the ability to search your own memory, but also everyone else's you can talk to. Just ask them if they remember something and, if you are nice, they will probably tell you. If they refuse, you can try to persuade them, likely with mixed results. Third, searching memory is fast. In fact, it's usually almost instantaneous: you see something and it immediately reminds you of something related. Accessing someone else's memory may be a bit slower, as you have to ask permission to conduct the search or, if they rebuff your request, try to persuade them. Fourth, memory's search function is very responsive. If the mind holds a bit of information, then the memory can precisely and rapidly retrieve not only just the right bit, but also all the bits that are related to it. The human memory's address system is remarkably flexible and efficient.

So speech is not searchable at all. Memory, however, is quite searchable. Searchable media, like memory, give rise to mapped networks. Assuming a certain degree of comity in a human group, each node (person) will make his or her storage and search capacities (memories) available to every other node, rendering the data therein visible to all. By the lights of our theory, mapped media networks should *amateurize* social practices. Here, "amateurize" means empowering the individual to do things independently, in this instance to look for and get information. The reason is this: since everyone in effect knows or can easily find out everything, everyone is an expert in everything, which is to say there are no experts, only amateurs.

We see this in intimate speech communities today. In the family, circle of friends, and workplace, we all do basically the same things, or at least a small set of different things everyone can see and is familiar with. Therefore, we know a lot of the same things. That which we don't all know is shared, so that everyone is "on the same page." Thus, everyone knows most everything important. Everyone is an expert, so no one is an expert. Such was probably the case with early human communities living in talking-only environments, only more so. In order for there to be unequal access to information, there has to be unequal distribution of information. Members of hunter-gatherer bands, however, all had similar experiences and therefore knew roughly the same things. Information was evenly distributed, at least compared to the era that followed (see Chapter 2). Naturally, different sorts of knowledge clustered in certain groups – elders knew things adolescents didn't, men knew things women didn't (and vice versa), and Big Men knew things Little Men didn't. But in comparison to the vast field of common knowledge shared by the entire band, these differences were minor. Thus, it was difficult to use knowledge as a basis for special status, at least in the long run. The primary exception would be the Wise Man. He claimed special, esoteric knowledge and used this claim as a basis for superior status. But even his position was not unassailable. In an oral environment, any declaration of esoteric wisdom could be challenged, as almost everyone had the ability and right to question anyone else. Moreover, even if the Wise Man survived a barrage of probing queries, he would be required to use his esoterica for the good of the group. This put him in a bind. If he refused, then the band would not grant him special expert status. If he complied, then he had to demonstrate the efficacy of his knowledge. What if he failed? What if his special knowledge proved useless? Again, the band would not grant him elevated status and might even call him a fraud. In early human communities, then, knowledge and status did not clump. Rather, they spread out among the members of the band, all of whom had some claim on them.

The fact that memory is highly searchable had a profound impact on hunter-gatherer values, as it does at present in intimate speech groups. The fact that knowledge was accessible to all accommodated, and it was via individualism, the idea that each person should be autonomous. Since everyone knew almost everything, and that which they didn't know they could find out, everyone knew all that was needed to live: how to hunt, how to cook, how to sew, how to pray, and so on. Any real person would know these things; if you did not, then your personhood was in doubt. People who were needlessly dependent on others were looked down upon. We see a similar ethic among intimate groups today. We share information freely with our family members, friends, and co-workers, and we expect them to be independent. Of course we would "do anything" for them, but we don't want to have to do it regularly. If we have to, then they run the risk of being called a "mooch."

In the nineteenth century, gentlemen-scholars were casting about for an omnibus name for the early human artifacts they had recently uncovered. They settled on "prehistoric," meaning "of the era before written history."[37] The choice was a sort of admission that their task – the reconstruction of human life from the moment *Homo sapiens* appeared to the emergence of writing – would be a difficult one. How, after all, do you write the history of people who could not write and left nothing but a scattered few mute artifacts in their wake? Over the past century, archeologists and anthropologists have offered many answers to this question, most of which focus on the detailed analysis of the ancient artifacts themselves as well as investigations of contemporary hunter-gatherers. We have offered another answer, one that focuses precisely on the fact that early humans were "prehistoric," that is, could not write.

Our thesis is that speech and memory shaped the way ancient hunter-gatherers lived in predictable ways, just as it does in our modern oral groups. Then and now, speech and memory had inherent physical attributes. Then and now, the attributes of speech and memory fostered talking networks. Then and now, talking networks promoted certain social practices and values. Table 2 sums up the entire theory as it concerns the impact of speech and memory on ancient hunter-gatherers and modern intimate circles alike.

It's important to note that speech and memory don't necessarily foster the social practices and values listed, or when they do, foster them in the same degree. They simply *tend* to produce them most of the time at some level. In fact, we can and do diminish or even completely override the natural tendencies of speech and memory at times, though only with great effort. Consider, for example, the military. Like any other large organization, the military is divided up into smaller working groups such as staff offices, combat units, and special details. Here

TABLE 2. *The Effects of Speech*

Speaking		Medium Attribute →		Network Attribute →		Social Practice →		Cultural Value
Accessibility	=	High	→	Diffused	→	Equalized	→	Egalitarianism
Privacy	=	Low	→	Connected	→	Opened	→	Publicism
Fidelity	=	Low	→	Symbolic	→	Conceptualized	→	Idealism
Volume	=	Low	→	Constrained	→	Economized	→	Asceticism
Velocity	=	High	→	Dialogic	→	Democratized	→	Deliberativism
Range	=	Low	→	Intensive	→	Simplified	→	Monism
Persistence	=	Low	→	Substitutive	→	Ritualized	→	Eternalism
Searchability	=	High	→	Mapped	→	Amateurized	→	Individualism

everyone works face-to-face and the primary mode of communication is talking. Under normal conditions, this fact would push military working groups in the direction predicted by our theory – members would begin treating each other as equals, knowledge would be shared, and decision making would be democratized. But the military cannot allow this to happen, for its work requires ever-present hierarchy, need-to-know secrecy, and to-the-letter obedience even in face-to-face contexts. In essence, the military has to foster social practices and values that run against the grain of the media environment in which they are realized. It does this by imposing a strict – and profoundly unnatural – behavioral code on face-to-face interaction. The code covers both gestures (salutes, standing at attention) and speech (use of honorifics like "sir," speaking only when addressed by a superior). It applies both to upward communication (from inferior to superior) and downward communication (from superior to inferior). The intention of all these rules is to ensure that inferiors do not refuse the commands of superiors and superiors do not treat inferiors "like brothers," that is, fraternize. The military – and not only the military, but many "total institutions"[38] – knows that in the absence of these strange, punitive rules, that is exactly what would happen. It's the natural course of things in predominantly oral groups.

Among our ancient ancestors, however, nature took its course. Thus, band members treated each other as equals and believed equality was proper. They communicated openly and held that knowledge was common property. They valued disciplined speech. They discussed common affairs and proclaimed that it was right to do so. They were similar one to another and understood conformity to be a good thing. They practiced many rituals and esteemed those who performed them correctly. They were autonomous in the sense that they could all do what needed to be done themselves, and they prized this autonomy greatly. Though we have arrived at this picture by considering the impact of speech and memory on contemporary intimate communities and reasoning back to hunter-gatherers, it is by and large supported by the work of paleoanthropologists.[39]

This, then, was Talking Culture, the product in large measure of talking itself. It was the most robust and productive media culture we've ever known, surviving basically unchanged for approximately

175,000 years and enabling *Homo sapiens* to populate nearly the entire globe. But nothing lasts forever. In the next chapter we will see how a peculiarly common set of circumstances placed burdens on Talking Culture that it could not bear, or rather bear alone. The result was the emergence of a new medium – writing – and with it Manuscript Culture.

2

HOMO SCRIPTOR

Humanity in the Age of Manuscripts

If men learn [writing], it will implant forgetfulness in their souls: they will cease to exercise memory because they rely on that which is written, calling things to remembrance no longer from within themselves.[1]

– Plato, *Phaedrus*, 275A

In Plato's time and place – Greece circa 400 BC – neither philosophy nor writing was particularly new. Understood in the generic sense of asking big questions, the former was as ancient as humanity itself. Understood in the sense of encoding spoken language, writing was already 2,500 years old. But the use of writing to practice philosophy was novel in Plato's day, and it was an open question as to whether the medium was up to the task. Plato didn't think so. He found the same fault with writing as he found with spoken rhetoric: neither allowed dialogue, the only means by which one could find the Truth. Like so many rhetorically adept politicians, written words "talk to you as though they were intelligent, but if you ask them anything about what they say, from a desire to be instructed, they go on telling you just the same thing for ever" (*Phaedrus*, 275D). Such monologues – spoken or written – were not only tedious, they were also the enemies of true understanding. But writing, Plato said, was worse than rhetoric, for it not only mislead people, it also made them pretentious fools. By "telling [readers] of many things without teaching them," Plato wrote, "[written words] will make them seem to know much, while for the most part they know nothing; and as men filled, not with wisdom, but with the conceit of wisdom, they will be a burden to their fellows" (*Phaedrus*, 275A). Writing's potential for causing harm was made greater by the fact that it separated speaker and speech. "Once a thing is put in writing, the composition, whatever it may be, drifts all over the place, getting into the hands not only of those who understand it, but equally of those who have no business with it; it doesn't know how to address the right people, and not address the wrong people" (*Phaedrus*, 275D). From Plato's point of view, this sort of wandering was unacceptable. In a dialogic context, philosophers can fight back against unwarranted attacks. But once their words are captured in writing, they cannot. The mute text is "unable to defend or help itself" (*Phaedrus*, 275D). For all these reasons, Plato said, "no intelligent man will ever be so bold as to put into language those things which his reason has contemplated, especially not into a form that is unalterable, which must be the case with what is expressed in written symbols" (*Epistle* VII, 343).[2] It's little wonder, then, that Plato makes no provision for the teaching of writing in *The Republic*.

It may seem paradoxical that Plato, enemy of supposed philosophic writing, wrote all this down. But it really isn't. True to his conviction that any form of monologue stunted intellectual development, he wrote dialogues. Others, however, were not so wise, and first among them were the rhetorically trained pseudo-statesmen he so despised. And why did they write their long, flowery speeches? The same reason they spoke them – for the sake of power and fame. To them, the written word was not a means to the Truth, but rather a tool of manipulation. As we will see, Plato was not wrong here. In the hands of elites, writing proved to be one of the most effective instruments of power ever invented. Rulers could not stop people from talking, but they could control writing, and with it meaning. The result was the end of the hunter-gather band and the birth of the kind of hierarchical societies with which we are all so familiar today.

WHY WE WRITE

In order to demonstrate that our "pull" theory of media evolution is correct in the case of manuscript-writing, we need to establish the truth of two propositions. First, we must show that the technical capacity to write preexisted writing by some significant period of time. If we find this to be the case, then we can conclude that people could have written but did not because demand for writing was too low. Second, we must show that some macro-historical shift made existing media – gesture and talking – insufficient for the purposes of some organized groups, and that this or these groups engineered a preexisting technical capacity – the ability to write – into a new medium.

What evidence, primary and secondary, can be brought to bear on these two propositions? As we saw, early Speech Cultures left very little to us and therefore we had to rely on an inferential method. In contrast, Manuscript Cultures left much more to us and thus we can rest our conclusions on a firm base of primary sources. True, these sources are few in the beginning, but they grow in number and richness as time goes on. Quite fortunately, they have been mined, sifted, and assayed by generations of scholars studying writing and reading in the Ancient Near East,[3] Classical Antiquity,[4] and medieval Europe,[5] that is, roughly the period 3500 BC to AD 1450. In all that follows we will rely on their work in testing our two theories.

Writing before Writing

We couldn't write until recently. But we clearly could have. It's possible that *Homo erectus* and certain that early *Homo sapiens* possessed the core capacity that stands behind all writing – the ability to associate graphic signs with thoughts, that is, to symbolize. We know this because both species were similar anatomically to us and, more directly, because they made symbols, or what look a lot like symbols. Some 300,000 years ago our ancestors apparently collected pieces of red ochre; we might reasonably guess that they used these early crayons for some symbolic purpose.[6] What that purpose was no one has been able to determine. About the same time, someone carved a rather nice minimalist design into an ox rib.[7] Like minimalist art today, no one can figure out what it means. Shells with holes bored in them dating back approximately 100,000 years ago have been found, evidently to be used as ornaments.[8] Doubtless they were fetching. There is ample evidence of symbolic production between 40,000 and 30,000 years ago, including beads, etchings, carvings, paintings, and burials.[9] The earliest of the famous French cave paintings, for example, come from this time or a bit later.[10] For the most part they are straightforwardly representational, depicting animals and humans, often in the process of killing one another.

So proto-humans and early humans could use things as symbols, but they apparently didn't need to very often. That started to change about 20,000 years ago.[11] The earth was then at the height of one of its periodic glaciations, meaning it was cold and dry. Things were not good for *Homo sapiens*, who generally prefers warm and wet. Happily, the globe gradually began to get warmer and the glaciers began to recede. But the good times didn't really start until around 14,500 years ago, when the pace of warming increased significantly. Warmth means more energy in the biosphere; more energy in the biosphere generally means more flora and fauna; and more flora and fauna generally mean happier hunting grounds. So it was that about 12,800 years ago, a new kind of human culture began to emerge – the Natufian.[12] The Natufians did something no other hunter-gatherers had ever done as far as we know: they settled down, or almost settled down. Apparently things were so good in their homeland – the Jordan River valley – that they stopped their ceaseless migrations from one food source to another and built permanent villages. They figured, "Why go to the food when the food will come to you?" These were popular sentiments, for the settlement movement spread. Today we find the remnants of the Natufians' little round huts, fire pits, bone piles (they clearly favored gazelles), and the faint traces of an astounding number of edible plants scattered over much of the Levant.

But it couldn't last. The earth being fickle, it suddenly got colder and dryer in an event climatologists mysteriously call the "Younger Dryas." From 11,500 to 10,300 years ago, times were hard for the Natufians. The food didn't come to them as it had, so most of them pulled up their stakes and returned to their wandering ways. Others, however, having grown fond of life in settlements, didn't fancy moving. They tried to stick it out by eating less appetizing things (like bugs) and, more importantly, by *making* food. We really don't know how they came to produce food in a systematic way. All hunter-gatherers lived with and off wild flora and fauna – grasses, fruits, nuts, tubers, and game of every variety. They knew a lot about them, more than we can probably imagine. One of the things they knew was that if you gather seeds and broadcast them – as they regularly did – nice edible plants will grow all on their own. They also knew that certain animals – like wolves – would just follow you around. To us, the leap from these facts to agriculture and animal husbandry seems small. To them it was huge. Who, after all, would trade the life of the open field for one that revolved around digging in the dirt among filthy animals, not to mention having

64

to live cheek-by-jowl with strangers? Moreover, there was no guarantee that such a mode of production would succeed. No one, after all, had ever tried it. It's not like you could run down to the model farm and see the new food production methods in glorious practice. Risk aversion was a smart play, as 170,000 years of experience showed.

The successors of the Natufians, the Neolithic farmers, eased into the new sedentary, food-producing way of life just to hedge their risk.[13] They began with a hybrid heavily favoring the old ways and, as flora and fauna domestication proved reliable, shifted their energies toward agriculture and animal raising. It may have been their skill, ingenuity, and perseverance that made it all work. Or it may have been the weather: beginning around 10,300 years ago, the earth's climate entered the "Holocene," a period of sustained warm and wet conditions that continues to this day (with a little help from us).[14] Wheat, barley, peas, lentils, and flax were domesticated around 9,500 years ago.[15] Within 1,000 years, goats, sheep, pigs, and cattle had been brought to heel.[16] As environmental conditions improved and news of domestication techniques spread, Neolithic farming migrated rapidly all over the Levant. Permanent villages of between 300 and 500 people became reasonably common.[17] Some of them – like Jericho, founded about 9,600 years ago – are still inhabited today.

These early Neolithic agricultural villages were in essence immobilized hunter-gatherer bands. But they couldn't be just that, for sedentary village life changed social organization in significant ways. On the range, the band generally held everything in common. No one owned the land or its resources. It was just there to be exploited. "Exploited" seems just the right word, for despite common myths to the contrary, hunter-gatherers do not – or at least did not – care much for conservation. Judging from the fact that hunting by proto-humans and early humans seems to have been responsible for the decimation of numerous faunal species, our ancestors never gave much thought to husbanding natural resources.[18] If it was around and made of meat, they killed it and ate it. Indeed, their rapacious carnivorousness in this regard was probably evolutionarily adaptive insofar as hunting on the savannah was a feast-or-famine affair. When the gazelle were running, you would do well to eat as many as possible because they weren't going to be running for long. Agriculture, however, is an entirely different game. Instead of killing and collecting food from a vast, divinely given pool, you have to breed it on a discrete plot of land or with a definite group of animals. Your labor – not somebody else's – gets invested. On the savannah, the sky lord grants you a good hunt; in the wheat field or pig sty, you reap what you sow.

This difference altered relations between families in the band. In the agricultural village, families had an economic incentive to pull out of the traditional resource-sharing scheme, proclaim their property private, and go it alone under the protection of tribal elders. Having hived off the band, the family was free to engage in independent, selfish, growth-oriented economic activity. It became a "household," a familial-economic unit, indeed one of the most durable in human history. It's still with us today. Interestingly, we can see when the transition from the band to the village *cum* collection of households occurred in the architectural footprints of successive cultural levels in early Levant villages.[19] The Natufians, as we've said, built round huts suitable for two people (a married couple) or one (an uncle, or grandfather). The early Neolithic farmers did the same about 10,000 years ago. But as their settlements grew over the next millennium, their dwellings became larger, rectilinear, and multi-roomed. These houses were for families and extended families: mom, dad, the kids, more distant relatives, and perhaps domestics. Significantly, storage facilities for grain begin to appear, suggesting the emergence of the family as an independent residential and economic unit. We also see the erection of the first public buildings, evidence of the rise of a common life and perhaps hierarchy on the level of the village.

"Pulling" Writing into Existence

These early public buildings are important for our story, because it was probably in them that the first true *system* of symbols in human history developed. The collective spirit of the band was not completely lost when the shift to agriculture and the emergence of households occurred. The Neolithic farmers still needed to cooperate, particularly in the production of public goods such as leadership, security, and spiritual care. These things were essential for the prosperity of every family, but no single family could provide them. There was no choice, really, but to create new public institutions to serve these functions and to pay for them collectively (though not necessarily equitably). Language enabled them to do the former, and the existence of an economic surplus enabled them to do the latter. Now, we should not think that this was some sort of early flowering of the democratic spirit. The Neolithic farmers may have composed some sort of social contract, or they may have been forced into an "arrangement" by some powerful family. In a sense, it doesn't really matter how they came to team up. The point is that if they failed to do so, by whatever means, they would probably perish.

Whether formed by compact or coercion, the new order had two important and novel consequences: social ranks and taxes. The former were held by princes and priests who supplied the aforementioned public goods, and the latter were levied from the beneficiaries of these goods. It was exactly in this context that humans first found good reason to make symbols systematically. That reason was to keep accounts. Princes and priests needed to record who had contributed what to the treasury and how much the treasury contained. Unaided memory wouldn't really do. As we pointed out, memory is good at boiling down information into gists. Typically, the mind reduces complex quantitative information to simple categories like one, two, and many. Keeping accounts in terms of one, two, and many is an invitation to disaster. Something much more exact was needed, namely, numerals: not one, two, many, but 24, 25, and 26. Alas, the Neolithic farmers had none. And even if they did, numerals alone wouldn't help much with the task at hand, because the memory doesn't store numerals well. You might be able to remember that one family deposited 26 bushels of wheat in the granary, but you couldn't remember the exact quantities that multiple families deposited, at least for long.

What the Neolithic people needed, and indeed all they could create without numbers, was a system of counting in which one physical symbol represented one physical item. In a word, they needed a token. And this is precisely what they created.[20] Being slothful, they "re-purposed" an old technology to do the job rather than inventing a new one. Craftsmen had been making clay trinkets for thousands of years. These could also be used as tokens. So, beginning in Mesopotamia around 10,000 years ago – just where and when we would expect – elites began to craft tokens representing goods. Though we don't know *exactly* how they were used, it seems that princes and priests employed them to track the receipts of taxes and offerings, for they are often found in the remains of palaces and temples. They were evidently marks of high status, for sometimes they are found in rich graves. The tokens fall into more than a dozen categories depending on their basic geometric shape (cones, spheres, disks, cylinders, etc.), and into additional subcategories depending on their markings (incisions of various kinds). In the course of time, they came to stand for many different sorts of goods: grain, oil, bread, cakes, animals, textiles, garments, vessels, tools, perfume, metal, and jewelry. Thousands of tokens have been found at over 100 sites around the Middle and Near East. The token system was remarkably durable. It was used for some 5,000 years, until it was replaced, as we'll see, by writing.

The token system grew in the context of the early agricultural village. Its successor, writing, grew in the context of the early tributary state.[21] In the fourth millennium BC, settlements of unprecedented size developed in Mesopotamia. They were trading centers, as well as centers of political and religious power. The amount of tribute an early city like Uruk handled put additional stress on the token system of accounting, and this led to innovation in information processing. The invention of the first system of pictographic writing was one of the results. In roughly 3,700 BC, Mesopotamian accountants began to place tokens into clay envelopes in order to create archival records of transactions. The envelopes, of course, were opaque, meaning the accountants couldn't learn what they contained without breaking them. That was inconvenient. So they began to impress the tokens into the envelopes before they hardened. If an envelope had four cones impressed on it, the accountant knew that it had four cones in it, no breaking necessary. The accountants eventually realized that the impressions on the envelopes made the tokens inside of them redundant. Thus, the envelopes were replaced by clay tablets with token impressions on them. The next step was to do away with the tokens themselves. It was discovered that one could make a pretty decent outline of any token with a stylus. You didn't need a set of tokens to record transactions, you just needed the stylus and some knowledge of what the tokens stood for. By 3,100 BC, the drawings of tokens on tablets had become stylized and regularized, and the writing system known as cuneiform was born.

An additional and important step was the invention – or discovery – of abstract numbers. The token system rested on a one-to-one correspondence between goods and tokens: to represent 10 measures of grain, you needed 10 tokens. The impressed tablet system rested on the same principle: 10 measures of grain were represented by 10 impressions. This was manifestly inefficient in terms of both space and computation, particularly when dealing with large numbers of goods such as those flowing through major Mesopotamian cities. Thus, some forward-thinking scribes invented symbols for *sets* of impressions. A sign like "X" was made to stand for 10 items, and "Y" was made to stand for 20, and "Z" for 30. To record that 10 measures of grain had been delivered to the temple, all the scribe needed to write was "X" next to the stylized sign for grain.

These were true numbers, and they made difficult accounting problems much easier. They also represented a revolution in communications. For the first time it was recognized that *any* symbol could be made to stand for *any* thing or idea. The symbol didn't need to look like the thing it represented – that is, have an iconic or pictographic quality – in order to be read, something that was quite impossible in the case of abstract concepts like numbers in any case. Rather, the only information needed to read the symbol was that it conventionally stood for this or that. Naturally, the pictographic principle remained useful and was still used: all of the early writing systems – cuneiform, hieroglyphics, and Chinese characters – are built on it. They began as picture writing. But once it was realized that the symbol and the idea or thing it signified need not be pictorially linked, a whole new universe of graphic representation emerged. You could simply make up new symbols and assign them meanings by associating them with ideas or things. Any idea or thing could be "written" using this technique.

Among the things that could be written in this way were spoken words. The idea that writing could be used to represent words was novel to the accountants of Uruk. They lived in a world in which writing consisted of pictures of things and, perhaps, ideas like "10." But once they discovered that writing could be used to record speech, they developed logographic scripts, either by associating existing pictographs with spoken words or by inventing new symbols for words. For the first time, it was possible to record exactly what a person said and to write things that were never said as if they had been. Once written, anyone who knew the table of symbol-to-word equivalencies – what we call a dictionary – could decode them simply by "playing them back," that is, reading them. Of course, the table of equivalencies was difficult to learn. A rich logographic script has tens of thousands of arbitrary symbols, each of which must be memorized. This is not, however, impossible – indeed, it is done by millions of Chinese school children every year, albeit with the help of a kind of phonetic crib sheet (*Pinyin*).[22]

But there is a different writing technique that makes it possible to recognize what word a particular symbol stands for with much less effort, or at least memorization. Instead of using a unique symbol to represent each word, you could use a unique symbol to represent each of the *sounds* that make up all words. Speech is a combinatorial system – it uses combinations of a small number of elements to create an infinite number of expressions. Just so, every language uses a small number of sounds – phonemes – to create a potentially infinite number of words. If you assign a symbol to each sound, you can combine the symbols to make up any word that can be spoken. That's a phonetic script, and to use it to record and "play back" texts, all you need to do is learn the small number of symbols for the phonemes in a given language. Scribes throughout the Levant realized the economy of this system of representing speech, and they adapted cuneiform and hieroglyphs accordingly. These writing systems, however, never became fully phonetic scripts, not due to any deficiency on the part of the cultures involved, but simply because reasonably complete phonetic scripts – syllabaries and alphabets –apparently were not needed. The progenitor of all modern alphabetic scripts seems to have originated in Egypt in the early second millennium BC.[23] For the next thousand years, however, the alphabet was little used.[24] Eventually it gained favor among the Phoenicians, who then spread it around the Mediterranean basin, where it was adapted to local languages. One of them was Greek, as we can see from Plato's writings.

The story we have just told, that of the gradual domestication of food sources, the organization of villages and cities, the rise of princes and priests, and invention of writing systems to serve them, was not unique to the Near East. It happened throughout much of the world in a relatively short period of time. It took humans six million years to evolve, 40,000 years to migrate all over the globe, but only a few thousand years to make the transition from the oral hunter-gather band to the literate "civilization." In addition to the Near East, this shift occurred independently in what is now Egypt, Pakistan, China, Peru, and Mexico, and probably not only there. In all of these places we see the emergence of agriculture, new forms of cooperative life (villages, cities, states, temples), followed by the development of counting devices, numbers, pictographic scripts, and sometimes phonetic scripts.[25] In light of this remarkable example of social evolutionary convergence, it hardly seems amiss to formulate a kind of law of human social evolution: if people turn to agriculture, they will often come to be ruled by princes and priests; and if they are ruled by princes and priests, they will often develop writing of one sort or another. Domestication, sedentization, princes, priests, and writing seem to go together. Indeed, they went together so well that they formed the basis for a way of life that dominated most of the world for nearly 5,000 years – "Manuscript Culture."

Writing and Human Nature

Humans took a very long time to develop writing, some 175,000 years. This is because, we argued, the historical conditions that "pulled" writing into existence were absent before the rise of princes and priests. Once writing was invented, however, it didn't spread very quickly or very far. Literacy was rare in all major Manuscript Cultures during the entire 5,000 years of their existence. There was nothing approaching mass literacy before for the nineteenth century, that is, well into the Print Era. The failure of literacy to saturate Manuscript-Era populations may have had something to do with the fact that princes and priests attempted to monopolize reading and writing. So far as we know, Manuscript-Era elites never promoted the teaching of literacy to the hoi polloi. On the contrary, they generally thought that widespread literacy might be quite dangerous. The minimal penetration of literacy in Manuscript Cultures might also be explained by the fact that reading and writing were basically useless for most purposes. Neither the peasant, nor craftsman, nor merchant needed to be able to read or write to do their business.

Yet there must be something more going on here. For the people of Manuscript Cultures not only didn't generally read or write, they seem to have purposefully *avoided* reading and writing. If humans find pleasure in something and it can be gained at a reasonable price, they generally do it. As we will point out shortly, it is probably the case that literacy training, not to mention the equipment necessary to read and write, were quite expensive in almost all Manuscript Cultures. The elites made them more expensive by intentionally limiting supply. Nonetheless, it is noteworthy that we never find a single case of mass literacy in any Manuscript Culture. Surely there were times and places in which the cost of literacy declined to the point that it was available to the person of moderate means. There are candidates: ancient Greece, early modern China, and medieval Western Europe. In all of these places, literacy training and literature (broadly construed) were reasonably widely available. Yet even here literacy rates – insofar as they can be guessed – were always very low by modern standards. Why?

The answer is plain: humans, by their nature, don't like to read or write. Natural selection gave us nothing, physiologically speaking, to prepare us for literacy. We were evolved to talk, which is why we have talking organs that make talking easy. We were not evolved to read or write, which is why we don't have reading or writing organs and why reading and writing are hard. In order to become literate we have to adapt organs – our eyes, minds, hands – that were obviously evolved for other purposes. This hijacking and rewiring process takes years to accomplish, is quite exacting, and is never really complete.[26] Even good writers and readers get tired eyes, headaches, and hand cramps. Moreover, evolution endowed us with a drive to talk, a drive that makes talking quite enjoyable. Evolution did not endow us with a drive to read and write, which is why most people throughout history have found both tiresome.

Surely, we tell ourselves, if the Manuscript-Era masses had *really* had the opportunity to become literate, they would have learned to read and write; and if they had had something *really* interesting or edifying to read, they would have read it. Of course, we can't know if these propositions are true or not, as they rest on counterfactuals – Manuscript-Era states did not have mass literacy programs, and Manuscript-Era writers, though they probably produced some interesting reading material, didn't produce very much of it. But given what we know about the way literacy spread in modern times – namely, through compulsory education – and what we know about modern reading habits – namely, that literate people generally don't read very much at all – there is no good reason to think that either statement is correct.

The needs of princes and priests "pulled" reading and writing into existence, but they could never "pull" it very far because, as it happens, humans don't like to read or write.

WHAT MANUSCRIPTS DID

In the Manuscript Era, what was an all-talking media environment became one characterized by talking and manuscript-writing. Before considering the impact of manuscript-writing generally, we need to make clear that writing did not in any sense *replace* talking. Rather, it supplemented talking. Neither should we think that writing came to dominate talking as the basic mode of human communication. That is simply false. As we've seen, only a small minority of people in the Manuscript Era could read or write; therefore, it must have been the case that most – indeed the vast majority – of all human expression, used for whatever purpose, remained oral. Indeed, the ways in which orality survived and affected writing is one of the primary concerns of Classicists and medieval historians.

By the lights of our "push" theory of media effects, manuscript-writing should have had a significant effect on social practices and values in these cultures; it should have laid the foundation of a distinct Manuscript Culture in a distinct Manuscript Era (3500 BC to AD 1450). As we noted earlier, there is sufficient primary and secondary evidence available to assess the theory, and we will do so presently.

Accessibility

Talking and listening are cheap. Writing and reading, however, are typically expensive. It doesn't seem that way to most of us. We went to school. They taught us to write and read. It wasn't pleasant, but it didn't cost anything, right? Of course it did. There is no free lunch, nor is there free literacy instruction. Ask anyone who's paying for their young son's or daughter's fancy private school. What does it cost to gain the power of writing? First, if you are going to write and read, you need the equipment: pen, paper, and a primer. Most people can afford these things today; in times past they couldn't. Once you've got the tools, you need to learn to encode and decode. That's not easy. It takes healthy children several years of instruction to gain moderate writing and reading proficiency in their *native* language. For reasons we don't quite understand, a significant minority of children will *never* learn to write and read well in their mother or any other tongue.[27] Once you've got the tools and skill, you need to use them. That's not exactly easy either. A competent manuscript writer can only produce something on the order of twenty-five words per minute, and she won't be able to keep up that pace for long.[28] In practice, and particularly on long projects, the rate is therefore much slower. It took Tolstoy seven years (1862–1869) to finish a version of *War and Peace* – coming in at 460,000 Russian and French words – he was happy with. That's 1.25 words a minute, assuming he worked night and day with no holidays. A competent reader can comfortably read with comprehension roughly 250 words per minute, depending on the legibility of the hand.[29] At that pace you could theoretically decode a manuscript of *War and Peace* in about thirty-one hours, though you might just die of exhaustion like the over-reaching peasant in Tolstoy's great story "How Much Land Does a Man Need?"[30] Incidentally, a recent book-on-tape version of *War and Peace* runs a languid seventy hours.[31] For whatever reason, both writing and reading have always seemed slow to us, which is why we have been inventing and using speed-writing and speed-reading techniques for ages. These are basically codes for codes, and none is very effective. Woody Allen famously quipped that he took a speed-reading course and then read *War and Peace* in twenty minutes. "It's about Russia," he reported.[32] Writing and reading, then, are naturally expensive. Interestingly, it's not terribly difficult to make them artificially more expensive. This can be done in two ways. First, you can restrict access to the equipment necessary – writing implements, media, and texts. In a modern environment, this is difficult because these items are so abundant and inexpensive. But in the Manuscript Era they were scarce and costly, so it was entirely possible keep these things out of the hands of would-be writers and readers. Second, you can segregate those who are literate and forbid them to teach writing or to write things you might not like. Again, this would be difficult today because so many people can read and write. But in the Manuscript Era and even after, it was a viable and often-used strategy. Queen Elizabeth I ordered a man's right hand cut off for writing something she didn't like.[33] Dismemberment doubtless made an impact on the man (whose name, ironically enough, was John Stubbs), but he still had his left hand to write with and two good eyes to read with. Much later, the rulers of the Soviet Union tried to prevent their subjects from writing and reading manuscripts, and enjoyed some success in this effort.[34] Nonetheless, underground literature (*samizdat*) flourished, and some of it was even quite good.[35]

The fact that literacy is expensive and can be made more expensive easily meant – and to some degree still means – that it is not a terribly accessible medium, particularly compared to speech. Nearly everyone has the equipment and skill to speak and listen, but only some people have the equipment and skill necessary to write and read. Because literacy is not accessible, the networks it engenders will be *concentrated*. Only a portion of those in a community will be literate and fully on the network; the rest will not. By the lights of our theory, concentrated networks should *hierarchicalize* social practices developed in and around them. Here, "hierarchicalize" means to engender informal and formal ranks. The reason is this: where assets are scarce and fixed, humans will attempt to monopolize them; if successful, they will use their unequal control over assets as a basis for unequal power, that is, to form ranks.

Both concentrated networks and hierarchicalized social practices evolved in the Manuscript Era. As we've seen, hunter-gatherers generally held assets in common, including the means of communication, speech. As humans settled down, new types of assets appeared. From our point of view, the most significant were tax-payers and sacred places. In the course of time, elites monopolized these assets and then used their unequal control as a basis for unequal power. Hierarchically administered social practices appeared, the most important being the palace and the temple. As the palace and temple grew more complex, they became more reliant on writing and reading for a whole host of reasons. Therefore, literacy itself became an *asset*. As demand for scribal services rose, supply lagged due to the aforementioned cost of equipping and training scribes. Therefore literacy became *scarce*. And as scribes set up shop where writing and reading were in highest demand, in urban areas, they became identified with and attached to places. Therefore literacy became geographically *fixed*. Because it was valuable, scarce, and fixed, literacy became a prime target for monopolization by those who benefited most from it. It's no wonder, then, that throughout the Manuscript Era, princes and priests sought to control writing and reading. Restricting access to literacy was not difficult because commoners weren't exactly clamoring for it – literacy was of no value whatsoever to the vast majority of Manuscript-Era people. Nonetheless, princes and priests put up barriers just in case. They were of several types. Since writing and reading rely on equipment, the elite tried to gain control of the requisite raw materials and the craftsmen who turned them into the instruments of literacy – hence monopolies on media (papyrus, silk, paper) production and copying. Since writing and reading must be taught, they attempted to gain control of those who could teach them, that is, the scribes themselves – hence the closed scribal caste. Since writing was a physical artifact, they attempted to limit those who could rightfully possess it or what could be written and read. Hence censorship. Once they added a bloody-minded penal code – the kind Queen Elizabeth I favored – the monopolists could be reasonably sure of their hold and the system of privilege that was built on it.

Princes and priests monopolized writing and thereby became more princely and priestly. That was the "is" of the situation from approximately 3500 BC to several hundred years ago, when literacy became a mass phenomenon. The "ought" developed to justify this state of affairs was elitism, or, more specifically, the belief that the world was the way it was – ruled by princes and priests who controlled writing – because that was the way the heavens intended it. This notion of divinely sponsored rule – or even divine rule itself – is enshrined in nearly every major political and religious doctrine that comes down to us from the 4,000-year period in which Manuscript Cultures dominated the earth.[36] In the third millennium BC, Sargon of Akkad claimed divine sanction; in the second millennium AD, King James I of England did the same. James went further, telling his subjects: "The State of Monarchie is the Supremest thing on earth: For Kings are not onely Gods Lieutenants upon earth, and sit upon Gods throne, but even by God himselfe they are called Gods."[37] Between Sargon and James, priestly princes and princely priests were standard equipment in almost all Manuscript Cultures. Nearly every Western religious tradition upholds the notion of divinely appointed kings. In the Jewish tradition, rulers are chosen by Yahweh: "And he changeth the times and the seasons: He removeth kings, and setteth up kings; he giveth wisdom unto the wise, and knowledge to them that know understanding" (Daniel 2: 21). In the Christian tradition, rulers are appointed by the Lord: "For there is no power but of God. The powers that be are ordained of God. Whosoever therefore resisteth the power, resisteth the ordinance of God" (Romans 13: 1–6). And in the Muslim tradition, rulers are appointed by Allah: "Allah has chosen him

[Talut] above you and has gifted him abundantly with knowledge and bodily prowess; Allah grants His authority to whom He pleases" (Surah 2: 247). Note that all these doctrines were (and are) *written*.

Privacy

As we said earlier, talking and listening to someone usually "gives away your position," that is, who you are and what you've communicated or heard. Writing and reading don't, at least not to the same degree. If you want, you can write a message to someone and be reasonably sure that she won't know it was you who wrote it. Naturally, you'll have to disguise your handwriting or typeface, alter your typical style or subject, and have a blind proxy deliver the note, but those aren't really hard things to do. Ted Kaczynski, the notorious Unabomber, took the first and third of these precautions but forgot to take the second. David Kaczynski recognized the "manifesto" published in the *New York Times* and the *Washington Post* as the work of his brother, Ted, and turned him in.[38] Ted is currently serving life in prison without parole, but you're not a madman so you can probably pull off a simple anonymous letter. Moreover, if, unlike the egomaniacal Unabomber, you want to limit the circle of people who read what you write, you can do that too. This is what "private correspondence" is supposed to signify, though you should be aware that once you're dead, your private correspondence is going to be a lot less private. Secretive bureaucracies – if that's not redundant – love to restrict the circulation of the copious paper they produce. For this purpose, bureaucrats have invented special stamps to denote whether a document is on or off limits. You've seen them, at least in movies: *Personal and Confidential, For Your Eyes Only*, or the ever-popular *Top Secret*. Perhaps the only advantage speech has over writing in terms of privacy is that it disappears. Talking to yourself doesn't "give away your position" because your words vanish immediately without leaving a trace, outside your memory, of course. Writing to yourself, however, might "give away your position" because it leaves a relatively permanent record of what you wrote. That's why people who work in criminal organizations, tyrannical governments, and the White House are strongly advised not to keep "private" notes. Rule number one: never write anything down. As for reading, it's generally easy to privatize: just get an anonymous post office box, an opaque bag, and close your door. When you are done, you might want to dispose of your reading material in a dumpster behind the mall. The FBI will look through your personal trash bins.

Writing and reading, then, can be made quite private. If you are careful, you can use writing to communicate anonymously to a restricted circle of correspondents. If you are careful, you can similarly ensure that what you read will not become known to anyone. When writing and reading are used privately, they create *segmented* networks, that is, networks that have restricted places in them. Information flows within the segment but cannot easily flow between segments. Our theory has it that segmented networks *close* social practices realized in and around them. Here "close" means tending to anonymize and remove from public view. The reason is this: if humans can benefit from concealing their identities or activities, they will often do so; segmented networks allow them to do this. Writing permits you to hide, and hiding can work to your advantage.

Both segmented networks and closed social practices evolved during the rise of reading and writing in the Manuscript Era. In the hunter-gatherer band, nothing could really be hidden because everyone could speak and hear. In Manuscript Culture, however, the princes' and priests' unequal hold on writing made hiding relatively straightforward. The elite could read and write; commoners couldn't. That gave the elite its own "private channel." The princes used it to privatize what had been public authority. Thus, *the* law became *their* law, though they continued to say that it was validated by tradition or divine sanction. The priests used it to privatize sacred power. Among hunter-gatherers, everyone could receive, understand, and interpret the sacred. Writing changed each of these things. In the Hebrew Bible, God told Moses he didn't want just anyone coming up to Mount Sinai to receive the law. Moses could ascend, and perhaps his brother Aaron, but the rest of the Israelites had to remain a safe distance below (Exodus 19: 20–24). If you were among that select group, you could talk to the Lord; if not, then not. Most people weren't. Upon his return from Mount Sinai, "Moses wrote down all the words of the Lord" (Exodus 24: 4). If you could read, then you could understand the Lord; if not, then not. Most people couldn't. By writing the sacred down, the priests segregated it; by segregating it, they were able to interpose themselves as readers between god and man. The question of interpretation remained, but it had an obvious answer: God had given the elite the ability to receive and understand holy words; therefore it should have the sole right to interpret them.

Princes and priests used literacy to privatize the public and the sacred. That was the "is" of the situation from the birth of civilization and remained so until government became "open" and church was separated from state – both recent phenomena. The "ought" elaborated to buttress de facto privatization was privatism, or, more specifically, the doctrine that God had given princes and priests an exclusive dispensation to receive, read, and interpret important texts. Such things, so it was held, were not and should not be given to laypeople. In their hands, the elite said, the words of the divine might be misinterpreted, and that might jeopardize the safety of the community and the souls of the faithful. Moses, Jesus, and Mohamed received the Word of the Lord (or, in the case of Jesus, *was* the Lord). You didn't. Their true disciples were entrusted with that Word. You weren't. Their rightful successors – rabbis, priests, and imams – know what the Word means. You don't. So all in all it's best to leave the Word where it is, firmly in the private hands of princes and priests.

Fidelity

Some writers are praised for their descriptive powers. Tolstoy provides an example. He could, so it is said, really "paint a picture." Actually he couldn't. He couldn't paint a picture because he wasn't painting. He was writing. With words. "Word pictures" are not pictures. You will never *see* Pierre reunited with Natasha in *War and Peace*. All you can do is read about it. The "mind's eye" is not an eye. Your mind can't see Pierre, Natasha, or anything else Tolstoy wrote about. All it can do is imagine. One might say that phonetic or logographic writing is a sort of "picture" of sound, or rather a small set of sounds arranged in a certain order. By reading a phonetically or logographically recorded sentence out loud – say, "When she smiled, there could be no doubt. It was Natasha, and he loved her"[39] – you can reproduce the sounds someone spoke, if someone spoke them. Ideographic scripts can't even do that, as they don't represent sounds in any direct way at all. Writing, then, isn't iconic. The written word "daisy" neither *looks* like the spoken word "daisy" – which doesn't look like anything – or a real daisy at all. Writing's signs are unmotivated by the things to which they refer: there is no *necessary* reason why the collections of symbols "d-a-i-s-y" should stand for the spoken word "daisy" or a daisy itself. Like speech, writing reduces the data of all five senses to one channel – vision – and therefore is what we call a five-to-one code. It encodes every manner of experience as little scribbles, even experiences that aren't little scribbles. In the process, lots of information is lost. Things get distorted. As Elvis Costello put it with reference to his own art: "Writing about music is like dancing about architecture."[40]

Writing, then, is a low-fidelity medium. What goes "in" is sight, sound, smell, taste, and touch; what comes "out" is sight, and encoded sight at that. Low-fidelity media give rise to *symbolic* networks. Such networks require quite a bit of effort to get on and use, and they tend to disfigure sense data transmitted over them. By the lights of our theory, symbolic media networks should *conceptualize* social practices that emerge within them. This means that concrete, individual entities perceived by the senses in the here and now – say those pretty flowers with yellow petals over there – will be removed from their context and placed under timeless conceptual categories like "daisies." The reason is that the symbolic network, built as it is on unmotivated signs designating categories, itself prompts humans to begin playing with the signs and building useful, shared representational systems out of them.

Literacy made symbolic networks more symbolic and conceptualized social practices more abstract in the Manuscript Era. Both speech and writing are five-to-one codes, so both speech and writing affected social practices in the same way, that is, by abstraction. But writing's impact was much greater for a simple reason: writing turns words into *things*. Spoken words are invisible and evanescent: you can't really do anything with them other than change the order in which they appear and immediately disappear. You "run" spoken words in one dimension (time) and in one direction (forward). In contrast, written words are visible and persistent: you can juxtapose them in all kinds of ways. You "arrange" written words in multiple dimensions (vertical, horizontal, depth) and multiple directions (up-down, right-left, back-forth). Using these characteristics of writing, princes and priests created much more elaborate schemata of social practices than was ever possible in the Talking Era. Oral laws and myths could only become so long and so complex before they surpassed the limits of memory; written laws and myths could expand almost infinitely and reach remarkable levels of complexity. With the intrusion of writing into the practice of modeling social practices, what was invisible became visible, what was simple became complex, and what was concrete became abstract. This not only changed the nature of once-oral social practices, but it also stabilized them. Within the hunter-gatherer band, social practices were ghostly and therefore always being renegotiated; within early Manuscript Culture, social practices were visible – you could read them – and therefore less subject to change. Naturally, people altered even written social practices, but writing's capacity to make words into things reduced the rate of change. Of course, this "slowing down" served the interests of those who benefited from the status quo, that is, princes and priests.

Princes and priests used writing to conceptualize social practices in law codes and sacred myths. That was the "is" of the situation and remained so until writing slipped out of the hands of the elite in the early modern period. The "ought" evolved to support written abstraction was idealism, or, more specifically, the doctrine that writing was a divine gift that linked humans to the all-important unseen world. The Sumerians believed that writing was brought from heaven by the deity Enki.[41] The Babylonians credited the discovery of writing to a descendant of Enki named Nabu. The Egyptians considered the goddess Seshat the inventor of writing. They said, however, it was Thoth, the deity of writing, who taught writing to men. Plato, incidentally, repeats the myth of Thoth (*Phaedrus*, 274C–275B),[42] whom most of the Greeks called "Hermes." The Romans, who cribbed most everything from the Hellenes, took Hermes and transformed him into Mercury, one of whose titles was "inventor of writing." Writing, then, was brought from the unseen world. As such, it could be used to gain access to the unseen world. It didn't matter whether the unseen world was populated by perfect forms (Plato) or a wrathful god (Moses). In either case it was better there than it was here. Since words were the bridge between there and here, they were not ordinary things – they were sacred. And as such they required "special handling" and became bogged down with a great variety of "dos and don'ts." We see this in Plato, who rails against the rhetoricians who misuse language and understand nothing of the Truth. And we see it in the Hebrew Bible, in which God issues all kinds of rules regarding the treatment of the Arc of the Covenant (Exodus 25: 10–22; Exodus 40: 3; Leviticus 16) and, later, the Torah.[43]

Volume

War and Peace is long, but – at 460,000 words – it's hardly the longest novel ever written. There are several contenders for this title. According to the *Guinness Book of World Records*, Marcel Proust's autobiographical *Remembrance of Things Past* (1913–27) takes the prize at 1.5 million words.[44] But according to Wikipedia (which, incidentally, is the world's longest encyclopedia),[45] Sohachi Yamaoka's historical epic *Tokugawa Ieyasu* (1950–67) and Mark Leach's science-fiction thriller *Marienbad My Love* (2008), each of which runs 10 million words, beat Proust hands down.[46] A graphomaniac named Richard Grossman has set out to end the controversy once and for all. When completed, he claims his experimental novel *Breeze Avenue* will run three million pages and comprise roughly one billion words. There are plans for a book tour.[47] But here's the most amazing part: somebody with a lot of time on her hands might even read *Breeze Avenue*. If you read 250 words a minute (a comfortable pace),[48] eight hours a day (you need your beauty rest), 240 days a year (weekends or holidays off), you'd be done in thirty-five years. If you read faster and stretched it out, it would be doable, though not really advisable. The point is this: a billion words probably approaches the upper bound of the length of a written message decodable by one person in one lifetime. Logically, we might guess that the lower bound is one word. In the case of a novel (or any story, for that matter), the practical lower bound is a bit higher. The shortest story Hemingway could write – and Hemingway was a big fan of brevity – consisted of six words, three periods, and five spaces: "For Sale. Baby Shoes. Never Worn."[49] So we have *Breeze Avenue* at one extreme and "For Sale" at the other. The rest fall in the middle, and the vast majority of them toward the "For Sale" end. As we noted in the last chapter, the capacity of a medium to carry information is determined not only by the typical length of messages, but also by the number of people who receive them. How many people can read your manuscript simultaneously? Well, that obviously depends on how many times you've copied it and how many people you've given it to who will actually read it. The answer is probably "Not very many" on both counts, because manuscripts are hard to reproduce and transmit. Copying is a pain. Your hand gets sore. Your eyes get tired. It's not for nothing that teachers use writing as a punishment ("Write 'I will not talk in class' 100 times on the chalkboard"). Carrying texts from person to person is not easy either. We *pay* postal officials to do this onerous task. And not all the folks who receive your text will read it. Reading is not the most exciting thing a person can do, which is why many people use it as a soporific.

It's no wonder, then, that writing is a low-volume medium: its messages are typically short and difficult to reproduce and distribute. Low-volume media give rise to *constrained* networks, that is, networks over which the number and size of packets of information moving between nodes is quite limited. Just how many and how large these packets are depends on the cost of production, reproduction, transport, and consumption. These costs have declined radically over the past several hundred years. In the Manuscript Era, however, making, copying, moving, and reading text were expensive. Therefore, the packets were few and small, and thus the resulting networks were constrained. According to our theory, constrained networks *economize* social practices developed in and around them. In these networks, people will consciously limit their use of scarce resources – bandwidth, to use a modern analogy – to essential activities because the network itself does not have the excess capacity to allow for playful use.

Literacy made already constrained networks more constrained and already economized social practices more economical in the Manuscript Era. Both speech and writing are low-volume media, so both had the same kind of impact on social practices, namely, economization. But writing and reading pushed things much further in this direction for one reason: they are, compared to speech, really quite hard to learn and do. The hand was not built for writing. The eye was not designed for reading. In order to write and read, humans have to adapt capacities that were evolved to do other work. That process is difficult, and we successfully avoided it for some 175,000 years. Then we invented writing. We didn't invent it for pleasure – far from it. We invented it because it was a *tool* we needed to do other things. "Tool" is just the right word, because for the first several thousand years of its existence, writing was used almost exclusively to do important, necessary work – keeping accounts, writing laws, copying scripture. An early Mesopotamian prince or priest would no more spend the expensive bandwidth afforded by writing for frivolous entertainment than he would make a gilded piss pot. Naturally, some ancients did use writing for non-utilitarian purposes, just as some probably urinated in golden pots. But the people who did so were most often the wealthy and powerful, and they often did these silly things simply to show they were wealthy and powerful. As we would say, they had "money to burn" and burned it to show they did. Most people, however, didn't, and therefore we find them using writing sparingly and only when it was really needed. A lot of texts survive from the first two millennia of writing, but only a handful are in any sense entertaining or, as we would say, "literary." About the year 1000 BC, literary activity seems to pick up. The "rich" Greco-Latin, Sanskrit, and Chinese literary traditions are born, traditions that continue to exist to this day. But we should not exaggerate their "richness": in the Manuscript Era, only elites read for pleasure, and very few of them at that. For most people, writing was just too precious to waste on fun. So they didn't.

Literacy in the Manuscript Era was a scarce resource and had to be used carefully. That was the "is" of the situation and remained so until mass literacy emerged in the late Print Era. The "ought" elaborated to support the judicious use of writing is asceticism, and more specifically the doctrine that some texts were quite harmful. It was one thing to study approved secular and sacred texts, what the Greeks called *paideia*. This was encouraged as it resulted in edification. But it was quite another to spend your time using the *lingua sacra* to amuse yourself and others. That was not encouraged as it resulted in corruption. When we think of censorship, our minds usually wander to the Papacy's *Index Librorum Prohibitorum* or the Nazis and their infamous book bonfires. But censorship was common and commonsense in the Manuscript Era.[50] Plato's teacher and hero, Socrates, was killed for what he believed and said. Yet Plato himself was a big supporter of censorship (*The Republic*, 382b).[51] The Romans, though they wrote some literature and seemed to have enjoyed it, institutionalized censorship.[52] Throughout the Manuscript Era, people agreed that writing certain kinds of things was immoral and reading them dangerous, therefore they should not be written or read. This opinion has lasted well into our own age.

Velocity

A famous quip often attributed to Pascal goes, "I'm sorry to have written you this long letter, but I didn't have time to make it short."[53] Short or long, writing – and reading – take time. As we already noted, a typical writer can jot down 25 words per minute, and a typical reader can digest roughly 250 words in the same time. Speed-writing and speed-reading can increase each of these rates by a small multiple, but only with a considerable loss of clarity and comprehension respectively. This, however, is not the worst of it. Ordinarily, when people say "the check is in the mail," they mean that it isn't. But it might be, because the mail is slow and everyone knows it. Unfortunately, words written on hard media (stone, clay, bark, reeds, fabric, paper) must be schlepped from place to place. Thus, their velocity is a function of the speed of the vehicle that carries them. In the Manuscript Era, that wasn't very fast. A fit adult with a light load can easily walk something on the order of 15 miles a day in good conditions, though he or she will be tired, hungry, and have blisters at the end of it. Running is faster, but not as efficient (see "The Tortoise and the Hare" for more). A horse with a light load can walk on the order of 30 miles a day in good conditions, but needs to eat along the way, meaning you either have to carry the fodder (which makes the load heavy and pace slower) or stick to green pastures (which isn't always possible). Galloping is faster, but not as efficient (see "Barbaro" for more). A well-equipped sailboat with an experienced crew can travel roughly 150 to 200 miles a day in the open ocean, though actual rates vary considerably (see "Doldrums" for more). And oceans are generally quite large. Once we enter the era of mechanically propelled craft, things pick up considerably. Trucks travel above 60 mph, trains above 100 mph, propeller-driven transport planes above 300 mph, and jet-powered transport planes above 600 mph. That may seem fast, but remember that the human voice moves at 770 mph, though admittedly over a much shorter distance. A data-bearing light wave speeds through a fiber-optic cable at about 124,000 miles per *second*, about two-thirds the speed of light in a vacuum. That means it can circle the entire world in about two blinks of an eye. Of course, no matter how you send your written words, they may never get to where you want them. That's infinitely slow. The disappearance of written messages is a particular problem on the surface of the earth, which is uneven, irregular, unstable, magnetized, irradiated, pressurized, and enveloped in a radically volatile, electrically charged mass of nitrogen, oxygen, argon, carbon dioxide, and vaporized H_2O. Carrying things around on it is tricky business. It's no wonder that the UK's Royal Mail reported in 2002 that it lost 500,000 pieces of mail a week.[54] "Neither rain, nor sleet, nor gloom of night . . . " Well, most of the time.

Writing and reading, then, are slow. You cannot produce, transmit, or consume a text very quickly. Slow media engender *monologic* networks, that is, networks in which it is hard to exchange information rapidly. Of course, you can trade information with someone by writing, and people do all the time. But if it takes you hours to write a short letter, the post office days to deliver it to the recipient, more hours for the recipient to read it and draft a reply, and more days for the post office to get it back to you and for you to read it, what you have is a "correspondence," which is how we say "slow-motion dialogue." The exchange is so leisurely that it may seem like nothing but a series of staggered monologues. In our theory, monologic networks *centralize* social practices realized in and around them. Here "centralize" means tending to concentrate power in the hands of the sender rather than the recipient of a message. The reason is this: if humans can use a media network to "speak" and make others "listen," they often will; monologic networks offer this opportunity.

Both centralized networks and centralized social practices grew with the arrival of literacy in the Manuscript Era. In the world of the hunter-gatherers, everyone in the band could speak to everyone else more or less simultaneously. In the world of the early Manuscript Cultures, this was no longer possible, at least when the "speaking" was done through writing. The elite "spoke," and the unlettered masses "listened." Princes and priests of the Manuscript Era issued written pronouncements that were then read aloud by proxies (messengers, heralds, criers). This is not to say that there was no room for exchange between the powerful and the petty in Manuscript Cultures. There was, but it occurred at a safe distance and was thoroughly ritualized. Just as God forbade the Israelites to ascend Mount Sinai, so the elite prohibited the illiterate masses from entering the palace and the temple. Occasionally, the elite would grant the hoi polloi an "audience"; however, the powerful required the humble speakers to bow and scrape before they said anything. In addition, they strictly limited what could be said and how it could be said. These were not "discussions." More generally, the elite demanded that the masses communicate their wants and needs through a conduit it could even more efficiently control, that is, writing. Nearly every Manuscript-Era polity had a formal petitionary procedure by which subjects begged "pardon and favor" from the powerful in textual form. Here again, the petitioners were required to humiliate themselves. In old Russian petitions, the petitioners described themselves as "lowly slaves" who "beat their heads" at the feet of "masters."[55] Since the petitioners were usually illiterate, they had to hire a notary to draft the document. Once the petition was submitted, it might or might not be answered. If it was, it wouldn't be soon and would usually be in written form.

Princes and priests used literacy to turn what had been dialogue into monologue. That was the "is" of the situation and remained so well into the Print Era. The "ought" created to legitimize top-down communications was dictatorism or, more specifically, the doctrine that princes and priests were authorized by God to "speak" to commoners via writing and that the latter could only under strict conditions "talk" back. We've already seen that the elite of Manuscript Cultures routinely propagated (and believed) the idea that its sovereignty, control of literacy, and the objects it wrote – especially laws and holy texts – were gifts from beyond given to it and only it. This was as it should be. It followed that the divinely sanctioned elite should be obeyed, that is, that its subjects should act with the utmost humility just as it would before God. Humility meant, among other things, not "talking" back. The idea that *some* people should have the privilege of speaking and writing their minds freely is found in Classical Antiquity, but almost always with reference to elites.[56] For everyone else, silent obedience was the rule. It was, however, a largely unspoken rule because there was no need to speak it – it was just obvious. The rule of silent obedience *was* spoken only when it was violated or might be, which was rarely. Thus, Paul found himself in the odd position of telling the Roman proto-Christians what they should have already known, that is, to shut up and do whatever the emperor told them (Romans 13: 1–6). Like all princes and priests, the Roman ruler was God's agent, so one had to act accordingly.

Range

Homer liked to put "winged words" into the mouths of his characters.[57] Achilles or someone would get all excited and "winged words" would come flying out. But as we've seen, "winged words" don't fly very far, and the farther they fly, the less they mean. Written words are another matter entirely, as the texts of the *Iliad* and *Odyssey* themselves demonstrate. Though wingless, they have flown from tiny Greece to points all over the world. It's only a slight exaggeration to say that these two poems are to be found wherever people are to be found. Moreover, the trip from Greece to everywhere doesn't seem to have done them any harm. Generally speaking, they land in the same form they took off, that is, with the words legible and in roughly the right order. One place you won't find the *Iliad* and the *Odyssey* is outer space. But that doesn't mean there's nothing to read there. When designing *Voyager I* in the early 1970s, engineers were concerned that, should the deep-space probe be encountered by extraterrestrials, it would have nothing to say. So, in striking confirmation of our thesis that humans just *must* be heard even if no one is listening, they placed a golden record on board with lots of information about the earth and its inhabitants. When *Voyager I* left Cape Canaveral in 1977, the record's label read "The Sounds of earth. United States of America. Planet earth."[58] Today, it is roughly 10 billion miles from the sun and probably reads the same way, not that anyone has read it or ever will. In the right conditions – and space is so empty that conditions are ideal – a textual message on a durable medium will just keep going, and going, and going. Its range is practically unlimited. Naturally, all conditions are not right and all media are not durable, especially on our little blue sphere. Things fall apart, the center cannot hold, and our written messages get effaced, broken, crumpled, torn, shredded, soaked, desiccated, burned, and otherwise made illegible all the time as they "wing" their way from here to there.

Often they make it. But that doesn't mean that they make it to many people. For, despite the fact that writing has excellent range, it has poor reach. Unlike the unaided human voice, which is a broadcast medium, writing is a point-to-point medium. There is an important difference in the way the reach of each is figured. Recall that the reach of a broadcast medium is a function of the area its signal covers. The stronger the signal, the more area; the more area, the more recipients. In contrast, the reach of a point-to-point medium is primarily a function of the cost of message reproduction and delivery. On the one hand, if a point-to-point medium allows for inexpensive copying and dispatch of messages to many parties simultaneously, then its reach will be wide. If, on the other hand, a point-to-point medium does not permit cheap reproduction and distribution, then its reach will be narrow. Writing clearly falls into the latter category. It's reasonably easy to write and carry a letter to one person. But it's much more difficult to copy that letter many times by hand and carry it to many people. In the Manuscript Era, only the powerful had the resources to extend the naturally limited reach of writing. Nonetheless, the fact that the elite could use writing to "broadcast" messages marked a real improvement over speech, for it meant that at least some messages could be distributed en masse.

Writing is a long-range medium with moderate reach, which is to say it can be transported over long distances with little loss of information to a moderate number of people. Long-range media engender *extensive* networks, ones in which nodes can be far apart, cover a large area, and unite many people. By the lights of our theory, extensive networks *diversify* social practices realized in and around them. Here "diversify" means to become composed of several different parts, and particularly ethnically different parts. The reason is this: people in extensive networks are more likely to encounter strangers than they are in intensive networks; sustained contact with strangers will often lead to practical cooperation and, eventually, toleration. In this instance, familiarity does not breed contempt, but rather its opposite, though usually quite slowly.

Diversification almost certainly occurred as writing spread during the Manuscript Era. Hunter-gather bands were small, relatively isolated, and homogeneous. The band's immediate successor, the agricultural village, remained small, isolated, and homogeneous. But as villages found reason to begin stable trade relations – trade being an easy and obvious way to increase well-being – they became linked. Surplus in the villages and trade between them naturally attracted bandits, violent "entrepreneurs" who figured it was easier to take than make. In an effort to stave off predation, the villagers sometimes formed defensive alliances. More often, the bandits themselves realized it was better to keep the goose alive and harvest the golden eggs than to kill it. So they made the villagers "offers they couldn't refuse" and set up what were in essence glorified protection rackets. Whether voluntary or forced, these extractive networks were the first "states." The early states needed a way to keep track of what had been "contributed" and to stay in touch with those far-flung officials who collected tribute. Speech was short-range so it wouldn't do. Writing, however, was long-range and worked well. What had been a trade network with a protection network superimposed upon it became an extensive media network, often knit together by safe roads and postal services. Moreover, these states were sometimes not content with the territory they already controlled, and so sought to bring "unprotected" settlements within their aegis by poaching the protected settlements of their competitors. This marked the beginning of imperialism and further expanded the written network. Naturally, the long process of state-building and imperial expansion brought many strangers together for the first time. The imperial center wanted to know who its various subjects and neighbors were, and the subjects themselves wanted information on foreigners united in the empire and on its outskirts. These parties began to gather information on foreigners, write it down, and circulate it through the empire. This was the origin of ethnography in the Manuscript Era.[59] One can find reasonably detailed descriptions of what we would call "ethnicities" in the writings of many ancient authors, including Herodotus, Aristotle, Strabo, Ptolemy, Pliny the Elder, Tacitus, and Sextus Empiricus, to mention only the most famous. One might also include the Hebrew Bible here, which includes many ethnonyms and descriptions of ethnic groups.[60]

Writing expanded and thereby pluralized the world – or rather the "world picture" – of the people who used it. That was the "is" of the situation and it remains so in our era, as the practice of ethnography itself attests. The "ought" developed to excuse diversification was pluralism, or more specifically, the idea that "our world" included many different kinds of people and things. Since these people and things were no longer "strangers," but rather the "them" in "us and them," we had a mild obligation to get to know them and, where they cooperated, be kind to them. Of these two propositions, the former – know "them" – is not attested in the sources, though it is implied by the very practice of ethnography. The latter proposition – kindness to "them" – is everywhere attested in the religions of the Manuscript Era.[61] For example, God instructed the Israelites, "Thou shalt not oppress a stranger: for ye know the heart of a stranger, seeing ye were strangers in the land of Egypt" (Exodus 23: 9). Christianity and Islam are even more ecumenical, insisting not only that "we" must be kind to "them," but that we must convert them, in essence making "them" into "us."

Persistence

Next time you're in London, stop by the British Museum. Take the stairs to the third floor and find your way to Room 55.[62] Look for a clay slab measuring 6 inches by 5.25 inches with a lot of tiny, geometric markings on it. The markings are writing, meaning the artifact is a document. By most accounts, the tablet is at least 2,600 years old. And here's the most remarkable part: it's legible. Twenty-six centuries after it was inscribed, you can still read it. Unfortunately, you'll have to learn to decipher the dead language of Akkadian encoded in the dead script of cuneiform to do it. But if you accomplish this feat, you'll find that the text is quite readable and relates an interesting story about a flood – actually *the* flood – from *The Epic of Gilgamesh*. The point is this: written words can be astonishingly persistent. Just how persistent they are depends largely on two things. The first is the substance on which they are written. Hard media like stone and fired clay are very durable. They are basically impervious to heat, light, and water. So, unless they are crushed or effaced, they are likely to survive for a long time. Soft media like papyrus, parchment, and paper are not as tough because they are made of organic material, just as you are for the most part. Heat, light, and water will destroy all of them in short order. Since it's hard to keep things cool, shaded, and dry on the surface of the earth, which is often warm, sunny, and wet, we possess only a few texts on soft media older than a millennium.[63] Whether hard or soft, all media of whatever sort will return to dust, just as we will. Happily, the life of the words they bear can be extended by copying them on a new substrate made of whatever you fancy. Naturally, copying may introduce errors, and texts that have been copied many times are full of them. But the upside of copying outweighs the downside. Think about this: were it not for the practice of serial copying, we would know next to nothing about the literature of the Manuscript Era. For example, we have no "first edition" of the *Iliad*. In truth, we have no contemporaneous edition of the *Iliad* at all. Rather, we possess a tenth-century copy, which itself is a copy of a copy of a copy ... and so on all the way back to Plato's day.[64] Good thing copyright is a modern invention. The second factor that determines the persistence of a text is the stability of the language and script in which it is written. We all realize that computer languages and codes come and go. You probably have computer files that can't be "read" by the computer you are using now. Functionally, your files are "dead." Human languages and scripts come and go too, often independently of one another.[65] Languages can die and their scripts live on (e.g., Latin and Latin characters), and scripts can die and their languages live on (e.g., Runes and German). If you know a language but not the script it's written in, then you have an encrypted code. If you know a script but not the language encoded in it, then (assuming the script is phonetic) you can vocalize a language you can't understand. In either case, the writing itself conveys no meaning, and writing that conveys no meaning is dead.

Writing, then, is persistent, or at least can be made persistent. If you record something on a reasonably durable medium, you can rest assured that it will be around for a while, and maybe even a long while indeed. Persistent media give rise to *additive* networks, that is, ones in which data accumulate. In additive networks, nodes in the present are in a kind of dialogue with nodes in the past. A reader on an additive network can pick up a document from, say, 2,600 years ago, and, if it is legible, read someone's words from 2,600 years ago. If you make some very reasonable assumptions (that there is a past, it's continuous with our present, and the relationship is temporally linear), then the reader in question has established a link across time and therefore across an additive network. There are some curious things about additive networks, the most important of which is that information can only flow in one direction over them, namely, from past to present. Outside science fiction, it's always now. You can't travel to the past and say anything in it. But the past can travel to you and does indeed speak after a fashion. There are lots of mind-bending philosophical puzzles to be worked out here, but all we need note is that additive media networks generally *historicize* social practices realized in and around them. Here "historicize" means to lengthen people's time horizons to such an extent that the past, present, and future become distinct. The reason is this: people in additive media networks are more likely to encounter meaningful, recognizable, datable artifacts from the past than people living in a substitutive network. This means that they have a more detailed understanding of the past than people in a substitutive network.

We can clearly see the impact of additive networks in early Manuscript Cultures. To hunter-gatherers living in an oral environment, data about the past – and especially the human past – were available to the present primarily as subjective memories, spoken words, and rituals. This meant two things. First, the messages "sent" from the past to the present would be few and unclear. Memory and ritual can only store a limited amount of information, and speech none at all. What they do store is usually compressed as gists, resulting in the loss of information. Naturally these gists decay, resulting in the loss of more information. For these reasons information in an oral environment does not accumulate easily. Second, the messages "sent" from the past to the present are not easy to move around. Subjective memories cannot be easily manipulated because of the limits of short-term memory. Even if you know calculus, you can't do it in your head. Spoken words cannot be moved around easily because they disappear. Speaking is a means of transmitting information, not recording it. Rituals cannot be easily manipulated because they are not consciously held in memory, but rather performed. They provide no signs to move around. Writing changed this situation dramatically. Since writing is persistent, it can store a lot of information for a long time. The more information stored, the more of the past is made available to the present. Human history appears with writing, as we can see in the case of the famous "Lists of Kings," compiled by Sumerians, Egyptians, Babylonians, and Assyrians.[66] The Hebrew Bible's "Book of Kings" is of a piece with these proto-histories as it essentially tells the stories of the rulers of Israel and Judah.[67] By the time we get to Herodotus, we have history as we would understand it: the empirical study of events that occurred at a specific place and specific (past) time.[68]

Writing not only provided the stuff out of which history could be constructed, it also offered a medium in which persistent symbols could be moved around. With writing, you can arrange signs liberally in two-dimensional space, hold them in place indefinitely, play them back, and then rearrange them. That means you can construct a vast range of symbolic "pictures," store them, reread them, and then touch them up. This activity is important for science. Let's be clear: humans have always thought scientifically and used language to do it. Writing simply provided them with a much better tool. And once they had it, they used it, as we can see in the explosion of scientific activity in the Manuscript Era.[69] Aristotle *alone* used writing to explore politics, ethics, logic, poetics, rhetoric, physics, astronomy, metaphysics, biology, and psychology. It wasn't as if people hadn't thought about these things before, or thought about them scientifically. They had. It's just that Aristotle had the right tool for the job, or at least a superior one.

In the Manuscript Era, people – though primarily princes and priests – exploited the persistence of writing to create persistent pictures of the past and the world. That was the "is" of the matter and remains so today. The "ought" evolved to support picture-making was temporalism, or, more specifically, the idea that the past, present, and future form a continuous, measurable, observable strip. In this world, you were no longer standing still on a still point. Rather, you were walking along a strip. As you do, things change in the "present," disappear in the "past," and appear in the "future." Your time horizon may be short – a dynasty – or it may be long – the life of the universe – but the essential rule of "travel" is the same: you must move forward at a constant pace. You can't go back, you can't stand still, and you can't slow down or speed up. Given this view of time, and the existence of a lot of evidence – written and natural – you might well want to know how you got to where you are and where you were going to go. People of the Manuscript Era did. Thus, they began to use writing to analyze the past with an eye to the future, or what we call "history." Listen to Cicero: "History is the witness of the times, the light of truth, the life of memory, the teacher of life, the messenger of antiquity."[70] Though he was more enthusiastic than most, the writing of history was clearly seen as a virtue in the Manuscript Era.[71] And people of the Manuscript Era began using writing to rationally analyze the present with an eye to the future, that is, to practice what we generically call "science." According to Aristotle, when someone asked Anaxagoras what the purpose of life was, he replied, "For the sake of contemplating the heavens and the whole order of the universe."[72] Aristotle did not necessarily agree, but he, together with countless others in the Manuscript Era, surely viewed the study of nature to be a virtue.

Searchability

The clay tablet now found in Room 55 of the British Museum was, not surprisingly, looted by a band of British antiquity hunters.[73] The group, lead by Austin Henry Layard, found the tablet circa 1850 in a tell near the modern-day city of Mosel in the modern-day country of

Iraq. They shipped it back to England because they thought it might be valuable. They could only guess, however, because they couldn't read it. The script and language of the tablet – cuneiform and Akkadian – were not fully deciphered at mid-century. Moreover, even if they could have read it, they probably couldn't have found it among the mass of tablets they were busily digging up and shipping off. Layard didn't just uncover a single tablet, he unearthed a whole library, that constructed by one King Ashurbanipal in the seventh century BC. Ashurbanipal apparently liked to collect texts, for his library had a lot of them. Thanks to the industrious if larcenous efforts of Layard and his successors, the British Museum holds more than 30,000 tablets from it. And that's only what has survived and been uncovered. With this in mind, it's easy to understand how the tablet of *The Epic of Gilgamesh* might just go missing, both in Ashurbanipal's day and in Layard's, for it was hidden in an ocean of other tablets. Perhaps Ashurbanipal's bibliographers compiled a kind of card catalogue that told readers where every tablet was in the library. If they did, Layard didn't find it, so all he could do was hunt and peck. As we've said, a misshelved book is a lost book. A tablet unearthed from a tell among thousands of others like it is pretty much lost as well, "lost" in the sense of "very difficult to find."

This is because written text in and of itself is hard to search through for a whole host of reasons. First, you have to have access to it to search it, and sometimes you don't. If you can't get to the tell, then your search for cuneiform gold is over before it starts. Second, texts usually have to be searched serially, meaning you look at items one after another until you find the thing you want. There are ways around this. Books have indexes and libraries have catalogues. These are some help, but tend not to be fine-grained – the index doesn't go very deep, and the catalogue doesn't get you "inside the book." Third, searching text is slow, at least with the equipment most of us have on-board. If our eyes and brains scanned text at a high velocity, then it wouldn't matter that we have to search text serially. We'd just fire through it like a computer fires through electronic text. But in fact our eyes and brains were not designed to "fire" through anything, especially tiny symbols crammed on clay tablets, papyrus, parchment, or paper. They are slow and tire easily. All of these problems add up to a fourth: textual search as done by humans is not very efficient in terms of information retrieval. A really efficient search is one that yields just what you want and nothing you don't. Visual searches of text necessarily produce a lot of stuff you don't want and a little of what you do. When searching text, you are going to do more looking than finding.

Text, then, is hard to search. If you don't have it, you can't search it. If you do, the process is going to be slow, tiring, and yield more noise than signal. Media that are hard to search generate *unmapped* networks, that is, networks in which either no system of addresses exists or, if it does, it is so incomplete that searching, finding, and retrieving stored data is difficult. Functionally, what this means is that data stored in an unmapped network will tend to become concentrated in certain nodes rather than being shared across many nodes. Some people will know things that others do not. According to our theory, unmapped media networks *professionalize* social practices realized in and around them. Here "professionalize" means tending to generate experts and expertise, that is, people who have – or claim to have – special knowledge and the special knowledge itself. The reason is this: people who have unequal access to information will often monopolize it in the hopes of increasing their power; unmapped networks allow this sort of monopolization.

Early Manuscript Cultures provide a good example. In hunter-gatherer bands, most people experienced the same things: life itself did not produce significant inequalities of knowledge. Moreover, when one person did gain (or claim) special knowledge, he or she was expected to share it and, practically speaking, had to. This equalized knowledge across the network. As humanity began to live in sedentary communities, and these communities were united in primitive states, *stable* vertical and horizontal difference appeared, two being ranks and occupations. Differences in life engendered differences in knowledge. Most of these "knowledges," so to speak, remained oral, and they could after a fashion be searched in the old way – remembering and asking others to remember. In some cases, however, they were reduced to writing. For example, princes wrote laws and priests drafted scripture. The practice spread: the Greeks – and all those who followed them – wrote treaties on many of the major arts, crafts, and sciences.[74] These writings constituted the first textual "disciplines." Sometimes disciplinary texts were gathered together in archives and libraries, and sometimes these repositories were even opened to the public. By and large, however, the disciplinary texts – which were, after all, valuable objects – were either privately held or accessible only to those who were authorized and able to use them (that is, the small minority of the population that was literate). Ancient Judaism offers an example of restricted access to texts. After giving Moses the law, God instructed him to build a fancy box to put it in (Exodus 25: 10–22). This was the Arc of the Covenant. God then told Moses to install the Arc in the Holy of Holies, a room within the Tabernacle (Exodus 40: 3). There only the High Priest, Aaron, brother of Moses, could enter and only on Yom Kippur (Leviticus 16). From that point forward, the descendants of Aaron were known as the *Kohanim* or "priests," and the office of High Priest remained in the Aaronic line until the destruction of the Second Temple by the Romans in AD 70. For the Israelites, the *Kohanim* had a special dispensation to keep the knowledge given to them by God. Writing enabled the *Kohanim* to restrict access to the special knowledge that became the basis of their authority. They could search it for meaning, and others could not. Of course, they could not search it efficiently for all the reasons we mentioned earlier. Nonetheless, they had physical access – and therefore power – and others did not.

Those who had special knowledge – professionals – recorded it in writing and hoarded it. That was the "is" of the situation and remained so until recently when, thanks to new media, expertise started to slip out of the hands of the experts. The "ought" evolved to support the emergence and existence of experts was, paradoxically, collectivism. The basic notion here is that human groups are not composed of autonomous individuals, as we saw was the case in the hunter-gatherer band, but rather are structured by dependencies. The social parts, each with its own function, work together to form the social whole. If one fails, then they all suffer. It is a short step from this concept of society to the idea that each social part has a divinely sanctioned obligation to the collective. This is the origin of the doctrine of "estates," as in "those who pray" (clergy, the First Estate), "those who fight" (nobility, the Second Estate), and "those who work" (peasants, the Third Estate). It is most familiar from medieval Europe but was common throughout the Manuscript Era.[75]

The same year Marshall McLuhan's *The Gutenberg Galaxy* was published, an altogether different book was issued under the clever title *How to Do Things with Words*.[76] It was the work of the British

philosopher of language, J. L. Austin, who tragically died before his
time in 1960. Whereas McLuhan tried to demonstrate that writing
"restructured thought," Austin sought to show that we *do* a lot of different things to other people with language. McLuhan may or may not
have been right, but Austin certainly was. We do, in fact, do many
different things to other people with words. Take a promise. It's a tool
we use to create an obligation. Or a threat. It's a tool we use to make
people fear us. Or a lie. It's a tool we use to fool someone. There are
hundreds of other examples. We've tried to point out in this chapter
that writing, too, is a tool that we use – often if not exclusively – to
do things to other people, to structure social relations and convince
others that certain things are good or true. But writing doesn't allow
us to do anything we like. Like any tool, it has more or less fixed characteristics that permit some kinds of use and discourage others. Taken
together, we argued, these attributes predictably led to the formation
of certain sorts of media networks in the Manuscript Era, and these
networks predictably led to the evolution of certain social practices and
values. Table 3 sums up the entire theory as it concerns manuscript-
writing.

We need to keep firmly in our minds that writing doesn't always
produce these effects or, where it does, always to the same extent. We
saw how the natural tendencies of speech could be blunted or even
scotched, though only with great effort. In principle, the same is true
of writing. One could make writing very accessible by means of free
schooling. One could make writing very public by forbidding private
reading and writing. One could make writing high-fidelity by teaching

TABLE 3. *The Effects of Writing*

Manuscripts		Medium Attribute →		Network Attribute	→	Social Practice	→	Cultural Value
Accessibility	=	Low	→	Concentrated	→	Hierarchicalized	→	Hierarchicalism
Privacy	=	High	→	Segmented	→	Closed	→	Privatism
Fidelity	=	Low	→	Symbolic	→	Abstracted	→	Idealism
Volume	=	Low	→	Constrained	→	Economized	→	Asceticism
Velocity	=	Low	→	Monologic	→	Centralized	→	Authoritarianism
Range	=	High	→	Extensive	→	Diversified	→	Pluralism
Persistence	=	High	→	Additive	→	Historicized	→	Temporalism
Searchability	=	Low	→	Unmapped	→	Professionalized	→	Collectivism

everyone to draw like an Old Master. One could increase writing's information-bearing capacity by making writing materials and the post free. One could make writing faster by creating a fast postal service, or even something like email. One could reduce the range of writing by making it illegal to transport texts. One could diminish the persistence of writing by instituting a universal burn-after-reading policy. One could make writing highly searchable by constructing an exhaustive index of everything written.

All this is possible, and some of it has even been attempted. But, as the historical record suggests, deflecting the tendencies of manuscript-writing takes a strength far beyond that possessed by most human groups. History is littered with tyrants, despots, and dictators, but none of them has ever had the power to reverse the currents of writing, at least in the long term. Despite their best efforts, writing usually did what writing naturally does. This is why Manuscript Cultures – despite the enormous cultural differences that separated them – all share a common set of characteristics. Princes and priests had access to literacy; almost no one else did or for that matter wanted to. Elites used their dominance of writing to privatize the secular and sacred, and everyone agreed that this was right and proper. They employed writing to create abstract models of the human and heavenly spheres, which in turn were used to rationalize those spheres. They deemed writing precious, used it sparingly, and put restrictions on its use. No one believed that one could or should write anything. They "spoke" to their subjects via writing, and their subjects almost never talked back. They employed writing as a tool of empire and science, gathering data about strangers and the strange. Thus their worlds expanded. They kept written records and wove "histories" out of them. Thus the "past" appeared and was used in the present. And they used writing to segment knowledge, thereby creating "disciplines." Thus did specialists gain power over laypeople in many important matters. These characteristics can be found in the Manuscript-Era cultures of the Ancient Near East, Classical Antiquity, and medieval Europe. Indeed, they are common coin among all agrarian societies wherever and whenever they are found.[77]

This, then, was Manuscript Culture, the product of manuscript-writing and the organized interests that "pulled" it into being. It proved quite durable and useful. For more than 4,000 years, Manuscript

Culture covered vast regions of the globe; with it, humans built enormous complex societies. In the following chapter, we'll see how people in one such society became dissatisfied with manuscripts and began to look for new media. The result was the birth of print, and with it, Print Culture.

3

HOMO LECTOR

Humanity in the Age of Print

The rulers will need to use a quite considerable amount of falsehood and deception for the benefit of those ruled. But we said, I think, that all such things are useful only in the form of medicine.[1]

    – Plato, *The Republic*, 459C

Plato believed that the only way to get to the Truth was by dialogue. Stentorian monologues wouldn't do the job, and neither would fancy writing. You had to talk to someone if you were really going to get to the bottom of anything. But talking wasn't all you had to do. Anyone could talk. In order to pursue philosophy, Plato said, you also had to have the right intellectual stuff. You needed to be smart and love – really *love* – the Truth. These intellectual and emotional characteristics were, however, rare. Only a few people possessed them, so only a few people were really cut out to be philosophers. To Plato, that was just a natural fact. In *The Republic*, he used this fact as the linchpin of his social engineering program. There he argued that the easiest way to create an ideal city was to put naturally superior people in charge, that is, those with the right intellectual stuff and a love of the Truth. The trick, of course, was finding and educating them. Thus, most of *The Republic* is given over to an explanation of how they might be discovered and raised. Once the philosopher-kings were found, trained, and placed over the citizenry, Plato claimed, the city would naturally flourish.

A knotty question, however, remained. Plato valued the Truth. He believed the pursuit of it was humanity's highest calling. He probably wished that everyone could have the capacity to find it, but as we've seen, he didn't believe this was so. Some did, some didn't. Clearly those who did should rule the ideal city, but should they tell the rest – the ignorant common people – what the Truth was? Didn't they have a right to know what was *really* going on? Plato didn't think so. Given their imperfect mental abilities and meager educations, they would just be confused by the Truth and their perplexity would disrupt the harmony of the city. In order to preserve said harmony, Plato recommended strict censorship and carefully crafted propaganda. What should the masses be told? Fairy tales like the cynical "Myth of the Metals" (*Republic*, 414B–415D). All people, so the fable goes, are brothers and sisters insofar as they are born of the earth. But they are not all equal. Not at all. Some are gold, some are silver, and some are iron and bronze, each being less precious than the last. Accordingly, those made of gold are rulers; those made of silver, auxiliaries; and those of iron and bronze, commoners. The lesson is transparent, as is its utility to the elite: the mighty are mighty and the meek are meek because that's the way nature intended it. Sensing that the meek might find the permanence of their sorry lot a bit disheartening, Plato offers them hope. It could happen, he says with a wink, that even though you are bronze your son or daughter might be gold, and if that is the case he or she will automatically be welcomed into the ruling class. Naturally, he adds rather more honestly, that probably won't happen, so don't get your hopes up and get back to work.

Plato's open embrace of censorship and propaganda may seem a bit odd to us, but they were common coin among the ruling elite of Manuscript Cultures. In that world, power rested on writing, and writing rested in the hands of the powerful. In this chapter, we will see what happened when the written word partially escaped from the elite's grasp for the first time in world history. With the spread of print and literacy in early modern and modern Europe, the hierarchs of old could no longer monopolize writing as they had for almost 5,000 years. They lost control of knowledge, and they lost control of the Truth. The results, as we'll see, were somewhat different than Plato anticipated.

WHY WE PRINT

If we are to show that our "pull" theory of media evolution is correct in the instance of print (and, just to be clear, we mean the "Print Revolution" that began in the West after 1450), we must prove two historical theses. First, we must show that the technical ability to print preexisted printing by some longish period. If this turns out to be true, then we can say that people could have printed in the modern way but didn't because they didn't need to or, rather, didn't need to enough. Second, we must show that some major social change made existing media – talking and writing – insufficient for the purposes of some organized group or groups, and that this or these groups developed a preexisting technical capacity – the ability to print – into a fully articulated medium.

What evidence, primary and secondary, can be brought to bear on these two theses? The primary evidence is plentiful, indeed, almost too much so. The libraries and archives of older Print Cultures – particularly those in Western Europe – are overflowing with millions upon millions of sources on printing and literacy. Historians generally love books, so it's not surprising that they have paid considerable attention to their production and consumption. Thanks to their efforts, we know much about the origin of print technology;[2] the birth of European print;[3] the early modern "Print Revolution";[4] talking in the age of print;[5] writing in the age of print;[6] the print business;[7] clandestine print;[8] the censorship of print;[9] print, education, and literacy;[10] and the origin of mass literacy.[11] In short, the ground has been well covered. We will take advantage of this fact in all that follows.

Printing before Printing

We could have written thousands of years before we actually wrote. Given the utility of writing in our own age, that must strike us as strange. But it's true. The case is rather different with printing. Not only could we have printed long before Gutenberg, we actually *did* after a fashion, though without the consequences that attended Gutenberg's invention. That must strike us as even stranger. But it's true, too.

Actually, Gutenberg didn't "invent" a whole heck of a lot. Almost all the elements of his printing system – the idea of stamping, movable type, a mechanical press, durable ink, and a stable medium – were present long before he set up shop. The basic concept behind printing – that you could use a crafted object to make a standard, reasonably permanent impression or mark on a surface – is ancient.[12] We'll begin with stamping. All early civilizations used seals and stamps, usually as authentication devices. The use of this technology to print texts is also old. By the fifth century at the latest, the Chinese were using carved stone to print text; by the eighth century at the latest, they were using woodblocks for the same purpose. In what was to become a typical pattern of diffusion, woodblock printing spread to Central Asia, then to the Islamic and Byzantine worlds, and finally to Europe. This printing technique was common in Europe by the fourteenth century, though it was almost always used to reproduce images. As for movable type, the Romans used it to create raised text on lead pipes, but never employed it to print on light media. The industrious Chinese used both clay and wooden movable type in the eleventh century. Korean craftsmen are generally credited with the creation of the first metal movable type, made of bronze, in the early fifteenth century. Movable type made it to Central Asia, but seemingly no further, though texts printed with movable type may have been seen by medieval European travelers. In the Manuscript Era, mechanical presses were ubiquitous and came in many varieties – beam, lever, and roller among them. The Romans invented the kind Gutenberg used, the screw press, in the first century. It was in widespread use in Europe by the year 1000, particularly in wine and olive oil production. Ink was also ubiquitous and came in many varieties in the Manuscript Era. Every literate civilization seemed to have its own favorite recipe – usually some combination of natural pigments, soot, gum, and water – but they all had it. Here, though, Gutenberg may be credited with a genuine invention. Traditional water-based inks didn't work well with his metal movable type, so he created a specially designed oil-based ink for printing. Finally, the Chinese invented paper in the first century. Over the next several centuries, it spread to Korea, Japan, and Central Asia. It migrated to the Islamic world in the eighth century, and from there to Europe in twelfth century. By the time Gutenberg set up his printing business, there were dozens of paper mills operating all over the continent, and paper had become a medium of choice.

Not only were the technologies required to print large numbers of texts at hand centuries before Gutenberg, in at least one instance they – or rather a subset of them – were put to exactly that use.[13] As we said, the Chinese were making rubbings from stone and wooden inscriptions well before the end of the first millennium AD. Prior to the eighth century, however, these techniques were not reengineered and deployed for the purposes of mass production because the Chinese "scribal pool," so to speak, was large enough to reproduce everything that needed to be reproduced. In the early eighth century, however, the Empress Wu (r. 690–705) ordered the mass reproduction and distribution of short Buddhist texts by means of woodblock printing. In fits and starts over the next several centuries, both a state-sponsored and independent printing industry grew. Wooden movable type became common in the twelfth century. Millions upon millions of texts were printed and found their way all over East Asia.

Yet there was no "Print Revolution" in East Asia. In Europe, the introduction of print was associated with a massive increase in the amount of text produced, in the speed with which texts circulated, and in the proportion of the population that could read them. In East Asia, it was associated with none of these things. Why the difference? One commonly cited explanation – that the Chinese script or the woodblock method made printing inefficient[14] – can immediately be dismissed. If that were so, then printed matter would not have been so inexpensive and plentiful in early modern China, and we know it was both.[15] No, there must be something else that paved the way for the odd explosion of print in Europe, something absent not only in East Asia but throughout the entire world.

This may have been a growing audience for text, and therefore growing demand. We have it on good authority that manuscript production – almost always religious – in the late medieval period was increasing.[16] There is also some indication, if rather uncertain due to lack of sources, that the era witnessed an increase in manuscript book ownership.[17] More books in more hands doesn't necessarily mean there were more readers doing more reading. But we also know that in some parts of Europe – particularly the Northwest – parishes and towns were opening more elementary and grammar schools.[18] This has led some to infer, not illogically though in the absence of anything like direct evidence, that literacy was increasing in the century or two before Gutenberg opened up his business.[19]

"Pulling" Print into Existence

New media are born of rising demand, and the evidence just presented concerning the expansion of the lay readership in late medieval Europe would certainly suggest rising demand. But that, according to our theory, is not really enough. The interests that stimulate and meet rising demand must be organized. In the Manuscript Era, the first such organized interests were Mesopotamian princes and priests. In the Print Era, they were Northwestern European capitalists, bureaucrats, and pastors. Each of these groups found reason to be dissatisfied with manuscripts as a means of communication, and each of them promoted – albeit irregularly – the adoption of print.

We'll begin with the capitalists.[20] Trade in most centralized Manuscript Cultures was severely restricted, both in the sense that it was dominated by political elites and starved for investment capital. These constraints made it hard for entrepreneurs to open new markets, and harder still to raise the funds necessary to exploit them. In medieval and early modern Europe, however, things were different. Thanks to the legacy of feudalism, political power there was divided among thousands of overlapping sovereignties and semi-sovereignties. At the top there were empires, below them kingdoms, then principalities, then duchies, then baronages, then counties, then domains – not to mention free cities, monasteries, colleges, universities, and guilds, all of which had some measure of autonomy. On the one hand, the jumble of jurisdictions divided markets. On the other hand, "Balkanization" ensured that no central authority could completely dominate all markets. Since each sovereignty was interested in increasing its tax revenue, and since tax revenue came primarily from imposts on trade, European authorities high and low found themselves competing for trade income. They could pursue a course of protectionism, capturing trade within their borders by imposing trade barriers. But the smarter move was to provide an economic climate conducive to commercial activity. The Northern Italian city-states – Venice, Milan, Florence, Genoa – did this most effectively in the fifteenth and sixteenth centuries. They were succeeded by the commercial cities of the Dutch Republic in the seventeenth century, and then London in the eighteenth. In order to take full advantage of new opportunities, European entrepreneurs, usually with the backing of political elites, invented new financial institutions to promote economic growth. These are now familiar to us, but were innovative in the fifteenth and sixteenth centuries when they first appeared: the commercial bank, the joint stock company, the insurance agency, and the entire financial infrastructure of a modern mercantile economy. With markets comparatively open and capital available, economic growth ensued. Thus, a new form of mass economic cooperation evolved – mercantile capitalism. Indeed, it evolved so rapidly that by 1776, one Adam Smith could lay down its basic laws in a book called *An Inquiry into the Nature and Causes of the Wealth of Nations.*[21]

Now let's turn to the bureaucrats.[22] As we've said, Manuscript Cultures were generally ruled by princes and priests. So were medieval and early modern European societies for the most part, but there princes and priests found it necessary to ask for a lot of help, so much that it eventually compelled them to reorganize the way they did business. Beginning in the seventeenth century, the costs of maintaining a competitive European sovereignty increased dramatically. This was in part due to "push" factors and in part to "pull" factors. In the former class we can cite rising military costs. Beginning in the sixteenth century, European states entered into an arms race that would last, intermittently, until the Second World War. In order to remain viable on the *champs de mars*, they had to build bigger, better equipped, better trained armies, navies, and eventually air forces than had ever been seen in the history of the world. Failure to do so meant extinction, or at least relegation to the rank of a second-class power, so all parties concerned took the race seriously. As everyone knows, armies are expensive, so in order to raise them, early modern European monarchs found they had to construct large organizations to extract the taxes necessary to pay for them and to recruit, arm, and train those in them. These were the first modern bureaucracies in Europe. As for "pull" factors, the same European elites who busied themselves building up their armies also took an interest in "improving" the societies from which those armies were raised. The two went hand in hand. In addition, a number of ideological currents stimulated their desire to use the state as an engine of social improvement. Among them we can name: Humanism, with its emphasis on education; Republicanism, with its focus on training good citizens; Cameralism, centered on the notion that the state should be well-ordered; and eventually Socialism, concentrating on the improvement of the material conditions of the downtrodden. We should of course mention Christianity itself, with its sundry duties to be merciful, just, and kind in the service of God. Whatever their motivation, early modern European rulers, particularly in the eighteenth and nineteenth centuries, embarked on "enlightened" campaigns of social improvement. They built roads, founded schools and universities, opened hospitals and orphanages, created postal services, reformed this, reformed that, and generally regulated everything they could. Their efforts may not have resulted in the hoped-for social progress, but they always produced large bureaucracies. These organizations had grown so bulky and intrusive by the end of the eighteenth century that they inspired spirited critiques such as that penned by the proto-anarchist William Godwin's in 1793, *An Enquiry Concerning Political Justice and its Influence on Modern Morals and Manners.*[23]

Finally, we have the pastors.[24] In many Manuscript Cultures, only priests (or those in their employ) could read, and only they were expected to read the holy scriptures. Indeed, much of their authority stemmed from the fact that they and they alone could read. All this was true of the Catholic and Orthodox Christian Churches of the High Middle Ages. That changed with the coming of the Reformation in 1517. Luther told his followers that scripture alone (*sola scriptura*) was the source of revealed truth and that they must, therefore, understand it if they wanted to receive the word of God. That meant reading it, something Catholic and Orthodox theologians almost universally believed was a bad idea. To facilitate reading by commoners, Luther himself translated the Bible into German, another no-no. Not surprisingly, it sold like hot cakes after it was printed in 1522. In the first two years of production alone, it was printed in fourteen authorized and sixty-six pirated editions.[25] Many other translations into the vernacular followed as Luther's "priesthood of all believers" grew. The Protestants' call to read and interpret the Bible had many effects, but the most interesting, organizationally speaking, was the fragmentation of Christianity itself. Not only did Protestantism hive off Catholicism and Orthodoxy, but it splintered into dozens and today hundreds of loosely aligned sub-denominations. If any believer can receive the divine word directly through the Bible, then it follows that any believer can found his or her own church based on his or her own revelation. And many, many have. In addition to Lutherans, of which there are many kinds, there are Calvinists, Anabaptists, Anglicans, Presbyterians, Pietists, Baptists, Methodists, Quakers, Pentecostals, Adventists, and Congregationalists, among others. The number of nameless, forgotten storefront Protestant churches past and present is too large to count. Protestantism isn't really an "organized religion" at all. It's less a church than a network of churches, less a faith than a discussion of faith, less a dogma than a stand against dogma.

The simultaneous rise of mercantile capitalism, the bureaucratic state, and reading religion in early modern Europe provided the historical context within which Print Culture could evolve, for each of these new developments stimulated the learning of letters and the adoption of print.

Mercantile capitalism required literacy to operate effectively. Think about the paper trail that capitalist production and exchange leaves: catalogues, contracts, sureties, indemnities, orders, delivery schedules, transit papers, bills of lading, inventories, receipts, invoices, account books, tax documents, bank statements, and so on. Reading and writing became a cost of doing business in early modern Europe, and businessmen actively patronized the schools and universities that produced the literate workers they needed. Print offered traders compelling efficiencies. First of all, it enabled them to inexpensively distribute news about markets or political conditions that might affect markets.[26] Manuscript newsletters with a commercial bent had been circulating in Europe for some time when the first printed proto-newspapers appeared in the sixteenth century. They included reports on commodity and currency prices, items of obvious interest to businessmen. By the first quarter of the seventeenth century, periodical newspapers were to be found in many major European cities, including Basel, Frankfurt, Vienna, Hamburg, Berlin, Amsterdam, Antwerp, and London. They continued to spread in the eighteenth and nineteenth centuries until they virtually covered the continent and were read by millions.

Similarly, bureaucracy necessitated literacy to run right. Modern offices process a huge amount and many different kinds of paper: laws, regulations, guidelines, directives, writs, summons, warrants, reports, white papers, memos, registers, indexes, and so on. Administrators must be literate to work in this environment, as is true of those who are administered. Thus, states became heavily involved in not only training literate bureaucrats, but making sure subjects themselves could read and write. For this purpose they opened and patronized countless schools and academies. In the eighteenth and nineteenth centuries, improving states launched full-blown literacy campaigns.[27] Print also provided new opportunities for states and their administrators, principally as a means of public announcement and propaganda. Print allowed edicts, regulations, and law codes to be distributed far and wide at reasonably low cost, something difficult – though hardly impossible – in a Manuscript Culture. Moreover, print could be used to shape emergent public opinion. Early modern rulers knew, of course, that some of their subjects read books and newspapers, so they regulated and censored both aggressively (just as Plato suggested they should). In principle, nothing could be printed without a government-issued license, and nothing distributed unless it had gone through the hands of a censor. Naturally, printers were careful not to run afoul of the powers-that-were, and therefore usually printed items that were favorable to them. A more aggressive tact was for the state to use a newspaper as a semi-official mouthpiece for the government line. This was not as difficult as you might imagine. Since the government was the source of most of the really valuable news anyway, all it had to do was make a sweetheart deal with a particular newspaper to get its bidding done. Throughout the entire early modern period, governmental administrations fed newspapers in this way to make sure that their message got out. American presidents had their own semi-official newspapers in Washington until the mid-nineteenth century.[28] Russian leaders still do.[29]

Finally, reading religion naturally needs literacy to do its godly work. Luther himself went back and forth on the issue of whether every believer was "priest" enough to interpret scripture in his or her own way. But he let the cat out of the bag, so there was little he or any Protestant theologian could do to stop the lay priests from reading the Bible – if, of course, they could read. Luther's followers went to significant lengths to see that they could. Throughout the early modern period, Protestant sects subsidized existing schools and founded new ones precisely for the purpose of teaching the faithful to read. They had, however, a rather limited view on what the faithful should read, as anyone who's been to Sunday school will know. The Reformation prompted the Counter-Reformation, and Catholics soon got into the literacy business as well. The Jesuits can be credited with the creation of the first "school system" in Europe in the sixteenth century, and they still consider education to be one of their primary missions. Europeans of every confessional stripe also had a stake in printing, for it seemed to be an excellent way to propagate the faith or, from the Catholic point of view, to prevent the propagation of the *new* faith. Luther was probably the first living author to become a bestseller in print. His many pamphlets quickly sold out, went through multiple printings, and were widely translated. By one estimate, Luther's thirty publications between 1517 and 1520 sold "well over 300,000 copies."[30] Luther is reported to have called print "God's highest and most extreme act of grace, whereby the business of the Gospel is driven forward."[31] During and after the Counter-Reformation, Catholics also embraced the printing press, so long as it was used to publish approved texts. Just so everyone would know which books were evil, the Papacy regularly printed lists of proscribed texts, the famed and feared *Index Librorum Prohibitorum*. If you printed, possessed, or read a book on the *Index*, you were asking to be summoned to the Inquisition. Catholics took printing and reading seriously: the *Index* was not abandoned until 1966, and then with great reluctance.[32]

The unprecedented confluence of capitalism, bureaucracy, and reading religion in early modern Europe lead to the explosion of the world's first Print Culture. Gutenberg opened the first European print shop of which we have record in Mainz around 1439. The shop failed, but the press was a success.[33] By 1480, there were printing presses in 110 Western European towns; by 1500, they were in 236. As the sixteenth century drew to a close, presses were to be found throughout the continent and overseas as well. The first substantial book printed by modern methods was Gutenberg's famous 42-line Bible of 1454. More quickly followed. Something on the order of 30,000 editions (that is, separate titles) were published in Europe before 1500, though some of these were pamphlets rather than books. It's estimated that somewhere between 150,000 and 200,000 editions (again, separate titles) were printed in the sixteenth century. Gutenberg printed approximately 200 copies of the 42-line Bible. The number of books increased suddenly and dramatically thereafter. Bibliographers believe that some 20 million books were printed before 1500, and between 150 million and 200 million in the sixteenth century. Given that the population of Europe outside Russia and the Ottoman Empire was roughly 78 million in 1600, that's three books for every person then living.[34] They were not, however, evenly distributed. Only the well-heeled could afford books until the eighteenth century, and only they were likely to be able to read. But there was a flood of cheaper printed material that was within the reach of the literate (and listening) middle and lower classes. These items generally took the form of broadsheets and chapbooks – ephemeral texts that catered to the tastes of common people, that is, reported miracles, mysteries, monstrous births, and the sort of thing one often finds in tabloid newspapers today. They were not meant to last, and for the most part they haven't. We have no idea exactly how many were printed. All we can say is that there were probably a lot of them. The same holds true in part for printed proto-newspapers and newspapers. They first appeared in the mid-sixteenth century as single-event newssheets and quickly evolved into periodicals covering many events. The first weekly newspaper appeared in Paris in 1631, in Florence in 1636, in Rome in 1640, and in Madrid in 1661. The first daily was issued in Leipzig in 1660. There were over 200 newspapers in operation in the German-speaking regions of Europe in the seventeenth century. Paris had 35 periodicals in 1779; by 1789, it had 169. London had 169 periodicals in 1779; by 1789, it had 205. It's estimated that 16,500 newspapers were printed daily in London in the mid-eighteenth century. In 1712, there was one stamped (taxed) newspaper printed for every two adults in England; in 1760, there were three for every two; and in 1800, there were three for every adult.

Literacy rates grew as well. Before we see how, we need to bear in mind that measuring literacy is a complicated business, particularly before the twentieth century. Though we often speak of people or populations as being more or less literate, "literacy" is not just a single dimension. Rather, it is a set of skills, all of which can be mastered to a greater or lesser degree, often independently of one another. You don't need to know how to write in order to read, and you don't need to be a good reader in order to sound out words. We need to be aware of these differences when we speak of "literacy." Moreover, Manuscript- and Print-Era societies did not administer standardized tests to measure reading and writing ability. In fact, they generally didn't measure reading and writing ability at all. Therefore, historians must rely on proxies of various kinds that suggest to various degrees how many people were literate and to what extent. These proxies fall into two categories: *indirect* measures such as the number of schools, production and sale of books, and property inventories including books; and *direct* measures such as the ability to sign one's name. Even here there is a lot of room for error: going to school doesn't necessarily mean learning to read, and signing one's name doesn't necessarily mean one can write. When estimating literacy rates, we should always recall the distance between the imperfect tool we use to measure reading and writing and the actual rates of reading and writing.

Having said all that, both indirect and direct measures strongly suggest that literacy made significant advances during the early modern period, particularly in Northwest Europe. The number of primary and secondary schools grew, at first ad hoc and then as a result of direct state intervention in education. According to one estimate, between one-fifth and one-third of all children in Western Europe had the opportunity to attend school in the eighteenth century. In Northwestern Europe and areas such as Prussia, the figure topped 50 percent.[35] As for higher education, it too experienced significant growth. Spain, for example, had six universities in 1450 and thirty-three by 1600. In the German-speaking lands, there were twenty universities in 1600, twenty-eight by 1700, and thirty-one by 1760. In England, Oxford and Cambridge remained the only two universities, but even they expanded by adding numerous new colleges. All in all, more than 184 universities were in operation at one time or another in early modern Europe. The number of college students rose. The University of Padua matriculated 300 students a year in the 1550s; by the 1610s, that number had reached 1,100. Cambridge University enrolled some 1,300 students in 1564; in 1622, it enrolled 3,000. The German universities taught 3,200 students in 1500; by 1600, they taught 8,000. Part of the rise in enrollments was due to increases in the general population, but the *rate* of university attendance was growing as well. About 1 percent of Western Europeans attended university circa 1500. A century later, that figure had increased to around 2.4 percent in England and 2.8 percent in the United Provinces of the Low Countries. It's true that the attendance rate rose and fell from decade to decade, but the general trend was probably slightly upward. More primary, secondary, and tertiary students meant more readers, and more readers meant higher demand for printed material. We've already seen that the number of printed books, newspapers, and ephemeral items grew rapidly over the entire period. The price of printed matter declined continuously, and as a result, ownership of printed text spread throughout society. Owning a book was virtually unthinkable for most Europeans around 1500; by 1800, it was quite common. Reading spread more quickly and widely than writing, but writing itself made significant gains. According to one estimate, more than 50 percent of adult males in Northwestern Europe could sign their names in 1800. More could read a simple text. As the state became more heavily involved in education in the nineteenth century, literacy rates continued to climb until most adults could read and write at least on a basic level.[36]

Printing and Human Nature

Mass literacy, largely built on the power of print to provide texts and the state to make people learn to read and write, arrived in Western Europe in the eighteenth and nineteenth centuries and then spread to much of the rest of the world in the twentieth century. It was, however, a long time coming. People could print long before the Print Era, but generally they didn't use print as a means of mass textual reproduction. Even when they did, as in the case of early modern China and Renaissance Europe, people did not rush to learn to read. And, even more strikingly, when European states made literacy training both available and indeed mandatory, people still avoided literacy. Why?

The answer is essentially the same one we gave for the remarkably late arrival and low penetration of manuscript literacy: humans really don't like to read and write very much. As we said, we were evolved to talk – that's why it is easy for us and we so like to do it. We were not evolved to write or read – that's why we find both so difficult and tiring. These facts did not change with the arrival of printing in China, Europe or anywhere else. We have no natural inclination to read manuscripts, and we have no natural inclination to read printed texts. Printing produced more texts and the state provided – indeed mandated – that people learn to read them. But neither the one nor the other could make reading any more useful or enjoyable.

Again, we tend to think that if people are given the chance to learn to read, they will learn. We also are inclined to think that if, once literate, they are given some good reason to read or something interesting to read, they will read it. In the Manuscript and Print Eras we could not test these propositions. But in our own age we can and, in effect, already have. For the past century at the very least, both of the previously mentioned conditions – inexpensive literacy training and useful, cheap reading material – have been met over all of the industrialized world and much of the rest of it. Yet a remarkable number of people are still illiterate. According to a recent UNESCO report, around 18 percent of the world's adults can't read or write at all.[37] Most of them live in places where the state's educational arm does not reach very far, Central Africa being the primary though not only example. But even in the developed and developing world, a small but stubborn percentage of people choose not to learn to read or write even though doing so is free and valuable. More compelling is the fact that even when people can read, they don't, at least not very often. In a 2002 survey, 43 percent of adult Americans reported that they had not voluntarily read a book in the past year.[38] According to the American Time Use Survey (2007), adults in the United States spend on average about twenty minutes every day reading on weekdays for pleasure.[39] They spend about twenty-three minutes on weekends and holidays. Since Americans spend roughly three hours a day watching television, it might make sense to say that humans have some sort of evolutionarily implanted appetite for watching. But it is crystal clear that we have no such ingrained hunger for reading – whether the text is written by hand or printed.

The needs of capitalists, bureaucrats, and pastors "pulled" mass printing and mass literacy into existence, but they could never really complete the job because, as we've said, most people don't like to read or write very much.

WHAT PRINT DID

In early modern Europe, then, what was a mixed-media environment characterized by talking and manuscripts became even more mixed by the addition of mass print. Again, we need to stress that mass print did not *replace* talking or manuscripts. Major media generally accumulate; they do not supplant one another. We also should emphasize that mass print did not at any point or in any place become the predominant mode of communications. For several centuries after the introduction of mass print, literacy rates remained low. People who can't read – and that was the majority of the European population until the late nineteenth century – do not read manuscripts *or* printed texts. They talk. Orality, though not primary orality, survived well into the modern era even where print and literacy spread fastest and penetrated most deeply.[40] And even among people who were literate, talking and manuscripts hardly disappeared once printing and printed matter became widely available. For many – and perhaps even most – purposes, it remained easier to talk to someone than to write a note to them, and easier to write a note to them than to print one. For example, people continued to write letters after print.[41] Erasmus wrote about 2,000 of them;[42] Linnaeus wrote over 2,400;[43] Darwin wrote over 7700.[44]

According to our "push" theory of media effects, print should have altered Manuscript Era social practices and values in these cultures; it should have formed the basis of a distinct Print Culture in a distinct Print Era (1450 to 1850). As we saw earlier, we have ample primary and secondary sources available to test these propositions, and we will use both in all that follows.

Accessibility

The cost of acquiring the equipment and skill necessary to talk and listen is low, meaning speech is highly accessible. In contrast, the cost of gaining the equipment and skill required to write and read manuscripts is high, particularly in marginal economies, meaning manuscript literacy is inaccessible. Traditional printing – that is, reproduction with a press, movable type, ink, and paper – falls somewhere between the two.

On the send side, the tools and skills required to print are costly. The equipment needed – a building, a press, movable type, frames, paper, and ink – to run even a primitive printing operation are not cheap; modern printing presses, the kind used by book publishers and newspapers, are hugely expensive. Once you have the equipment, you've got to learn to use it. That means, first of all, learning to write and read in the printed language. That takes years. Then you have to learn how to operate the printing machine. That will take more time. Once you've learned to use it, you've got to use it. Printing presses are complicated, need ongoing maintenance, and are subject to frequent breakdowns. All in all, they are not a lot of fun to operate. It's hardly surprising, then, that few people use printing presses when they want to relax, the way someone might sing a song or write a letter. Printing, then, is an expensive proposition. Moreover, it's not terribly difficult to make it artificially more expensive than it naturally is. This is because printing presents would-be monopolists with a fair – though not excellent – logistical bottleneck, that is, a place in the production chain that is narrow and therefore easily dominated. With printing, the bottleneck is precisely access to printing equipment and skill. Tyrannical governments restrict access to both. There is something about printing that makes tyrants nervous.

On the receive side, the equipment and skills necessary to read printed texts are comparatively inexpensive. The primary tool necessary for reading is the text itself (though eyeglasses and a good light source are also helpful). Since the printing press can produce texts quickly and inexpensively, it drives down the cost of this reading material. The press has the potential to put texts in the hands of the many, rather than – as in Manuscript Culture – the few. The primary skill necessary for reading is, well, reading ability. The press does not have any direct impact on the cost of literacy training, though it did have an indirect effect insofar as it made text more abundant and therefore increased the opportunity to study reading. A manuscript literacy primer was probably more expensive than a printed literacy primer. Also, it is reasonably difficult to make obtaining printed texts and learning to read them more expensive than it naturally is. Once printed texts slip through the bottleneck (as we'll see they frequently do), they are a lot like water that has run over a levee. If you block it here, it will flow over there. Try to pick it up, and it runs through your fingers. Even totalitarian states have trouble keeping books out of the hands of their subjects. This is primarily because printed texts – like all texts – are easily hidden and can be passed through "private" channels, a topic we will discuss later. As for learning to read, pretty much anyone who can read can teach someone who can't. So if there are a lot of readers, then it will be expensive to prevent the teaching and learning of literacy. The passage of reading skills is a bit like the passage of secrets: they move stealthily and it's hard to tell just by looking who has them.

Printing, then, would seem to be inaccessible on the send side and accessible on the receive side. But it's clear that the accessibility of print changed radically over time, at least in the early modern and modern West. It began as relatively inaccessible – few printers, small print runs, few readers – and became much more accessible – many printers, larger print runs, more readers. For this reason, we'll treat it in its mature form as accessible on both the send and receive sides. According to our theory, accessible media engender diffuse networks, and diffuse networks tend to *equalize* the social practices and values that grow with them. We'll see this was the case in the early modern and modern West.

In late medieval Europe, the elite – princes and priests – controlled manuscript production de facto and de jure, just as we would expect in any Manuscript Culture. When printing was introduced, they made every effort to dominate it as well, again as we would expect. By the early sixteenth century, nearly every European state had imposed a scheme to license and censor the logistical bottleneck in the printing system – presses and printers. By and large, these attempts at monopolization proved reasonably effective in that they limited who could print and what could be printed. Hierarchy was thereby maintained. Nonetheless, the princes and priests eventually lost control of the press because it was just too slippery. This proved to be so for a number of reasons. First, it was generally easy to move printed texts across Europe's many borders. If a European printer couldn't print something in one jurisdiction, he could always go to another and export his product. Second, really aggressive attempts to control the press were impossible or unreasonably expensive, both economically and politically. The best an English king or Dutch *Stadtholder* could muster was a low-cost licensing and censorship system under which the printers' and booksellers' guilds policed themselves. As this complaint regarding illegal printing issued by Parliament in 1643 indicates, it often didn't work.

Very many, as well stationer and printers as others of sundry other professions not free of the Stationers' Company, have taken to set up sundry private printing presses in corners, and to print, vent, publish and disperse books, pamphlets and papers in such multitudes that no industry could be sufficient to discover or bring to punishment all the several abounding delinquents.[45]

According to one estimate, as many as a third of all books in early seventeenth-century England were unauthorized.[46] Finally, good control of the press wasn't really good enough. You needed to get them all. Effectively censoring ninety-nine out of one hundred presses sounds like a job well done, but a single press – producing thousands of copies – could do a lot of damage.

It took some time, then, for the European elite to lose their hold on printers. In contrast, they almost immediately lost all control of readers. The Inquisition and similar censoring bodies might have worked in the Manuscript Era, when both texts and readers were few. But in early modern Europe, this was not the case. The facts were simple. Demand for written material was steadily rising as Western Europeans became wealthier, more literate, and increasingly accustomed to having their textual tastes gratified. Supply followed rising demand thanks to a healthy, responsive, and sometimes devious printing industry. Readers and printed texts multiplied. The result was the slow but steady democratization of reading, especially though not exclusively in Northwestern Europe. Remember that print production presented a bottleneck the elite could exploit – printers, few in number and easy to find, could be hounded and their presses destroyed. But in a world of millions of readers and millions of texts, the consumption of print offered no easy chokepoint. Russians have a nice expression: "A word is not a sparrow. Once you've let it go, you can't get it back."[47] The same might be said of printed texts. Once they have escaped into the public, they cannot be easily retrieved. This was obviously true in the countries of early modern Western Europe (and later North America) where both custom and law prevented the state from illegal searches and seizures of property, and especially property found in one's residence. But it was also true in despotisms where such customs and laws, though they might be on the books, were not respected. Both the Russian and, later, Soviet governments did their best to censor what their subjects read; still, underground literature was widely available in both.[48]

The democratization of printing and reading in early modern Europe had a profound impact on a number of social practices, but clearly the most significant was on the social practice of government. In the Manuscript Era, princes and priests monopolized writing and reading and were able, then, to use text as an instrument of control. In the Print Era, their monopoly was broken and the instrument based on it destroyed. Suddenly the ruling elite's "voice" was one among many, albeit the strongest. Parties, confessions, regions, towns, classes, business interests, guilds, and all the other component parts of traditional societies could now "speak," not only to power but to each other. And "speak" – or rather argue – they did in the host of religious, political, and politico-religious conflicts that punctuated the early modern period: the Reformation, the English Revolution, the Dutch Revolt, the American Revolution, and the French Revolution, to name only the most significant. Each of these contretemps generated a flood of partisan printed material: discourses, treatises, tracts, broadsides, chapbooks, ballads, pamphlets, and newspapers. Many of them, like Locke's famous *Two Treatises of Government*, are still read today.[49] It was out of this new chorus of voices that limited monarchy emerged, and out of limited monarchy that liberal democracy as we know it today emerged. To be sure, the accessibility of print did not uniquely "cause" the birth of free government, but it surely served as its midwife.[50]

That was the "is" of the situation: by the eighteenth century at the latest, the Western European elite's hold on text slipped away and with it the elite's hold on power. The "ought" moved from one stating that the press should be licensed and restricted – elitism – to one stating that the press should be free – a sort of egalitarianism.[51] The new "ought" manifested itself in many forms, but among the most important was the doctrine of the "marketplace of ideas": the notion that the truth is best arrived at through an open exchange of opinions. Milton famously laid it out in 1644: "And though all the windes of doctrin were let loose to play upon the earth, so Truth be in the field, we do injuriously, by licencing and prohibiting to misdoubt her strength. Let her and Falshood grapple; who ever knew Truth put to the wors, in a free and open encounter?"[52] Eighteenth-century revolutionaries took Milton's sentiments to heart and enshrined freedom of the press in the U.S. Constitution and the French Revolutionary "Declaration of the Rights of Man."[53] By the middle of the nineteenth century, the idea that the free and open "contest of ideas" was basic to good government was dogma. Writing in 1869, John Stuart Mill expressed the hope that "the time... is gone by, when any defense would be necessary of the 'liberty of the press' as one of the securities against corrupt or tyrannical government."[54] Thus did the press become the "Fourth Estate," a bulwark of liberty, in the first half of the nineteenth century.[55] Some, like Oscar Wilde, didn't believe – or said they didn't believe – that the press protected anything.

In old days men had the rack. Now they have the press. That is an improvement certainly. But still it is very bad, and wrong, and demoralizing. Somebody – was it Burke? – called journalism the fourth estate. That was true at the time no doubt. But at the present moment it is the only estate. It has eaten up the other three. The Lords Temporal say nothing, the Lords Spiritual have nothing to say, and the House of Commons has nothing to say and says it. We are dominated by Journalism.[56]

But Wilde was in the minority, and a shrinking one at that. The notion of just what constituted a contribution to the "marketplace of ideas" expanded mightily in the late nineteenth and early twentieth centuries.[57]

By the end of the twentieth, all you had to do is say that your writing was "art" – which naturally makes such a contribution – and it was protected.[58]

Privacy

Speaking and listening are usually public. Manuscript-writing and reading are often private. Again, traditional printing falls between these two stools.

On the send side, recall that a handy medium would make it easy for *senders* – in this case, printers – to hide their identities and the content of their correspondence. Traditional print makes it relatively hard to do either of these things. Kidnappers use print to hide their identities with their signature "ransom note" style of cutout print letters. But that's not really printing. If you are printing, then you face the following problem: as the number of copies of a text you print goes up, so does the difficulty of hiding your identity. The reason is purely physical. Small presses that produce a few copies at a time can be hidden, a fact that has enabled revolutionaries, radicals, and pornographers to print their underground wares without too much notice (though probably too much for them) for the past several centuries. But big presses – the ones that can produce thousands of feet of print per minute – fill entire warehouses, require teams of technicians to run, and must be fed by a long logistical supply train. You can't hide them. When the revolution begins, the first thing the revolutionaries do is take over the big newspaper and rename it something like "The People's Voice." They know right where it is, and so will the counter-revolutionaries when they strike back. That said, if you are willing to use a small press with limited reproductive capacity, then you can hide your identity. Now let's say you want to conceal the contents of what you've printed from those who are not designated recipients. This might seem odd, given that the usual purpose of printing is precisely to publicize your message. But nonetheless, there have been times and places in which hiding printed messages has been deemed necessary. One of them, not surprisingly, was the Soviet Union. There, "sensitive" printed items – banned books, magazines and newspapers, internal government reports, Party memoranda – were kept in special closed collections that restricted access to those who "needed to know."[59] Copies "for official use only" were often numbered to ensure that they all were accounted for, and if borrowed, would be returned. Of course this still left open the possibility that "wreckers" would somehow reproduce the item and return the numbered original, and in fact some people did this. But the Party had a solution to that problem as well: they simply made sure that copiers – a dangerous technology in an authoritarian state – remained under strict government control.[60] Copiers are anti-communist. Nevertheless, hiding the contents of printed texts is hard, and it gets harder the more copies you print. Most texts aren't hard to hide, and people like to pass them around. If they are short enough, they can be memorized (prisoners in the Gulag did a lot of this) or copied by hand (Soviet citizens did a lot of this).

On the receive side, recall that a handy medium would allow recipients – in this case, the readers of printed texts – to hide their identities as well as the contents of the messages they receive. Neither of these tasks is difficult. To get reading material anonymously, you only need to follow a few simple rules. First, stay out of bookstores, libraries, or anyplace where someone might see you get a book you don't want people to know you have, say *The Anarchist Cookbook* or *The Devil Wears Prada*. You might go to one of these places to get books you *do* want people to know you have just for misdirection's sake. *Profiles in Courage* or *Tom Sawyer* would be excellent choices. Second, when you must get a book from someone you don't know, order it by mail using a phony name and post office box. The post office knows that there's big money in providing this kind of cover for men who want girly magazines, so they make it dead simple. Third, whenever possible get your books from people you know well and trust. Make sure they don't work for the secret police. If they don't, chances are they won't rat you out. Finally, do all of your reading in private and discuss it with no one outside your trusted circle. Do no "public readings" and avoid "book clubs." If you have questions about any of these rules, seek out a Russian, Cuban, or basically anyone who has lived in an authoritarian country. They are well practiced in private reading and will be able to explain everything to you.

Printing, then, would seem to be semi-public. If you do it, people will probably notice, though not always. But reading print is, or at least can be, private. If you are cautious, you won't ever be observed doing it. As we saw was the case with the accessibility of print, however, the privacy of print changed considerably over time in the early modern and modern West. It began quite public and, as presses became more widely available and reading more common, became more private. Thus, we will treat it in its modern form and classify it as relatively private on both the send and receive sides. According to our theory, private media foster segmented networks, and segmented networks *close* social practices and values. We will presently see that this was the case in the eighteenth-, nineteenth-, and twentieth-century West.

In the Manuscript Era, the privacy of writing enabled the elite to accomplish two important things: to privatize political affairs and to gain control of sacred power. Because they and they alone could write, the princes and priests of the Manuscript Era could conduct their business (which, as it happened, was everyone's business) and control the *lingua sacra* in private, out of the view of their ordinarily illiterate subjects. At the beginning of the modern Print Era, the elite continued to enjoy private dominance over political and religious matters due to their command of printing itself. But over the course of the early modern period, the princes and priests allowed the print channel to slip from their grasp. Printers made printing more and more private, thereby removing it from the gaze of the authorities and creating a relatively safe channel through which subjects could engage their fellows regarding the *res publica* and *res sacra*. Paradoxically, then, the privacy of printing enabled once muted subjects to break the elite's monopoly on political and religious power and to become political and religious powers themselves. In so doing, they created what we now call the "public sphere" – the open forum in which affairs common to all are rationally discussed by all, or at least those with printing presses.[61]

The press helped open the public sphere, but it also solidified and expanded the private sphere. In the Manuscript and early Print Eras, reading – itself an elite activity – was surprisingly public.[62] First, people read out loud. Like musical notation, writing was understood to be a set of prompts that allowed speech to be "played back." Second, people read in front of others. Reading was a performance, and performances were to be conducted before audiences. Finally, readers performed texts of interest to the public, which, being elite, itself was quite small and uniform. Because the audience was homogeneous, so were the texts. With the advent of print, however, reading became much more private, and the very notion of "privacy" was articulated in a modern way.[63] Unlike manuscript writers and performers, early modern printers were in the business of producing many texts for a varied audience made up of readers of all different skill levels. Thus, the printers needed to make technical accommodations for marginal readers. Fonts would need to be clear and large. Words and sentences would need to be separated. Language would need to be simplified, and even translated out of little-known idioms (Latin, Greek) and into the vernacular. Similarly, the printers would have to expand the range of topics in their catalogues. Religious texts and classics remained at the top of the "list," but they were joined by romances, histories, dramas, adventures, travels, and tall tales of every sort. Finally, printed materials would have to be made affordable, which is to say made badly. Thus, the leather-covered, board-bound book was joined by various sorts of "ephemera" – chapbooks, broadsheets, and the like. As the printers went "down market," they liberated common people from the necessity of listening to elites read aloud; the half-literate masses could just read cheap, legible texts to themselves *by themselves*, out loud or silently.

Making the book private allowed printers to exploit a huge and untapped market – the trade in guilty pleasures. Guilty pleasures, of course, are things you do for personal enjoyment but don't feel so good about and, usually, don't want others to know you are doing. In strict, patriarchal, religion-bound societies like early modern England or France, the demand for guilty pleasures was no doubt high, but the supply was low precisely because it was difficult to hide the naughty bits you were pursuing. Books, however, could be hidden and consumed in private. And so books became filled with every manner of guilty pleasure. The archetypal case is the pornographic book, a "published" artifact that can really only be enjoyed in private.[64] The famous English diarist Samuel Pepys bought *The School of Girls* for private enjoyment on February 8, 1688. The next night he "read" it:

We sang till almost night, and drank my good store of wine; and then they parted, and I to my chamber, where I did read through *L'escholle des filles*, a lewd book, but what doth me no wrong to read for information sake (but it did hazer my prick para stand all the while, and una vez to decharger); and after I had done it I burned it, that it might not be among my books to my shame.[65]

As we can see, Pepys was conflicted about the book. It was fun, but it was bad. Moralists, politicians, and clergy were generally more consistent, at least in public: pornography was just bad. But as much as they railed against the reading of naughty books, they could not stop people from reading them.

That was the "is" of the situation: the privacy of print allowed people to enter the public sphere and do as they liked in the private sphere. The "ought" that followed was composed of two parts, one already familiar to us and the other not. The former is the doctrine of the "marketplace of ideas." It served as a justification for the right of private subjects to print in the public sphere. The "marketplace of ideas" was, however, primarily intended as a defense of the "right" to print high-minded political and religious texts. But what of the low-minded printed texts that the public so avidly consumed in private? Some defense of the "right" to read tasteless, offensive, and obscene texts had to be mounted if the public was to be given what it wanted and print could provide. That defense took the form of privatism, the notion that information need not be shared. It manifested itself in several doctrines, all of which are known to and hallowed by right-thinking people everywhere.

The first was the "right to privacy" itself. In public, hierarchy should be maintained, and thus some should be more equal than others. But in private, hierarchy was erased, and everyone was equally free to act as they wished, and more particularly read as they wished. This idea seems to find its origins in the seventeenth-century debate concerning the right of the state to intervene in "private" confessional matters, though there is some disagreement on this score.[66] In any case, it was certainly established by the American Revolution, for the Founding Fathers wrote it into the "establishment clause" of the First Amendment, a doctrine more commonly known as the "separation of church and state."[67] The notion that you could read *anything* in the privacy of your own home came much later and is still debated, but it came nonetheless.[68]

The second was the "harm principle," the notion that governments should not forbid people from doing things that harm no one but the doers. It finds its origins in Mill, though he never intended it to cover the vast and somewhat disturbing range of "victimless" naughtiness that it came to protect.[69] In truth it was rather late in coming, and might well be thought of as a product of the Audiovisual Era. But it was first tested on "obscene" literature and therefore rightfully belongs, at least in part, to the Print Era. Of course, whether things like pornographic literature are damaging or not is an open question.[70] But, judging by what one finds in the popular press, there is little public sympathy for the idea that it is in most Western democracies.[71] Some have even gone further and suggested that pornography, far from being harmful, is beneficial.[72]

The third doctrine follows from the second. For, if everyone has the right to read whatever they like in private, you have the obligation to let them. This is the principle of "obligatory tolerance." It, too, was late in coming, though it is also bound to print. In 1953, for example, the American Library Association and the American Book Publishers Council endorsed a statement of principles entitled "The Freedom to Read." Among the many reasons it gives to guard this "freedom" generally, one finds this:

To some, much of modern expression is shocking. But is not much of life itself shocking? We cut off literature at the source if we prevent writers from dealing with the stuff of life. Parents and teachers have a responsibility to prepare the young to meet the diversity of experiences in life to which they will be exposed, as they have a responsibility to help them learn to think critically for themselves. These are affirmative responsibilities, not to be discharged simply by preventing them from reading works for which they are not yet prepared. In these matters values differ, and values cannot be legislated; nor can machinery be devised that will suit the demands of one group without limiting the freedom of others.[73]

In other words, every citizen has a duty to tolerate any manner of print expression no matter how "shocking" it might be.

And finally, we have a fourth doctrine, "aesthetic populism." This is the notion that the people should be given what they want, that the popular is the same as the good, and that public opinion is the arbiter of taste. It means that no printed text, no matter how distasteful to some, can be banned on aesthetic grounds. It was also a late arrival. In the first half of the nineteenth century, Tocqueville noticed it among Americans (and was disgusted).[74] In the second half of that century, the English critic Matthew Arnold found it among his countrymen (and was also disgusted).[75] Today it reigns supreme. Those who argue against it are routinely denounced as "snobs" and "elitists."[76]

Fidelity

Most writing is a sort of picture of speech. Most printing is a sort of picture of writing. As such, a printed copy of a clean manuscript of *War and Peace* should be semantically identical to its handwritten source. Both the one and the other reduce several kinds of sense data – here about Russia between 1805 and 1813 – to one encoded visual channel, that is, written language. Thus, you can no more "see" Natasha and Pierre in the printed *War and Peace* than you can in the manuscript. You can only read about them and imagine "seeing" them. This is to say that both manuscript-writing and printed texts are five-to-one codes, and both consequently are low-fidelity media. But there is an important difference. It's not between the manuscript text and the printed copy of it – these, as we just said, are semantically equivalent – but between *copies* of the manuscript text and *copies* of the printed text. After his many dalliances with young peasant girls, Tolstoy settled down and got married to one Sofia Andreyevna Behrs. The "conscience of Russia" was apparently a good husband, but he did ask Sophia to do something a bit above and beyond the call of wifely duty, namely, to copy the manuscript of *War and Peace* seven times.[77] Though comparing all seven manuscripts would be laborious (though perhaps not too laborious for a graduate student in comparative literature), it stands to reason that such an exercise would reveal them all to be different from one another and from the printed first edition. It really could not be otherwise: no mere mortal can exactly copy almost half a million words without making a few mistakes – not even once, let alone seven times. If, however, one were to compare all the printed copies of the first edition of *War and Peace* – a task too troublesome for even a graduate student – one would probably find them all to be virtually identical. There might be differences, but they would be few (and highly collectable).[78] This leads us to the following conclusion: a copy of a printed text is usually an exact picture of the printed text. When used as a means of reproducing text, writing creates *editions*, while printing produces *facsimiles*. The difference in faithfulness is even greater when it comes to the reproduction of images. We've said that both writing and printing are five-to-one codes, but that's true only in the case of written and printed *text*. Both writing and printing can be used to produce and reproduce images, that is, motivated signs like a picture of a daisy. You can hand-draw a daisy and make a copy of the drawing. You can make an engraving of a daisy and then print a copy of it. When used in this mode, writing and printing are four-to-one codes: they reduce sound, smell, taste, and feeling to vision, while the visual channel itself is not encoded (or at least *as* encoded). A drawing or engraving of a daisy is an *icon* of a daisy – it doesn't need to be "read," only recognized. Though formally similar, the potential of each medium to reproduce these icons is vastly different. In order to make *one* mediocre reproduction of the *Mona Lisa* by hand, you need to have talent and a lot of time. But in order to make *thousands* of mediocre reproductions of the *Mona Lisa* with a press, all you need is one mediocre etching of the *Mona Lisa*. Once you have the ability to take photographs and print those, then you can produce thousands of good copies of the *Mona Lisa*. And once you can do this, printing moves from low fidelity to high, at least in the visual channel.

As concerns text, print is low fidelity: what comes out (inked symbols) doesn't look, sound, smell, taste, or feel like what goes in (sense data). As concerns images, print has somewhat higher fidelity: what comes out (inked icons) looks more or less like what comes in (sights). Given these attributes, print networks will be primarily symbolic and secondarily iconic. Like writing, print's forte is – or at least was until relatively recently – the reproduction of text. Print is superior to writing in terms of its ability to reproduce images. We would expect, then, that the principal impact of a print network, or rather the dominant symbolic aspect of it, would be the *conceptualization* of social practices. Print provides more symbolic material to more people than any medium before it, and therefore prompts more abstract representation and systematization than any medium before it. We would also anticipate, though, that the iconic aspect of the print network would *sensualize* social practices. The reason is this: if humans are given the opportunity to use a medium for sensual gratification at low cost, then they usually will; the ability of print to reproduce images offers them this chance, though in a limited way.

We see both conceptualization and sensualization of social practices in the Print Cultures of early modern and modern Europe. As to the former, the clearest example is the systematization of organizations of all kinds. In a Manuscript Culture, most organizations had a sort of accidental character. They grew and evolved in accordance with the peculiarities of time, place, and personality. There was rarely if ever an overarching plan; rather, there were only adjustments from moment to moment. Take medieval European feudalism.[79] Its exact origins are obscure, though it seems to have evolved *circa* 1000 out of a kind of semi-customary compact between the powerful (princes) and the less powerful (vassals) by which both would rule and tax the power-less (townsmen and peasants). Feudalism was less an imposed system than an emergent phenomenon, the almost spontaneous appearance of rough order out of even rougher disorder. Everywhere it went it was adapted to local conditions on an *ad hoc* basis. Like a tree, it grew where it could, withered where it couldn't, and thereby took on a kind of gnarly, twisted, organic form. It's interesting to note that the people who lived under feudalism had no name for the "system" itself: the word "feudal" was invented by French lawyers in the sixteenth century, just as the thing itself was breathing its last.[80] In the centuries that followed, feudalism was finally killed in Europe by rationalizing bureaucrats, that is, people who liked to plan and organize things and used print to do it.[81] They saw it as their mission to take the gnarled tree and make of it neatly stacked wooden planks. Their new science of administration went under various names in different ages: cameralism, merchantilism, economics, political science, and sociology.[82] Its theorists are well known: Colbert, Montesquieu, Justi, Smith, Condorcet, Saint-Simon, Owen, Fourier, Compte, Marx, Spencer, Durkheim, and Weber. For these men and those who thought like them, print – all right angles, straight lines, and clear logic – was a model for the way human affairs *should* be organized. But print was also a means to bring society into order. Their printed books, each like every other, would teach men and women the ways of rational, systematic organization. The abstract plan would thereby become concrete reality. When applied with subtlety, systematization worked. Governments, businesses, and churches were, as Weber put it, "rationalized" over the course of the seventeenth, eighteenth, and nineteenth centuries, at least in Northwestern Europe and North America.[83] But when applied with brute force, systematization failed dramatically. There can be no clearer case of this than that of the Soviet Union. All the Bolsheviks had when they took power was an abstraction, for no communist society had ever existed.[84] When they proceeded to impose their untried plan on the all-too-organic Russian empire, the results were disastrous. Yet – and this is the remarkable part – the print-aided dream of universal rationalization through social engineering did not die. It was tried in China, Vietnam, North Korea, Cuba and elsewhere, again with ruinous consequences.[85]

That was the "is" of the situation: people – and especially intellectuals – were going to use print to create and disseminate abstract models of virtually everything on earth and in the heavens. The "ought" that followed was a modern form of idealism that generally goes under the name "rationalism." It held that the rational systematization of ideas was the best means to the good life. This incredibly influential doctrine finds its modern origins in the Enlightenment.[86] For the *philosophes* and those who followed them, the application of reason to reality – what we might simply call "science" – was the basic motor of human progress. To apply reason to reality was to systematize. In the famed *Discours préliminaire* to the *Encyclopédie*, d'Alembert says as much in his praise of the "systemic spirit."[87] Indeed, it probably would not be too much to say that all of post-Enlightenment science has been one long effort to reduce the observed world to systems, interlocking sets of propositions that explain what goes on around us. Almost no one today seriously doubts that this effort has been beneficial to mankind and should be further pursued, not even most mainstream religious authorities.[88]

The ability of print to reproduce images sensualized social practices from the beginning. The earliest printed items contained images. They were almost always highly representational – the things depicted could be immediately recognized, if not really understood, by anyone. This style was taken up both because many viewers would be poorly educated and because realistic depictions were simply more sensually powerful than abstract ones. Early printers realized that not all images were equally popular. It seemed that the more transgressive the picture, the more people enjoyed it (and the more the authorities paid attention to it). Viewers wanted to *see* things that they could not or did not want to experience. Thus, many of the printed images – particularly those aimed at popular readerships – were violent, sexual, or both. For example, a German pamphlet of 1561 reporting atrocities committed by Russian troops in Livonia includes a woodcut of the soldiers nailing the "tender little hearts" of slaughtered children to trees and shooting arrows at the "privy parts" of freshly ravished virgins.[89] There is no doubt that such images were meant to stimulate feelings, not thoughts, and no doubt that they succeeded. Naturally, the most reliably and pleasurably stimulating images were, then as now, pornographic. As anyone who has ever studied Greek vases or Roman murals knows, the Ancients demanded pictorial porn and got it, though not much of it.[90] Medieval Europeans may have demanded it as well (though, lust being a sin, they hide it away in their hearts), but they had no ready supply of it.[91] Early modern engravers and printers were happy to enter the market and fulfill their desire, so to speak. Though they were constantly under the gun of prudish secular and clerical authorities, pornographers managed to publish a reasonably large catalogue of dirty texts with many dirty pictures, including most famously *The Sixteen Pleasures* (1524), *The School of Girls* (1655), *Memoirs of a Woman of Pleasure* (1766), and, inevitably, de Sade's *Justine or The Misfortunes of Virtue* (1791) and *Juliette or the Fortunes of Vice* (1797). With the invention of photography in the 1830s, the history of pornographic images entered a new phase. For, although etchings could be realistic, particularly in the hands of skilled craftsmen, they were not as realistic as photographs. In a photograph, the viewer had the impression of seeing things as they are, and that really matters with pornography. Not surprisingly, the female nude became a popular subject among photographic "artists." In the 1840s, William Fox Talbot figured out a way to make copies of photos at a reasonable cost and the industry of photo-porn was born.[92] Artsy "postcards" were an early vehicle and millions were produced in the second half of the nineteenth century.[93] Modern printed photo-porn emerged with the invention of halftone reproduction in the 1880s.[94] By the first decade of the twentieth century, one could buy magazines full of nude photographs catering to the interests of artists, nudists, and health nuts.[95] Whether any artists, nudists, or health nuts bought them is another matter. What followed was a short process in which cultural inhibitions went down, photographic quality went up, and everything came off. The tale can be told in titles: *Esquire* (1933), *Playboy* (1953), *Penthouse* (1965), and *Hustler* (1974).[96]

That was the "is" of the situation: people were going to look at all manner of tasteless printed pictures no matter what. Not people like you, of course. The "ought" that followed was a collection of ideas generally called "Romanticism." Romanticism is a very messy concept; there are many different Romanticisms.[97] But all of them share the notion that the senses, not the intellect, are the key to living the good life. You could not think your way to the Truth, as Plato taught; you needed to feel your way to it, as Hugh Heffner taught. According to Nietzsche, Romanticism put "the cult of feeling ... in place of the cult of reason."[98] Understandably, it has been associated with the Counter-Enlightenment's attack on overreaching rationalism.[99] The Romantics wanted to feel, and anything that allowed them to do so – be it passionate poetry, erotic images, or hard drugs – was just fine with them.[100] Romanticism was perhaps the most influential ideology of the nineteenth century. Our culture is drenched in it, so much so that Romantic production and sensibilities have essentially become synonymous with culture. Poetry, erotic images, and hard drugs don't really give us that "oceanic feeling" anymore, though. We prefer new-age music, sex toys, and espresso machines.[101]

Volume

The length of the manuscript of *War and Peace*, a very long written message, is 460,000 words. The length of the printed version is the same. The length of a manuscript of Hemingway's "For Sale," a very short written message, is six words. The length of the printed version is the same. The fact of printing doesn't enable people to write any more or any less than they could in the Manuscript Era. Hands still get tired; eyes still get sore. Yet print has a much higher carrying capacity than manuscript-writing for one simple reason: it's better at making copies. Imagine you have a 1,200-word composition. If you copied 25 words a minute (a reasonable pace) for 48 minutes out of every hour (you need to rest), you could produce 10 copies a day. If you were an early modern printer, you could produce 500 copies in the same time. If you were using a modern web-fed printing press, the kind they use to print newspapers, then you could produce something on the order of 14.5 billion copies in a 10-hour day.[102] That's more than two copies for each person on earth. The print "pipe," as they say, is wide indeed. Just how wide is not known for the world as a whole, but good statistics are available for the United States. There are something on the order of 80,000 book publishers in the United States. They issued 276,000 new titles in 2007; 411,422 if nontraditional "print-on-demand" publishers are included.[103] In 2006, 3.1 billion books were sold in the United States.[104] In the same year, there were 1,452 daily newspapers in the United States with weekday circulations averaging around 35,000; about 53 million Americans buy newspapers every day.[105] In 2007, there were over 19,000 magazines (titles) printed in the United States and Canada.[106] Americans buy almost 370 million magazines a year (comic books not included).[107]

Print is indeed a high-volume medium. Though the messages you can produce with it are not typically any longer or shorter than those you can write, you can produce a lot more copies of them. High-volume media engender unconstrained networks, that is, networks in which there is transmission and storage capacity to spare. This is certainly true of printing: on a cost-per-unit basis, printing is inexpensive. In our world, print is so cheap that we often give it away and, after we've used it, throw it away. According to our theory, unconstrained networks will *hedonize* social practices developed in and around them. Here "hedonize" means to use for the sake of entertainment or enjoyment. The reason unconstrained networks hedonize social practices is this: if humans can use a medium for diversion at low cost, then they will; print drives down the cost of such use dramatically.

The hedonizing impact of print in early modern European culture is everywhere apparent. In medieval Europe, as in any Manuscript Culture, texts were expensive. This meant that most of the bandwidth of writing was "owned," so to say, by the elite and used for high-value documentation – legal papers, administrative materials, ceremonial texts, and, above all, scripture. Of course, there was "literature," that is, writing meant to be read for pleasure. But there was comparatively little of it, both in terms of the number of titles and number of copies of those titles. You might not get this impression when taking a class on the ancient literary tradition of this or that culture, for they sometimes give the impression that "literature" then was something like "literature" now. It wasn't. Even texts that are today considered classics were extraordinarily rare in most Manuscript Cultures. *Beowulf*, for example, comes down to us in a *single* manuscript copied circa 1000.[108] If it was popular in its time, we would expect to find many more copies of it. Yet we don't. The reason is clear: few could read, those who could weren't interested, and those who were interested probably didn't have the money to subsidize the creation of a manuscript copy. All that changed with the coming of print. Many more people could read, many more people were interested, and print's remarkable fecundity drove the cost of catering to those interests further and further down. Print had the bandwidth required to accommodate both the serious stuff – like law and theology – and a whole host of new types of fun-to-read writing: myths, tales, stories, poems, ballads, songs, tragedies, histories, biographies, comedies, farces, romances, news, satires, parodies, encomia, jeremiads, blasts, counterblasts, allegories, plays, adventures, mysteries, horrors, thrillers, fantasies, and pornography in abundance. The first professional writer was born in this era (probably John Dryden, the seventeenth-century English wordsmith),[109] as was the passionate reader (and I do not use the word "passionate" loosely). Profit-minded printers were only too happy to put the two of them together. The "authorities" might not like it, but as we've seen, the logistics of print production and consumption made censorship an expensive proposition.

That was the "is" of the situation: people were going to use the wide bandwidth supplied by print for the purposes of entertainment, and there was little anyone could do about it. The "ought" that followed was a modern hedonism captured by the notion of "self-improvement" and particularly self-improvement through reading. It holds that the act of reading itself, almost no matter what you read, is a means of bettering yourself. Plato thought that reading was a waste of time, but by the nineteenth century, most educational reformers, like, say, Horace Mann, thought it was quite the opposite. Teaching people to read, literacy advocates claimed, made them, *ipso facto*, better people. Mann argued that reading itself made them more productive.[110] One might well think that "this message was brought to you" by the very people who sell you printed matter, as they had the most to gain by your believing that reading and virtue were identical. But, historically speaking, that's not so: the progressive state propagated the "cult of reading" because progressive administrators really believed that reading was a kind of ennobling patriotic act. "Literacy is the path to communism," read an early Soviet poster.[111] It wasn't, but it was the path to more reading. Naturally, neither educators nor administrators thought that all literature was equally salutary: some of it was so unwholesome as to be banned. But the general drift of opinion tended toward the notion that reading in and of itself was "good" no matter what you read. That includes trashy novels, dirty stories, and really bad poetry. That's not only because all reading makes you "more literate," but also because reading will improve your health, mental and otherwise, or so some psychologists claim.[112] Thus was a vice – idle pleasure-seeking or even sloth – transformed into a virtue. Interestingly, no one has ever seriously argued that "*all* television watching is good."

Velocity

The velocity of a medium is primarily determined by the speed with which messages can be created and transmitted. Speech is fast. You just think of something to say, say it, and your words travel at the speed of sound to your interlocutor (if, of course, your interlocutor is in earshot). In contrast, writing is slow. Once you think of something, you have to write it down and then carry it, or have it carried, to the recipient. For most of its history, printing has been even slower than writing. Print didn't change the amount of time it took to conceive of something brilliant to say, but it made almost everything that followed take longer than it had before. You can write eight pages in a couple of hours. It took early modern printers approximately 10 hours to set eight pages of type and another 10 hours to print the first copy made from it. Then the printed text had to be physically moved to the reader. From the fifteenth through eighteenth centuries, this meant carrying the documents by foot, transporting them by horse, or sending them by boat. All of these means of transport are sluggish, especially on routes overrun with bandits, traversed by bad roads, or plagued by rough seas – that is, most places. Beginning in the nineteenth century, industrious printers developed new technologies – linotypes, powered presses – with which they could set type and print copy faster. These industrial-age printers were also able to move printed text more rapidly thanks to new vehicles – trains, motor-driven ships, trucks, and airplanes – and more safely thanks to secure routes. Even with these improvements, though, the rate of production and transmission remained (and remains) leisurely by electronic standards. Eventually the post office helped quicken the pace of delivery. Postal systems are ancient, but *good* postal systems, the kind that reliably transmit text anywhere at a reasonable speed for a reasonable price, are a product of the nineteenth century. It's rather shocking to recall that the humble postage stamp was not invented until about 1840 and took the better part of a century to spread over the globe.[113] From the perspective of printers and their customers, however, a good postal system itself doesn't entirely do the trick, because being able to send something by post and being able to afford to send it that way are two different things. Although newspapers, magazines, and books are reasonably light compared to, say, stone tablets, they are heavy compared to paper letters. Thus, they cost more than letters to transport. For decades after the organization of the modern postal services, the cost of transmitting printed wares priced most would-be readers out of the market. It was only with the introduction of special print rates in the later nineteenth century that it became economical to send and receive bulky printed matter. You have government subsidies to thank for the fact that you receive newspapers, magazines, and books by "snail mail."

Print, then, is a low-velocity medium. Low-velocity media give rise to monologic networks, which is to say that traffic over them tends to move in one direction. The senders send and the recipients receive. These roles are difficult to reverse due to the time and effort it takes to reply, especially in medium-kind. You might just be moved to write an angry letter to the dunderheaded editors of *The Pretty New Republic*, but you certainly are not going to buy a printing press, learn to use it, and print a response. The folks on the masthead of the TPNR talk to you; you really don't get to talk back to them. The editors of *The Really New Republic*, who disagree with everything they read in *The Pretty New Republic*, might well print a response in their pages, thereby creating a kind of "dialogue" with their mortal enemies. If there are enough magazines like the TPNR and TRNR, something like a "discussion" might take place among their editors. But calling this sort of back-and-forth a "dialogue" or "discussion" rather strains the terms. By the time you get TRNR's counterblast to TPNR's blast, you may well have forgotten what all the fuss was about. By our theory, monologic networks *monocratize* social practices evolved in and around them. This is to say they blunt the natural impulse of humans to exchange information rapidly and, in its place, impose a unidirectional structure on communications.

Print did not alter the basically monologic pattern established by written networks in medieval Europe, but it did lead to the creation of many *more* such networks. The medieval elite – princes and priests – was reasonably successful in monopolizing written communications. They "spoke" through writing to the largely illiterate masses, who in turn were compelled by their illiteracy and lack of power to "listen."

To put this point in structural terms, a few nodes communicated with many nodes that could not themselves respond. As we've seen, however, early modern European elites were not completely successful in controlling the printing press: they could guide it, but not really monopolize it. Throughout the early modern period, powerful princely and priestly interests remained the loudest voices in the land. Their print-based monologic networks were larger and more persuasive than any others. But there *were* others, and as time went on, there were more and more of them. Beginning in the Reformation, opponents of this or that began to use the press to issue messages that were in one way or another critical of the status quo. In so doing, they created a large number of unofficial, interconnected monologic networks, a "public sphere." These networks were ordinarily evanescent. One thinks, for example, of the many pamphleteers who rapidly entered and exited the political scene during the English Civil War, the American Revolution, or the French Revolution. Others, however, proved to be lasting, first among them newspapers. By the eighteenth century, newspapers had become institutions in their own right. Democratic politicians, who often wrote for them and published them, saw newspapers as fortresses of freedom and sought constitutional protection for them. They were right to do so, for the press played a crucial role in the creation of limited, representative government. Yet we need to remember that print networks, for all they aided the democratic cause, were (and are) themselves monologic. This is most obvious where tyrants destroy the free press and replace it with party papers, as in the case of the Soviet Union or Cuba. *The Workers' Voice* usually isn't. But even in democratic states, media moguls, corporations, and officials manipulate the press for their own purposes. They are able to do so precisely because of the monologic structure of print networks: they "speak" and we "listen."

That was the "is" of the situation: it was difficult to have any sort of meaningful exchange by means of print, thus those with presses "talked" and those without "listened." This reality was a tricky thing to accommodate in the relatively liberal political cultures of eighteenth- and nineteenth-century Western Europe. For, if "the people" were sovereign, as democratic theory held, why didn't *all* the people get to "speak"? This paradox was accommodated by means of a kind of dictatorism, that is, the notion that some should speak for others. It came in two variants. In its mild version, it simply stated that those with presses were somehow the victors in the "marketplace of ideas." They had better ideas, so they were entitled to "speak." If you thought differently, you were free to write a letter to the editor or even buy a press and enter the marketplace yourself. Of course this is ludicrous, but it served the purposes of those with presses, who were powerful, and was consistent with the idea that the press should be private, which remained sacrosanct in liberal governments. In its harsh version, invariably found in authoritarian and socialist regimes, the idea of freedom of the press was said to be a plot to oppress "the people." Listen to Lenin: "The capitalists have always used the term 'freedom' to mean freedom for the rich to get richer and for the workers to starve to death. And in capitalist usage, freedom of the press means freedom of the rich to bribe the press, freedom to use their wealth to shape and fabricate so-called public opinion."[114] Lenin knew just what to do about the capitalists' abuse of the press: "The first thing to do to win real equality and genuine democracy for the working people, for the workers and peasants, is to deprive capital of the possibility of hiring writers, buying publishing houses and bribing newspapers. And to do that the capitalists and exploiters have to be overthrown and their resistance oppressed."[115] In Lenin's mind, the Vanguard Party should control the press because it knew what "the people" wanted and could "speak" for them. If you disagreed with what the Party said, you could complain to the local Party cell or even begin your own underground press, but you would probably be well advised not to do so.

Range

Many people feel guilty that they don't know enough about what's going on abroad. They should, for a mass of accessible information *from* abroad is available at many corner newsstands. If you've got a good one in your town – and most of us do – you'll find newspapers and magazines from all over the world: London, Cairo, Moscow, Delhi, Beijing, Tokyo, Sydney, Sao Paulo, Mexico City, New York and on and on. And even if you haven't got a first-rate foreign news-seller in your town, you can probably easily find out how to order newspapers from abroad and have them delivered right to your door. You've got no excuse. After a bit of reading you will have a diplomat's knowledge of global affairs. Or you'll just scratch the entire self-improving project and remain in the dark with the rest of us. In any case, it's clear that we owe the ability to bone up on what's going on in the world to print. This may seem surprising, because in terms of range, print is no better or worse than manuscript-writing. Both have the two properties that are necessary to give any physical medium long range. First, stability: information carried by writing or print does not decay if the substrate on which it is inscribed is of reasonable quality. Second, transportability: manuscripts and books are neither bulky nor terribly heavy, meaning you can move them easily. Thus, there is no practical limit to the range a manuscript or printed page can travel if it is made of the right stuff and carried by the right vehicle. Although the ranges of manuscripts and print are the same, their reach is very different. Because writing is a point-to-point medium, our ability to use it to send messages to many people simultaneously is constrained, as we said, by the expense of reproduction and transmission. Manuscripts usually cannot be copied inexpensively, so they are not a suitable means of mass distribution. In stark contrast, printed copy can be reproduced cheaply, so it is easy to use for the purposes of mass distribution. You won't be the only one reading *The Times of India* outside India. Thousands of others will as well, due precisely to the reproductive power of print.

Print, then, is a long-range medium with significant reach: you can send it across the globe and, if you are Rupert Murdoch, to millions of people. Media with these characteristics generate extensive networks, which is to say networks that enable senders to distribute messages widely in both the geographic and demographic sense. Murdoch has an extensive print network indeed. According to our theory, extensive networks should *diversify* social practices and values, meaning they will become more varied, especially in the ethnic sense. Extensive networks bring strangers in contact with one another at a greater rate than intensive networks. Moreover, they often compel or encourage strangers to cooperate with one another. This sort of familiarity breeds understanding and thereby fosters an expanded, diverse world picture.

Diversification was one of the hallmarks of early modern European history. In the mid-fifteenth century, when print was born, Europe was an astoundingly parochial place. The vast majority of common people were illiterate peasants who were born, lived, and died "with their own." They traveled little and knew less about what was going on even a short distance from their places of birth. They rarely met strangers, and when they did, were profoundly suspicious of them. Naturally there were exceptions. The elites – capitalists, princes, and pastors – knew more of the wider world, and perhaps had seen some of it. But even among them the degree of provincialism was, by modern standards, astounding. Most people are aware that Europeans did not know the Americas existed prior to Columbus's famed journey of 1492. But fewer people know that they, or at least those who live west of the Elbe River, did not know Russia existed before approximately that date. As far as the Spanish, English, French, and even German elites were concerned, what lay beyond Poland was *terra incognita* every bit as much as the territory beyond the great ocean to their west. That's why, once they "discovered" Russia in the sixteenth century, they put accounts of it right next to descriptions of America in books with titles like *Novus Orbis*, the "New World."[116] It isn't the relative isolation of the sixteenth-century Europeans that should draw our attention, for that was a common characteristic of all Manuscript Cultures all over the globe. Rather, it is the very existence of printed books like *Novus Orbis* and the social practices they reflected. Europeans were on the move – exploring, conquering, and colonizing. And as they did so, they brought back news, which they disseminated with the aid of print. Thousands of ethnographic reports about parts foreign were printed in the early modern period, hundreds about Russia alone.[117] As they were printed, scattered, and read, the European demographic picture expanded mightily. What had been a small, homogenous world made up of families and neighbors, parishes and counties, became an enormous, diverse world comprising tribes and peoples, kingdoms and empires.

Print not only diversified the extra-European world, but the inner-European world as well. Capitalists needed information about European markets, rulers needed information about their allies and competitors, and pastors needed information about European souls that might be saved. The press provided it all, and no vehicle was more effective than the print newspaper.[118] From its beginnings as the one-off "relation" in the sixteenth century, the newspaper grew rapidly into a mighty organ of information dissemination. It was a kind of "difference engine" in that its stock and trade were differences. Where things were the same, there was nothing to report. But where they were different, there was a story. It made little difference how far away the story was, for the agents of print could get to it (and, more importantly, get back). Neither did it make much difference whether 100 or 100,000 people wanted the story, for print could reproduce and, as the means of transportation improved, disseminate it to those who could read and afford it. And, as literacy spread and the price of print dropped, the number of people who could do the one and the other ballooned.

That was the "is" of the situation: print made the world a much more varied, information-rich place. The "ought" that followed was, predictably, a modern form of pluralism that is nicely captured by the doctrine of "toleration." It held that there were no "strangers" in the sense of unclassifiable people or things to be assiduously avoided. Everyone and everything was of one type (known), but could be subcategorized as "us" or "them," the "thems" being further subcategorized as "them A," "them B," "them C," ad infinitum. The doctrine's origins can be traced to the debate over religious toleration in sixteenth- and seventeenth-century Europe, the conclusion of which was the general sentiment, backed up by law, that religious toleration was a good thing.[119] Thereafter it began to assume its modern form as a kind of "one-world-ism" in which differences of all kinds would be respected. The kernel of this idea can be seen in Kant's proposed community of nations in his *Perpetual Peace* (1795),[120] though it did not find mature expression until the League of Nations (1920) and the United Nations (1945). The UN's "Universal Declaration of Human Rights" (1948) is a particularly forceful statement of universal toleration. Article two states:

Everyone is entitled to all the rights and freedoms set forth in this Declaration, without distinction of any kind, such as race, colour, sex, language, religion, political or other opinion, national or social origin, property, birth or other status. Furthermore, no distinction shall be made on the basis of the political, jurisdictional or international status of the country or territory to which a person belongs, whether it be independent, trust, non-self-governing or under any other limitation of sovereignty.[121]

In other words, "We are the World." But not only "us." This also means everything on the world and the world itself. Just ask member of the animal rights movement or the environmental movement.

Persistence

In the last chapter, we took a trip to the British Museum to look at a 2,600-year-old tablet upon which part of *The Epic of Gilgamesh* was inscribed, and we noted that, despite its considerable antiquity, the text was still legible. That's the case because the stuff upon which it is written – clay – is very sturdy, the script in which it is written – cuneiform – has been deciphered, and the language encoded in the script – Akkadian – is known today. The persistence of any written document is determined by these same three factors: substrate, script, and language. By and large, print is persistent. If you've ever had the opportunity to handle early printed books, then you will know that they were printed on tough stuff – mashed, bleached, cotton rags.[122] Think of a pressed, starched, white dress shirt and you'll get the idea. Indeed, except for a bit of yellowing and the occasional worm hole, even fifteenth-century books still look pretty good. In the nineteenth century, printers began to use new kinds of low-cost, flimsy "pulp" paper.[123] Such stuff is still used for newspapers today. But most good publishers now use archival quality, acid-free paper that is meant to last hundreds of years. The scripts used in printed books are also stable. Though the world has thousands of languages, it only has hundreds of writing systems. And though there are hundreds of writing systems, only a fraction of them have been printed. In fact, most of the world's printing is and has always been done in scripts based on a few character sets: Latin, Cyrillic, Arabic, Indic, Chinese foremost among them. Since millions – and in some cases billions – of people use these scripts on a daily basis, they aren't going to disappear any time soon. The same might be said of the languages they are used to encode: only a few of the world's many languages are printed with any regularity, and they tend to be the ones spoken by millions of people. They aren't going to go away, either. As a result of the stability of modern scripts and languages, one would be hard pressed today to find even a single printed document that couldn't be sounded out or understood by someone. Yet the persistence of print is even greater than that of manuscript-writing for another reason. The British Museum's ancient tablet inscribed with part of *The Epic of Gilgamesh* is unique or close to it. If this chunk of clay is destroyed – heaven forbid – then it will be lost forever. *The*

Epic of Gilgamesh, however, will not be lost. Thanks to print, the text itself exists in thousands of copies in dozens of scripts in hundreds of languages scattered all over the globe. It would take a catastrophe of biblical proportions – a bit like the flood described in the text itself – for all of these copies, scripts, and speakers to be lost.[124]

In short, print is a persistent medium. It's true that paper, the primary substrate used in printing, is not as robust as stone. Paper burns, rots, and fades. But it makes up for this disadvantage by incredible redundancy. Printed items are almost never unique. Persistent media give rise to additive networks. These are webs of connected nodes in which information accumulates as it is created and transmitted. If you recite *The Epic of Gilgamesh* from memory, and then recite it again, you still only have one copy. Since it's stored in your head, it will perish when you do if you fail to pass it on orally. If you print *The Epic of Gilgamesh*, and then print it again, you have two copies. Since the text has been recorded in a stable medium, it will survive your passing, and probably the passing of several generations after you. According to our theory, additive networks *historicize* social practices evolved in and around them. People in additive networks are constantly confronted with the human past, and especially the past as recorded in writing. Because of this fact, their time horizons begin to recede and the past, present, and future become clearly separate, alterable entities.

Early modern Europe was historicized to a degree never before witnessed in world history, and the reason has everything to do with print and the additive networks it engendered. In Manuscript Cultures, manuscripts accumulated, but not very quickly because so few of them were created and they were so difficult to copy. Thus, manuscript messages from the past to the present were comparatively few. In Print Cultures, printed texts accumulated rapidly because so many of them could be inexpensively produced and reproduced. Take books, for example. The number of titles printed annually in England increased from several hundred in the early 1500s to several thousand circa 1800.[125] It was really only at that point, however, with the introduction of machine-powered presses, cheap paper, and the rapid increase in literacy that print production took off.[126] In the United States, for example, over 6,000 titles were being published annually by 1900;[127] today 275,000 are produced annually.[128] The number of books accumulated at an incredible pace. It seems sensible to say that between one million and two million books were produced annually in the sixteenth century.[129] Something on the order of a billion were printed in the United States in 2007.[130] All of these books accumulate. WorldCat, a union catalogue including the holdings of about 70,000 libraries, contains about 110 million records (titles) and references 1.3 billion items (books, journals, etc.).[131] According to the American Library Association, America's 100 largest libraries collectively house 526 million volumes.[132] If you walk into one of these great textual repositories – or any other great print archive, for that matter – you are in a sense walking back in time. You are surrounded by artifacts from the past that "speak" to you in the voice of the past. It's hardly surprising that the historical profession as such emerged with print, for only print could supply the historical material and means of scholarly communication necessary to sustain it in its modern form.

But it wasn't only history that emerged as a result of print – it was modern scientific practice in general. We noted earlier that writing enabled people to rearrange signs in space, fix them indefinitely, replay them, and then amend them in accordance with new observations. This, we said, was the essence of scientific practice. Yet it was not enough to engender scientific practices of the kind we know today – professional training and standards, scholarly societies and journals, research-oriented facilities like labs and libraries. These came into being only after print made it possible to accurately reproduce and disseminate theories to increasingly large numbers of proto-scientists for "testing." Manuscript Cultures had few "scholarly communities" in the sense of coherent, intergenerational groups of widely scattered experts working on the same material; those they had were almost uniformly focused on religious questions. Manuscripts were too few and their contents too variable for such communities to emerge and sustain themselves. In the world of print, however, scholarly communities could form around key printed texts, each identical to the next, that focused the attention of readers on common problems. A crucial development here was the creation of the scientific society and its journal in the seventeenth century. The former gave scientists a home and the latter offered them a common script – a "literature" – to keep up with, test, and amend. The journals in particular established a clear chain of evidence that led from past beliefs to present, from good to better, from wrong to right, from imperfection to perfection. In their pages the very notion of scientific progress appeared. Indeed, anyone who read past issues of the *Transactions* of this or that scholarly society would know this to be the case: new theories replaced old ones that were then replaced by still newer ones. And so the cycle of improvement proceeded.

That was the "is" of the situation: print promoted the pursuit of history and science. The "ought" that followed was a sort of temporalism centered on the idea of progress. The Manuscript Era knew both the notion of linear time and the idea of progress, though neither was the dominant conception of the age despite what some historians have written.[133] The Ancients were besotted with the notions of the (lapsed) Golden Age and the Eternal Recurrence.[134] Some authors find the origins of the idea of progress in early Christian eschatology, but this is a difficult case to make as Christian time has a beginning and end and so must Christian progress.[135] "Our" progress, however, may have a beginning but it has no end, just like "our" time itself. To find a widespread, fully articulated understanding of open-ended progress, one must look to the Print Era, just as J. B. Bury said in his classic treatment of the idea.[136] Renaissance scholars nibbled at open-ended progress, and the *philosophes* – especially Turgot and Condorcet – made of it a tasty side dish. But it wasn't until the nineteenth century that it became the main course, so to speak. For Saint-Simon, Comte, Hegel, Marx, Spencer, and the rest of the "big thinkers" of the age, the idea that history was one more or less inevitable upward swing was dogma.[137] The "motors" that these gentlemen identified as "driving" history *cum* progress varied: sometimes they were ideas, sometimes classes, and sometimes technologies. But the notion of limitless advance was shared by all and became common coin in the Victorian era.[138] As we saw earlier, Cicero proclaimed "Historia magister vitae est."[139] It was a suitable pronouncement for the Manuscript Era, but was outmoded in the Print Era. George Santayana seems to have realized this when he wrote, "Those who cannot remember the past are condemned to repeat it."[140] The telling word here is "repeat," for repetition of past mistakes is exactly what the study of the past and present was intended to avoid. And if you don't repeat past mistakes, then how can you not progress?

Searchability

After you're done reading the ancient though remarkably well-preserved flood story in Room 55 at the British Museum, pop by the British Library. It's not far, you can walk. Go to the circulation desk and ask if you can get in the stacks. The rules say you can't, so they probably won't let you. But let's say the librarians allow you in. Now look for, say, *War and Peace*. They have it, which is good. But they also have around 13 million other books, which is bad. Happily, the tireless bibliographers at the British Library have carefully catalogued every volume in their vast collection. They know where every book is, or at least should be, and have recorded the address in an electronic database that you can search. But let's say you decide, just for fun, to look for *War and Peace* without reference to this remarkable finding-aid, or any finding-aid for that matter. If the books are randomly distributed (and let's just say they are), then the chances the first book you look at will be *War and Peace* are one in 13 million. As you look, you will eliminate books, so your chances get better: the chances the next book is *War and Peace* are one in 12,999,999, the book after that are one in 12,999,998, and so on. If you look at one book a second without interruption, then the amount of time it will take you to find *War and Peace* will fall between one second (very lucky) and 150 days, 11 hours, 6 minutes, and 40 seconds (very unlucky). You better use the electronic catalogue.

No less than manuscript text, printed text is difficult to search for a number of reasons. You have to have access to it. If the librarians say "no," your search is over. Text must be searched serially. Even the best physical finding aids won't get you very "deep" into the text. Searching text is slow. Our eyes and brains aren't very good at scanning text quickly. And, finally, searching text is inefficient in terms of retrieval. You are going to get a lot of chaff and only a little wheat. All this is true of search in manuscripts – it's just as hard. But there is an additional problem with searching through printed texts, namely, their volume. It is one thing for you to look through your box of letters for the embarrassing one you sent to your high school sweetheart. It's quite another for you to go to the British Library in search of *War and Peace*. As the number of items you need to go through goes up, so does the time it will take to find the item you want. You aren't much of a correspondent, so your letter box contains thirty items. You'll find the awkward missive you want quickly. But the acquisitions librarians at the British Library are very acquisitive, as we've seen. It will take you the better part of a year to find *War and Peace* without one of their handy finding-aids.

Like writing, then, print is not a very searchable medium, and it becomes less searchable the more of it there is. It might be fun to "Google" yourself in the universe of printed text, but you just can't. Egomania is a long, hard slog in the printed world. According to our theory, media that are hard to search produce unmapped networks, that is, networks that do not have a handy, efficient system of addresses with which one can easily track down information. On such networks, finding and sharing information is difficult, so data tend to become concentrated in certain nodes. By the lights of our theory, unmapped media networks *professionalize* social practices developed in and around them. As information pools in some nodes, unmapped networks naturally generate information inequalities. These give those with precious information – experts – power over those who need it. The experts tend to band together in order to perfect their knowledge and to maintain their privilege, that is, they professionalize.

The early modern period witnessed the birth of the modern professions. Professions of a sort existed prior to Gutenberg, but they were neither very many nor well organized. In most Manuscript Cultures, theologians, scholars, soldiers, and artisans of many kinds all made credible and somewhat enforceable claims to expert knowledge. They plainly knew things other people did not, and sometimes they were members of organizations – churches, universities, armies, guilds – that limited access to special knowledge and restricted use of this knowledge in practice. If these experts didn't just "know" something, then they could find what needed to be found in the repositories of manuscripts they controlled. Print weakened some old professions, but more importantly created many strong new ones. An example of de-professionalization is found in theology. Once held tightly by the medieval clergy, the Scripture was, after Luther, available to a massive number of European readers. Since they were all "priests" who could read and understand the word of God for themselves, each became an expert after a fashion. The authorized expertise of the Catholic clergy lost value, and the faith splintered into many dominations. An example of radical professionalization is found in the university. In the medieval period, subjects of study were few – grammar, rhetoric, dialectics, arithmetic, music, geometry, and astronomy – as were specialized faculties – theology, law, medicine.[141] Plato might have recognized the medieval university as the successor of his Academy. He would not recognize the modern university. Beginning in the nineteenth century, largely in Germany, scholarship began to professionalize and simultaneously diversify.[142] Educational reformers created serious systems of accreditation, a host of new academic disciplines, and research facilities to support their work – first and foremost libraries. By the end of the nineteenth century, students could choose from hundreds of courses, arranged in many disciplinary tracks, all leading to professional qualifications that gave their holders the right to "practice." Academic credentials became the *sine qua non* of expert status in a bewildering host of new disciplines, some old like medicine but most new like marketing, mortuary science, and cosmetology.[143] Each of these novel areas of expertise came to have its own faculty, professional organization, and literature – printed and housed in university libraries.

That was the "is" of the situation: it was hard to find things in print and this permitted people to horde valuable knowledge. The "ought" that followed was a modern version of collectivism manifested in the notion of professional duty, or simply "professionalism." Of course the idea of civic duty – that one was bound to serve the common interest – predates the Print Revolution by centuries: it is found in a well-elaborated form among the ancient Athenians, for instance.[144] So too is the related notion that some occupations entail higher obligations: the Hippocratic Oath, written in the fourth century BC, offers a ready example.[145] But the concept that all occupations, professional and not, entail civic obligations of a higher sort is a modern one. Weber noted this in his discussion of the Protestant origins of the idea of occupational "callings."[146] The essence of the ethic of professionalism is that everyone in society is obliged to everyone else and that the nature of citizens' obligations is determined by the work they do. In 1893, Emile Durkheim captured this essence perfectly when he wrote that industrial societies were held together by means of "organic solidarity," that is, the cohesion which arises from the division of labor.[147] The butcher depends on the expertise of the baker for bread, while the baker depends on the expertise of the butcher for meat. They cannot live well without one another and are therefore obliged to one another. The idea of professional obligation evolved in two directions. The "weak" version, predominant in capitalist countries, held that it was virtuous though not necessary to trade expertise. If the baker didn't want to sell bread to the butcher, that was her "right," though she would probably suffer a certain amount of opprobrium for neglecting her "professional responsibility" as defined by the Bakers' Society. The "strong" version, found in socialist countries, held that it was both virtuous and necessary to trade expertise. The baker has no right not to sell bread to the butcher. Rather, she has an obligation to contribute her baking expertise to the collective. As Marx himself put it, "From each according to his ability, to each according to his need."[148]

Printing hardly appeared revolutionary in the first decades after Gutenberg. Rather the contrary, it seemed terribly conservative. The Catholic Church embraced the press as a means of spreading the faith. With the help of numerous like-minded princes, the Holy See controlled much of what was printed. The majority of texts printed were naturally religious, for example "Books of Hours" and "Lives of Saints." Of course, they were in Latin, the *lingua sacra* of the age. Early printed works even looked like manuscript books. It's clear now, however, that those who thought Gutenberg's "invention" would anchor Manuscript Culture were wrong, for in a few short centuries print destroyed the old European order. This is somewhat surprising, for written and printed texts are quite similar from a purely formal perspective. Both are linguistic codes inscribed on substrates that are usually portable and often quite durable. Yet print has physical attributes that make it a very different tool than manuscript-writing. In this chapter we've tried to point out these attributes, to show how they led to the creation of particular kinds of media networks, and to suggest that these networks had a significant impact on social practices and cultural values in early modern and modern Europe. The sum and substance of what we have said in this regard is sketched in Table 4.

Of course, print doesn't necessarily nurture these effects or, when it does, to the same degree. The natural tendencies of any medium can be blunted with enough effort, and print is no exception. One can imagine a scenario in which a few people controlled all printing presses, which in turn were few in number. That would make print inaccessible. One can

TABLE 4. *The Effects of Print*

Print	Medium Attribute	→	Network Attribute	→	Social Practice	→	Cultural Value
Accessibility	= Moderate	→	Diffused	→	Equalized	→	Egalitarianism
Privacy	= Moderate	→	Segmented	→	Closed	→	Privatism
Fidelity	= Low/ High	→	Symbolic/ Iconic	→	Abstracted/ Sensualized	→	Idealism/ Realism
Volume	= High	→	Unconstrained	→	Hedonized	→	Hedonism
Velocity	= Low	→	Monologic	→	Centralized	→	Dictatorism
Range	= High	→	Extensive	→	Diversified	→	Pluralism
Persistence	= High	→	Additive	→	Historicized	→	Temporalism
Searchability	= Low	→	Unmapped	→	Professionalized	→	Collectivism

further imagine that these few presses and the material they produced had some peculiar characteristics, namely: they are impossible to hide – making print very public; they produced nothing but text – making print low fidelity; they produce few texts – making print low volume; they dispatch text at great speeds though not very far – making print high velocity but low range; they print with vanishing ink – making print very ephemeral; and, finally, they automatically produce a universal index of terms – making print very searchable.

In principle, all this is possible. In practice, however, it is futile, or at least very difficult. Organized interests – churches, states, parties, corporations – have tried to rein in print for centuries. They have done so in the pursuit of godliness and godlessness, democracy and domination, liberalism and conservatism, capitalism and communism. But nowhere have they ever really succeeded. In almost every case, print did what print naturally does. This is part of the reason why modern societies, from North Korea to the United States, all look "modern" as regards print. They uniformly have large, diversified print industries. Some are government-run and others private, but all are nominally devoted to enlightening and entertaining "the people." These industries produce a huge amount of printed material for a far-flung and usually highly literate public. The leaders of all modern societies agree that literacy is a necessity and reading a virtuous act. By and large, printed matter is produced in public and consumed in private, usually through silent reading. The right to free expression and private consumption is recognized, though not uniformly respected, the world over. Some of what is printed is text, some of it pictures, and some of it both.

Low-brow content – melodrama, celebrity gossip, eroticism – is most popular in both liberal and conservative states. There is also, however, a place for the high-brow. That place is the university, where high-brow print is made, and the library, where it steadily accumulates. These institutions are universal. In all modern societies, the professions are highly developed, and each profession has its own "literature" that is known well to professionals alone.

This, then, was Print Culture, the product of print itself and the organized interests that "pulled" it into existence. It was tremendously successful. Print Culture spanned the globe very quickly, and everywhere it went human societies became, eventually, more productive, better governed, and more humane. But, as it happened, its reign was short, lasting a mere 450 years. As we will see in the next chapter, the Print Era was cut short by the arrival of a medium that did what print could not – give people seemingly direct access to "experience."

4

HOMO VIDENS

Humanity in the Age of Audiovisual Media

But I once heard a story I believe, I replied: How Leontius son of Aglaion, coming from Piraeus under the outer north wall, perceived corpses laid out near the gallows. He wanted to look, and at the same time he was disgusted with himself and turned away; he fought with himself for awhile and covered his face, but, overcome by desire, he held his eyes wide open and ran up to the corpses and said "Look, damn you. Take your fill of the lovely sight!"[1]

    – Plato, *The Republic*, 439E–440A

Plato didn't like artists, but he truly *feared* actors. Why? Because their craft corrupts otherwise good people. Drama pretends to show us life in all its richness, and it succeeds so well that it can and does trick almost everyone. When viewers see an actor pretending to be in pain, they are likely to feel as if they are witnessing *actual* pain. The really frightening part, though, is that we *enjoy* sympathizing with dramatists pretending to weep and wail, snort and chortle, and behave in all kinds of undignified ways. Thus, we find ourselves delighting in actions that we would ordinarily condemn. Eventually, Plato predicts, drama will corrupt us: if we view enough of it we will begin to act like the actors, that is, badly. Our moral decline is inevitable so long as the actors remain in the city, for so long as they do, we will compulsively seek vicarious gratification in their productions. Drama appeals so mightily to our base instincts that we won't be able to help ourselves. Thus, almost all actors must be sent away if the city is to survive.

Most modern folks rightly find Plato's arguments against drama unconvincing. That said, Plato makes one very good point about drama: as an artistic medium, it is – or at least can be – extraordinarily compelling. We can put down a book when we don't want to read it. We can tune out poetry or music when we don't want to listen. But when we hear or see people, particularly if they are saying or doing something odd, we feel we have to listen and look – just like Leontius in Plato's story. Leontius didn't want to look at the corpses, but he *had* to. Plato feared that if people were afforded the opportunity to see whatever they wanted, then they, like Leontius, would lose control of themselves. In this chapter, we will see that Plato's fears were not misplaced. By the mid-twentieth century, audiovisual media made it possible for anyone to see almost anything. The consequences were just as Plato predicted, for people did after a fashion lose control of themselves.

WHY WE WATCH AND LISTEN

To demonstrate that the "pull" theory of media evolution is valid in the case of audiovisual media, we need to establish two things. First, we must show that we knew how to "do" audiovisual media before we "did" them, at least very often or widely. If this was so, then we can confidently conclude that people could have employed audiovisual media but didn't because demand was too low. Second, we need to show that some significant historical disjuncture made existing media – talking, writing, and printing – insufficient for the purposes of some organized group or groups, and that this or these groups developed a preexisting technical capacity – in this case, audiovisual know-how – into a real medium.

What sorts of evidence, primary and secondary, bear on these two propositions? Since audiovisual media are both relatively new and by and large persistent, the sources available to study them are much greater than even those left to us by the Print Era, themselves very considerable. Thus, it comes as no surprise that the secondary literature treating the origins and progress of telegraphy,[2] photography,[3] telephony,[4] recorded sound,[5] radio,[6] motion pictures,[7] and television[8] is itself voluminous. That literature includes, fortunately, a number of excellent surveys of all the audiovisual media.[9] Moreover, and in contrast to the literature on the Talking Era, Manuscript Era, and Print Era, scholars have paid abundant attention to ways in which electronic media have shaped modern society. For the past half-century, it has been commonplace to say that the introduction of the "mass media" (sometimes including print, and sometimes not) brought on a "communications revolution" (sometimes "information revolution") that created an "information society" (sometimes "information age").[10] Whether, how, and to what degree audiovisual media actually did change the patterns established during the Print Era is precisely the question we will try to answer. In so doing, we will depend on this prodigious body of scholarship.

Audiovisual Media before Audiovisual Media

As we will point out in a moment, humans really like to watch and listen. They have a natural and ineradicable hunger to see and hear certain things. For most of human history – 140,000 years to be exact – this hunger seems to have been satisfied by simply watching and listening to what was naturally all around them, including each other. In this long era, there were no artificial visual or sonic media, at least as far as we know. That began to change about 40,000 years ago when our ancestors started to draw, paint, and sculpt things.[11] Judging by what they drew, painted, and sculpted, they were very interested in what we are still very interested in: sex, food, drink, power, wealth, conflict, and violence. One of the earliest pieces of statuary archeologists have uncovered, the 24,000-year-old Venus de Willendorf, is a straightforward depiction of a naked lady.[12] And that was only the beginning. Wherever representational art flourished in the Ancient World – Mesopotamia, Egypt, India, China – we find depictions of what might be called "racy things." The best known examples are doubtless the erotic murals of Pompeii and Herculaneum, both of which were buried and thereby preserved by the eruption of Mount Vesuvius in 79.[13] These depictions, often of sexual acts, were clearly meant to arouse and not for any "higher purpose." In addition to the visual arts, our ancestors also used the performing arts to represent this common set of racy things. Just when they began to do so we do not know, for nothing survives. But it stands to reason that prehistoric peoples performed rituals in which dramatic events were reenacted. Why wouldn't they? The same logic applies to early civilizations. We have scant evidence of Mesopotamian, Egyptian, Indian, or Chinese dramaturgy, but it would be surprising if none existed given the sophistication of these places. What we do know without doubt is that by the time of Plato – the fifth century BC – the dramatic arts were both highly developed and very popular in the Hellenic World.[14] They were also controversial, as we can see in Plato's spirited condemnation of them.[15] Plato didn't like drama for a variety of reasons, but one of the most salient relates precisely to the playwright's favorite subject: people behaving badly. Arrogance, lust, greed, envy, hatred, spite, malice, and cruelty – these were the dramaturge's best friends. We know the reason: these were the things people wanted to see.

This was true in ancient Athens and after. Yet, for nearly 1,500 years, the technology designed to deliver representations of racy things remained unchanged. You could draw them. You could sculpt them. You could enact them. But that was all you could do. And actually "you" probably couldn't do any of these things, at least very well. The graphic, plastic, and dramatic arts are, well, arts. Performing them with any proficiency requires talent, training, and resources. Most common folk in the Manuscript Era didn't have any of these things. Thus they were consumers, not producers, of high-quality art. But high-quality art wasn't easy to come by for two reasons. The first was economic: really good representations – well-wrought paintings, sculpture, and drama – were going to be expensive. The elite could afford them, but most plebs couldn't. The second was logistical: even in the cases where good art was affordable, there were real limits on the size of the audiences that could view it. Stadia, hippodromes, amphitheaters, and circuses could only be so numerous and so big, a fact we will return to later.[16] These two considerations – scarcity and audience size – meant that many people in the Manuscript Era were not going to get to see or hear the things they wanted to see or hear. This was true in Plato's time and it remained true more than a millennium later in Shakespeare's day. To put the quandary in terms only an economist could love: by creating a limited and inelastic supply of stimulating fine arts, Manuscript- and Print-Era cultures systematically generated "excess demand" for them. The bright lights of Uruk, Athens, Rome, and London whetted appetites, but could not slake them.

Yet common people did not riot over the high cost of fine art or theater, at least the way they rioted over the cost of bread when it was dear. They made their own fun of the representational sort, most of which is lost to history. Throughout the Manuscript and Print Eras, the commoner's calendar was full of festivals, fairs, and games, all of which allowed ordinary folk both to let off steam and to see things represented that they could not in their daily lives.[17] This tradition still survives in the form of the annual Purim celebrations in the Jewish world and Carnival celebrations in the Christian world. Your local county and state fairs might also be cited in this regard. These folk traditions went some way toward satisfying people's appetites for aural and visual stimulation, and thereby reduced social pressure. But just as important were the positive measures taken to reduce the appetite itself. From Plato to Shakespeare and even after, the authorities – especially literate princes and priests – told people that some representations could do tangible harm and should, therefore, be strenuously avoided.[18] Graven images, depictions of heaven, polyphonic music and such might offend the deities, which would naturally provoke their wrath. No one wanted that. Masques, mummers' plays, and political ditties might offend powerful persons, which would provoke their wrath. And no one wanted that. So it was more or less taken for granted in the Manuscript and Print Eras that there were certain things that one could not safely draw, sculpt, or play because they were "unholy" or "dishonorable."

But the basic problem remained, an endemic characteristic of Manuscript and Print Cultures: too much demand for audiovisual stimulation and not enough supply. To right this imbalance, some means had to be found to lower the cost of producing representations of racy things. As we've seen, the purveyors of print – experts at lowering production costs – were the first to attempt a solution. From the earliest days of printing, publishers realized that pictures helped push their textual products.[19] Thus, they made sure to complement their printed texts with engravings, the more suggestive of immorality the better. They also pushed for ever more accurate pictures, but this almost always meant the employment of better etchers and etching techniques. Photography never occurred to them. Of course it never occurred to anyone, or almost anyone, before the early nineteenth century. The notion that you could mechanically capture what your eyes had seen was an odd one, as we don't experience anything like it in nature beyond shadows and reflections – and they disappear. Nonetheless, by the seventeenth century both of the ideas necessary to produce photographs – the pinhole camera effect and the photochemical effect – were floating around Europe, waiting for someone to put them together.[20] Nicéphore Niépce finally did in the 1830s.[21] Thereafter, there was a rush of activity aimed at bringing photography bearing racy things to market. Photos could be inexpensively reproduced as early as the 1840s and were. Photos could be printed in newspapers, magazines, and books by the 1880s and were.[22]

But it still wasn't enough, and entrepreneurs knew that. Yet, much like the printers before photography, they opted for more of the same. Most historians recognize the nineteenth century as the moment at which leisure was commodified in the Western world, or at least became a lot more commodified than it had ever been.[23] Folk art, folk theater, and folk music had always existed in Europe. But generally speaking, these were not things people paid for, or paid very much for. The only form of "popular entertainment" that required the expenditure of brass was drinking, and it was the most popular entertainment of all. In the nineteenth century, though, entrepreneurs expanded the concept of entertainment for hire beyond its traditional boundaries. They did it by going down-market with up-market things, giving the rising middle classes – who had money to spare and time to spend it – what their betters had had all along, though at a cheaper price. These entrepreneurs opened opera houses, professional theaters, music halls, variety shows, seaside resorts, mountain retreats, and country reposes. It was all very respectable, indeed, a bit too respectable for the tastes of some (predominantly male) parts of the audience. They wanted to see and hear more, and the mavens of entertainment were only too glad to accommodate them if the censors would play along. In the end, they did, and so vaudeville, cabaret, burlesque, and striptease were born.[24]

With both prosperity and population on the rise, more of the same was not going to do the job. Entertainment entrepreneurs needed to find a way to supply large audiences with cheap audiovisual diversions. The technologies they needed to accomplish this feat were available, but they were generally buried too deeply in esoteric scientific discoveries and crude prototypes for anyone to realize it. This accounts for the lag between the discovery or invention of sound recording, movies, radio, and TV and their commercialization.[25] The first device capable of recording sound was Edouard-Leon Scott's "phonoautograph" in 1857. Sound recordings were not brought to market before Thomas Edison's phonograph cylinders in the 1880s and Emile Berliner's gramophone discs in the 1890s. The precursors to motion pictures – the flip book, the Zoetrope – were all in circulation decades before Eadweard Muybridge began his experiments with "serial photography" in the late 1870s. It wasn't until the late 1890s that Edison and the Lumière brothers succeeded in commercializing film, and it was long after that before the movies assumed their modern form. It's impossible to tell who "discovered" radio, because bits and pieces of it were conceptualized or demonstrated by several scientists over a long period. David E. Hughes (1879), Heinrich Rudolf Hertz (1887), Nikola Tesla (1893), Oliver Lodge (1894), Jagdish Chandra Bose (1894), and Alexander Popov (1895) could all reasonably be called the "inventors" of wireless. After being granted a patent in 1896, Guglielmo Marconi began to sell the technology, primarily for ship-to-shore communications. The first recognizably commercial radio stations, however, were not organized until the 1920s. It's also hard to say who "discovered" television because so many people did. Paul Nipkow (1884), Vladimir Zworykin (1923), John Logie Baird (1925), and Philo Farnsworth (1927) are all good candidates for the honor – if such it be – of "Inventor of Television." The first commercial television broadcasts were not made until the 1930s, and the technology was not really widely adopted until the 1950s.

Although it took some time for corporations to see the potential of audiovisual technologies and to organize the industry, when they did, audiovisual media spread at a rate faster than any medium in history. By the 1920s, both gramophones and records were common items in middle-class households in the industrialized world.[26] The music industry stagnated during the Great Depression and World War II, but by the late 1960s, it had recovered to the point that "stereos" and "LPs" were ubiquitous. So they remain today, though both the playback devices and recordings are digital. The story is much the same for film.[27] By 1930, some 80 million Americans, or 65 percent of the total population, were going to the movies once a week.[28] Attendance rates dipped during the Great Depression, rose again beginning in 1933, and then started to fall after World War II with the proliferation of television. Of course, in that same postwar period, the consumption of movies in all formats (film, video, DVD) increased and the habit of movie-watching spread all over the world. According to one estimate, in excess of 9.6 billion movie tickets are sold worldwide each year.[29] And the tale is similar for radio and TV.[30] In the United Kingdom, where we can track diffusion with reasonable accuracy thanks to state regulation, 125,000 radio reception licenses were issued in 1923. Twenty years later, around 10 million were being issued annually. In 1947, 15,000 TV licenses were given out in Great Britain. Twenty years later, over 14 million were issued.[31] Today, nearly every household in the developed world has at least one radio and TV, and most have more than one. According to an estimate in the *CIA World Factbook*, there were over 2.5 billion radios and 1.4 billion televisions in the world in 1997, the last date for which data are available.[32] One imagines that there are many, many more today.

"Pulling" the Audiovisual Media into Existence

Beyond the fact that people are genetically predisposed to enjoy listening and watching, and beyond the fact that the technology to make listening and watching easy was available, why did audiovisual media take off with such rapidity in the twentieth century? According to our "pull" theory of media adoption, the answer should be that newly evolved organized interests, having found existing media insufficient for their purposes, began to forcefully seek out – indeed create – new media, in this case of the audiovisual variety. It's not at all difficult to demonstrate that this was the case. Print was "pulled" into being by the advent of mercantile capitalists, state administrators, and pastors – all of whom found the new medium very useful. By the late eighteenth century, it was evident that all three of these organized interests were undergoing significant change: mercantile capitalism was becoming industrial capitalism, the bureaucratic state was becoming the welfare state, and reading religion was becoming cultural liberalism. It is in these transformations that we will look for – and find – the increase in demand that "pulled" audiovisual media into widespread use.

First, consider industrial capitalism.[33] The essence of mercantile capitalism was trade, the movement of goods from a place where they could be purchased for a low price to another place where they could be sold for a higher price. Buy spices here cheaply; transport them there and sell them dearly. Mercantile capitalism required a lot of paperwork, and therefore those who practiced it had to have some facility with reading and writing. The essence of industrial capitalism was production, the organized manufacture of goods to be sold in a market. Make widgets and sell them to people who need widgets. This practice, too, required literacy. But it required other skills as well. The most important of these for our purpose was what we might call "market creation." Unlike the mercantile capitalist who connected existing supply and demand – spices and a hunger for spices – the industrial capitalist actively looked for new supplies to fulfill as yet unrecognized demands. The merchant capitalists asks, "What do people want, and how can I find it and bring it to them?" The industrial capitalist asks, "What use might there be for this thing, and how do I convince people that they need it?" To put this difference in mentality and practice in the shortest possible terms: the mercantile capitalist transports, while the industrial capitalist makes and sells.

Engineering and marketing are the handmaidens of industrial capitalism. We can see how they worked together in the nineteenth and twentieth centuries to stimulate demand for audiovisual media. By the mid-nineteenth century, European cities were filling up with people who had both the means and desire to be entertained. Entrepreneurs met this demand by building more theaters, music halls, and resorts. But, as we've seen, it wasn't enough. By the last quarter of the nineteenth century, it was clear to forward-looking engineer-entrepreneurs such as Edison, Berliner, and Marconi that a technical "fix" to the problem was within reach. They went about implementing it in the way that had become customary in industrial economies: they filed patents, held exhibitions of their "inventions," sought financial backing, formed public companies, and hired publicists to convince politicians that their products would serve the national interest and convince consumers that they could not really do without them. They succeeded beyond their wildest dreams. Why? Because there was immense latent demand for the products they wanted to bring to market. That hidden hunger, however, had existed unfulfilled for a very long time. We can be pretty sure that Plato would have listened to records, gone to the movies, tuned into the radio, and watched TV had he the chance. He never did, and neither did anyone else in the Talking, Manuscript, or Print Eras. The explanation for this, we like to say, is that the technical capacity to build audiovisual technologies didn't exist then. That's true. But it is also – and perhaps more importantly – because nothing like industrial capitalism existed then. Industrial capitalism gave men like Edison, Berliner, and Marconi a reason to create marketable new technologies and a means to build companies to produce and sell them. Industrial capitalism worked a kind of magic: it transformed hazy mass desire into effective demand.

Second, consider the welfare state.[34] The early modern European state was dedicated to two activities: making war and collecting taxes so it could make war. The princes knew more or less how to fight battles, as that was really all their forbearers, the medieval aristocracy, did. But collecting taxes, especially the very large amounts of revenue that early modern armies required, took them into new administrative territory. They found that in order to ensure a sizeable and steady flow of cash, they needed to field large bureaucracies. Large bureaucracies, in turn, meant increased demand for literate bureaucrats; hence, demand for the skills of reading and writing. The literate bureaucrats were still there when the European states took on a new mission in the late nineteenth century. That mission was public welfare. In medieval and early modern Europe, most princes ruled by some sort of divine right. They did God's will first and the people's will second. If the two coincided, good. If not, then you just had to put up with it. The American and French Revolutions marked the beginning of the end of all that. After these epochal events, only governments "of the people, by the people, for the people" (in Lincoln's memorable phrase) would be deemed truly legitimate.[35] There had been murmurs and more of this new mission before 1776 and 1789. The eighteenth-century Prussian absolutist Fredrick the Great, for example, reportedly proclaimed that he was merely "first servant of the state."[36] He apparently thought that serving the state meant making war as often and as violently as he could, for that is what he did. His late nineteenth-century successors had different ideas of state service. Otto von Bismarck was no lover of liberalism or socialism, yet he found it expedient to create national labor laws, health insurance, disability insurance, and pensions for masses of Germans.[37] He found it expedient exactly because he feared the liberals and socialists were winning popular support by advocating these paternalistic policies. That was something to be avoided, so he stole their thunder. He was hardly alone. By the end of World War I, the entire Western political spectrum was shifting toward soft or hard socialism. Both liberal and conservative regimes answered the popular call for the creation of a social safety net.

The newly powerful masses also clamored, however, for "modern" conveniences. Among these we find audiovisual media, and particularly the telephone, radio, and television. People saw these things and they wanted them. Politicians saw that there was political hay to be made by helping constituents get them.[38] Moreover, there were compelling economic reasons for some sort of central coordination of these emerging networks. Combine these two reasons with the fact that European regimes already controlled telegraphy – the first electronic network – and you have a compelling case for state support and control of the new audiovisual media. So it happened that European countries generally opted for state-run telephone networks, as well as taxpayer-subsidized national radio and television broadcasting services, the BBC being the most familiar example. The film industry was also heavily subsidized in Europe, and is to this day. The United States took a different path, electing for predominately private telegraphy, telephony, film making, radio, and TV. Yet, even in the land of free enterprise, government regulation was extensive, as evidenced by the formation of the Federal Radio Commission in 1927 and its powerful successor, the Federal Communications Commission in 1934. And outright federal support of broadcasting is hardly unknown in the United States, as can be seen in the examples of National Public Radio and the Public Broadcasting Service. Modern states are welfare states, and welfare states make sure their citizens have things to listen to and watch.

Finally, consider cultural liberalism.[39] The pastors of early modern Europe generally wanted their flocks to be able to read and write. They made efforts to see that they learned, and were generally supported in their pro-literacy activities by princes. Literacy rates rose. But it certainly was not the case that princes and pastors wanted their subjects to write and read *anything*. On the contrary, they had reasonably serious – and by our standards very restrictive – notions of what was proper and improper written material. Every early modern European regime and faith practiced censorship. So too did they regulate, or attempt to regulate, what could be heard and viewed.[40] Theaters were licensed, popular entertainments monitored, and even dress was regulated by "sumptuary laws." As we've pointed out, restrictions on what could be written, read, heard, and seen began to fall away with the rise of the idea of the free press in the early modern period. In hindsight, we can see that if ever there was a conceptual and legal slippery slope, the notion of the free press was it. For once it was conceded that (a) the government's power to censor representations could be abridged and (b) representations have no obvious corrupting effect, so then (c) it became very difficult to halt the expansion of the "freedom of expression." The first threshold was crossed in the seventeenth century when political speech was granted as a right, at least to some and in some circumstances.[41] This act opened the door for formerly outré expressions by giving them legal cover. Thus, obscene political cartoons came to be seen as less obscene and more political. What might be called the "sticks-and-stones" doctrine ("Sticks and stones may break my bones, but words will never hurt me"), however, was not fully articulated until the later nineteenth or even early twentieth centuries, though it was not fully accepted even then. Members of the Free Speech League (1902) in the United States, for example, argued that "obscenity" was a matter of taste, that it was not at all obvious that "obscene" material harmed its consumers, and that it seemed certain that it didn't harm anyone else if consumed privately.[42] These were good arguments, and they were hard to rebut in the progressive legal climate of the day. But they were not found persuasive by the self-appointed guardians of public morality or the courts.[43]

They were, however, found compelling by most people, at least those who flocked to the movies to see every manner of impropriety. Even in the beginning of cinema sex and violence sold. Despite the fact that the people had voted with their feet, however, neither the government nor the wardens of propriety had given up the battle against "obscenity."[44] In the United States, for instance, the states could and did censor films well into the twentieth century. American secular and religious groups mounted sustained attacks on what they deemed "immoral" films. In order to protect their booming industry, then, the movie moguls needed to do something to appease the censors and critics. This gesture took the form of the famous Hay's Code of 1930, under which the studios agreed to censor themselves. What needs to be recognized, however, is that although we look back on the Hay's Code as outright censorship, it permitted a lot more than it banned. You could go to the movies in the 1930s, 1940s, and 1950s and see all the sex, violence, and illicit behavior you wanted, though everyone kept their clothes on and refrained from cursing. It wasn't propriety, but the veneer of propriety. And that's just the way everyone wanted it, from the guardians of morality to the Supreme Court to the average moviegoer.

Audiovisual Media and Human Nature

Audiovisual media, once properly engineered for mass consumption, took off very quickly. There was, as we expected, a lag between the capacity to "do" audiovisual things and the creation of full-fledged audiovisual media. But it was comparatively short. It took about 175,000 years for manuscript-writing to become established, and even then its penetration was low. It took roughly 1,000 years for printing to become established, and even today its coverage is not complete. But it took only a few decades for audiovisual media to cover the world and saturate all the populations in it. A significant number of people today cannot read or write. A significant number of people today do not read or write though they can. But virtually everyone alive, if they are healthy, can watch and listen to audiovisual media – and they do, a lot. Part of the reason for the rapid spread and remarkable penetration of audiovisual media no doubt has to do with the power of modern states and enterprises to provide them cheaply to the masses. But obviously this is not the whole story. If it were, then everyone would be able to read and would do so often, for states and enterprises also provide literacy and literature at low cost. No, there is something about the audiovisual media that is different. And we know just what it is: humans love to watch and listen. Not to everything, but to a certain class of things. As we'll see, this fact goes a long way toward explaining why we watch and listen in the way that we do.

We talk compulsively, though we don't really realize it. The same is true of listening and watching. Most of us think that we listen to what we want and look at what we will. It's a comforting notion insofar as it conforms with our rather prideful belief that we have unfettered free will. It has the further benefit of being partially true, which is never a bad thing for a notion to be. Forcing someone to listen or look at something attentively is difficult. In Anthony Burgess's dystopian novel *A Clockwork Orange*, the evil state, believing that wayward people could be "rehabilitated" by prolonged exposure to horrible sounds and images, built an elaborate contraption to do the job.[45] Criminals were strapped into chairs, had their eyelids mechanically peeled back, and were given drugs to heighten awareness. In the real world we use similar attention-focusing techniques of a much milder sort: schools confine students to classrooms, churches confine congregants to pews, and companies confine employees to cubicles. As everyone knows, these methods often fail. Who hasn't slept in a classroom, a church service, or at work? But the fact that no one can really compel you to listen to or look at something doesn't mean that you can listen or look at anything you like. Your ability to do so is constrained by two factors. First, there's only so much material available in any given time and place. If you are in a large art museum, there's a lot to see. If you are on the frozen tundra, there's not. Second, and much more important, there are some sounds and sights that seem to draw our attention whether we like it or not. These might be called "intrusive stimuli." Some are sonic: whispering, lisps, bad music, good music, crying babies, shrieking girls, shouting men, barking dogs, hissing cats, alarms, gunfire. Some are visual: surpassing beauty, unclaimed money, low-cut blouses, drooling, celebrities, explosions, disheveled street people, disfigured faces, open wounds, bloody brawls, car accidents, dead bodies, guns. What all these things have in common is that they are "ear catching" and "eye catching." We are drawn to listen to them and look at them even though we sometimes don't want to. We want to tune them out. We want to turn away. But we can't. Just as we must talk, we must listen and we must look.

The similarity is deeper. Just as we are compelled to talk about certain kinds of things, so too are we compelled to listen and look at certain kinds of things. In fact, they are essentially the same – the relevant ones. As we explained, human speech and reason evolved in part as the result of an age-old competition to gain allies. In what we called the "relevance game," our ancestors attempted to prove their worth to others by presenting relevant facts, that is, interesting tidbits of information that would improve the fitness of their interlocutors. The more relevance individuals brought, the better allies they would be, and the more allies they would have. The number and quality of allies in turn translated into increased reproductive success. What's important to remember is that success in the relevance game depended not only on the ability to present and test relevance – both of which relied on speech and reason – but also the capacity to *uncover* relevance to be presented. Those who were better at finding relevance would naturally enjoy greater reproductive success than those who were worse. This difference, and the advantage it entailed, stimulated the evolution of sensory hardware and software that made the hunt for relevance more efficient.

This is to say no more than that the human ears and eyes, together with the software that runs them, were specially tuned to pay close attention to certain kinds of aural and visual signals, namely, the relevant ones, the ones that matter to us and to people we might talk to. In Chapter 1, we said that these intrusive signals could be grouped under two general headings: anomalies and puzzles. Nothing will draw our attention like something that shouldn't be there. The human mind is a remarkable pattern-building and pattern-recognizing machine. It is so primed to create models that it often sees regularity where there is none, as is evidenced by the fact that people habitually see patterns in random processes where they do not exist. If you roll a six-sided die three times and get six on each roll, you will somehow expect a six on the next roll, though there is no good reason to do so if the die is fair. Even if you understand the laws of probability and *know* that the die is unweighted, you will somehow sense that it may not be fair after all. You intuit that there is something wrong, something that doesn't "add up." This in turn triggers your inborn reflex for puzzle-solving. You will attempt to "figure it out," to square the anomaly with your world-picture. What's most interesting is that you will do this even at considerable risk to yourself, even where your investigative behavior doesn't appear to be rational in terms of cold, hard cost-benefit analysis. Measuring the die might be a rational way to investigate the fairness of the game, as it is low risk. Calling the person who handed you the die a cheater might not be, but you might do that anyway just to judge his or her reaction. Hopefully it won't be a poke in the nose, but you can never tell.

Your ears and eyes, then, are designed to draw your attention to anomalies and make you investigate them whether you like it or not. But there is good reason to suspect that there is another class of much more specific intrusive stimuli that you were pre-programmed to hear and see. This is easy to demonstrate. In our world there is nothing anomalous or puzzling about a picture of a naked lady. Such pictures are practically everywhere. But despite their commonality, if you are a heterosexual male, your attention will be drawn by these images almost whenever and wherever they are presented. Even in cases where you feel ethically uneasy about looking at them, or feel that tangible harm will come to you if you do, you will still be drawn to look. As in the case of Leontius, your reason tells you one thing – do the moral thing, protect yourself – but your eyes and instincts tell you another – look, look now. Often, however, conscious reason never comes into play because it all happens too fast: the image appears, you unthinkingly look, and only then do you feel you've done something immoral or unsafe. For heterosexual males, pictures of naked ladies fall into the category of "relevance reflexes": signals that almost always trigger an automatic perceptual response. Although the exact catalogue of such signals is unknown, our own experience provides us with a fair guide to the basic set. In addition to sexual imagery, we can reasonably add food, drink, power, wealth, conflict, and violence – the "racy things" we mentioned earlier. During our evolution, these specific stimuli were always relevant because they often had a tangible impact on our fitness. Their importance was so universal that there was no reason for the mind to waste energy deciding whether they mattered or not. They almost always mattered. Thus, over the course of millions of years, our response to them became reflexive. They were made part of the elementary program that guides human behavior, not unlike the program embedded in the autonomic nervous system. In this limited sense, we have no more control over what we listen to and look at than we do over whether our hearts pump or our lungs breathe.

Industrial capitalism, the welfare state, and cultural liberalism "pulled" the modern audiovisual media into existence. They were able do this so rapidly and completely because we love to watch and listen. The purveyors of manuscript literacy and print opened a door and forced people through it; the purveyors of the audiovisual media opened a door, and people, of their own volition, rushed in.

WHAT AUDIOVISUAL MEDIA DID

In the modern era, then, the media environment comprised of talking, manuscript-writing, and print became even more complicated with the addition of audiovisual media. Bear in mind that the latter did not supplant the former – media, as we've said, accumulate over time. Neither did audiovisual media come to dominate human communications. Older media remained very useful in the era of movies, radios, TVs, and the rest. People talked, and perhaps even more than before thanks to the telephone. In 1990, at the height of the Audiovisual Era, Americans were making 9.5 billion calls a day.[46] People wrote, and doubtless even more than before thanks to mass literacy and marked improvements in the post. In 1990, the U.S. Postal Service handled over 166 billion pieces of mail.[47] Just how many of them were handwritten letters we don't know, but even if it was a tiny fraction, say 1 percent, that amounts to 166 million manuscripts. And of course people produced and read print, again more than before thanks to mass literacy and improvements in printing technology. In 1990, almost 43,000 new books and editions were published in the United States.[48] That's book *titles*, not copies. If the average print run was in the range of 1,000 copies, that would amount to 43 million books in that year alone.

Our "push" theory of media effects predicts that audiovisual media should have altered the social practices and values of Print Culture; they should have generated a distinct Audiovisual Culture in the distinct Audiovisual Era (1850 to 1990). As we've already noted, there are ample primary and secondary sources available to test these predictions, and we will use them liberally in all that follows.

Accessibility

We noted previously that print was both accessible and inaccessible, depending on whether you were a sender or recipient of it. The same is true of audiovisual media, only much more so.

Beginning on the send side, anyone who has ever seen the inside of a modern radio or television station knows that the tools and skills necessary to produce and send audiovisual signals are expensive. The equipment itself – sound stages, microphones, cameras, transmitters, signal towers, satellites, and so on – does not come cheap. You can't afford it if you are not Ted Turner. Even if you had a fully equipped studio and the wherewithal to send signals from it, you wouldn't know how to use any of it without extensive training. A degree in television or radio production would come in very handy. Once you had your studio and knew how to use it, you'd still have to produce something to broadcast. This is no easy feat. You don't just whip up an evening news broadcast or a sitcom. So you'll need degrees in journalism and the dramatic arts as well. Yet you'll never be able to acquire and learn to do all of these things. No individual could. That's why audiovisual media are produced and transmitted by large teams of people. Directors get all the credit for great films, but it's the army of people on the crew who do all the heavy lifting. Not only is audiovisual production naturally expensive, it's not that hard to make it more costly by artificial means. This is because audiovisual media, like print, present those who would control it with a nice logistical bottleneck, a stage in the production and distribution process that is particularly vulnerable. With audiovisual media, it's the studio and transmission facilities themselves that cannot (with the partial exception of radio) be hidden. This is why tyrannical governments *always* control the airwaves and fill them with self-serving garbage. In such an environment, the cost of private transmission is death, and that's a high price to pay.

On the receive side, the tools and skills necessary to get and understand audiovisual signals are generally cheap. In terms of equipment, all you need is a box, either a radio or a TV. Like almost all mass-produced electronics, these items became less expensive as the twentieth century progressed. Eventually, even people of moderate income could afford them, and they became nearly universal in the free, developed world. Today, radios and televisions are everywhere. As for skills, you need none. You do not have a reading organ, so you need to learn to read. But you do have listening and watching organs, so you don't need to learn anything at all to listen to the radio or watch the TV. It's possible that there are people who, for whatever neurological reason, just don't "get" the box. They don't understand where the voices come from, or how large, three-dimensional people become small, two-dimensional people. But if such unfortunates exist, they are rare exceptions. A comprehension test of audiovisual media has now been performed on billions of people, and the results are clear: almost everyone "gets" radio, TV, and the movies immediately. Now, the degree to which people "get" them varies considerably. You may not "understand" an art-house movie due to a "cultural barrier." If it's in a foreign language, then you may not "understand" it due to a "language barrier." But your lack of full comprehension doesn't mean you don't "get" it at all. Billions of people all over the world consume audiovisual media – particularly American music, television, and films – that they don't "understand" in either of these senses. But they seem to "get" them enough to enjoy watching or listening to them, for they both watch and listen avidly. Not only are audiovisual media cheap to get and consume, they are difficult to make more expensive than they naturally are. This doesn't mean it can't be done. A despotic government could make it illegal to own a radio and TV receivers. But even despots are loath to take this step because it would deny them the opportunity to use radio and TV for propagandistic purposes. The trouble is that, once the boxes are widely disseminated, they can be used to receive "subversive" foreign broadcasts. The Soviet leadership made the reception of foreign broadcasts illegal and even attempted to jam their signals.[49] Nonetheless, millions of Soviet citizens daily tuned into Deutsche Welle, the Voice of America, and the BBC. Finnish television was very popular as well (it aired the TV series *Dallas*).[50]

Thus, audiovisual media are inaccessible on the send side and accessible on the receive side. As such, they foster a dual network. On the send side, the network is concentrated: control of the means to produce and transmit audiovisual signals is held by a few nodes. On the receive side, the network is diffused: a large percentage of those in the network will have the ability to receive signals. This is what is commonly called a "one-to-many" network, meaning that a few nodes send messages to many nodes, and the many nodes do not send messages back. Such a description fits audiovisual media perfectly. Following our theory, a dual network will both *hierarchicalize* and *equalize* social practices evolved in and around it. Concentrated networks encourage the formation of ranks, while diffused networks work in the opposite direction.

On the send side, hierarchicalization can clearly be seen in modern audiovisual networks. After an initial scramble, the motion picture industry in the United States simplified to a number of big players all coordinated into the "Hollywood system": Fox, Paramount, Warner, MGM, and RKO (the "Big Five") plus United Artists, Universal, and Columbia (the "Little Three").[51] Similar concentration took place in the radio industry, with NBC (1926), CBS (1927), and ABC (1943) emerging as the dominant players.[52] When television was finally launched en masse in the 1950s, the "Big Three" networks dominated it as well. Outside the United States, the situation was different as governments almost uniformly initiated or nationalized radio and television networks.[53]

That was the "is" of the situation: a few nodes in the network would control all production and transmission of broadcast audiovisual materials. The "ought" depended on the way hegemony was established. In the United States, it was argued that corporate domination of

audiovisual media was a natural result of the operation of free enterprise and free speech, both of which were hallowed principles. In this
peculiarly odd view, the big media companies were simply victors in
the marketplace and the "marketplace of ideas." If anyone thought
they could do better, they were free to try. "Market entry," as the
economists have it, proved singularly difficult until the era of cable television, and even then was no easy trick. The "marketplace of ideas,"
therefore, did not (and does not) operate as the Founding Fathers or
Mill might have hoped.[54] In Europe, members of the Vanguard Party
argued that the state had to control audiovisual media in order to protect "the people" from harmful private interests, precisely the kind that
dominated the media in the United States. This logic had the odd effect
of making politicians into art critics, a role they were singularly unfit
to play. Sometimes the result of taking audiovisual media from "the
people" in order to make it the "people's media" were benign, as in
the case of the UK's BBC. Other times it wasn't, as in the case of the
USSR's ITAR-TASS.

On the receive side, equalization is just as apparent. We see it most
notably in the formation of the "masses" or "mass society." In the
Manuscript and Print Eras, there were many different audiences: literate and oral, elite and common, this confession and that confession,
this region and that region. In the nineteenth century, with the introduction of mass print publications and the rise of mass literacy, this
began to change. Ever larger audiences began to form, a phenomenon
noted early on by many observers. In 1932, for example, José Ortega y
Gasset wrote of the emergence of the "mass man."[55] The rapid spread
of the audiovisual media, particularly following World War II, accelerated this process of "mass-ification." Both capitalist enterprises and
communist parties saw the value in audiovisual media and worked to
make sure that everyone would have access to them. To be sure, their
motives were quite different: the capitalists wanted to sell soap and the
communists wanted to sell the party line. But the result was the same:
nearly universal access to a small set of audiovisual signals. The varied,
smallish audiences of Manuscript and early Print Culture were thereby
united into mass audiences of "listeners" and "viewers," all of whom
are equal and all of whom have one "vote" (their attention). This phenomenon, too, was noted by observers. In 1956, for example, C. Wright
Mills wrote a classic treatment of "mass society."[56]

That was the "is" of the situation: everyone was going to listen and watch, and moreover to the same (often bad) things. The "ought" that followed was a peculiar twist on egalitarianism by which the mass consumption of audiovisual media was intertwined with the notion of democratic citizenship. The idea that the free press – both the right to send printed materials and to receive them – was essential to democracy and cultural enrichment had already been established in the nineteenth century. Free-press doctrine was applied to the audiovisual media as well but it meant different things on the send and receive sides. On the send side, it was a merely formal right: any citizen was free to transmit audiovisual signals within the confines of the state's regulatory structure, though only those with the means – that is, the very wealthy or powerful – could actually do so, at least to large audiences. On the receive side, however, it was, or rather became, a substantive right: any citizen *could* listen and watch the audiovisual media. Now most of what was "on" – music, game shows, sitcoms, sports – had nothing to do with the workings of democracy or cultural enrichment. But some of it did: news, election coverage, government announcements, and the various high-brow offerings like those found on Soviet television and American PBS. Programming of this sort was enough to allow politicians and industry lobbyists to claim that listening and watching constituted "participation" in the democratic process and national cultural life. This argument provided the opening necessary for state regulation and public subvention of the audiovisual media: the government needed to make sure the right things were broadcast and that everyone had access.[57] Thus, access to the media – and television in particular – became a sort of tacit right.[58]

Privacy

We saw that printing is usually public, but reading print is private, or at least can be made so reasonably inexpensively. It's the same with audiovisual media: transmitting is public, receiving is private, or at least often so in practice.

On the send side, it's difficult to hide the fact that you are broadcasting signals from a radio or television station. The reason is that you are broadcasting signals from a radio or television station. Occasionally we hear about things like "pirate radio" and "pirate TV."[59] In the popular imagination, these operations are run by radicals shacked up in secret locations with primitive equipment. Said radicals "appropriate" bandwidth from "the man" and therewith broadcast their scratchy radicalism to the masses yearning to be free (or listen to weird music). It's all very outré. It's also very risky business because the authorities – the folks who license the airwaves – usually have no difficulty locating and closing down the pirate operations. Actually, pretty much anyone with a radio direction finder – not a complicated or expensive piece of equipment – can make their way to the source of a radio or television signal. Once they find the source, they are going to find you, and your "cover" is going to be blown. So you can't hide your identity very easily in the world of broadcast. But can you hide your message, that is, transmit it to a closed audience? You only have two options for accomplishing this feat: limiting reception and limiting comprehension. There is no way to do the former while broadcasting: anyone with the proper equipment can pick up an airborne signal. You can, however, constrain reception by transmitting your signal over a closed circuit; that way only those "in the loop" will be able to receive it. But this won't really work for a large network because it will have too many loose ends to monitor. Someone will hack in. As for limiting comprehension, this can be accomplished by encrypting your signal whether you broadcast it or send it over a closed circuit. If you have the cipher, you can decode the signal. If not, then not. Again, this won't work well on a large network because too many people will have the cipher to secure it properly. Somebody will leak it. All this talk of closed circuits and codes may sound far removed from your humdrum life, but it's not. If you have cable TV, you are both on a closed circuit and have a decoder. If you aren't paying for your cable TV, then you have joined the millions of viewers who have hacked through both.

On the receive side, it's entirely possible for someone to tell whether you are listening to the radio or watching TV in the "privacy" of your own home. Both kinds of receivers give off signals that can be detected through walls and from some distance. Just ask anyone who lives in Britain. The United Kingdom sells annual licenses to the owners of TV sets in order to fund the BBC. These licenses aren't cheap: £142.50 for a color TV and £48.00 for a black-and-white one.[60] Naturally, some people don't pay, or at least try not to. So the TV Licensing office (TVL) has a fleet of unmarked vans with ultra-secret detection equipment that roam the streets looking for what might be called "TV pirates." According to a TVL spokesperson, the vans are "so powerful they can tell if a TV is in use in as little as 20 seconds. And once the television is detected, the equipment – which works from up to 60 meters away – can pinpoint the actual room that the television set is in."[61] The TVL catches over 400,000 "TV pirates" a year, though how many are caught with the vans is not certain. If this sort of equipment is commonly used in a democratic state like the United Kingdom, one can only imagine that it was and probably is used in despotic governments as well. The rulers of the former Eastern Bloc, as well as those of contemporary China, Iran, and Cuba, don't want their subjects being "corrupted" by foreign broadcasts. In June 2008, a street vendor in Zimbabwe, then ruled by the tyrant Robert Mugabe, was arrested for listening to the Voice of America.[62] All this may sound a bit like something ripped from the pages of Orwell's *1984*, but the reality is quite different. In most of the world, governments make no attempt at all to monitor or control what people listen to or watch in their homes, and those that do try to surveil and limit radio and TV use have failed. Although it's really impossible to know for certain, there is good reason to believe that tens of millions of East German subjects tuned in to West German radio and TV daily.[63] Penetration was also high in the remaining Eastern Bloc countries, including the USSR.[64] Although the Chinese government has not entirely given up on radio and TV censorship, it has certainly loosened its grip (or rather, had it loosened by increasing public demand for foreign broadcasts).[65] Satellite dishes are illegal in Iran, but many people seem to have and use them.[66] Only the North Koreans have had real success in controlling what their subjects listen to and watch. Every "Hermit Kingdom" brand radio and television comes conveniently and permanently preset to government stations and sealed to prevent tampering.[67] In North Korea, the TV watches you.

So you won't be able to broadcast audiovisual signals without "revealing your position," but you will probably be able to privately listen to or watch whatever you like from the comfort of your pleather Barcalounger. Here again we encounter a dual network. Audiovisual networks are connected on the send side: the senders are few, known to one another, and constitute a coherent group. In contrast, they are segmented on the receive side: recipients are very many, not known to one other, and are clustered into "audiences." Our theory has it that such networks will simultaneously *open* social practices on the send side due to the practical impossibility of hiding transmission and *close* them on the receive side due to the ease with which reception can be hidden. Both opening and closing are apparent in the history of societies that have adopted audiovisual technologies.

From almost the very beginning of audiovisual media, broadcasters had no choice but to operate in the open. As we've seen, American media companies in all three spheres – movies, radio, and TV – quickly grew, consolidated, and became nationwide and later worldwide brands. Just as quickly they came under intense public scrutiny.[68] After repeated calls for state censorship, the movie industry created the Motion Picture Producers and Distributors of America in 1922 and instituted the self-limiting Production Code in 1930. Radio and TV were not as successful in fending off state regulation, largely because of the federal government's nationalization of precious bandwidth. The Federal Radio Commission was created in 1927 with the right to assign frequencies and issue broadcast licenses as it pleased. In 1934, it was renamed the Federal Communications Commission (FCC). Under the watchful eye of the FCC, not to mention the press and the public, the audiovisual industry quickly came to dominate American national consciousness in a way no one could have imagined. Amazingly, the exploits of its gray-suited executives – Samuel Goldwyn, Louis B. Mayer, David O. Selznik, Darryl Zanuck, Howard Hughes, Walt Disney, David Sarnoff, William Paley, Barry Diller – became objects of public fascination. The personal lives of its stars, far too numerous and well-known to mention here, were followed by millions with an intensity bordering on mania. The case was much the same, if somewhat more muted, in countries that heavily subsidized or nationalized the film, radio, and TV industries. Even tyrannies got into the act. Their ministries of culture created auteur-directors, national stars, and lavish (if often kitschy and propagandistic) productions of every kind. The North Korean despot Kim Jong-il liked movies so much that he kidnapped a famous South Korean director, Shin San-ok, and ordered him to make films for the benefit of the hard-working, long-suffering people of North Korea.[69] He made seven movies, with the Dear Leader serving as executive producer of each.

That was the "is" of the situation: broadcast audiovisual production and distribution were open, public affairs. The "ought" took the form of a new publicism according to which movies, radio, and TV were believed to be public or quasi-public property. Whether they were held by private companies as in the United States, or by the state as in much of Europe, the broadcast media were seen as somehow beholden to "the people" because they were intrinsically public on the send side. In contrast to writing and print, broadcasts could not be hidden. That meant they *could* be regulated. Politicians, pundits, and concerned citizens argued that they *should* be. They claimed that regulation would, variously, save children, educate the public, protect decency, promote culture, preserve neutrality, limit commercialism, and so on and so forth. But all of these reasons boiled down to the belief that the broadcast audiovisual media were shared resources, something that belongs to everyone. The public does not own writing or print, but it does own the airwaves.[70]

In contrast, consumption of audiovisual media began as a quasi-public affair and became more private and closed as the century progressed. The original nickelodeons and movie palaces were public places where crowds of people went to watch in public.[71] Similarly, early radio (1920s) and TV (1940s) were enjoyed in public settings, though they were generally smaller than those at movie houses.[72] Even in the first years of audiovisual media, however, entrepreneurs realized that there was a sizable market in private viewing. As early as the 1890s, movie makers were producing proto-pornographic shorts to be viewed in single-viewer Mutoscopes and Kinetoscopes. Soon they were doing a thriving (if clandestine) trade in coin-in-the-slot peep shows and "stag films."[73] The privatization of audiovisual consumption, however, didn't really take off until mid-century, when two crucial developments took place. First, automobile manufacturers began to put radios in cars and cars themselves became ubiquitous.[74] Although we don't usually think of it, the car is one of the few places one can truly be alone without drawing attention to the fact that one is alone. No one is put off when you go for a drive by yourself. And since you are riding solo, you might as well listen to the radio. Second, television manufacturers began to produce TVs every homeowner could afford.[75] Thus, the "TV room" found its place in every middle-class house.[76] Although the TV room was not a place to be alone (that would be suspicious), it was a locus where the family could gather in private around the "electronic hearth."

In the 1970s, the notion that every member of the family should have his or her "own space" and hence own room further privatized the consumption of audiovisual media. When everyone has their own TV, there is no fighting over the remote control (or "dominator" as it's sometimes rightly called). The final moment in audiovisual privatization came with the Walkman and the videotape.[77] With the former, you could listen to your music in your private space whether you happened to be alone or not. With the latter – which was much more culturally significant in the long term – you could order anything you liked anonymously and, with the right equipment and a private space, view it alone. Naturally, this was a boon to pornographers, whose business had long suffered under the logistical requirement that they sell their wares in public.[78] The days of stealing into the dirty movie theater were over. All you had to do in the age of the videotape was get a post office box and fill out a form. As we've seen, no prude or politician was likely to try to stop you, and even if they did, they would probably fail.

That was the "is" of the situation: people were going to listen to and watch what they wanted in the privacy of their own homes. The concomitant "ought" added additional weight to already well-established Print-Era doctrines such as the "right to privacy," the "harm principle," "obligatory tolerance," and "aesthetic populism." Whether you were a citizen of the Soviet Union or the United States, you were more or less formally free to listen to or watch whatever you wanted in your own home. Yet this was not much of a concession on the part of the aforementioned regulators, for practically speaking you could only listen to or watch what the broadcasters broadcasted, which is to say what the regulators wanted you to hear or see. If you fancied something else, you were free to record it or film it within the confines of the law. But of course you couldn't do that very easily. And it goes without saying that you couldn't distribute your music or film even if you managed to produce it because then you would be subject to regulation. The advent of non-broadcast audiovisual media – especially videotape and cable – presented the regulators with a problem, as they could be produced, distributed, and consumed in private. After attempting to control this new audiovisual channel for a time, the regulators either disappeared, as in the case of the Soviet Union, or gave up, as in the case of most of the liberal democracies. Thus, in the second half of the twentieth century, it became both legal and acceptable to consume, for example, audiovisual pornography so long as it didn't travel through the "public's" airwaves.

Fidelity

In 1824, the famous German historian Leopold von Ranke enjoined his colleagues to represent the past "as it really was."[79] Alas, neither he nor is colleagues had the right tool for the job. They wrote, and written words are a poor way to represent anything other than themselves. As we've said, the word "daisy" looks like the word "daisy," but it doesn't look like a daisy. In this regard, audiovisual media are different. They don't appear to be representations of anything. Rather, they seem to be experience itself. This sense is reflected in the way we speak. We "read" written or printed texts, and they are the only things that can really be read. But we "listen" to recorded music just as we would listen to live music, and we "watch" recorded moving pictures just the way we watch life go by. Reading text seems unnatural. Listening to and watching recorded audiovisual media seem natural. Of course, from a purely technical standpoint, *both* are unnatural insofar as both are encoded signals. The difference is that you must laboriously learn to decipher the code to understand a text, while you just "get" the audiovisual code without conscious effort. The reason we automatically "get" audiovisual code is that it's iconic. Written and printed words are symbolic.[80] They don't appear like anything but words. Their only use is to "stand for" something other than themselves. But a recorded voice *sounds* like a natural voice. A photographed image *looks* like a natural image. They don't seem to "stand for" something, they appear to be something.

This is to say that audiovisual media don't reduce sense data to an obtrusive code. Rather, they "capture" it for playback, and in this sense they are really best thought of as one-to-one codes. Sound-recording media encode sound for playback as sound. Visual-recording media encode vision for playback as vision. Now in principle, audiovisual media can be used as five-to-one codes, just like writing and print. The results of such use, however, are often hard to "get." Ferde Grofé's "Grand Canyon Suite" may somehow *sound* like the Grand Canyon *looks*, but you just don't "get" the reference the way you do when you look at a picture of the Grand Canyon. "Purple Haze" is not purple, "More than a Feeling" is not a feeling, "Smells Like Teen Spirit" doesn't smell like anything, and "A Taste of Honey," were you to take a bite of the 1963 Beatles' album on which it appeared, would taste like old vinyl. These things *sound* like something, namely themselves. We should add one detail about audiovisual media: like print, they can be reproduced easily and accurately in very large numbers at very low cost. "Reproduced" is surely the right word for audiovisual recordings like records, films, tapes, CDs, and DVDs, for these things are copied. Whether one should call a broadcast received by a radio or television a "reproduction" is rather a sticky philosophical point. It's clear, however, that the sounds and sights audiovisual transmitters transmit travel through space and then appear in many different places at the same time. Given this fact, it makes at least some sense to say that the transmitted item is an "original" and the received versions "copies," albeit evanescent unless recorded.

Audiovisual media, then, are very high fidelity, at least in the audio and visual channels: what goes in comes out the same way. High-fidelity media create iconic networks, that is, ones that carry messages that require little or no effort to decode. Iconic audio and visual signals are not "read" but "recognized," not "deciphered" but "experienced." According to our theory, iconic networks *sensualize* social practices developed in or around them. Humans naturally seek sensual pleasure, but in ordinary circumstances their pleasure-seeking drive is blunted by high costs. Iconic networks lower the cost of seeking and receiving sensual pleasures of certain kinds, thereby leading to sensualization of social practices and mores.

Sensualization is one of the hallmarks of modern life, both in the institutional and moral sense. To be sure, Manuscript and Print Cultures had their pleasure palaces. These included brothels, public houses, gentlemen's clubs, not to mention a calendar full of riotous, drunken, and often bawdy festivals. But in most cases their "entertainments" were not mediated. Prostitutes, publicans, club managers, and carnival masters ran what consultants sometimes call "high-touch" businesses. Everything is done face-to-face, and a premium is put on personal – sometimes very personal – relationships. This fact necessarily limited market size: a high-touch service provider can only provide so many services without a drastic reduction in the quality of the "product."

For this reason, high-touch services tended to be expensive, and so might be called "costly thrills." In the Manuscript and Print Eras there was only one way to radically reduce the cost of costly thrills – theater. Entrepreneurs took personal, sensual services and made "live" representations of them that could be shown to many people at the same time. The representation wasn't as good as the real thing, but from the perspective of the punters it was cheap and reasonably safe. For a few pennies you could see a man tame a lion without risking getting eaten. Theater proved popular, but it still suffered from two drawbacks. First, only so many people could watch. The Romans' fabled Circus Maximus could hold several hundred thousand people.[81] That's a lot, but one wonders exactly what the poor folks in the cheap seats really saw. Remember, neither the Romans nor anyone else had PA systems or JumboTrons. The larger the audience, the less you saw; the less you saw, the less sensual the experience. Second, the authorities had good reason to be worried about theater, and so they restricted it. The moralists among them, like Plato, didn't like what was shown. The rulers among them didn't like the threat they posed to public order.[82] From a ruler's perspective, the difference between a rowdy audience and a rebellious mob can be subtle. For all these reasons, cheap, vicarious thrills were hard to come by in the Manuscript and Print Eras.

Audiovisual media changed all that. By making iconic sound and sight portable, audiovisual media – or rather that part of it known as the "entertainment industry"[83] – made high-touch businesses low-touch. In the audiovisual world, the stimulator no longer had to be in the physical presence of the stimulated. This separation revolutionized the sensation industry by radically reducing the risks associated with sending and receiving sensual signals. This is true in a physical sense: sex workers can rip off johns, and johns can beat up sex workers, but neither can harm the other directly in an interaction mediated by a pornographic film. But it's also true in a psychological sense: people will do things and watch things "alone" that they would never do or watch in public for fear of embarrassment. Not only did audiovisual media make the exchange of stimulation safe, it also made it remarkably inexpensive. Neither high-touch sensual services like prostitution nor low-touch sensual services like live theater could be mechanically reproduced; therefore, they remained comparatively expensive and undemocratic. They were, as we said, costly thrills. In contrast, audiovisual media could be mechanically duplicated and so became inexpensive and democratic. They engendered the first "cheap thrills." In the Manuscript and Print Eras, hundreds of well-born people occasionally watched plays in public amphitheaters. In the Audiovisual Era, billions of common people constantly watch TV in their own homes. They aren't watching plays, but other quasi-sensual, dramatic material: romances, thrillers, comedies, talk shows, fashion shows, cooking shows, and sports of every variety. They cannot and will not stop because it feels too good.

That was the "is" of the situation: people were going to stimulate themselves with audiovisual media. The "ought" needed to justify self-stimulation was not immediately obvious. Written and print signals are often constitutionally protected speech; broadcast audiovisual signals usually are not. Therefore, a "freedom of expression" rationale wouldn't work. You have the right to consume any written or print signal in private; so too do you have the right to consume any broadcast audiovisual signal in private. So "right to privacy" and related justifications would work in principle. But there was a hitch: many audiovisual signals were either intrinsically public (broadcast radio and TV) or hard to make completely private (recorded music and videos). Thus, other people were going to know what you were listening to or watching, and therefore you would be open to public censure if you listened to or watched the wrong things. Clearly, the only option was to change the criteria for what the wrong things were. That was accomplished by expanding the notion of Romanticism. The late eighteenth- and nineteenth-century Romantics had hammered out the idea that it was fine to feel, and that things that made you feel more were fine as well. Most of them had poetry, paintings, and opium in mind. The postwar Romantics of the Audiovisual Era went further. Frank Sinatra, Hugh Hefner, Aldous Huxley, among others created what might be called "Softcore Romanticism," that is, a way of life built around the night club, mild eroticism, and "mind-expanding" drugs.[84] It was very sophisticated and therefore could be consumed in public. In turn, their successors – Sid Vicious, Larry Flint, and William Burroughs, et al. – went even further. They founded "Hardcore Romanticism," a cultural style built on hard-core music, hard-core pornography, and hard-core drugs.[85] It wasn't sophisticated. Rather, it was "intense," which is to say very stimulating. And since everything stimulating was good, it too could be consumed in the open.

Volume

An intuitive way to measure the volume that speech, writing, and printing can sustain is to find the number of words in a typical message and then multiply it by the number of recipients. With this simple method we reached the sensible conclusion that speech and writing, neither of which can be mass-reproduced, were low volume, while printing, which can, was high volume. This formula, alas, won't work terribly well for audiovisual media because their "content" is not limited to words. In addition to words, they truck in sounds and images. Sounds and images can't really be counted, at least very easily. One could reckon the bits and bytes typical audiovisual messages contain, but that figure doesn't really yield a good approximation of the quantity of information received by the listener or viewer. A highly compressed, small digital sound file can sound as good as an uncompressed, very large digital sound file – it all depends on the compression software and the sensitivity of the listener.

Since audiovisual messages flow past the passive consumer in time, duration might provide a logical metric for message size. The longest "song" regularly broadcast is probably Mahler's *Symphony No. 3*, coming in at 110 minutes; the shortest is the grind-core band Napalm Death's "You Suffer," coming in at 1.316 seconds.[86] The longest movie ever shown in theaters is the German film *Heimat II*, which runs 25 hours and 32 minutes; the shortest is called *The One Second Film*.[87] The longest continuous radio segment was hosted by Switzerland's Christoph Stöckli and lasted 105 hours; the shortest was a commercial that ran under a second for none other than *The Guinness Book of World Records*.[88] The longest continuous TV segment was hosted by Croatia's Kristijan Petrovic and ran 36 hours and 15 minutes; the shortest TV segment was a commercial that ran one-sixtieth of a second for a Canadian music retailer.[89] All this is interesting, but not really very enlightening because audiovisual messages – particularly those that are broadcast – don't really come in discrete packages like spoken "speeches," written "letters," and printed "books." Rather, they stream 24 hours a day, 365 days a year, year in and year out. In that sense, the longest audiovisual messages have been running and will be running for decades. Nobody listens to or watches them continuously. The longest anyone has ever watched TV at a stretch was 69 hours and

48 minutes. This feat was accomplished by Suresh Joachim during a stunt staged by – that's right – a TV program, the *Live with Regis and Kelly Show*.⁹⁰ In 2006, the average American household watched TV for 8 hours and 14 minutes a day, though the average American only watched for 4 hours and 35 minutes.⁹¹ Still, the signal was always there, incessantly piping audiovisual information into millions of homes.

Perhaps a better way to judge the capacity of the audiovisual pipe is by counting "channels," that is, streams of more-or-less continuous sonic and visual output that reach – or can reach – some considerable number of people. In the beginning, these were few and had relatively short range. Around 1900, records and phonographs were uncommon, movies and movies theaters were rare, and there was no commercial radio or television. By the turn of the twenty-first century, all of these media flowed through multiple channels, many of which reached millions of people. The number of devices, albums, movies, radio stations, TV stations, and now video games available is astounding. There are now in use in the world today hundreds of millions of machines that play back sound, and billions of things (records, tapes, CDs) to play back on them. In a bit over five years, Apple has sold 100 million iPods, and its iTunes music store has sold in excess of 2.5 billion songs. Both numbers are rising.⁹² In 2007, the people of the United States bought 500 million albums (records, tapes, CDs), though that number is declining due to music piracy and online sales.⁹³ The number of movie screens worldwide is enormous and hard to figure. According to the annual statistical report of the *Cahiers du cinema*, the United States had 38,974 screens, Europe had 25,028 screens, and India had 14,000 screens in 2007.⁹⁴ The world total probably approaches 150,000 screens. There's a lot to be seen on them. According to the same source, India produced 1,146 films, Europe 1,095 films, and the United States 603 films in 2007.⁹⁵ The world total would seem to be around 5,000 films. The number of radio stations in the world is not known but doubtless very large. In 2006, there were about 1,400 licensed broadcast stations in the United States.⁹⁶ Urban markets in the developed world commonly have several dozen stations. The number of television stations in the world is not known but, again, doubtless sizable. In 2006, there were approximately 2,200 in the United States.⁹⁷ The average home in the United States receives 118 TV channels.⁹⁸

Audiovisual media, then, clearly are very high volume. They deliver millions of messages, long and short, continuously flowing through thousands of channels to billions of listeners and viewers. As new technologies come online – particularly fiber-optic cable and next-generation satellites – they will have the capacity to deliver even more messages through more channels to more people. High-volume media engender unconstrained networks, that is, ones with a lot of spare capacity. Audiovisual networks fit the bill not only because the audiovisual pipe is enormous, but also because it is only one of four pipes. When audiovisual media came into existence, speech, writing, and especially print already provided considerable bandwidth to senders and recipients. Together, this aggregate "legacy" pipe offered all the volume needed to perform high-value, necessary communications work and more. Audiovisual media provided even more spare capacity, a flood of cheap bandwidth that could be used as senders and recipients saw fit. In our theory, unconstrained networks like those created by audiovisual media *hedonize* social practices developed in and around them. They do this precisely by affording people the opportunity to use the medium for the purposes of entertainment at low cost. Like no other medium before, audiovisual media provided this opportunity.

The results were dramatic, as the history of entertainment in the twentieth century shows. In Manuscript Cultures, most of your time was consumed by family life and work, and most of the communication you did was related to those two spheres. This situation changed somewhat with the coming of industry and the advent of mass print. The former raised living standards, reduced working hours, and created the opportunity for what we now call "leisure," a new sort of structured, sanctioned activity. The latter gave people something to do in it, namely read for pleasure. But that wasn't all people in the nineteenth century did with their leisure time. Entrepreneurs realized that additional brass in pocket and time on hand created commercial opportunities for those who might provide safe, accessible, and sometimes clean amusements. Thus was the "live" entertainment industry born. Businessmen expanded theaters, created music halls, and opened seaside resorts, all of which became very popular in the Victorian era. But it wasn't enough. There was still plenty of excess demand for entertainments, especially inexpensive ones that could be consumed quickly and conveniently. The recorded music, film, radio, and TV industries were all born of this excess, unmet demand.[99] Technicians such as Bell, Edison, Westinghouse, Tesla, Marconi, Fessenden, Zworykin, Farnsworth, and the rest all understood the commercial potential of audiovisual media. They knew people wanted to listen and watch. They actively sought patents and financial backing so that their technological innovations (one can't really in most cases call them "inventions") could be commercialized. As we've already pointed out, the men who did the commercialization are household names, as are the companies they ran: Paramount, MGM, Warner Brothers, Disney, RCA, NBC, CBS, ABC and so on. The Berliners, Goldwyns, and Sarnoffs laid the audiovisual pipe and simultaneously produced entertainment to flow through it. The result was an explosion of cultural production the likes of which the world had never seen. Thousands of singers, musicians, writers, actors, and technicians of every kind were trained and put to work feeding the pipe. They produced thousands upon thousands of songs, movies, radio shows, and programs. As they did, demand rose with standards of living. By the mid-twentieth century, daily life in the developed world had been transformed. You no longer had to "make your own fun." Now you bought it or – even better – it was given to you for the price of watching a few silly advertisements. Playing recorded music, going to films, listening to the radio, and watching TV became things that literally everyone did for several hours or more each day.[100]

That was the "is" of the situation: people were going to have their MTV no matter what. The "ought" devised to rationalize audiovisual hedonism had to be different from that rolled out for literary hedonism: almost no one seems to be able to stomach the idea that pop music, porno films, and trash TV are, like reading, modes of "self-improvement."[101] This is not to say that critics said all of it was bad for you. On the contrary, they claimed some high-brow audiovisual entertainment – Bach records, French art films, BBC costume dramas – could be edifying.[102] But most of it was deemed garbage, the aural and visual equivalent of junk food. People, however, really like junk food, so some pretext for eating it (or rather, listening to and watching it) had to be found. This wasn't difficult. Even before Freud, psychologists had said that modern life was unnaturally stressful and, thus, that a period of daily relaxation was necessary for good mental health.[103] The audiovisual industry was ready and able to step up and help by providing many hours of relaxing sounds and sights for the stressed-out worker. Of course, said worker could quietly meditate, but – so the argument went – watching TV for three hours accomplishes the same thing and is much more entertaining. The downside is that stimulation of the relaxing sort, so to speak, can be addictive, but no matter.[104]

Velocity

In 1964, the legendary Canadian animator Richard Williams began making a movie called *The Thief and the Cobbler*.[105] He worked on it and then didn't. He got funding, then lost it. He landed a distribution deal and then that slipped away. At one point, *The Thief and the Cobbler* was seized by creditors. In 1995, the film was finally released in the United States under the title *Arabian Knight*. The new name didn't help. It flopped. Thirty-one years is a long time, much longer than it takes to produce most films. But the case of *The Thief and the Cobbler* is proof that audiovisual messages are not made overnight. Most aren't even made over many nights. Feature films can take decades to produce, albums can take years, radio shows months, and TV shows equally as long. That's part of the reason you hear about them (and hear about them and hear about them) well before they appear. With some effort, audiovisual messages can be put together quickly, sometimes with surprisingly good results. Roger Corman's cult comedy *The Little Shop of Horrors* (1960) was shot in two days.[106] The Beatles recorded most of their debut album *Please Please Me* (1962) in about 10 hours.[107] But generally speaking, professional-quality audiovisual messages can't be fashioned that fast. You might think that "live" broadcasts – ones in which performance and transmission are simultaneous – are an exception. They aren't. Most of them take extensive preparation – rehearsals – before they are "ready for primetime." The fact is, you just aren't very likely to find anything "spontaneous" on live radio or TV, unless you are listening to the college radio station or watching the local public access channel. From the perspective of audiovisual executives, departing from the script is dangerous. From the perspective of consumers, it's usually just bad. Although the production of audiovisual messages is slow, some of them move very quickly. Those recorded on portable media don't: movies, videos, tapes, and CDs have to be physically moved from wherever they were made to wherever you are. If the means of transportation are good, then they will arrive quickly. If not, then you will wait. But the others move like lightning. Like all electromagnetic waves, radio and TV signals in a vacuum travel at close to the speed of light, that is, 186,000 miles per second.[108] Coaxial and fiber-optic cable propagates electromagnetic waves at over 110,000 miles per second.[109]

Despite their remarkable transmission speed, audiovisual media are low velocity because they take a long time to produce, at least the way we generally like them produced. Low-velocity media engender monologic networks, that is, networks in which it is relatively easy to send information, but not easy to respond, especially in medium-kind. If Lush Rimbaugh or some other blowhard says something you don't like on the radio or TV, you might call the station and vent. It is unlikely, however, that you will try to mount a radio or TV show called "Lush Rimbaugh is a Very Corpulent Buffoon" for the sole purpose of blasting Rimbaugh off the air. That would take a long time, not to mention a lot of money. By the date you got the show ready and issued your scorching rebuttal, no one would really remember what you were on about. In the real world of audiovisual media, Rimbaugh lectures you and you don't get to lecture him back. Rimbaugh's *bête noire*, Foul Rankin, can respond in kind because he has a production company at his disposal (or at least he used to). But he's not going to be able to fire back immediately. The wheels of audiovisual production, as we said, grind slowly. He's going to have to run the idea by the producer, get the writers to work on it, fit it into the already-filled schedule, and then tape it. That might take a day, or it might take a week. The result will not exactly be a face-off between Rimbaugh and Rankin, but instead, two monologues separated by a considerable period of time, the second of which makes extensive reference to the first. This is why albums don't generally respond to albums, movies to movies, radio shows to radio shows, and TV shows to TV shows or really any of these media to each other – they are just too slow to make the "dialogue" apparent, except to acolytes, aesthetes, and academics who make a game of searching out "homage." By our theory, monologic networks like those engendered by audiovisual media *centralize* social practices evolved in and around them. These networks suppress the natural human inclination to engage in dialogue and impose on it one-way communications – information flows from one node to another (or many others), but not back.

Written networks such as those characteristic of Manuscript Culture were essentially monologic: elites used writing to communicate to other elites and the unlettered masses. There was little written dialogue to speak of because writing was too slow and too rare to sustain it. After 1450, print networks – also monologic – either replaced or were added to existing written networks. There was still no real dialogue, although the number and size of monologic networks expanded appreciably, the consequence of which was the birth of the public sphere. The coming of audiovisual media in the first half of the twentieth century had much the same impact as print. There was still no dialogue, but the number and especially size of monologic networks grew. We can see this clearly in the experience of the United States. The motion picture networks were first. Paramount, MGM, Warner Brothers, and the rest produced pictures for distribution to chains of movie houses that they often owned. The radio networks were next. NBC, CBS, and ABC produced radio programming for distribution in stations they owned or were affiliated with. Then there were the television networks. NBC, CBS, and ABC used their experience in radio and accumulated capital to create TV networks, and produced shows for their own and affiliate stations. Beginning in the 1970s, the growth of cable and satellite transmission brought a further expansion in the number of networks. Counting both TV and radio, these now number in the hundreds in the United States. If the primary result of the spread of print-based monologic networks was the emergence of the public sphere, that of the rise of audiovisual-based monologic counterparts was the appearance of what might be called the "entertainment sphere." Its structure is like that of the public sphere in that a relatively small set of strong nodes send messages to very large sets of weak nodes, who cannot respond in kind (or often at all). The difference is rather in content than form: communications in the public sphere tend to be a means to an end, whereas those in the entertainment sphere tend to be an end in themselves. We read the newspaper because we think we should in order to become better citizens (or some such). We watch TV because we enjoy it, full stop. Newspaper editors give you homework assignments; TV producers give you games to play during recess. In both cases, however, it's important to recognize that the activity is structured by the shape of the network: the editors and producers "speak" to you; you don't get to "talk back," at least directly.

That was the "is" of the situation: broadcasters would broadcast and recipients would receive. The "ought" needed to justify this lack of dialogue was already at hand, namely, a form of dictatorism that dictated some should rightfully speak for (or to) others. The Print Era had evolved this doctrine to deal with the concentration of presses in the hands of a relative few. The Audiovisual Era pushed it further to deal with the concentration of broadcast media in the hands of a relative fewer. Again we have two versions: the liberal one, under which those who speak through the audiovisual media are somehow winners in the "marketplace of ideas," and the illiberal one, under which those who speak through the audiovisual media know the Truth. Interestingly, in both cases the fiction of popular control is maintained: in liberal democracies, the "people" vote with their dollars and attention; in socialist one-party states, the "people" and the Vanguard Party are one and the same.

Range

Electromagnetic waves, including radio and TV signals, can travel a long way. Astronomers have detected infrared EM waves from celestial bodies 13.2 billion light-years from our sun.[110] The space probe *Voyager I* regularly sends super-high-frequency EM signals more than 10 billion miles back to earth.[111] They take 14 hours to get here. EM waves travel through space so well because they move in a straight line and nothing much gets in their way. The earth, however, is curved and covered with a soupy atmosphere, meaning that terrestrial EM broadcast won't travel as far. Still, if you have the right tools and some know-how, you can exchange them at considerable distance. "DXers" – enthusiasts who make a sport of pulling in distant radio and TV signals – can tune in stations thousands of miles away in good conditions. The signals bounce off the ionosphere and back down to earth, where the DXers pick them up with very sensitive equipment. Most people don't have this sort of equipment, but then again they don't need it. Good commercial broadcast stations can transmit signals between 10 and 50 miles, and any commercial radio and television can tune them in. But if you want to get radio from Australia or television from Taiwan, you can. You just need to buy a satellite dish or get cable and you'll get feeds from every part of the globe. We hardly need to point out that everyone within range – which is everyone – who has the proper equipment – which is not everyone, but most people – can receive a "copy" of whatever is being transmitted. That means enormous audiences, particularly for single events. On September 9, 1956, an estimated 60 million people tuned in to see Elvis Presley shake, rattle, and roll on *The Ed Sullivan Show*.[112] On September 26, 1960, a reported 75 million viewers watched the Nixon and Kennedy presidential debate.[113] On July 20, 1969, something on the order of 600 million people tuned in to see Neil Armstrong make one giant leap for mankind.[114] On September 6, 1997, a remarkable 2.5 billion people apparently watched some of Princess Diana's funeral.[115] Periodic events, like the Super Bowl and World Cup games, routinely gather audiences between 50 million and 100 million.[116] Primetime shows draw millions daily.[117]

Audiovisual media, then, has long range and great reach. Under the right conditions, speech can reach hundreds of people, manuscript-writing thousands, and print hundreds of thousands. Audiovisual media, however, reach many millions of people scattered all over the globe as a matter of course. Media such as these engender extensive networks, that is, networks in which information is passed over great distances and through large populations. We proposed that extensive networks would *diversify* social practices and the values accompanying them. Geographically large and demographically inclusive networks promote interaction among strangers more readily than those that are small and monochrome. Populations mix, and as a result both institutions and worldviews become diverse, or at least tolerant of diversity.

Diversification is everywhere apparent in the Audiovisual Era. In the Speech and Manuscript Eras, people's knowledge was more or less confined to what they experienced in their own daily lives, which were almost always narrow. You knew your people and what they did. What others did, you could not know. Print broadened people's horizons to some degree by bringing them "foreign" experiences to read. You had never hunted sperm whales in the Atlantic, traveled by caravan over the Silk Road, or had tea with the Queen at Buckingham Palace. But you could read about doing all these things from people who had, or at least could convincingly pretend they had. As a diversifying agent, however, print had drawbacks: it was comparatively difficult to distribute, not everyone could decode it, and there were many different and mutually unintelligible codes. Print's reach, therefore, was limited. Not so audiovisual media. They truly "democratized" experience."[118] Radio and TV could be beamed anywhere: physical transportation was in most cases unnecessary. Anyone could "get" it: you didn't have to learn the code because you already knew it. And the cultural barrier was low: the visual code was universal, and the audio code often unnecessary for enjoyment. Audiovisual media brought whaling, caravanning, high tea, and everything else anyone had ever experienced or imagined experiencing to the masses at a cost they could bear and in a language they could understand. With audiovisual media, you could really "see" the world and never leave your couch. Of course, all of your experiences would be vicarious. But what did it matter? Real experiences were expensive, uncomfortable, and often boring. Audiovisual experiences were always cheap, unthreatening, and carefully chosen precisely for excitement.

That was the "is" of the situation: the audiovisual media allowed people to trade experiences and therefore broaden their experiential horizons in a way previously unimaginable. The "ought" developed to legitimate this mixing and expansion was a new form of pluralism that generally goes by the name "multiculturalism."[119] Multiculturalism is essentially the Print Era's doctrine of toleration adapted for a new media ecology. Both share the central notion that there are no "strangers" in the sense of unclassifiable people or things. We and everything around us are "us" or "them." But there are subtle differences. Toleration emphasized the similarity of "us" and "them"; multiculturalism stresses the differences. Toleration looked forward to a point at which people, however different to begin with, might become one; multiculturalism insists on preserving "diversity" now and forever. Toleration was premised on a qualified acceptance of behaviors; multiculturalism's permissiveness is nearly unbounded.

Persistence

Here are some remarkable facts. You can see one of the first photographs ever taken, a "heliograph" of a Dutch engraving – that is, a picture of a picture – produced by Nicéphore Niépce in 1825.[120] You can listen to one of the first sound recordings, a "phonautograph" of a French folk song produced by Édouard-Léon Scott de Martinville in 1860.[121] You can watch one of the earliest silent films, the so-called *Roundhay Garden Scene* produced by Louis Aimé Augustin Le Prince in 1888.[122] You can enjoy one of the earliest "talking pictures," Lee De

Forest's "phonofilm" of a barking dog of 1921.[123] You can listen to one of the first radio broadcasts, Frank L. Capp's recording of President Woodrow Wilson's Armistice Day Speech in 1923.[124] You can watch the first recorded TV signal, a shot of a dummy taken by the Scottish inventor John Logie Baird in 1927.[125]

In the last chapter, we noted that the longevity of any manuscript is a function of substrate, script, and language. The persistence of audiovisual media is also determined by only three factors: the medium in which they are recorded (the equivalent of writing's substrate); the means used for playback (a bit like writing's script); and, if they record writing or speech, language (just like writing). As the aforementioned examples indicate, audiovisual recordings are quite persistent. The recording media aren't necessarily very durable: vinyl, celluloid, magnetic tape, plastics all decay, and in some cases quite rapidly. The type of celluloid on which early films were recorded is both unstable and highly flammable. Needless to say, early films were lost in great numbers.[126] But audiovisual recordings can be easily transferred to more robust media – for example, from analog film to digital files – and thereby preserved indefinitely. Since the copies can be reproduced rapidly and cheaply, audiovisual recordings are also protected by remarkable redundancy. With something on the order of 100 million copies of Michael Jackson's album *Thriller* floating around, it's doubtful that it will ever be lost.[127] The techniques used to play *Thriller* back – analog recording onto vinyl disks or magnetic tape – are, however, rapidly becoming obsolete. If you can't play an audiovisual recording, then you have no audiovisual recording. But re-recording solves this problem as well. You can just take the old, nearly obsolescent format and re-record it in the new, very common one. Record companies, movie studios, and TV networks have been updating formats for some time. The current wave of updating – "digitization" – not only helps these companies preserve their product, but also enables them to sell you the same product *twice*. You bought *Thrille*r from them on vinyl. Now you can buy it from them again on CD. That's quite a business plan. Or is it? Unfortunately for audiovisual companies, new technology enables almost anyone to make and distribute multiple copies of their products, so they may never have the opportunity to sell you anything ever again. But we're getting ahead of ourselves. As for language obsolescence, it's really not an issue as of this moment. To be sure, there are recordings of extinct languages, and there will surely be more if current trends continue.[128] But the vast majority of all audiovisual productions have been and are recorded in major languages spoken by millions of people. None of these idioms is at risk of dying or morphing into something unintelligible, at least for the next several hundred years.

Audiovisual media, we can safely conclude, are quite persistent. Your embarrassing collection of '70s disco records will disappear, but – alas – disco itself will never die. Persistent media give rise to additive networks, that is, those in which data accumulate rapidly. If you take your unloved disco albums to the thrift store, they will take their place in the bins next to all the other unloved disco albums. In places where disco is still the rage, even more disco albums are being produced, adding further to the awful total. According to our theory, additive networks *historicize* social practices evolved in and around them. In such networks, the artifacts of the past build up in the present, making progressively more of the past visible and manipulable. Time horizons recede; history is written and rewritten.

There can be no doubt that audiovisual media historicized social practices. Writing made the human past more visible than speaking. Printing made it more visible than writing. But in neither case could one really "see" or "hear" what had happened before. Audiovisual media changed that. They transmitted the sights and sounds of the past to the present so that the past could be "replayed" in a stream that anyone could "get." This ability – to travel, as it were, to the past and see it and hear it as it was – proved extraordinarily attractive to the powerful, the powerless, and everyone else interested in re-experiencing what had happened "before." The result was the practice of audiovisual "documentation." The idea of documentation – "the accumulation, classification, and dissemination of information"[129] – was conceived in its modern form by bibliographers in the early twentieth century.[130] Its object was paper, or rather the data on paper. But the term quickly migrated to nonfiction film. In a review of Robert Flaherty's 1926 film about Samoans, *Moana*, the Scotsman John Grierson wrote that the film had "documentary value."[131] The name "documentary" stuck. By 1932, the British Commission on Education and Cultural Films could report "A deliberate documentary film must be a transcript of real life, a bit of what actually happened, under approximately unrehearsed conditions."[132] Around the same time, "documentation" migrated to folk music, just, as it happens, as the American Works Progress Administration launched a massive project to "document" – that is, record – American folk songs.[133] Audiovisual "documentation" began as an elite phenomenon, the kind of thing film-makers and government-funded musicologists did. But as the price of cameras and recording devices declined following World War II, audiovisual "documentation" became a mass phenomenon. By the late 1960s, almost anyone could make a "documentary" of their family (that is, a "home movie") and any would-be Woodie Guthrie could record his songs (that is, make a "basement tape"). If you were born after, say, 1970, it is quite likely that you or one of your kin have a relatively complete audiovisual record of your life, or at least the major events of your life. With it, you can travel back in time to hear and see yourself, or so it seems.

The most significant historicizing impact of audiovisual documentation, however, was mass surveillance. Of course, suspicious people have always been listening, watching, and recording (usually by writing) what they heard and saw. But until the advent of audiovisual media, they had to do it in person or by proxy. That made surveillance expensive – hiring people to inform on other people is not cheap – and ambiguous – oral and written reports tend to be fuzzy. Affordable bugs and video cameras made mass surveillance inexpensive and seemingly unambiguous.[134] It's hardly surprising, then, that they proved quite useful to those with an interest in listening and watching. In the past several decades, surveillance devices have spread to a host of public spaces: parks, shops, offices, roads, and just about any other place where anyone might do something wrong. They are found in many private spaces as well, for example, in the homes of people who use "monitors" to listen to and watch their children and those who take care of them.[135] The ubiquity of audiovisual surveillance, in turn, has changed the way we act. We all know that we can be "caught" by these machines, and therefore we behave accordingly. You might be able to refute a written account of you running a red light, but "pictures don't lie."

Interestingly, our faith in the probative value of the audiovisual record spawned an interest in how that record might be manipulated for one greater good or another. The Soviets took an early lead. Since Lenin didn't really like the way the Winter Palace was seized in 1917 – a walk-over followed by a drunken riot – he had it restaged in 1920 and made a propaganda film.[136] As far as many Soviet citizens knew, the film *was* the storming of the Winter Palace as it actually happened. But what to do about embarrassing historical photos, like the ones that showed Lenin and Stalin working hand-in-glove with "Enemies of the People" like Trotsky? Stalin knew.[137] If Trotsky is in the photo, take him out. No Trotsky, no problem. Richard Nixon's aides did a similar sort of thing with the so-called Watergate Tapes, that is, tapes of conversations between the president and his lieutenants recorded in the Oval Office.[138] The tapes apparently had something quite damaging on them, so Nixon had an 18.5-minute segment erased. No tape, no problem. Over time, the art of doctoring audiovisual records became much more sophisticated. Today that art is so advanced that recordings, photos, and film no longer have the same "documentary" value that they once had. You never know whether a recording has been "remixed," a photograph has been "Photoshopped," or a film has been "green screened."

That was the "is" of the situation: audiovisual media enable us to capture and preserve more of the present than was ever possible with speech, writing, or printing. The "ought" evolved to justify audiovisual archiving was a robust form of temporalism that we might call "vigilism." Recall that the central idea in any mode of temporalism is that things change over time. Vigilism takes this idea and adds another: that we *should* record things as they change so that we can compare past and present. Sometimes vigilism is innocent, as when we compile garage-band recordings, family photo albums, and home movies. Here, vigilism tells us not to miss the "Kodak moment." But, more often, vigilism serves as a justification for keeping other people in line. Here, vigilism tells us that we must be watchful or we will suffer at the hands of others, that we will need an incontrovertible, permanent record of their misdeeds should they act badly, that this "proof" may be our only defense against chaos. Of course we value our privacy, but vigilism tells us that we must sacrifice a major part of it so that good order can be preserved. And besides, "we" have nothing to worry about, because "we" aren't going to do anything wrong.

Searchability

Like unrecorded speech, broadcast audiovisual messages can't be searched at all because they vanish into the ether. Recorded audiovisual messages can be searched, but it's not easy. Many of us have probably had the following frustrating experience. You want to show someone a scene in a movie, for example when Bogart says "Play it again, Sam" in *Casablanca*. You've got the videotape cued up. But where is the scene, exactly? All you remember is that it's in the first half of the film. There is no scene index telling you when Sam plays "As Time Goes By," because videos don't have such finding aids – almost no audiovisual media do (though that's changing). So you begin to hunt and peck. Fast forward. Watch. No, not there. Back up. Watch. No not there. Start again. Finally, you've found it. Only your recollection has deceived you. Bogart doesn't say "Play it again, Sam." Instead, he says, "If she can stand it, I can! Play it!"[139] This is one of the most memorable – and most misremembered – scenes in all of film history. Finding it should have been a snap. But it took some time, because you didn't really know where it was and there was nothing to tell you. Now imagine trying to locate a random scene – say footage of a three-legged dog – in a vast film archive. How would you do it? Well, you need to gain access to a vast film archive. There aren't many of these and they don't let just anyone in. But let's say you find an archive and they let you in. Now you have to search through the films. If there are no good finding aids (and there usually aren't), that means you are going to have to watch them one after another until you come upon your hobbled dog, if it's there at all. That is going to take time, particularly if the archive is large. Before you find the crippled dog footage, if you find it at all, you are probably going to have to watch a lot of films, meaning you are going to "find" a lot of "non–three-legged-dog" before you find any "three-legged-dog." That's not very efficient. But then again, neither is the entire process. It would probably be faster just to find a three-legged dog and film it yourself.

Audiovisual materials, then, are not very searchable, or at least they haven't been until recently.[140] In most cases, you simply have to go through them in order to get what you want. That's time-consuming and yields a lot more noise than signal. Media that are not readily searchable generate unmapped networks, ones that do not have an accurate, fine-grained system of addresses. Because information on the network as a whole cannot be easily found and recovered, it tends to clump in particular nodes. Our theory predicts that unmapped media networks will *professionalize* social practices evolved in and around them.

Since information becomes concentrated in certain nodes, inequalities of knowledge appear. Some know more than others, and those who do often join forces to perfect, protect, and otherwise restrict access to their special knowledge.

In the last chapter, we saw how the spread of print worked to both weaken some professions (theology) and strengthen many new ones (those taught in the university). Audiovisual media had a similar effect, though all in all, much milder. Although the live entertainment industry was hardly destroyed by the advent of records, movies, radio, and TV, it was appreciably changed. The theater, music hall, vaudeville circuit, burlesque show, and their live cousins came to occupy a small niche in a huge, audiovisual-centered entertainment market. The special knowledge that was required to put on one of these shows was no longer in high demand, and so these "professions" shrank and faded. More accurately, they were winnowed and concentrated in audiovisual production units run by record companies, movie studios, radio networks, and television networks. In the beginning, the only acts these outfits could broadcast were ones that had been developed in the old world of live entertainment. Music hall singers, theater company actors, vaudevillians, and Borscht-Belt comics were all staples of the early audiovisual broadcasts.[141]

But the studios soon began to develop their own talent. "Develop" is exactly the right word, for it gets to the heart of the difference between the old live theater world and the new broadcast world. In the theater world, performers toured widely and only occasionally had the opportunity to appear before very large audiences or even the same audience many times. The act was often more important than the performer, though there were exceptions (e.g., Sarah Bernhardt). In the broadcast world, performers would be – or, rather, could be – seen by millions many times. As audiences grew and faces were committed to memory, viewers began to do something somewhat unexpected: they strongly identified with the performers. The star became just as important, or more important, than the act. It didn't take long for the studios to realize that stars could be *made* if the right promotional techniques were employed.[142] They set about building the legal, technical, and artistic infrastructure of the modern star system. Raw talent would be taken and re-fashioned into an image that tested well. Proto-stars were put under contract, that is, required to do what the studio said. They were re-named (Rock Hudson *né* Roy Harold Scherer Jr.), given new biographies, and told to embody certain personae.[143] Special vehicles were written and produced to suit their characters, be they tough, loving, sexy, sentimental or what have you. Promotional campaigns were carefully crafted, replete with leaks that weren't leaks and scandals that were made up. Thus, the "dream factory" was built. The degree to which it operated in any given sphere of audiovisual media varied. The movie studios were the most proficient star-makers, with the record companies, radio, and TV networks lagging but putting in a good effort. The point to remember, though, is that only these nodes in the network had the resources and know-how to make a star. They made "show business" a modern business. And they were and are very good at what they do, as they can make almost anyone – whether they have "talent" or not – into a star, or at least a reasonably well-known and therefore bankable celebrity. How else do you explain Pamela Anderson?

That was the "is" of the situation: those who knew how to make stars made them and those who didn't listened to and watched them. The "ought" deployed to justify this clumping of useful knowledge was a form of collectivism that stressed the essential and highly valuable contribution that audiovisual "professionals" made to the commonweal. They were allowed to use the public airwaves, were permitted to serve as guardians of the pubic culture, were paid handsomely by the public itself, and were, therefore, bound to act in the public interest. They had, as the saying goes, a "civic duty." Once more we see two variants on this doctrine, both born in the Print Era. According to the weak version, found in capitalist nations, the moguls and the stars they made were simply encouraged to contribute to the betterment of the nation, though they were under no strict obligation to do so. If they didn't, of course, they would likely suffer at the record store, box office, or in the ratings game. So when they were asked to pony up, pitch in, or come around, they usually did.[144] According to the strong version, found in socialist countries, the moguls and stars had no choice in the matter: they were the people.[145]

In Plato's story, King Leontius could not help himself. Even though he was a reasonable man, reason could not restrain his curious eyes. He had to look at the corpses rotting under the gallows, and he felt ashamed that he could not stop himself. In one sense, audiovisual media have made Leontiuses of us all. We all have to look, even when we know in our heart of hearts we shouldn't. The reason is that there is something deeply psychologically compelling about audiovisual media, something more forceful than talking or reading. This fact is demonstrated every day of our lives. We live in a world of relatively unconstrained media choices. In our own free time, we can talk, read, listen, or watch as we choose. And what do we choose? The answer is obvious: we listen and watch more often, for longer, and more pleasurably than we talk and read. Further proof of this native preference is the fact that the choice is largely independent of content. When faced with reading a good book or watching an awful TV show, most people will watch the awful TV show. And here we come to the difference between Leontius and us. He felt guilty about his compulsion to look at things not deserving of his attention, things that might do him harm, things that teach nothing. We don't. We say everything is worthy of our attention – only snobs think otherwise. We say nothing heard or said can do us harm – only prudes think otherwise. And we say everything teaches something useful – only the narrow-minded think otherwise.

We may or may not be right in holding these opinions. But as we've tried to point out in this chapter, there is good reason to believe that they are themselves a product of audiovisual media. The audiovisual media – like all media – have physical attributes that engender particular kinds of networks, networks that in turn produce certain kinds of social practices and values. Table 5 summarizes this process with regard to audiovisual media.

Naturally, audiovisual media do not necessarily generate these results and, when they do, do not generate them to the same degree. The impact of media can be blunted and, with great effort, even eliminated. Try to picture a society in which everyone owned, say, a television broadcaster-receiver. That would make TV very accessible on both the send and receive sides. Let's say, further, that these personal TV broadcaster-receivers had some strange attributes. They can be simply concealed, making TV private on both the send and receive sides. They can transmit nothing but text, making them low fidelity. They can transmit only short messages irregularly, making TV low volume. They broadcast only over a short radius, making TV short range. Everything

TABLE 5. *The Effects of Audiovisual Media*

A/V	Medium Attribute	→	Network Attribute	→	Social Practices	→	Values
Accessibility	= Low (Send)	→	Concentrated (Send)	→	Hierarchicalized (Send)	→	Elitism (Send)
	High (Receive)	→	Diffused (Receive)		→ Equalized (Receive)		→ Egalitarianism (Receive)
Privacy	= Low (Send)	→	Connected (Send)		→ Open (Send)		→ Publicism (Send)
	High (Receive)	→	Segmented (Receive)		→ Closed (Receive)		→ Privatism (Receive)
Fidelity	= High	→	Iconic		→ Sensualized		→ Realism
Volume	= High	→	Unconstrained		→ Hedonized		→ Hedonism
Velocity	= Low	→	Monologic		→ Centralized		→ Authoritarianism
Range	= High	→	Extensive		→ Diversified		→ Pluralism
Persistence	= High	→	Additive		→ Historicized		→ Temporalism
Searchability	= Low	→	Unmapped		→ Professionalized		→ Collectivism

they transmit is recorded, making TV persistent. Finally, what they transmit is well indexed, making TV highly searchable.

In theory, all this could be done. In practice, however, it hasn't been and probably can't be. As was the case with print, many powerful organized interests – churches, states, parties, corporations – have sought to control audiovisual media or alter their natural effects. And as with print, they have done so in the name of ideas across the entire political spectrum. But they have all failed. Almost everywhere, audiovisual media did what audiovisual media naturally do. Thus, modern societies, whether they be capitalist or communist, democratic or authoritarian, developed or primitive, seem awfully similar as regards the way audiovisual media are deployed. Everywhere we find audiovisual media concentrated in the hands of a relative few. Those few, however, are at least nominally dedicated to providing a public service. Everywhere we find people consume audiovisual media primarily in private according to their own tastes. The right to watch and listen to what you will is enshrined in the laws and customs of almost every nation on the planet, although of course it is often disregarded. Everywhere we find the audiovisual media dominated by entertainment, usually of the low-brow variety. Content through the audiovisual channel is usually meant to stimulate, not educate. Everywhere people consume audiovisual media, but they almost never produce it. No one really talks back to their TV set, nor do they seem to want to. Almost everywhere we find incredible variety in the audiovisual media – it spans the globe and brings the globe into your living room. The exception here, and it's an important one, are illiberal regimes that impose censorship on foreign broadcasts. They, however, are dying. Everywhere we find vast repositories of audiovisual materials, not only in the hands of consumers, but also in libraries and archives. These cultural "treasures" are often protected by the state in the interests of the public. And finally, everywhere we find what amounts to a guild of audiovisual producers, a cast of professionals who know how to "do" audiovisual magic. People do not themselves know how to produce audiovisual items, and they do not generally want to learn how.

This, then, is Audiovisual Culture, the product of the audiovisual media and the organized interests that brought it into being. Judging its success is made difficult by the fact that it is not very old and really still with us. It seems likely, however, that it will not be with us for long (see the following chapter). So on that score – longevity – it is a failure compared to Talking Culture, Manuscript Culture, and Print Culture. Whether it is – or was – good for humanity is an open and much debated question. No one seems to doubt the value of talking, writing, or print for the human project. Many critics, however, wonder whether the audiovisual media have contributed anything of lasting worth to our collective endeavor. And it must be admitted that these critics have a point, for the audiovisual media seem to naturally appeal to our desire for diversion rather than our need for edification. Audiovisual media may, as one detractor says, cause us to "amuse ourselves to death."[146] But we will never find out, for the Audiovisual Era is passing out of existence even now. It is, as we will presently see, being pushed aside by a medium whose message is even more mixed – the Internet.

5

HOMO SOMNIANS
Humanity in the Age of the Internet

– Next then, I said . . . Picture people as dwelling in a cavernous underground chamber, with the entrance opening upward to the light, and a long passage-way running down the whole length of the cave. They have been there since childhood, legs and necks fettered so they cannot move: they see only what is in front of them, unable to turn their heads because of the bonds.

– A strange image, he said, and strange prisoners.

– Like ourselves, I replied.[1]
> – Plato, *The Republic*, 514A

In Plato's cave, nobody sees what's really happening. They think they do, but they don't. Plato says we are like the cave dwellers. We think we see the Truth, but we don't. The difference is that we can see the Truth if we know how. Plato knew how and wanted to show us. But Plato also knew that we – or at least most of us – are either incapable of or uninterested in coming to grips with the Truth. Philosophers have the way and the will, but the rest of humanity doesn't. We are quite happy living in our pleasant illusions, far removed from the Truth. This is why we build the imaginary worlds – dramas – that Plato found so disturbing. For what are storytelling, literature, and theater but attempts to escape from reality into some fantasy? The storytellers, writers, and thespians all say we can learn something about ourselves from their productions. But what do we learn, really, if all that is depicted is fiction? Fiction cannot be the Truth, for it is the opposite of the Truth. And even those productions that claim to be something other than fiction – histories and the like – aren't they simply poor reflections of a reality that is gone and cannot be revisited, and therefore really fictions themselves?

Perhaps they are, and perhaps they aren't. In any case, Plato was on firm ground in asserting that we naturally seek the comfort of illusions. He would not, therefore, be at all surprised by what we have done with the Internet. For there we have created a cave of absolutely immense proportions. In it we see only the reflections of real people and things, the shadows they leave for us to observe on the screens before us. Unlike his prisoners, we are aware that they are there behind the electronic wall. Yet we don't know who or what they "really" are, and we don't much care. It's usually better if we don't know, for that makes the illusion more powerful. All that is important to us is that they provide gratification, that they present a virtual reality that is satisfying to us. Some part of it may not be agreeable, but the cave is so large and its variety so great that we can be certain we will find something diverting, amusing, or even useful in it. Just what that something is will happily remain our own business, because, although there are millions of us in the cave, we are functionally alone. The prisoners in Plato's cave cannot see each other. Neither can we see each other on the Internet, that is, if we don't want to be seen. We are free, therefore, to look where we will without regard for the judgments of others. An added benefit is that we, unlike Plato's shackled captives, can cast our own shadows. This is both enjoyable for us and pleasing to others. Whether our projections are truthful, reasonable, or dignified is largely beside the point. For the point of our virtual world is to entertain and be entertained, and that goal is sometimes best achieved by lies, foolishness, and impropriety. Most important, we believe that none of it matters precisely because we are in the cave and not in real life. We reject absolutely one of Plato's central premises, namely, that playing at acting badly and watching other people play at acting badly will somehow harm us.

Perhaps we are right, and perhaps we are not. Time will tell. It is certain, however, that we are currently in the middle of a significant change in the way we communicate with one another, a change brought by the Internet. As we will presently see, the change was sudden and is having a significant – though all in all, predictable – impact on the way we organize ourselves and think about what is right and what is wrong. Plato believed we should seek the Truth. The Internet suggests other ends.

In order to show that the "pull" theory of media evolution explains the rise of the Internet, we need to demonstrate two theses. First, we must show that the technology behind the Internet was available some time before the Internet itself. If it were, then it makes sense to conclude that people could have developed the Internet but didn't because demand was insufficient. Second, we need to show that some new moment in world history made existing media – talking, manuscript-writing, printing, and audiovisual media – insufficient for the purposes of some organized group or groups, and that this or these groups elaborated a preexisting technical capacity – in this case, the ability to network computers – into a new medium.

What evidence, primary and secondary, can be brought to bear on these two propositions? On the one hand, we have all the data we need at our fingertips because the Internet and the social practices and values we claim it engenders are all around us. Any careful observer of the Web and modern life should be able to judge whether and to what extent the theory we have presented is valid. On the other hand, our task is made difficult by the very fact that we are immersed in a new and evolving phenomenon. No one offered a compelling explanation of the impact of talking, manuscript-writing, print, or audiovisual media in the early days of those modes of communication. Although the literature pertaining to the effects of the Internet is already large and growing quickly, what's on offer – much of which is somewhat hyperbolic[2] – is disappointingly vague.[3] It may just be too early in the game to gain the perspective needed to offer an accurate assessment of what the Internet is doing and will do. Maybe, but probably not. As we'll presently see, in the instance of the Internet, the past is a remarkably good guide to the future.

The Internet before the Internet

The story of the Web properly begins in sixteenth-century Europe during the Scientific Revolution, for it was then and there that the project that would end in the Internet was conceived in its modern form. That project was the systematic collection, classification, and dissemination of knowledge for the purpose of scientific progress.[4] The initial spurs that urged European thinkers to pay close attention to data gathering, classification, and dissemination were two. The first spur was the revival of ancient Greek scientific interests and practices. Aristotle and his peers stimulated Europeans to think anew about the world of the senses, the more so now that their many works were widely available thanks to print. No better example of the new attention to data collection, classification, and dissemination can be given than that of Tycho Brahe, whose exact observations of celestial bodies helped his assistant, Johannes Kepler, formulate his eponymous laws of planetary motion and revolutionize our understanding of cosmology.[5] The second spur was imperialism. The people of the Renaissance had the good fortune of "discovering" (to put it very mildly) new worlds, and when they did, they imported new things from them by the ton. These novelties were often categorized and displayed in early museums of natural history – cabinets of curiosities (*Kunstkammern* or *Wunderkammern*). Scientifically minded elites created the first such institutions in the mid-sixteenth century.[6] By all reports they were big hits. The impulse to collect and catalogue was a characteristic of the age, as we can see in the path-breaking methodological writings of Francis Bacon, proto-information scientist *par excellence*. Bacon is most famous for the saying "knowledge is power."[7] He seems to have believed it. In a number of still-read books, Bacon outlined a program to banish ignorance and superstition by collecting, measuring, analyzing, and comparing everything. Like so many ambitious programs, it proved largely unworkable.

Happily, some of Bacon's fellows and followers were rather more practical than he. The founders of the early scientific societies not only theorized about collecting and exchanging data, they created organizations to do it. The result of their handiwork can be seen in the Italian *Accademia dei Lincei* (founded 1603), the English Royal Society (founded 1660), the French *Académie des sciences* (founded 1666), the Prussian *Akademie der Wissenschaften* (founded 1724), and the Russian *Akademiia nauk* (founded 1724).[8] Before these societies, natural philosophers had only very limited means to discuss their work with like-minded colleagues. The early scientific societies and state-sponsored institutions – especially research universities – improved this situation dramatically. Together they created the basic structure for handling scholarly information that persisted until the birth of the Internet. This system comprised three institutions. The first was the *library*, which allowed scientific information to accumulate in one place for easy access. The second was the *index*, which permitted information in the library to be retrieved. And the third was the *article* (in a book or journal), which allowed scientists to share information at a distance. The entire system worked in a loop: scientists produced journals that fed the libraries that were indexed by bibliographers who then supplied them to scientists who produced more journals, and so on.

The new system of scholarly communications constituted a real step forward, but it was by no means perfect. Far from it. Libraries concentrated information, which was good. But they also isolated it, which was bad. You had to go to the library, it could not come to you. So if you weren't near the library you needed or if you were near and couldn't get in, you were out of luck. Indexes helped you find information, which was good. But they also hid it from you, which was bad. Alphabetical or subject indexes generally do not penetrate – or do not penetrate very far – the items they index. In an ordinary card catalogue, you get the author, title, a few subject headings, and the book's location in the stacks. Almost everything between the covers is obscured. This is to say that you really had to know exactly what you were looking for before you started to look, and this is inconvenient if you don't know quite what you want. Articles provided a convenient means to share scientific information on a specific topic, which was good. But they shared the deficiencies of the library and the index, which was bad. That is, if you didn't have access to the article for whatever reason – a subscription cost too much, the library lost it, your dog ate it – it might as well not exist. And even if you did have access to it, there was no really efficient method to find out exactly what was in it other than to read it carefully – not a very efficient way to track down specific facts. In short, the entire thing didn't work well for people who: (a) didn't have access to a big library; (b) didn't know exactly what they were looking for; and (c) didn't have the time or patience to read everything that might have what they wanted. That pretty much describes everyone who wasn't a student or professor at a university.

The problem was recognized. As early as the eighteenth century, enlightened souls were trying to figure out ways to improve scholarly communications and bring trustworthy knowledge to the people who needed it. The French *encyclopedistes* felt that the existing mechanism of separating truth from superstition, disseminating the former and discarding the latter, was wanting. To rectify this sorry situation, Denis Diderot, Jean le Rond d'Alembert, and their *philosophe* allies revived an old (Greek, as it happens) idea – the encyclopedia.[9] They set themselves the task of compiling all that was true and useful in one place for all time. The result was the epoch-making thirty-five-volume *Encyclopédie, ou dictionnaire raisonné des sciences, des arts et des métiers* (1751–). Yet the *Encyclopédie* and its imitators (especially the *Encyclopedia Britannica* [1768–] and the *Brockhaus Enzyklopädie* [1796–]) were limited by the medium in which they were produced, namely print. Books are fine for many purposes, but if your object is to provide a universal store of knowledge in which anything can be found instantly and anything can be amended as needed, they are not ideal. Anyone who has every used a print encyclopedia knows that they are big but not complete; well-indexed, though not well enough; and often updated, though never really current.

Print not only limited the degree to which scholarly communications could be perfected, it also limited the imaginations of the men and women who were trying to perfect it. Diderot, d'Alembert, and the Enlightenment gang just couldn't conceive of a way to store, find, and transmit information outside the ink-and-paper paradigm. A bit latter, however, some began to see past the printed book. One such visionary was the French bibliographer and information scientist Paul Otlet.[10] Otlet didn't much like books. He felt – correctly – that they concealed as much as they revealed. They were full of data that was basically hidden from researchers and, more importantly to the progressive, Internationalist Otlet, hidden from humankind in general. To Otlet, the existing means of storing, categorizing, and conveying information hindered human progress. But Otlet had a solution – the humble 3 × 5 index card. Otlet and his colleagues wanted to use the index card to crack the book, that is, to extract from the standard scientific print medium every bit of discrete information it held. According to Otlet's plan, these unique bits would be recorded on 3 × 5 cards and classified according to an exhaustive universal index so that information could be found and easily retrieved. He called his index the "Universal Decimal Classification." It was a kind of Dewey Decimal System on steroids. Otlet even dreamed of creating a Rube Goldberg-esque workstation in which scholars would use levers to find and extract cards from his massive universal card catalogue. It was all quite mad. The engineering problems presented by print made Otlet's vision utterly impractical. For all that he was ahead of his time, Otlet was still thinking in terms of print.

New technologies such as microfilm inspired his followers to think past print, sort of. One of the most obvious problems with print as a mode of communications is its bulk and weight. A piece of paper is small, but thousands of pieces of paper are big. A piece of paper is light, but thousands of pieces of paper are heavy. Big, heavy things are expensive to transport. This makes them unattractive as media (cf. stone tablets). One way to surmount this problem, however, is to shrink the big heavy thing into a small light thing. Publishers have known this trick for centuries, and they have endeavored to test the limits of human vision by publishing ever smaller books with ever smaller type. Interestingly, if you are really devoted (not to say crazy), you can pack a lot of text into a very small place by hand. According to legend, followers of Mao inscribed the entire contents of his *Little Red Book* on a six-sided die. Such feats are impressive, but not very practical. The real breakthrough in tiny text came with the invention of practical photography by Louis Daguerre in 1839.[11] It took less than a year for one of Daguerre's admirers, the lens grinder John Benjamin Dancer of Manchester, to begin miniaturizing photographs for viewing under microscopes. In its early days, microphotography was nothing but a novelty. Rene Dagron of Paris was given the first microphotography patent in 1859. His chief product was a tiny image embedded in a tiny viewer embedded in a tiny trinket. Yet a few forward-thinking people at the time recognized that microphotography might be made to serve more practical purposes. In 1859, the same year Dagron patented his bauble, the *Photographic News* wrote that microphotography might allow "the whole archives of a nation [to be] packed away in a small snuff box."[12] Given the state of miniaturization at the time, it would have had to have been a very big snuff box. But no one needed to build such a box, because no one was really thinking of putting government archives on tiny bits of photographic paper – governments had more important things to think about.

Businesses didn't. In the early twentieth century, banks – theretofore used largely by rich folks and merchants – became truly retail businesses. Everyone began to use them, and thus they found themselves having to track millions of transactions, not only deposits and withdrawals (done at the bank, so easily recorded), but also checking activity (done off site with third parties, so more difficult to record). In the mid-1920s, New York banker George McCarthy saw in microphotography a potential solution to the bank's paperwork problem.[13] With this in mind, the plucky money man invented the "Checkograph," a device that produced microfilm copies of checks flowing through financial institutions. For obvious reasons, Eastman Kodak loved the Checkograph, bought it from McCarthy in 1928, and began to sell microfilming services under its Recordak brand. By the 1940s, governments, university libraries, and corporations began to microfilm their holdings. They did so with some urgency. Even as Recordak filmed, entire cities were being wiped off the map in World War II, taking entire government archives, academic libraries, and corporate vaults with them. The ordinarily upbeat President Franklin Roosevelt stressed that the United States needed to microfilm everything "so that if any part of the country's original archives are destroyed a record of them will exist in some other place."[14] He uttered these words a bit over a month after the Pearl Harbor attack in which, as a matter of fact, "original archives" had been destroyed by Japanese bombers. It seems he expected more of this to come. If he did, he was right.

The notion that microfilm might be used to preserve and disseminate *some* knowledge – banking records, government archives, and such – rather naturally led the futurist H. G. Wells to the idea that it might be used to preserve and disseminate *all* knowledge. Wells proposed the creation of a "Permanent World Encyclopedia" that would capture and convey all of the world's wisdom by means of very tiny text.[15] "At the core of such an institution," he writes, "would be a world synthesis of bibliography and documentation with the indexed archives of the world. A great number of workers would be engaged perpetually in perfecting this index of human knowledge and keeping it up to date. Concurrently, the resources of micro-photography, as yet only in their infancy, will be creating a concentrated visual record." Such a record is, he says, already being created by "American microfilm experts" who are making "facsimiles of the rarest books, manuscripts, pictures and specimens, which can then be made easily accessible upon the library screen." By means of this remarkable technology, he gushes, "there is no practical obstacle whatever now to the creation of an efficient index to all human knowledge, ideas and achievements, to the creation, that is, of a complete planetary memory for all mankind." One suspects that Wells did not have much hands-on experience of the "practical obstacles" presented by microfilm. Indeed, as anyone who has ever used it can attest, such enthusiasm for microfilm can only have been born of never having used it. Wells, it seems, never touched the stuff.

The next wave of information scientists had probably used microfilm, so they knew to look elsewhere for inspiration. The elsewhere in question was in the rapidly developing field of information-handling machines. The notion that one could use mechanical means – wedges, gears, levers, etc. – to store information and even solve mathematical problems was hardly new. The people who built Stonehenge over 4,000 years ago knew it; the Greeks who built devices to predict the position of celestial bodies in the second century BC knew it; the inventors of the slide rule in the seventeenth century knew it. So did one Vannevar Bush, engineer, science tsar, and technological visionary.[16] In the first of these capacities, Bush built the "Differential Analyzer" in 1927, a device that could solve complicated differential equations very quickly and accurately. In the second capacity, Bush ran the Office for Scientific Research and Development, the bureau that oversaw the Manhattan Project and all military research in the United States during World War II. In the final capacity, Bush wrote "As We May Think," an essay published in the Atlantic Monthly in 1945.[17]

Today Bush is remembered primarily for "As We May Think." It's little wonder, for it is a remarkably prescient essay. In it, he plainly says that gummed-up scientific communications are a huge problem. "Professionally," he writes, "our methods of transmitting and reviewing the results of research are generations old and by now are totally inadequate for their purpose." Researchers produce more useful information than ever, but more than ever is simply lost due to an antiquated system of storage, search, and retrieval. "The summation of human experience," Bush complains, "is being expanded at a prodigious rate, and the means we use for threading through the consequent maze to the momentarily important item is the same as was used in the days of square-rigged ships." In a word, the print paradigm – libraries, indexes, and articles – just wasn't doing the job anymore, if it ever did.

Bush proposed that the basic problem was the linear way that information was stored, indexed, and retrieved in print. Finding a "record" in a library catalogue was like walking a narrow, confined path: you could go forward or backward, but you couldn't leave the trail. "The human mind," Bush pointed out, "does not work that way. It operates by association. With one item in its grasp, it snaps instantly to the next that is suggested by the association of thoughts, in accordance with some intricate web of trails carried by the cells of the brain." Bush dreamed of a workstation that could store and retrieve huge volumes of information, but which mimicked the way the brain related bits of data by subtle "associations." In the former aspect, Bush's "Memex" looks a lot like Otlet's data contraption, replete with levers, gears, buttons, and plenty of microfilm. It is the latter aspect – sorting by fuzzy, expandable, and user-directed association – that makes Bush's Memex noteworthy. Like Otlet, Bush dreamed of cracking the book, that is, finding a way to extract and isolate every bit of useful information in it. But his "associations" went beyond Otlet, for they allowed researchers to freely create new sources that could then be cracked by other researchers. "It is exactly," Bush wrote, "as though the physical items had been gathered together from widely separated sources and bound together to form a new book."

Bush was ahead of his time, not only in terms of his ideas but also in terms of the technology available to realize them. Yet help was on the way. It came from the U.S. Defense Department.[18] After World War II – which, as you will recall, had gone pretty badly for all sides involved, though worse for some than others – the American military became concerned about preventing "another Pearl Harbor." The U.S. generals had good reason to be worried, as the potential consequences of a sneak attack had grown much more terrible in the terrible nuclear age. So, they wisely set up a system of radar installations designed to detect airborne incursions from sea to shining sea. The radar bases worked fine, as radar itself had been thoroughly battle-tested during the aforementioned world war. In fact, the bases worked a little too well, that is, they provided too much information too fast for even the smartest generals to handle in a reasonable amount of time. And said generals did not, in fact, have a reasonable amount of time to sort through the reams of data and decide what to do, for the attacking planes – flying very fast – would arrive at their targets only minutes after the radars detected their presence. Something needed to be done to improve what the military calls "command and control" or, they said, we'd all be blown to hell. So the defense establishment decided to build a computer-aided information network, the world's first. Made operational in 1959, SAGE (Semi-Automatic Ground Environment) brought everything the decision makers needed to know – including radar images, an innovation – to central locations so the deciding could be done. SAGE also assisted the decision makers – via automation, another innovation – in scrambling fighters and guiding them to their airborne targets.[19] Once again, science and technology had made America safe.

But then another problem arose, a hypothetical one posed by one of the many professionally paranoid people governments employ to dream up nightmarish hypothetical scenarios. What would happen, this thinker of the unthinkable asked, if one of the enemy's bombers got through the radar-based, electronically linked, computer-assisted early-warning system and managed to drop a bomb on the system itself?[20] The answer was plain: the system would crash and take America's ability to make good decisions about what to do next with it. This just wouldn't do. So, in the early 1960s, the government decided to invest some effort in creating a more robust network, one that wouldn't collapse like a house of cards if one of its cards were pulled away (or blown to bits, as the case may be). Happily, there were some very smart young scientists working on just this problem at various well-thought-of universities around the globe. They proposed an ingenious solution: break the system's messages up into chunks, send the chunks through multiple paths in the network, and reassemble them at the end. That way, if any path were destroyed, the several parts of the message would still get through by traveling along other paths and could be reassembled as if nothing had happened. Humpty Dumpty *could* be put back together again. This disassembly-reassembly system was called "packet switching" over a "distributed network."[21] It seemed to be a good solution to the problem of network fragility, and the American government was pleased to fund and implement it.

But scientists working on the new communications system pointed out yet another problem, as scientists will. It's fine to switch packets and distribute networks, but the computers doing the switching and distributing have to be able to talk to one another. Computers, you may recall, were sort of new at the time, and a lot of people were building them. Computer companies generally built computers that could talk to the ones they built, but not to the ones that other people built. So there were a lot of computers that couldn't talk to one another, many of them in the American defense establishment itself, as it was the primary market for expensive computers. This was bad. But it wasn't the only difficulty, the scientists warned. Rather more selfishly, they noted that not only were mute computers bad for the nation's defense, they were also bad for science itself. You see, mathematicians, engineers, and physicists – all the folks who are so vital to America's security – love to talk to one another. They must do so, and often, in order to accomplish their work efficiently and effectively. If their computers couldn't talk to one another, neither could they, and science would suffer. So the scientists proposed a solution that would solve both the generals' problem and theirs: a set of computers and computer protocols (a sort of *lingua franca* for machines) that would link not only the defense establishment's computers in a distributed network, but theirs (or rather, those owned by their research institutes and universities) as well. The American government, being wealthy, worried, and respectful of scientists, decided to fund and implement this program too. So was the Advanced Research Projects Agency Network (ARPANET) born in 1969.[22]

Alas, neat though it was, ARPANET wasn't very useful if you weren't a general or a computer scientist. This was true for a variety of reasons, but the chief one was that you couldn't get to ARPANET from your network, wherever your network was. And there were several good ones in different places around the country and world. Just as a lot of computer companies were producing computers that couldn't talk to one another, there were serious establishments (especially scientific institutes and universities) creating networks that couldn't talk to one another. The military didn't care much, because it had its own network and, prizing secrecy as military folk will, didn't really want anyone else on it. But communications-hungry scientists did care, because they wanted to trade information in the service of scientific progress. What was needed, they said, was a network of networks, a massive grid that would enable every scientist to talk to every other scientist no matter what network he or she was on. As many parties and interests were involved, it took well over a decade, a lot of negotiation, and a boatload of money to create this "inter-network." But by the mid-1980s, the network of networks – the "Internet" – was alive and well, linking most big institutes and universities in the nation, and some overseas.[23]

Although the Internet was much bigger and more accessible than ARPANET, it was still pretty hard to use. You could exchange messages, files, and even run some programs remotely, but beyond that you couldn't really do much unless you were an expert. This bothered an English fellow named Tim Berners Lee. He worked at a big Swiss physics laboratory, and it was his job to make it simple for scientists to collaborate. Since it plainly wasn't simple, he set about designing a way to make the Internet useful as a collaborative tool. He figured that what people really wanted out of a network was access to things on computers, not computers themselves. After all, when you use the phone, you want to talk to someone, not simply connect to another phone. It's the same with the Internet. You want to use it to get information in documents, not to connect to computers. So in the early 1990s, he and a French colleague designed a system that used the Internet to store, receive, and send documents, and he called his invention the "World Wide Web."[24] On the World Wide Web, you seem to move from document to document, reading what you want and moving on. The computers are just where they should be, in the background. Technical people almost immediately recognized that the Web was extremely useful, and they made it a kind of a standard.

At this point, the Internet and the Web that ran on top of it were still obscure. People in the computer industry knew about it, because they make their living building gadgetry. Scientists knew about it, because they enjoy collaborating with colleagues in distant places. And, finally, geeks – especially young geeks – knew about it, because young geeky people make it their business to know about the latest technical advances. While the computer-builders were busy building networked computers for the collaborating scientists, a team of young geeks in Illinois had a monumental insight.[25] First, they noted that a lot of people were buying desktop PCs running the Windows or Macintosh operating systems, not UNIX, which was standard in "serious" computing. Second, they noted that these PCs could be hooked up to the Internet by phone lines. Third, they noted that our frustrated English fellow in Switzerland had already created a kind of software that made it easy to send, receive, and store multimedia documents on the Internet, although his program was kind of clunky and not very pretty. So these college students put one, two, and three together and set about creating a really intuitive, clean, multimedia "Web browser" for users of PCs.

The browser was something like a combination of a glossy magazine – full of pictures and text – and a TV beamed right into your home. It made the Internet easy to understand. In 1993, these college students *cum* entrepreneurs began to give their graphical Web browser away under the name "Mosaic." Suddenly it was not only easy to get on the Internet, but once you were there, it was easy to get around. By the mid-1990s, "surfing the net" was an activity like reading the newspaper, listening to radio, or watching TV, although there wasn't much in the way of newspapers, radio, or TV on it.

"Pulling" the Internet into Existence

And so the Internet was born. Its deepest roots, as we've pointed out, were scientific. In this sense, the Internet is the fulfillment of the 400-year-old dream that information might be collected, stored, and sifted easily, efficiently, and endlessly. Yet science itself did not "pull" the Internet into existence in the last quarter of the twentieth century. No, there were larger systemic forces at work, all of which are hinted at in the story we have just told. Generalizing, they were three: information capitalism, the surveillance state, and cultural privatism.

First, there was information capitalism.[26] Industrial capitalism, a product of the eighteenth century and one of the motive forces behind the spread of audiovisual media, is about producing goods. It still exists, as we still need things produced industrially, for there is no more efficient way to make them. But, beginning in the twentieth century, industrial capitalists noted two things. First, they saw that the data-handling requirements of modern business were becoming a drag on productivity and, more important, on profitability. Second, they understood that the return on investment in research and development could be significant, particularly in a legal framework that protected intellectual property and an economic framework – the public company – that allowed rapid financing and development. These two insights put a new and higher premium on information production, manipulation, and storage. Knowledge might be power, but information was money. Companies became interested in what were aptly called "business machines." Calculating engines had been around since the seventeenth century. Both Pascal and Leibniz built them.[27] By the 1880s, they were being produced commercially, and by the 1890s, they were becoming common in offices throughout the developed world. The companies that made calculators and other early data-processing machines (punchers, tabulators, sorters) are still with us today: IBM, NCR, Burroughs (now Unisys).[28] They invested resources in researching and developing new products and supplied a steady stream of them to businesses seeking to make their operations more efficient. Somewhat surprisingly, computers were a relatively late addition to the game. First built in the 1940s, they – "mainframes" – long remained much too expensive for most businesses. With the advent of time-sharing by dial-up connection in the 1960s, more businesses began to use computers in their operations. But it was really only after the introduction of the PC in the late 1970s that computers become a staple of office work.

It was the spread of the PC that was to be businesses' primary contribution to the rise of the Internet, for, by giving computer manufacturers an incentive to produce low-cost, portable, easy-to-use machines, they put computers within reach of large numbers of consumers. This provided a kind of mass "base" for the rapid take-off of the Web in the 1990s. Some thought was given to how networked computers might aid collaborative work, in business and out. Examples include Ted Nelson's "Project Xanadu" (1960s), Murray Turoff's "Electronic Information Exchange System" (1976), Irene Greif and Paul Cashman's "Computer Supported Cooperative Work" (1984), and Charles Findley's "Collaborative Networked Learning" (1986).[29] But, by and large, businesses were caught off guard by the rapid expansion of the Internet. However, once they saw it for what it was – both a new place and a new way to conduct business – they very quickly exploited the opportunity it provided, thereby hastening its expansion.

The "pull" of information capitalism, however, paled before that of the surveillance state.[30] The welfare state was all about providing goods and services at a minimum level to its citizenry. In order to fulfill this mission, however, it needed to collect and crunch a huge amount of data. If you are going to send pension payments to everyone over 65 years of age, you need to know (a) where the money is going to come from; (b) who is going to process it and how; and (c) where the money is going to go. That might not seem like a lot of information until you consider that it requires you to know a host of other things: who works where, what they do, how much they earn, where they live, what they own, what they owe, what sorts of families they live in, to whom they are related, how old they are, and sundry other difficult-to-anticipate items. Then multiply the task by many tens of millions. As the scope of the "safety net" expanded to include educational entitlements, health insurance, unemployment insurance, survivor's benefits, and all the other "rights" afforded to citizens, so too did the information-handling requirements of the state grow. It's not surprising that the enterprise that became IBM got its start building machines to tabulate the results of the U.S. censuses of 1890 and 1900.[31] Neither should it be unexpected that government bureaucracies remained the best customers of the makers of business machines throughout the twentieth century.

The pursuit of national welfare, however, was not the only reason modern states needed to ramp up their information-collecting and data-handling capacities. There were less savory grounds as well. One we have already touched on was the need to find more efficient ways to kill people and prevent them from being killed. The U.S. Defense Department funded virtually all of the research that led to the production of the first American computers, the first American computer networks, and the immediate forerunner of the Internet, ARPANET.[32] This investment was by far the most powerful factor "pulling" the Web into being in the second half of the twentieth century. Another factor was "state security," or rather insecurity. Governments have been spying on their subjects for eons, but the scope and intensity of clandestine state surveillance expanded radically during the twentieth century. This was especially true in the socialist world, where enemies were suspected under every rock, and party dictatorship ensured that every rock would be picked up without objection from the public. But it was also the case in democracies and semi-democracies, particularly during the periodic "Red Scares" that marked the century. Time and again, free governments set civil liberties aside in order to surreptitiously surveil the free citizens in whose interest they supposedly governed. Sometimes they had reason. Sometimes they didn't. But in either case the task of surveillance put an additional load on the state's information-handling capacity, and thereby helped "pull" the Internet into existence.

Finally, there was cultural hedonism.[33] In the first half of the twentieth century, cultural liberalism helped bring the modern audiovisual media into being by putting a fig leaf on impropriety. You could show most anything in public, so long as bodies remained clothed, speech clean, and messages "wholesome." The Hay's Code and its fellows made most everyone a hypocrite, which was fine with most everyone. Appearances had to be maintained. Until the 1950s. For reasons that go far beyond the scope of this book, polite hypocrisy began to fall out of favor in that decade in much of the Western world. Like Holden Caulfield, a lot of people suddenly found themselves surrounded by "phonies."[34] Some of these people are cultural icons today: Hugh Heffner, who founded *Playboy* in 1953; Aldous Huxley, who issued *The Doors of Perception* in 1954; Jack Kerouac, who published *On the Road* in 1957.[35] In a sense, all three of these men were hinting at the same thing: appearances don't need to be maintained because they aren't being maintained as it is. We should, therefore, do away with appearances and openly embrace what is "real." And that, for the proto-pornographer, the advocate of drug use, and the poet of loafing about, was raw experience. The rising generation, it turned out, was very receptive to this notion.[36] It became central to the shift in mores that took place during the 1960s, the wake of which we still live in today. Heffner's, Huxley's, and Kerouac's philosophy (if it can be called such) rested on a utilitarian logic that was as compelling as it was simple: all you know and are is what you feel, and therefore the "good life" should be spent in the pursuit of feelings, especially the good ones. Combined with a convenient cynicism toward "the man" – that is, the real world – this doctrine exploded into full-blown hedonism under the thin guise of "mental expansion," "consciousness-raising," and "getting back to nature." Whether any minds were expanded, consciousnesses raised, or natures gotten back to in the 1960s and 1970s is not at all clear. It is certain, though, that a lot of sex was had, drugs were taken, and loafing about done. Not surprisingly, the people who, moving far past anything Heffner, Huxley, and Kerouac ever imagined, trumpeted the virtues of radical hedonism became heroes to the merrymakers and were made celebrities by the press. The names of Timothy Leary, Ken Kesey, and Hunter Thompson still ring today.[37] They were, after a fashion, serious people, or at least famous people, which increasingly amounted to the same thing. The intellectuals of hedonism added a veneer of high-mindedness to the pursuit of raw experience.

The problem, however, was that once right-thinking people had agreed to condone high-minded hedonism, they were defenseless against the low-minded variety. Any such differentiation would make them hypocrites, and recall that it was the fight against hypocrisy that started the slide into hedonism in the first place. If you approved of Hugh Heffner, Aldous Huxley, and Jack Kerouac, it was hard to consistently disapprove of Larry Flint, Snoop Dogg, and Charles Bukowski. These "free spirits" were all just "doing their own thing," which is what everyone was supposed to do. The courts more or less agreed. By the mid-1970s, only two classes of expressions could be constitutionally censored in the United States: (1) those that were likely to promote "imminent lawless action" (*Brandenburg v. Ohio*, 1969); and (2) those that a community deems obscene *and* a reasonable observer would find lacking in any serious "literary, artistic, political or scientific value" (the Miller Test, 1973).[38] In practice, this meant that nothing beyond credible death threats and kiddy porn was banned. The FCC could censor more, but really only on the public airwaves. The 1960s and the birth of cultural hedonism set the stage for the Internet. By the moment of its birth, people were ready for a channel in which they could hear, see, and say anything. Print and audiovisual media could not supply this. The Internet could and did.

Human Nature and the Internet

We saw earlier that whereas writing and printing spread slowly, audiovisual media took off in a few decades. The reason, we said, was in part because we have a natural disinclination to read and write and an inborn inclination to watch and listen. Interestingly, the Internet took off even more quickly than the audiovisual media. In the span of a few years, it covered the globe and penetrated every nation on earth. The preexistence of an audiovisual infrastructure explains much of this rapid spread and remarkable reach: the Internet "piggybacked" on other networks, and so did not have to wait for new networks to be built, as was the case with audiovisual media. But that doesn't explain the entire phenomenon. It seems sensible to say that there is something about the Internet that appeals to our natures, a drive that makes us want it. Is there?

The answer would seem to be "yes." While it would not be fair to say that the Internet pushes all our evolutionary buttons, it certainly pushes more of them than any other single device in history. As we've said, humans were designed to look for anomalies and solve puzzles. The Internet is full of anomalies and puzzles. The world is a very big place and people are doing all kinds of things. You don't know about most of them. But now they are putting them on the Internet for you to find. Just about any search you perform, no matter how specific, is likely to return results that surprise you and present you with things to figure out. It's all there: the odd, the weird, the strange, the peculiar, the curious, the bizarre, the uncanny, the mysterious – everything. What is more, because you are on the Internet, you can quickly and easily do some research to clear things up. That's the idea, at least. So you surf from link to link to link, uncovering more and more and more information. Yet, as you do, you uncover new anomalies and puzzles that lead you in new directions. A book is a machine for focusing attention; the Internet is a machine for diffusing it. A book takes you on a trip from here to there; the Internet takes you on a trip from here to God-knows-where. Getting lost is half the fun of it. Most of us have had the experience of casually going to look something up on Wikipedia and ending up, an hour or more later, in a place we never imagined, learning about something we never knew existed. In truth, you don't so much look things up on the Internet as just look at things. This is something we clearly like to do, an end in itself. So compelling is our desire for anomalies and puzzles that some of the most popular sites on the Web are devoted to their collection. Some of them are low-brow, like Fark.com, and some are high-brow, like Metafilter.com, but they all exist precisely because we naturally find the unusual, curious, and just plain weird entertaining.

These link-presentation sites exist for another reason, also evolutionary in origin. Not only do we need to find what we called "relevance," but we are driven beyond reason to share what we find with others. We usually do this by talking, but the Internet has provided us with a much larger forum in which to present our trophies. Some commentators make the mistake of calling what happens on the Internet "exchange" and wax lyrical about how the Internet has unleashed a long-repressed human desire to "collaborate."[39] But the truth is that both exchange and collaboration on the Internet are *results* of the native drive to present relevance to others, not the cause. Ultimately speaking, we do not talk because we want to trade information or work together; rather, we talk because we naturally enjoy it, and we naturally enjoy it because talking – the presentation of relevance – increased our fitness eons ago. Similarly, we do not put things on the Internet because we desire to swap information or cooperate with each other; rather, we do it because we naturally enjoy putting things on the Internet, and we naturally enjoy it because this sort of behavior – the presentation of relevance – increased our fitness eons ago. Posting is the continuation of talking by other means.

This is easy to demonstrate. People often wonder why anyone contributes to Wikipedia. Indeed, it's something of a puzzle if you look at it in terms of cost-benefit analysis, as least as cost and benefit are usually understood. What are the costs? Well, there is the time and effort you spend editing. But you spend a lot of time on the Internet anyway, so that's a minor expense. More significantly, there is the very real possibility that your edits will be erased *and*, to add insult to injury, that you will be abused by angry strangers whose hardheadedness is matched only by their ignorance. Wikipedia can be a rough place. What are the benefits? Well, you certainly don't get paid, which is the way most people who work expect to be rewarded. Neither do you attain glory, for most contributors edit Wikipedia anonymously or at least pseudonymously. Contributing just doesn't add up. Yet thousands of people do it. There are probably many reasons – the desire to participate in something "bigger than yourself," the fellowship of the "collaborative community," or the simple alleviation of boredom. But the basic reason people contribute is that they find it enjoyable, and they find it enjoyable for easy-to-understand evolutionary reasons. The Internet is like a great game of show-and-tell, and we like show-and-tell a lot.

Another button that the Internet pushes is our desire to experience what we called "intrusive stimuli." These, it will be recalled, are a class of sounds and sights that we are preprogrammed to pay close attention to, whether we like it or not. They include depictions of sex, food, drink, power, wealth, conflict, and violence. From an evolutionary point of view, these stimuli are always relevant and therefore instinctively draw our ears and eyes. It goes without saying that the Internet is brimming over with material of this sort. Obviously, there is more pornography in more flavors than one can easily comprehend. But not only that. Even "mainstream" sites often have a quasi-pornographic visual style. They show you things that you want to see but don't have the opportunity or stomach to see in "real life." In the former category – opportunity – one would put all the commodity porn that populates so many commercial sites: gadgets, cars, houses, clothes, and "bling" of every kind. In the latter category – stomach – one would put the frequently disturbing pictures and videos of misfortune that litter the Web: pratfalls, car accidents, airplane crashes, and even people being beheaded. Looking at the one and the other you often get a kind of rush. The feeling may be superficially pleasurable or unpleasurable. But in either case it is a feeling, a kind of stimulation, that you desire on some very deep psychological level. If you didn't, you wouldn't look. And you always do.

Information capitalism, the surveillance state, and cultural hedonism "pulled" the modern Internet into existence. They succeeded in doing so rapidly and thoroughly in large measure because we are inclined by nature to like – even to the point of personal harm – what the Internet allows us to do. Once the door to the audiovisual media was opened, we ran through it. Once the door to the Internet was opened, we ran through it and, sometimes, stumbled.

WHAT THE INTERNET DID (AND IS DOING)

Not even two decades ago, then, the world of the "Old Media" – talking, manuscript-writing, printing, broadcasting – became the world of the "New Media" – those carried by the Internet. In truth, that's a bit of an exaggeration in two senses. First, despite what you might have heard, the "Old Media" have not and probably will not disappear, *ever*. All the historical evidence suggests that major media are remarkably persistent: new media don't displace the old, they join them. Second, and again despite what you may have heard, the Internet is not the dominant mode of human communications today. Far from it. About 80 percent of Americans currently use the Internet regularly. On average, they spend 17 hours a week online.[40] Almost all Americans chat, read, and watch TV. Every week they spend on average 13 hours chatting, 2.5 hours reading "for pleasure," and 23 hours playing couch potato.[41] Assuming they aren't doing these things simultaneously, Americans live in the world of the "Old Media" a lot more than they live in the world of the "New Media" (21.5 hours a week more, to be exact).

According to our "push" theory of media effects, the addition of the Internet to the mix should have altered social practices and values in Audiovisual Cultures; it should have produced a distinct Internet Culture in the distinct – and ongoing – Internet Era (1990 to the present).

As we saw earlier, our experience itself gives us abundant evidence to test this thesis, and our experience over the past quarter century is exactly what we will use to prove it.

Accessibility

There was a time, now dimly remembered, when computers were very expensive and Internet access was rare. The IBM PC, released in 1981, cost around $2,000;[42] the original Apple Macintosh, released in 1984, ran $2,500.[43] Neither had modems. These cost around $225 in 1980.[44] The Internet was in its infancy and there were no Internet service providers (ISPs), but you could access bulletin board systems (BBSs) for a few dollars a month. Today, you can buy any number of new, fully functional PCs – computer, screen, keyboard, mouse, modem – for less than $400.[45] The philanthropic organization "One Laptop per Child" is building a machine that will cost around $200.[46] If you don't mind used computers, you can get one for the price of shipment. Internet access will cost you about $10 a month at home, but you won't have any trouble finding someplace where it's free if you live in the developed world. Every school, public library, café, and many cities offer *gratis* wired or wireless access. And of course you get it at work for nothing, if you don't count the working part.

There was also a time, perhaps not so dimly remembered, in which learning to use a PC and navigate the Internet was hard. Many of us remember the wonders of config.sys, autoexec.bat, and the "blue screen of death." More of us, alas, know what TCP/IP and DHCP stand for. In the main, however, the tendency has been for both "usability" and "connectivity" to increase – that is, become easier – over time. Many computers are now truly "plug and play," though occasionally they have to be re-plugged and re-played. The era in which the tech guy was a god-king is not gone entirely, but it's fading fast. Proof that PCs and Internet access have become less costly in financial and training terms is borne out by the number of people who use them. It's estimated that there are more than one billion PCs in use worldwide today, and that number will double by 2015.[47] Something on the order of 1.4 billion people have Internet access.[48] Both numbers are rising. There are 6.7 billion people on the planet.[49] The digital divide, it would seem, is closing rapidly.[50] We should add that would-be monopolists will have a hard time making Internet access any more expensive than it naturally is, for the Internet's logistical chain has no readily exploitable bottleneck. Computers are made in too many places for production to be controlled. They are small enough that they can be transported relatively easily and secretly. Once in operation, they can be hidden. Some Internet traffic moves over telephone and cable lines, which can be cut, but only at the loss of other important services. Internet signals that are transmitted over satellites and picked up wirelessly are difficult to interrupt. Some tyrannical states have attempted to limit Internet access.[51] Not surprisingly, only North Korea has been really successful, largely because it has no telecommunication infrastructure to speak of.[52] The country code for North Korea is +850, but don't try to call because almost no one has a phone.[53] Satellite dishes and even cell phones are periodically banned. The frightened leaders of China, Iran, Cuba, and other shackled countries censor the Internet, but their ability to do so in the long haul as satellite-delivered service expands seems doubtful.

The Internet is a marvel of accessibility. If you want to get on it and use it, you probably can. If you can't now, you'll be able to soon. Accessible media foster diffused networks, that is, ones in which the ability to send and receive messages is shared by a large proportion of the population. In the developed world – Canada, the United States, Western Europe, Japan, South Korea, Australia – 40 to 80 percent of the population have Internet access.[54] In the less developed though developing world – Mexico, South America, the Middle East, Russia, China – 20 to 40 percent of the population have it. In the undeveloped world – Africa, Central Asia, Southern Asia, Southeast Asia – between 0 percent and 20 percent do. Overall, about 20 percent of the earth's population can get on the Internet. According to our theory, diffused networks *equalize* social practices and values evolved in and around them. Diffused networks give everyone roughly equal power to send and receive messages. Thus, it is difficult for any particular sender or receiver to monopolize communications and use unequal control to create unequal power.

There are ways in which the Internet is not democratic at all. Governments regulate it, telecom companies own it, search engines dominate it, and big corporations manipulate it. But having said all that, it's probably the most democratic "place" in the world, at least in the sense of having equalized social practices. In the real world, you are a person with lots of traits – gender, race, class, and all of their subspecies – that differentiate you from others; on the Web, however, you are most often just a "user" like any other. Offline, Bill Gates is very rich and you aren't. But online, Bill Gates is a "user" and so are you. Citizenship is to offline democracy as "user-hood" is to online democracy. Since both you and Bill are "users," everything you do together online – play games, talk software, write encyclopedia articles – is going to be on a "peer-to-peer" basis. Actually, *all* virtual social practices are equalized in the sense of "more equal than in the real world." They are not, however, equal for at least two reasons. First, the real world bleeds into the online world. So Bill's offline cred – if the "user" is *really* offline Bill Gates – is going to win him points in the software discussion site that you can't score. Second, reputation matters in the online world. Bill might really know what he's talking about and develop a good reputation, while you might be a "troll" and develop a bad one. Bill's online "peers" are going to listen to him and they aren't going to listen to you (in fact, they may ask the "mods" – moderators – to ban you). If you behave, however, you and everyone else will get a voice, just like your "peer," Bill Gates.

That is the "is" of the situation: everyone is on the Internet (or soon will be) and everyone is more or less equal on the Internet. The "ought" that followed was a peculiarly radical form of egalitarianism that took the Print Era notion of the "marketplace of ideas" to an extreme. In Print Cultures, everyone *theoretically* had a voice. But in practice, only those who were willing and able to bear the cost of print expression actually "spoke." It was generally agreed that this restriction of voices was a good thing: the "marketplace of ideas" would work only if those trading ideas had some investment in them and knowledge of them. In Internet Culture, everyone – or nearly everyone – *actually* has a voice. The costs of expression are so low that anyone can "speak," and everyone does. The "marketplace of ideas" can work only with difficulty in this cacophonous environment, so some additional justification for everyone "talking" at once had to be found. It was in the form of the "wisdom of crowds," according to which large, uncoordinated groups of independent people "know" things that even experts don't.[55] An important conclusion follows: if more people always know more, then there can be no reason to restrict anyone from weighing in. By this logic, more is better even when it's not. Not surprisingly, some people just don't buy it, at least as it applies to the Internet.[56]

Privacy

It's the most famous cartoon ever produced about the Internet. It's been reprinted thousands of times. Everyone has seen it. "On the Internet, no one knows you're a dog."[57] In the real world, everyone knows who you are. Here's why. First, you don't get to decide who you are. Others do that for you. You can't elect to be blue if you're born green. You can try to pass as someone you aren't, and some have. But the difficulty and psychological toll are great. Witness Michael Jackson. Second, you only get one identity at a time. You can try to lead a double (or triple, or quadruple) life. This feat, however, is notoriously difficult to pull off, and usually ends in divorce, incarceration, or an extended stay in a mental hospital. Third, you don't get to change identities. You can attempt to remake yourself. But if you really want a new identity, you have to enter the FBI's witness protection program. That, alas, involves saying bad things about some very mean people, a risky endeavor in itself. Finally, you often have to present your identity to others in person. You can avoid the *tête-à-tête* with intermediaries, letters, and the telephone. But when the deal is finally done, you are often going to have to look the other fellow in the eye.

None of these rules applies on the Internet. You get to decide who you are. Just pick a user name, "Bob," and make up a false profile. You get to have multiple identities simultaneously. Just make up another user name, "Betty," and another false profile. You can switch from one identity to another easily. Toggle back and forth: Bob-Betty-Bob-Betty. You never have to meet anyone face to face, for everything you want to do can be done at a distance. Even having sex (of an electronic sort). This doesn't mean that you can't be tracked down. Unless you're an expert, you can be found. But it's going to take a lot of effort to get from Bob and Betty to you if you are at all careful. As for your correspondence, it's relatively easy to conceal. Imagine some unauthorized someone wanted to see a file you've placed on the Internet. They would have to know where the file is. Happily, there is software available that will make a file functionally invisible. If they knew where the file was, they would need to get to it. Firewalls can stop them. If they manage to get to it, they would have to be able to open it. Passwords can prevent them from doing that. If they managed to open it, they'd have to be able to read it. Encryption will prevent that. Someone really dedicated and smart will probably be able to hack the file, but, again, they are going to have to go to a lot of trouble.

The Internet, then, is very private indeed. With just a little effort, you can hide who you are and what you've communicated behind multiple layers of deception and security. People do it routinely. Private media engender segmented networks, that is, ones in which information can flow in confined, restricted spaces but not between them. According to our theory, segmented networks will *close* social practices evolved in and around them. For a whole variety of reasons – some noble and some base – people like to hide what they do, and the Internet enables them to do this like no medium before it.

The Internet has allowed people to accomplish something unprecedented: the creation of private though public social space. This may seem like a contradiction in terms, but that's only because most of us have never had the experience of being unidentifiable in public. If you've been to a masked ball, then you've come close. But even there, you can probably be identified because masks don't mask very well. On the Internet, however, you can achieve true anonymity: your offline self will remain private, while your online self – your "avatar" as it is sometimes called – remains open for all to see. When you are anonymous, *all* of the social practices in which you engage are closed in the sense that they cannot be identified with your offline self. If you want a partial "second life," all you need do is pick a pseudonym. If you want a complete "second life," you can find it in any number of online virtual worlds.[58] In either case, you needn't worry at all about what others think of you, because "you" are separated from your actions. You – that is, the real you – are not accountable.[59] It's well understood that when people are not accountable, they do things they ordinarily wouldn't and probably shouldn't. "When the cat's away, the mice will play," as the proverb has it. It's no surprise, then, that the Internet is full of such bad behavior, or at least behavior that is deemed bad by offline standards.[60] Yet, even if you decide to enter the online world using your true offline identity, you can still easily create a closed space and a closed social practice within it. You simply build what is commonly referred to as a "walled garden," that is, a network that cannot be penetrated from the "outside." Within the garden, you and the other "users" will be able to do as they please without regard for "public" censure. Clearly, the possibilities for such closed "collaboration" are endless and somewhat disturbing.

That is the "is" of the situation: people are going to do all manner of things – good and bad, wholesome and sick – with the cover provided by the Internet. The "ought" evolved to justify this wide range of hidden behaviors was an old mode of privatism expanded to encompass new "digital" forms of expression. Offensive speech, pictures of naked ladies, and really tasteless art were all enjoyed by people of the Print and Audiovisual Eras. So too are they enjoyed by people in the Internet Era, though in vastly greater quantities and varieties. No new legitimating doctrine, therefore, was needed, for the "right to privacy," the "harm principle," "obligatory tolerance," and "aesthetic populism" were already on hand, gifts of Print and Audiovisual Culture. The Internet did, however, give rise to new forms of extreme "private" expression that didn't seem to have any direct equivalent in those earlier ages and therefore might not be covered by the inherited doctrines. Virtual child pornography is the clearest and most disquieting example. In a 2002 decision, the United States Supreme Court ruled that it, too, was protected by the First Amendment.[61]

Fidelity

Many people speak of the Internet as if it were a radically new mode of communication. In some ways it is, as we've seen and as we will see later on. But in other ways, it's not new at all. Take the kinds of data it delivers. There's speech: you can talk to people over the Web using Skype. There's writing: you can correspond with them using email. There's print: you can read all manner of printed material on the Web. And there are audiovisual media: you can listen to music, look at pictures, and watch videos on the Web. The Internet, then, is a telephone, a post office, a library, a radio, a photo album, and a TV all rolled into one. Which of these is new? None of them. "New" would be a medium that carries tastes, smells, and feeling. Sense-o-Rama may be coming, but the Internet isn't it. Despite what the boosters say, what we have in the case of the Internet is old wine in new bottles, at least in terms of data-type. On the Internet, speech, writing, and print are still five-to-one codes: they reduce every kind of experience to linguistic symbols born by sound (speech) or vision (writing and print). Internet "word pictures" still aren't pictures. On the Internet, audiovisual media are still one-to-one codes. Internet sounds are sounds; Internet pictures are pictures. Enthusiasts will object that the Web enables people to do all kinds of artsy new things with these media, things that were impossible in the old world. At best, that's an exaggeration. At worst, it's just untrue. Decades before the Internet, artists were mixing, mashing, and otherwise manipulating speech, writing, print, and audiovisual media for fun and profit. Go to MOMA or any collection of modern art and see. What is definitely true is that *computers* – not the Internet – have made messing about with the traditional media a lot easier than it was when Andy Warhol made art out of soup labels. If Andy had had Illustrator and Photoshop, he could have saved himself a lot trouble. But the Internet wouldn't have made much difference.

In terms of the kinds of information it delivers, the Internet is nothing but the sum of its parts. These are two: a low-fidelity channel carrying speech, writing, and print, and a high-fidelity channel carrying audiovisual messages. Hence, we have a dual network. When used to send and receive messages through the low-fidelity channel, the Internet will generate symbolic networks. Users on these networks have to "know the code" – that is, how to read – in order to use them effectively. Some of them will, some of them won't, and some of them will fall in between. When used to send and receive messages through the high-fidelity channel, the Internet will generate iconic networks. Users on these networks have to know a code, but it is so natural – listening and watching things "as they are" – that no conscious decoding will be required. They will just "get it," and they will all do so to roughly the same degree. According to our theory, symbolic networks *conceptualize* social practices developed in and around them, while iconic networks *sensualize* them. The Internet is a dual network, so it should do both.

It does, but even this is not entirely new. The Internet is not the first medium to deliver two channels, one low- and the other high-fidelity. In principle, writing can deliver two: a writer, for example, can draft text *and* draw pictures in a sketchbook. In principle, audiovisual media can deliver two: a TV producer can create a broadcast with both text and images, for example, a film with subtitles. These, however, are really marginal cases, for in the instance of writing, words dominate, while in the instance of TV, pictures do. We read writing and watch TV; we almost never watch writing and read TV. The first medium to approach a balance between the two channels was print, especially in recent times. The modern glossy magazine – *Time, Sports Illustrated, Playboy* – definitely has two channels. You get words and you get pictures. You never get one without the other, even in really wordy magazines like *The Atlantic Monthly, The New Yorker,* or *The Economist.* These considerations suggest a surprising conclusion: the Internet looks a lot like a "slick," as they say in the magazine trade. It's pretty hard to find web pages that are *only* words or *only* sounds and images. You almost always get both. Yet there is a difference between the way channels are employed in print and on the Internet. It's one of weighting. By and large, in print the low-fidelity channel (text) dominates, thus print networks are primarily symbolic, and therefore the most pronounced effect is the conceptualization of social practices and values. In contrast, on the Internet the high-fidelity channel (sounds and images) dominates, thus Internet networks are primarily iconic, and therefore the most pronounced effect is the sensualization of social practices and values.

And sensualization is just what we find. Earlier we saw that audiovisual media engendered social practices centered on the consumption of "cheap thrills," that is, stimulating, low-cost entertainments. The Web continues and amplifies this trend by further reducing the costs of the production and consumption of "cheap thrills." Some of these are genuinely new – the multiplayer online games, for example – but most are traditional, which is to say they are images, music, or video. On the production side, the Internet (and attendant computer technologies) enables almost anyone to create or at least copy a picture, a song, or a movie. These items, in turn, can be distributed to millions upon millions of "users" via "file-sharing" sites. Thus, we find millions of amateur "cheap thrills" on the Internet, as well as many that would seem to be made by professionals and nominally protected by the laws of copyright. On the consumption side, everything on offer, whether copyrighted or not, is free because all the "users" were doing was sharing. Add the fact that all of these free "cheap thrills" could be consumed in private, outside the censorious gaze of the public, and you have the recipe for an explosion of entertainment unprecedented in the history of the media. If you find it stimulating, you can find it on the

Internet – all the time, for free, and probably in quantities and varieties you never imagined.

That is the "is" of the situation: people are going to use the Internet to stimulate themselves in every imaginable way. The "ought" developed to excuse self-stimulation was a form of realism that we might call "virtual Romanticism." Here again we see very little that is new: the Audiovisual Era's soft-core and hard-core Romanticism, premised on the notion that any sound or image that makes you feel good is "enriching," was simply transferred to the online world. The principal difference between the old Romanticism and the new virtual version has to do with acquisition of "cheap thrills." In the Print and Audiovisual Eras, there was no way to get "cheap thrills" except by paying for them, and so it was generally agreed that people should pay for them so that the people who created them would create more of them. That was the basic reason for copyright – to stimulate the production of entertainment. As we've seen, though, the Internet made it possible to get "cheap thrills" for nothing by simply copying and distributing them, which is exactly what millions of "users" began to do. This "is" caused many right-thinking people to wonder whether stealing might not be stealing, at least in this case.[62] They muster a number of arguments to support this odd view. They claim copyright is unnecessary: the "creative class" will create even without it. They claim copyright is broken: the Internet has made the protection of intellectual property practically impossible. They claim that copyright itself is stealing: you can't really own ideas, as they belong to everyone. And they claim that the victims of copyright infringement will become its ultimate beneficiaries: the emerging "economy of attention" will make it so. Reasoning in this way, they conclude that the mass infringement of copyright is not stealing. How could it be stealing if it's good for us and good for the copyright holder? Of course, not everyone is convinced.[63]

Volume

In the previous chapters, we measured the capacity of media to carry information in terms of chunks and flows. Speech, writing, and print messages come in chunks, discrete packets of a typical size. The larger they are and the more of them that can be delivered, the higher the volume. Audiovisual messages generally (though not always) come in flows, continuous streams of data all of the same size from the consumer's perspective. The more of them there are, the higher the volume. What's curious about the Internet is that it turns chunks into flows. Not all chunks: Voice Over Internet Protocol (VOIP) "calls," for example, still come in discrete bursts of a certain size and duration. They start, things are said, and then they stop. But the Internet definitely moves writing and print toward the flow end of the spectrum. Take writing. Although email messages are discrete, email itself is always "on." The line is always open. Your inbox is filling up. You can always check it and, if need be, respond. Thus, the conversation – as opposed to a particular conversation – never ends. It simply flows on and on. Take print. Although web pages are also discrete entities, that's not really the way you experience them. You "surf" through them one after another in a continuous stream. You stop when one grabs your attention, read a bit, then move on. But there is always one there in your browser, awaiting your attention, approval, or disapproval. It's true that writing and print don't flow on the Internet in the same way as sound and sight. In the former case, you have to make the media flow by clicking, while in the latter case, they flow past you automatically. Nonetheless, the effect of both is nearly identical: a continuous stream of texts, sounds, and sights. In this sense, surfing the Internet is like watching captioned TV, with one crucial difference: there are millions of channels on the Web. Just how many millions, no one knows. More than 100 million registered domain names are currently active.[64] According to one recent estimate, there are in excess of 170 million websites (although only about 700,000 are active).[65] Since any of these sites can have many pages, and many do, the number of total web pages runs well into the billions. One rough estimate is that there are over 27 billion pages on the indexed Web.[66] And that's only the part of the Web search engines can see. The "Deep Web," that part which has been hidden (see "Privacy"), is probably much larger.[67]

The Internet, then, has extraordinarily high volume. It currently has too many channels to comprehend, and more are being added at a fantastic rate. This is hardly surprising. Anyone with a wired computer, a little know-how, and something to say can add their own drop to this electronic ocean. Since just about everybody has all three, the electronic ocean is expanding rapidly. High-volume media engender unconstrained networks, that is, ones that have plenty of spare capacity above and beyond what is deemed necessary for essential communications. According to our theory, unconstrained networks will *hedonize* social practices and values developed in and around them. The reason is this: people are pleasure-seeking. Thus, if a medium has extra bandwidth, people will use it for the purposes of pleasure. The Internet has ample spare capacity and has, as a result, hedonized social practices and values.

In the last chapter, we saw that the excess capacity of audiovisual media allowed people to create the social practice of "leisure," that is, a time for relaxation and, more than likely, the consumption of audiovisual stuff. The Internet has even more excess capacity, so we shouldn't be surprised to learn that it engendered even more "leisure." It did this in two ways: by changing the way entertainment is made and changing the way it's delivered.

First, consider entertainment production. In the Talking, Manuscript, and Print Eras, we generally made our own fun and little of it involved the media. In the Audiovisual Era, we paid people to make our fun for us and it was the media. In terms of entertainment, the Internet Era is like the one and the other: we make our own fun, but we use the media – or rather the Web – to do it. This isn't to say we don't hire people to entertain us on the Web. We certainly do. All the traditional entertainment companies – publishers, record companies, film studios, radio stations, TV channels – make their products available on the Web, usually for a fee. The difference is that they do not dominate the Internet in the way they ruled print and audiovisual media. The reason is simple: bandwidth. Print and audiovisual media don't have much of it, comparatively speaking, so only big companies can afford it. The Internet has an infinite amount of it, so anyone can get into the entertainment game. You've written the great American novel but can't get a contract? Post it online. You've penned the greatest song since "Puff the Magic Dragon" but can't find a distributor? Post it online. Your one-minute remake of *Star Wars* isn't getting any attention from the studios? Post it online. We tell our children to think they are geniuses-in-the-making, teach them to emulate geniuses-in-fact, and then tell them to sit down and shut up. It's hardly a surprise that there have long been millions of frustrated Hemingways, Dylans, and Scorseses out there who just needed a break. Now the Internet has given it to them and to all of us.

Second, there's delivery. In the Audiovisual Era, entertainment was what we might call "then-and-there." *I Love Lucy* was on at 6:00 PM on Mondays in your "TV room." You had to be "then-and-there" to enjoy it. This being so, audiovisual companies made sure that their best programming was broadcast when and where people had free time at home. Thus TV, for example, colonized evenings, that is, "primetime." On the Internet, however, entertainment is "always-and-everywhere." You don't have to enjoy it at a particular time and place; you can enjoy it any time and any place, or some approximation thereof. You, not some programmer at a big media company, decide when and where to look, listen, or watch. The liberation of entertainment from time and space, however, had a peculiar effect: it allowed "leisure" to colonize all the times that were not otherwise occupied by work and traditional media. These periods tended to be short: a few minutes waiting for the doctor, riding the bus, or between tasks at the office. But "short" is just what the Internet offers. Articles, picture essays, songs, games, videos – they can all be enjoyed in a few minutes. The result is that the Internet has increased the total time people spend at "leisure." Since a lot of this increased "down-time" is spent at work, employers and economists are worried about the cost of "workplace Internet leisure browsing," or "cyberslacking," as it's sometimes called.[68]

That is the "is" of the situation: people are going to use the infinity of Internet bandwidth to produce and consume entertainment like never before. The "ought" developed to justify this behavior was a form of hedonism composed of two parts, one old and the other new. The old part was the Audiovisual Era's notion that modern life was so stressful that you needed to relax in order to remain healthy. Surfing the Internet is an aspect of necessary "self-care." The proof of this doctrine was born out by some suspiciously comforting studies that demonstrated that surfing the Internet at work increased productivity.[69] The new part revolved around the idea of "self-expression." Of course, the notion that self-expression is essential to self-development is not new: the Romantics loved it.[70] The Internet didn't so much alter the self-expression-is-self-discovery line as democratize it. It's one thing to tell children, as Maria Montessori did, that self-expression would unlock their protean selves when, as adults, they wouldn't do a whole lot of self-expression, at least in public.[71] It's another to tell children the same thing when they can, as both children and adults, simply go online to express themselves to millions. Yet that is precisely what we tell our children and precisely what they are doing. They are making their own entertainment and at the same time becoming better people, or so we say. Not everyone is impressed with the result.[72]

Velocity

Email and chat have always been fast. It doesn't take long to compose messages and, once sent, they arrive almost instantly if everything is running according to spec. Thus, you can easily "talk" to someone over them. Web pages are a different story, or at least were. For most of the 1990s, making and editing web pages was a slow process because every alteration had to be hand-coded, that is, you had to write the HTML. If you didn't know HTML, and most people didn't, then updates were especially slow. "Slow" here means hours, which may be fast to you and me, but is an eternity in Internet time. In any case, hours between updates meant that you couldn't really have a conversation on or between web pages. Rather, you could have a series of monologues, and that really isn't very satisfying. So, in the late 1990s, some impatient programmers with a lot to say invented tools that allowed them to edit web pages quickly and easily.[73] Thus was the Blog born, and with it the flood of read/write web pages that are now ubiquitous on the Web. You've probably heard the term "Web 2.0."[74] You may not have heard the phrase "read/write Web." They mean the same thing – it's just that the former is an opaque buzzword promoted to sell electronic soap, while the latter is a pretty good description of what many people do on the Web today, and have since the early 2000s. You read something on a web page and then you write something about what you read on the same web page. Then other people read what you just wrote and they write back. The back-and-forth can happen instantly, just like talking to someone; or it can be drawn out, like an email exchange. But in either case it is what it is: a conversation. These days you are not limited to reading web pages and writing to them. You can listen, look, or watch, and then respond in kind. So a more accurate description of the Web today would be the read-listen-look-watch/write-record-photograph-video Web. One doubts that clumsy tag will catch on, but the point is the same: the Internet allows you to create and transmit messages in several formats very quickly, and thereby facilitates discussion.

The Internet, then, is a high-velocity medium: you can compose and send messages very quickly, and others can respond to them. This you cannot really do with writing, print, and audiovisual media. High-velocity media generate dialogic networks, ones in which messages can be quickly and easily exchanged between nodes. The "turn-around time" on such networks is short, or at least can be short. You compose a message and send it. It arrives quickly and is understood. And the recipient composes and sends a response. Thus, messages flow back and forth over the network rapidly and easily. According to our theory, dialogic networks *democratize* social practices developed in and around them. By "democratize" we mean to encourage deliberative and consensual decision making. People like to talk, and they like to be heard. Dialogic networks give them the opportunity to do both at a low cost.

The Internet is a huge dialogic network made up of millions of smaller dialogic networks – an Inter-network, a network of networks. Wikipedia, for example, is one of them. Most people would say Wikipedia is an online encyclopedia. It sure looks like one. It's comprised of short descriptive entries, just like an encyclopedia. They are written in a "stick-to-the-facts" style, just like an encyclopedia. They cover a remarkably broad range of topics, just like an encyclopedia. Wikipedia, however, clearly isn't an encyclopedia in the traditional sense, and some critics say it's not an encyclopedia at all. The reason most commonly cited for Wikipedia's "un-encyclopedia-ness" is that it is written by amateurs rather than experts. But that can't really be right, for in point of fact many amateurs contribute to *Britannica* and many experts to Wikipedia, though the proportion of each is surely different in the one case and the other. The real difference between traditional encyclopedias and Wikipedia is the medium in which they are realized and the way in which those media shape their form.

As we've said, writing and print are inherently monologic because they do not permit the rapid production and exchange of messages. The traditional encyclopedia is a perfect example. An artifact like *Britannica* takes many years to organize, write, edit, typeset, print, and distribute. And once it's done, it's done: the articles themselves cannot be edited. It is true that the production of the next edition will involve an exchange of information. The new authors will enter into a "conversation" of sorts with the old authors – and the "literature" in general – as they go about updating entries. But is a "conversation" that takes place over decades or even centuries really worthy of the name? No matter what we call it, one thing is clear: the lag between "call" and "response" – a function of the logistical characteristics of the medium – seems unnaturally long. In contrast, the Internet as it exists today is inherently dialogic in that it not only permits rapid exchange of information but encourages it. Imagine you've been asked to write a *Britannica* entry. It might take you a short time – you just slap something together. Or it might take you a long time – you write a carefully crafted, informed article. When you're done, as we said, you are done. Now imagine you want to write a Wikipedia entry. The goal is the same, and it's your choice how you want to pursue it. You can settle for "good enough" or strive for excellence. The difference is that when you're done, you aren't done. In fact, you – or rather the article you've started – is never done. Ever. This is because anyone can edit "your" article at any time or leave comments about it. It is this ceaseless back-and-forth about articles that really makes one wonder whether Wikipedia is an "encyclopedia" and its articles are really "articles." Might it not be more accurate to say that Wikipedia is a never-ending discussion about everything, neatly topically arranged for everyone's convenience? And might not one say the same of the Internet in general? What is it but a boundless forum for dialogue, discourse, and conversation, for negotiation, cooperation, and collaboration, for deliberation, disputation, and debate? Imagine a space so large as to comfortably accommodate everyone in the world. A space in which everyone is near everyone else, but no one can touch anyone. What do you think people would do there? They'd talk, of course.

That is the "is" of the situation: people are going to use the Internet to rapidly exchange messages about every possible subject and to every possible end, even encyclopedia-writing. The "ought" developed to justify this behavior was a multipart form of deliberativism. The kernel of this doctrine is Mill's notion that deliberation is the best way to get to the truth.[75] It is almost universally held by "users." Of course, there are limits. Not every form of expression is deliberation. In Internetese, "trolls" are those who enter into discussions just to provoke other "users" and generally disrupt the deliberative process.[76] Such people sometimes get banned by moderators precisely for their disingenuousness. But in general, users and mods are willing to tolerate most anything in the name of deliberation. More novel is the idea of a "beta" version, or the "perpetual beta." In software engineering, a beta is a version of a program that has passed internal testing and is ready to be released to "users" for further testing until it is officially launched. The idea is that the users will help perfect the software by finding things wrong with it ("bugs"). This being so, the sooner you release the program to the users, the less work you and your internal testers will have to do. So it makes sense to "go live" as soon as possible.[77] This attractive idea migrated to other content on the Web, and soon many things – encyclopedia entries, blog posts, comments of every kind – could be seen as betas awaiting improvement by users. Peculiarly, this doctrine turned the meaning of deliberation on its head in the name of more deliberation. Most people would probably define "deliberation" as careful consideration, a kind of slow weighing up or mulling over of some matter. But this is not what happens in a beta release at all. Rather the opposite: ideas are put up for "deliberation" before they have been carefully considered, and they are subject to a kind of rapid-fire, off-handed criticism that is more akin to a water-cooler conversation than a true "deliberation."

Range

When we talk about the Internet, we usually mean the World Wide Web. The former is a system of pipes; the latter is one of the kinds of data – HTML documents – that runs through the pipes. The distinction, however, is now largely lost. Most people use the terms "Internet" and "Web" synonymously. In a way, that's good, because as a descriptor "Internet" is obscure. It's short for "Internetwork," a non-word that isn't really much clearer. "Web" is much more telegraphic, as it is metaphorically connected to things with which we are all familiar – weaving, fabric, and even spiders. It's easy to imagine the Internet as a gigantic spider's web blanketing the earth, connecting everything to everything else through multiple, interconnected strands. Of course, the "web" – in the generic sense of a communications network – is not new. It was brought into being hundreds of thousands of years ago the moment one human talked to another. Over time, humans invented new media and used them to create new webs, each larger than the last. They superimposed the new webs on the old: writing on talking, print on writing, audiovisual media on print, and finally the Internet – *the* Web – on audiovisual media. Although the Internet web is probably larger geographically than the audiovisual web, the two are very roughly the same size. You can retrieve HTML files from servers all over the world; but you can also place calls all over the world, listen to radio stations from all over the world, and watch TV from all over the world. What really makes the Internet web different from the audiovisual web is not its extent, but rather its density. The Internet web is thicker, bushier, woollier than the audiovisual web. More people are connected to more places at fewer removes more of the time on the Internet than on, say, a telephone, radio, or TV web. This relates to our previous discussion of channels. The Internet's billions of channels are "served" from computers all over the world. You can go to any of them, any time. The audiovisual networks have thousands of "broadcasts" from stations over most of the world. You can go to some of them, some of the time. Audiovisual channels typically have much larger audiences than Internet channels, but the coverage of the Internet web as a whole is greater than that of the audiovisual web. As the audiovisual channels themselves migrate to the Internet (so-called convergence), the superiority of the Web will become all the greater.

The Internet, then, has global range and unexcelled coverage. It goes everywhere and soon will reach everyone. Media with these character-istics engender extensive networks, which is to say networks that bring diverse places and peoples together. According to our theory, extensive networks *diversify* social practices and values evolved in and around them. On extensive networks, strangers confront one another, learn from one another, and assimilate one another to their worldviews. What was smooth becomes rough, what was plain becomes mixed, what was monochrome becomes multicolored. It's not always pretty. Sometimes this confrontation leads to conflict. But over extended periods of time it often leads to the softening of edges and the acceptance of diversity.

There is no doubt that the Internet mixes things up in a new way. Everything is there: every nationality, culture, language, dialect, creole; every political viewpoint, economic theory, scientific school; every reli-gious creed, spiritual belief, and ritual practice; every taste, aesthetic, and sensibility; every ethic, moral code, and law. All and more are found together on the Web. Some are real; some are imaginary. Some are serious; some are silly. Some are sensible; some are so wacky as to confound belief. But they are all there, each exactly one click away from the other. The Web scotched the notion that people and things are the same, or even similar, everywhere for good. But it also engendered a new kind of voyeurism. In the Print and Audiovisual Eras, the presentation of documentary exotica – that is, depictions of the strange that were uncontrived or "natural" – was enough to satisfy the curiosity of most readers, listeners, and viewers. There seemed to always be more of it, so what was on offer simply created anticipation for what came next. The Internet, however, demonstrated that the well of "natural" variation was not bottomless. In fact, it was quite finite, and that which is finite and known is not as interesting as that which is infinite and unknown. The finitude of "natural" variation, then, created a desire for what we might call "artificial" variation, that is, exotica that is purposely contrived simply to surprise, astonish, or shock. Some of this is benign, or at least relatively so, for example the "virtual worlds" created by online gamers. But some of it is very disturbing, particularly that which involves real people doing dangerous, degrading, or disgusting things simply for the sake of attention. You can see such material in abundance on YouTube and any number of fetish porn sites.

That is the "is" of the situation: people are going to use the Web to see everything there is – natural, imaginary, and contrived. The "ought" we might call "transculturalism." Recall that the doctrine of toleration was born of the Print Era and multiculturalism of the Audiovisual Era. Transculturalism moves beyond both by positing an identity that is "beyond culture," that is, envisions a kind of identity that is not rooted in a historical culture (Russian, Vietnamese, or what have you) but rather is an amalgam of many historical and invented cultures.[78] Transculturalism might seem like a variation on Enlightenment "citizen of the world" cosmopolitanism, and they are in fact similar. But transculturalism includes an element of self-fashioning that cosmopolitanism did not. Transculturalism permits and even encourages the creation of new *sui generis* identities. These include both offline and online selves, the "real" as well as the "imaginary." Identity is completely plastic and any identity assumed is, so long as it does not obviously violate the "harm principle," acceptable. Perhaps the most familiar transnational identities are found in offline subcultures, such as bikers, goths, skinheads, nudists, gangbangers, metalheads, hipsters, punks, skaters, deadheads, hackers, hippies, trekkies, and so on.[79] Since the Internet makes it much easier to assume an identity than it is in the offline world, we shouldn't be shocked to learn that there are many more such transnational subcultures (or "communities" as they are often called) there.

Persistence

In spring 2007, Bear Stearns hedge-fund managers Ralph Cioffi and Matthew Tannin were pretty bullish about the prospects of the securities they were hawking. At least that's what they told the investors who bought them. Secretly, however, they knew the funds were dogs. Tannin told Cioffi so in an email:

> [T]he subprime market looks pretty damn ugly. . . . If we believe [our internal modeling] is ANYWHERE CLOSE to accurate I think we should close the funds now. The reason for this is that if [our internal modeling] is correct then the entire subprime market is toast. . . . If AAA bonds are systematically downgraded then there is simply no way for us to make money – ever.[80]

They didn't close the funds – they kept on pitching. And they didn't make any money – ever. But they did get indicted on charges of conspiracy, securities fraud, and wire fraud. Thus, Cioffi and Tannin joined the ranks of Henry Blodget (Merrill Lynch), Jack Grubman (Citigroup), Frank Quattrone (Credit Suisse First Boston), and other Wall Street crooks who, while quite smart, forgot one of the basic rules of life on the Internet: email is forever. So is most everything else on the Internet. It's not really the case that the Internet never forgets. It does. But it remembers a heck of a lot.

The reason is twofold. First, it can. Unlike spoken words, writing, printing on paper, and audiovisual signals on tape, digital files – the kind that are stored on the Internet – can be copied and archived very quickly, very accurately, and very cheaply. Practically speaking, there is no limit to the amount of information that can be stored on the vast array of devices that make up the Web. Second, we live in a world where archiving information is the safe bet, at least most of the time. You never know when you are going to need that document for some purpose. So you archive it. Many people, however, are lazy about backing up their files. Horror stories abound. Don't worry, though, there are powerful organizations making sure that everything gets saved. Your company, for example, has probably hired people to make sure that its digital files are routinely archived. That includes the emails you send from your work address. Then there are the folks at the Internet Archive. They've been taking periodic "snapshots" of the Web since 1996 and making them available to the public. Although the Internet Archive is not complete, it's still awfully large. As of 2008, it contained 2,000 terabytes of data and over 85 billion web pages.[81] According to one estimate, an academic research library – the kind with millions of books – holds about two terabytes.[82] The print collection of the Library of Congress, arguably the largest library in the world, contains about 10 terabytes.[83] And then there are all the private corporations that record and archive what you do on the Internet in order to sell you more soap. They do this using "tracking cookies" – little pieces of software that are downloaded to your computer – that essentially spy on you. Google's cookies, for example, tell the main office what you searched for, when you searched, which of the results you selected, and so on. They save it all, mix it up with other user data, crunch it, and then use the results to try to figure out what sort of soap you and people like you want. Then they sell advertising space on your browser to your soap company. That's a good trick. Just how long all of this data will last we don't exactly know, but it will probably be a long time. The medium in which it is recorded doesn't decay very rapidly. The means used to read it – hardware, software – changes from time to time, but engineers are for the most part pretty aware of the need for "backward compatibility." And the languages recorded are very big and stable: English, Chinese, Japanese, etc. Besides, any file in danger of becoming illegible due to decay, format obsolescence, or language change can be recopied, re-formatted, and translated. It wouldn't be surprising if the "snapshots" of the Internet taken by the Internet Archive today were legible in 1,000 years. If we're still here to read them.

The Internet, then, is a persistent medium. It's like a trillion elephants all linked together in a sort of Vulcan mind-meld. Don't forget that next time you decide to bilk your investors out of their hard-earned cash. Persistent media engender additive networks. These are networks with a significant capacity to accumulate information. Like your crazy grandmother, they don't throw anything away – they just put it in the basement. According to our theory, additive networks will *historicize* social practices and values developed in and around them. This means that both awareness and the importance of the past will be heightened. The past – represented in artifacts or imagined – will be in a constant dialogue with the present.

In the previous chapter, we saw how audiovisual media engendered the practice of pervasive (and often intrusive) documentation. The Internet continues this trend. Since at least 1996, the Internet has been recording a good percentage of the *new* spoken, written, printed, recorded, photographed, or filmed messages that passed over it. Thus, it comprises a remarkable record of what we have done online for the past decade or so. But just as significantly, the Web is assimilating the pre-Internet past as well. For well over a decade now, institutions of every shape, size, and purpose have busied themselves with the digitization and posting of artifacts that were not "born digital." The scope of this project is mind boggling: every government record, every corporate record, every clerical record – pretty much everything ever written, printed, or photographed by an agency of one sort or another. Google and a consortium of academic libraries alone plan to scan and make available somewhere around 32 million books.[84] This may seem like a lot of information, but it may be exceeded as individuals and their families get into the act. People are already scanning and uploading their family photo albums to the Web. It won't be long before they begin to scan old letters, personal paper, and even the family Bible. Like some enormous gravitational force, the Internet is sucking the past into its vast memory banks. That digitized past will be affixed to the ever-expanding present of born-digital information, at which point the "what came before" will be one seamless digital archive.

The Internet will enable us to preserve more of the past than ever before. It will also expand the capacity for mass surveillance by creating a vast permanent record for every "user."[85] Every email you send, every post you make, every site you visit, every search you conduct, every profile you view, every article you read, every file you download, every file you upload – all of it can be recorded and stored for "later reference." And it's not only your online behavior that will find its way online. All of the "real world" records you generate will be there as well: your commute times, your arrival and departure from work, your credit card purchases, all of your other bills, your phone records, and all those video surveillance tapes that you appear on. Interestingly, none of this – or almost none of it – is Big Brother's doing. We are active participants in the creation and maintenance of the permanent record machine. We don't mind the cookies, we like the nifty transaction records, and we feel safer because of the security cameras. Of course, the collectors of this information assure us that it is secure and will never be used for nefarious purposes. Not everyone is convinced.[86] The creation of the electronic dossier has lead, predictably enough, to an expansion of the practice of "reputation management." In the Audiovisual Era, corporations used reputation management in order to protect their brands.[87] They needed to do this because they were public entities and were, therefore, closely watched. Any misstep could cost them dearly. In the Internet Era, everybody needs to practice reputation management because everyone is a public entity and is closely watched. You, so the business gurus say, are a brand.[88] If you let someone sully your image, you may not be able to clean it up. That, of course, could cost you dearly. So you need to monitor and perhaps even edit, say, your Wikipedia entry to make sure that it tells your version of the truth. But don't get caught managing your reputation in this way, for that in itself could damage your reputation.[89]

That is the "is" of the situation: people will, whether they know it or not, use the Internet to create electronic dossiers on everything and everyone. The "ought" that attended this behavior is an odd variation on temporalism that could be called "passive vigilism." Recall that the Audiovisual Era saw the development of vigilism, that is, the notion that we should record and archive ongoing events as they happen, both so that we can enjoy re-viewing them and can use them in forensic contexts. Being vigil in this way was an active process. We had to record the sounds and visions, store them, and then search through them in case we needed something from them. Being vigil on the Internet, however, is a passive process. We don't really collect and store data; rather, "data are collected and stored." We don't make the universal archive of electronic dossiers; rather, it seems to simply "appear" as if by itself. This, so we say, is generally fine because it makes things very convenient (it's nice when a website knows your name and credit card number) and safe (should anyone misbehave, we can "go back in time" and catch them).

Searchability

The ability to store a lot of information is useless if you can't find anything in it. As we've said, written, print, and audiovisual archives can be quite capacious, but it's hard to find anything in them. The reason is that we don't have a special tool we can use to look through the data – all we have are our eyes and ears, and they were designed to do other things. In contrast, computers, which can store even more information, do have a specialized tool to search for data in their archives – the find command or something similar. As everyone knows, computers store all their data as zeros and ones – the two digits in "digital." The find command tells the computer to go through data looking for a specific series of these zeros and ones. Functionally speaking, this is no different than you looking for a string of characters on a page, in a book, or in a library. The difference is that the computer can do the operation really, really fast. We can't. Since we can't, we construct indexes: tables of one sort or another that tell us where the information we want is. Computers do the same thing – they just do it much faster and arguably better. Librarians laboriously construct indexes – catalogues – that tell us where every book in the library is. By analogy, the computer automatically constructs an index that tells it where every word in every book in the library is, as well as where many possible combinations of words are. In a sense, a search engine works like a computer. It "crawls" across the Internet gathering information and then uses that information to construct a massive index. When you tell the engine to find something – such as a string of characters like "William" – it mechanically looks through the indexes and return addresses – URLs – to web pages that you might want.

The crucial term here is "might," for given that your search term is probably short and the index is very large, you are probably going to get a lot of URLs that have nothing to do with what you are actually searching for. If your intention in searching the string "William" was to get web pages about William Shakespeare, you might be disappointed. The engine could return a lot about "William" and only a little, if any, about William Shakespeare. Here, however, the search engine has an advantage over the personal computer, because it can anticipate what you were looking for even when you were vague, as in the previous example. It does this by comparing your behavior to everyone else's. We noted that a search engine records all the strings everyone searches and what they select after the results are returned. This enables it to compile a ranking based on click-through rate. If it turns out that many people who search the string "William" click a link having to do with William Shakespeare, then the search engine will respond to your "William" query by presenting you with William Shakespeare pages on the sensible presumption that you are more or less like everyone else. Since you are, you will get what you want despite the fact that you were vague. Click-through rate is only one of the factors that the search engine can consider when deciding how to rank URLs returned. It might also consider the amount of traffic a site gets, the number of inbound links a site has, the amount of time people spend on a site, the number of pages they look at on a site, or the rate at which they return to the site. All of these factors are packed together in a search algorithm, a kind of formula the engine uses to guess what you are really looking for when you type "William" into the search box. The results can be sort of spooky, because the search engine seems to know something about you that you didn't tell it. That's because it does.

The Internet is a supremely searchable medium. Unlike, say, the British Library, its doors are always open. Unlike the British Library, it has a remarkably detailed index. Unlike the British Library, its index can be searched with blinding speed. And, unlike the British Library, the search results are highly relevant and the materials themselves are immediately accessible. It's no wonder that the British Library and every other library on earth is rushing to put its holdings online. Searchable media generate mapped networks, that is, ones that have a fine-grained address system that allows users to locate archived items easily. These sorts of networks *amateurize* social practices developed in and around them. By allowing anyone the ability to find and retrieve what they need to know, they blunt the attempts of "experts" to monopolize special knowledge and use it as a basis for professionalization. The line between amateurs and experts thus becomes blurred.

The Internet is blurring this line remarkably quickly. Only a quarter century ago, if you wanted to learn something specific and specialized on your own, you were going to have a hard time doing it. Most people didn't have access to those great repositories of knowledge, academic research libraries. Even if they managed to get in, they probably didn't have the background knowledge to find what they wanted and, more important, needed. And even if they located it in a book or article, they wouldn't likely be able to retrieve it without special permission. None of that is true today. If the Internet has not already supplanted the academic research library as the primary archive of knowledge, it soon will. In some cases, the institutions that control these repositories are themselves abetting this process of democratization, as in the case of the consortium of libraries that have joined the Google Books project.[90] In other cases, they are resistant, as in the case of many academic publishers. In the end, it won't matter because the information will "leak" out of these sources through multiple channels. The same forces that are pushing copyright-protected audiovisual materials onto the Internet will force copyright-protected intellectual materials there as well. They may not be in a form that can easily be traced or recognized, for example in Wikipedia entries or on blog posts, but the substance will be the same. You can be pretty sure that what you need to know is somewhere on the Internet. To find it, all you will need is some "Googlefu" – the ability to use a search engine efficiently – and a search engine.[91] You may not know exactly what you need to know – that is, be faced with what former U.S. Secretary of Defense Donald Rumsfeld called an "unknown unknown."[92] The search engines, however, know what people *like you* typically need to know and will lead you in that direction. If this "wisdom of crowds" technique fails, you can rely on the wisdom of individuals to tell you what you need. There are, as we've already noted, thousands of communities of interest on the Internet in which real people are trading knowledge of every kind, from how to deal with cancer to how to get a date. On these sites you can ask very general or very specific questions and receive tailored advice. If you don't learn what you need here, then you can take a final step and ask an expert directly. There are countless thousands of credentialed experts on the Web who are giving away advice. They do it for various reasons: because they want attention, because it makes them feel good, because they are bored. The remarkable thing is that they are there and will provide you a professional service for free.

That is the "is" of the situation: people will use the Internet to find out what they need to know, or at least what they think they need to know. The "ought" developed to justify this behavior is a species of individualism that goes under the odd name "prosumerism." The word is a portmanteau of the words "producer" and "consumer" and means, broadly, a person who is involved in both the production and consumption of a product. The term was coined in this sense by the Futurist Alvin Toffler in 1980, but wasn't used with reference to the Internet until the mid-1990s.[93] The core idea in online prosumerism is that there really shouldn't be any separate "producers" and "consumers"; rather, everyone should be a "collaborator." By extension, prosumerism suggests that there shouldn't be any "experts" and "amateurs"; rather, there should just be people who know different things and are willing to combine them in various ways for the good of all. This philosophy was anticipated by the Free Software Movement in the 1980s; it was formalized by Open Source Initiative in the 1990s; it was adopted by Wikipedia in the early 2000s; and it is the credo of those who champion "user-generated content" today.[94] Those who oppose it charge "anti-elitism."[95] Proponents of prosumerism dismiss these charges as "whining" issuing from the "reactionary core of the academy."[96]

People have been waiting for virtual reality for years. They needn't wait any longer, because it's here. It's not an immersive environment, but rather a set of web pages through which we can "live." On these web pages we can chat up strangers, go on dates, have sex. We can read books, watch movies, and play games. We can go to museums, visit foreign countries, or land on the moon. We can go to school, do our work, and get paid. We can buy stuff, sell stuff, and trade stuff. We can be professors, lawyers, and doctors, or at least "know" what they know. We can do all this and never leave our seat in front of the computer. Of course, as Plato would point out, it's all a sort of illusion, for none of it gets to the essence of things, none of it is True. Nonetheless, it has many real-world implications, some of which we have tried to flesh out in this chapter. The Internet is a new medium, but it is a medium all the same. As such, it has physical attributes that permit people to use it in certain ways and prevent them from using it in others. These logistical characteristics, we argued, predictably led to the formation of certain sorts of media networks, and these media networks in turn engendered specific social practices and values. Table 6 summarizes all that has come before.

TABLE 6. *The Effects of the Internet*

Internet	Medium Attribute →	Network Attribute	→ Social Practice →	Cultural Value
Accessibility =	High →	Diffuse	→ Equalized	→ Egalitarianism
Privacy =	High →	Segmented	→ Closed	→ Privatism
Fidelity =	High →	Iconic	→ Sensualized	→ Sensualism
Volume =	High →	Unconstrained	→ Hedonized	→ Hedonism
Velocity =	High →	Dialogic	→ Democratized	→ Deliberativism
Range =	High →	Extensive	→ Diversified	→ Pluralism
Persistence =	High →	Additive	→ Historicized	→ Temporalism
Searchability =	High →	Mapped	→ Amateurized	→ Individualism

It goes without saying that the Internet doesn't necessarily engender the effects listed and, when it does, engender them in the same degree. The Internet's effects could be buffered or even eliminated altogether with enough effort. Call to mind a society in which only a few have access to the Internet – a kind of cyber-priesthood. Now imagine that this low-access Internet has some odd and rather un-Internety characteristics: it can only be used in public, so that everyone knows who and what is being transmitted; it can only send text, and not very much of it, very quickly, or very far; its transmissions disappear without a trace shortly after receipt; since it has no archive, it can't be searched at all.

All this is technically feasible. But realistically it cannot and will not ever be done, at least not all of it. Most of the world's nations seem to have learned the lesson taught by print and audiovisual media: media will do what media do, and attempting to go against their grain will probably lead to nothing but trouble and failure. This acceptance is one of the reasons the Internet is now virtually everywhere, and virtually everywhere the same. There are nations that have not learned this lesson. They are uniformly the last remaining illiberal, undemocratic, tyrannies left on the planet. And – with the exception of those that almost completely block access to the Internet – none of them is succeeding in bending the Internet to its will, at least to any great degree. Moreover, where they have succeeded, we can be reasonably sure they will eventually fail, and suffer for their failure. For the Internet will do there what the Internet has naturally done everywhere else. It will spread until almost everyone has it and everyone believes everyone should have it. It will foster the formation of many private groups and a belief that individuals have the natural-born right to opt in or out of these groups. It will be used primarily for pleasure and without penalty or shame. It will engender dialogues both within and between groups at a level heretofore unimaginable, and it will lead to a general (though not necessarily laudable) democratization of everything. It will grow to include everyone, everywhere, and thereby break down barriers. It will save everything, make everything saved findable, and thereby make us at once vulnerable and knowledgeable.

This, then, is Internet Culture, brought into being by the Web and the organized interests that "pulled" it into existence. Whether its run will be long and whether it will be good for humanity, we do not know. In the next and final chapter, we will consider just these questions.

CONCLUSION

—

THE MEDIA AND HUMAN WELL-BEING

In our days, everything seems pregnant with its contrary: machinery, gifted with the wonderful power of shortening and fructifying human labor, we behold starving and overworking it.[1]

    – Karl Marx, 1856

Marx worshiped technology. Thanks to labor-saving machines, he predicted, one day we would all be free to "hunt in the morning, fish in the afternoon, rear cattle in the evening, criticize after dinner."[2] One day, but not in his day. Marx looked around his mid-nineteenth century world and saw, much to his horror, that capitalists were using the technical instruments of emancipation to bind their fellow men. "At the same pace that mankind masters nature," he wrote, "man seems to become enslaved to other men."[3] The problem was not the tools. They had "revolutionized industrial production," thereby setting the stage for a new epoch of human fulfillment.[4] The problem was the way we – humanity – used these tools. Marx told a story of technical progress, and so have we. He described the "forces of production" marching to ever greater heights, and we have described the "forces of communication" doing the same. But Marx, as we've seen, was careful to distinguish technical progress from moral progress. He saw a lot of the former and very little of the latter. We would be remiss not to make the same distinction. It may seem obvious to us that each successive media – writing, print, audiovisual devices, and the Internet – has been "better" than the last. In a technical sense, this is true. But in an ethical sense, the case is much less sure. A tool is only as good as the purposes to which we put it. It seems only fitting, then, that we conclude our consideration of the media by asking whether we have been using them to improve our well-being or not.[5]

In order to answer this question, we need to be rather specific about what we mean by "improve our well-being." That is not easy. People have been arguing about just what makes people "happy" – to put a word on it – for millennia. More than 2,000 years ago, Aristotle, who proposed his own theory on the subject, noted there was a lot of disagreement about just what happiness is.[6] There's just as much today.[7] Is it better to be an unhappy Socrates or a happy pig?[8] To answer that question, you'd have to know what happiness is, and nobody seems to know. You'd also have to talk to a pig, and nobody seems to know how to do that, either.

It's much easier to say *when* happiness – whatever it might be – is likely to arise. There is general agreement on this score. If we are starved, tormented, or guilt-ridden, we probably aren't going to be happy; if we are well-fed, joy-filled, and guilt-free, we are quite likely to be happy. This being so, we can say with some confidence that the conditions under which happiness is most likely to materialize are at least three. The first condition is *material* well-being, that is, being well-fed, clothed, and sheltered. The second is *sensory* well-being, that is, feeling – in the physical sense – good. The third is *spiritual* well-being, that is, having a sense that we are acting rightly in relation to our fellows and the universe. In what follows, we will use this simple measure to see whether the media have improved our lot or not.

THE MEDIA AND MATERIAL WELL-BEING

Have the media improved the material well-being of humankind? The answer is "yes." We know this, as we will explain, because (a) we know that we are much better off, materially speaking, than we were even 100 years ago – standards of living have risen; (b) we know why we are better off – improved economic productivity; and (c) we know why economic productivity has improved – improved tools, media among them.

In purely material terms, we live in a golden age. Our ancestors' lives may have been nasty, brutish, and short, but ours are likely to be pleasant, refined, and long, at least by comparison. In the year AD 1, the average person earned the equivalent of about $500 per year; today he or she earns more than $7,000.[9] Moreover, the *rate* of income growth has been quickening over the long haul. Not only do we earn more each year, but the size of our annual raise is increasing. What's most remarkable about this boom is that it occurred *despite* an explosion in world population. In the year AD 1, there were roughly 170 million people on earth; in the year 2000, there were more than six billion. And the *rate* of population growth is also increasing: not only are there more of us each year, but the size of the annual bump is growing as well.

The simultaneous rise of income and population may seem odd. After all, you might think that more pie-eaters would mean *less* pie per person. That's the way it works around the dinner table, anyway. But it's not the way it works in long-term economic history: more pie-eaters meant *more* pie per person. The number of pie-eaters grew, but the amount of pie grew faster. And not only that: the rate at which pie-eaters and pie has grown has itself been rising. There can really be only one explanation for this odd occurrence: people are getting better at making pies, and the rate at which they are getting better is accelerating.

Why? There are several ways to raise economic productivity, but the best – or at least most powerful in the long term – is to improve the tools you use to make pies. The other "inputs" – labor and capital – don't increase productivity as well because they are subject to severely diminishing returns. Adding bakers *might* increase the number of pies produced per baker for a while, but eventually it won't. Adding more pie capital to the production process might increase the number of pies baked per unit of capital, but eventually it won't. Adding better technology – and here we mean tools and know-how in the broadest sense – will definitely increase productivity, and it will do so in an open-ended fashion. Technology is the only economic gift that seems to keep on giving. Using better tools, the same number of bakers can take the same amount of pie capital and make more pie.

Technology has been driving improved productivity for a very long time. We know this, surprisingly enough, because of the increase in global population itself. Prior to the demographic transition in the nineteenth century, people almost always turned extra food into extra progeny. They didn't save and consume more like we do; they had more babies. For this reason, premodern populations usually hovered

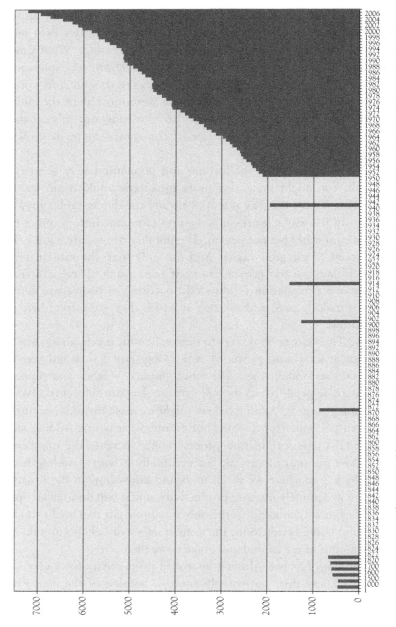

Chart 1. World GDP per Capita: AD 1 to AD 2006 (1990 International Geary-Khamis Dollars).

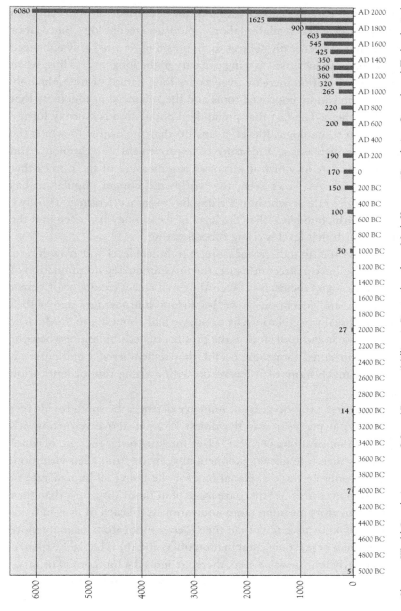

Chart 2. World Population: 5000 BC to AD 2000 (Millions). Data taken from Mark Kremer, "Population Growth and Technological Change: One Million B.C. to 1990," *Quarterly Journal of Economics* 108:3 (1993), 683.

around their carrying capacity, that is, they "carried" as many children as they could, given available labor, capital, and technology. Since labor and capital are generally subject to diminishing returns, only enhanced technology can increase carrying capacity in the long term. Thus, when we see a population increase over a very long period of time, the only explanation can be improved tools and the enhanced productivity that comes of them. The fact that premodern population is a proxy for the premodern technological level means (a) that the degree to which the population increases is a measure of improvement in technology; and (b) that the rate at which it increases is a measure of the rate of that improvement. As we've seen, the worldwide human population has risen and the rate at which it is rising has been accelerating. Thus, we can say with confidence that the level of technology has risen and the rate at which that level is rising is accelerating.

Population is an indirect measure of technical level and growth rate. But we also have a direct measure, the production and accumulation of new technologies themselves. According to a recent catalogue of "great discoveries and inventions," we began our journey ages ago with a handful of really useful tools; by 2000, we had about 8,500.[10] Much of this increase in our tool stock is the product of accumulation: when our ancestors invented something useful, they remembered it and passed it on.[11] But much more of it has to do with a rising rate of innovation over time.

For the first 150,000 years of human existence, the species-wide rate of innovation per year was the tiniest fraction above zero; now it's around 50 innovations per year. Over the long term, the rate of innovation has therefore grown exponentially. Aside from alien visitation, there can only be three explanations for the rising all-human rate of innovation over time: (a) there are more of us innovating now than then (more innovators meaning more innovations); (b) each of us is individually more innovative now than then (better innovators meaning more innovations); or (c) some combination of (a) and (b). The right explanation is clearly (c). As we've seen, there are indeed a lot more of us innovating now than then: 7,000 years ago there were perhaps five million people on earth; now there are billions.[12] We are also better innovators. Around 10,000 years ago, the rate of innovation per year per billion people was 0.75; now it's 6.68.[13] If one focuses on people in the developed

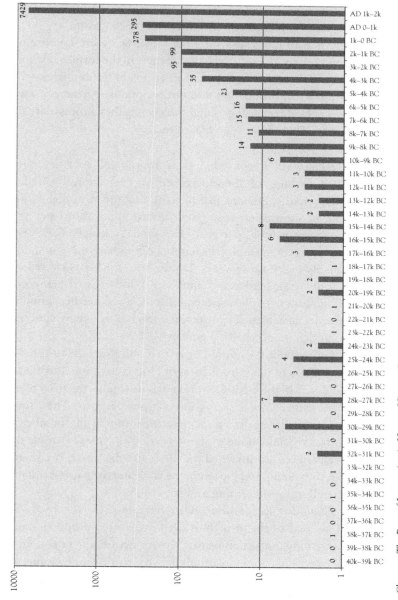

Chart 3. The Rate of Innovation in Human History (Innovations per 1,000 Years: 40,000 BC to AD 2000 [Semi Log Scale]). Based on data provided to the author by Jonathan Huebner. On that data, see Huebner, "A Possible Declining Trend for Worldwide Innovation," 981.

257

world – that is, where most of the innovation is accomplished – then the increase in per capita rate of innovation is much greater.

Of course, not all innovations are the same. Some are important – the plow – and others less so – the letter opener. In the former category, we should put those technologies – or rather sets of technologies – that spawn new modes of production and discontinuously greater productivity. These epochal technologies and the epochs they brought are not hard to identify. There have been five of them.

1. The "Behavioral Revolution" circa 50,000 BC to 10,000 BC. So-called because of the emergence of "behaviorally modern humans," that is, humans just like you and me.[14] In this period, the rate of innovation rose from 0.0001 innovations per year to 0.0033 innovations per year. The annual average growth rate was 0.06 percent, meaning the number of innovations would double roughly every 1,167 years. During this era, we perfected old stone tools (e.g., blades and hand axes) and created many new ones (e.g., bows, arrows, spears, buttons, awls, needles, grinding implements, ornaments, figurines, paintings) out of new materials (bone, antler, ivory, shells, pigments).[15]

2. The "Agricultural Revolution" circa 10,000 BC to AD 1000. So-called because of the introduction of crop cultivation and animal husbandry.[16] In this period, the rate of innovation rose from 0.006 innovations per year to 0.295 innovations per year. The annual average growth rate was 0.44 percent, meaning the number of innovations would double about every 159 years. During this era, we perfected or invented the plow and the sickle, bricks and mortar, the spindle and the loom, the yoke and the harness, mining and metallurgy, and writing and papyrus.[17]

3. The "Capitalist Revolution" circa AD 1000 to AD 1700. So-called because of the growth of market-oriented production and trade, predominantly in Europe.[18] In this period, the rate of innovation rose from 0.52 innovations per year to 4.85 innovations per year. The average annual growth rate was 1.19 percent, meaning the number of innovations would double about every 59 years. During this era we perfected or invented stirrups, heavy plows, waterwheels, flywheels, windmills, modern ship rigging, pumps,

compasses, clocks, guns, printing presses, calculating machines, other very useful tools.[19]

4. *The "Industrial Revolution" circa AD 1700 to AD 1940.* So-called because of the introduction of artificially powered production and trade. In this period, the rate of innovation rose from 5.8 innovations per year to 30.2 innovations per year. The average annual growth rate was 1.75 percent, meaning the number of innovations would double every 40 years. During this era, we perfected or invented all manner of energy sources (coal, oil, atomic), energy transmission devices (railroads, cars, electricity), engines (steam, internal combustion, electric), and built them into machines of every kind.

5. *The "Information Revolution" circa AD 1940 to Present.* So-called because of the introduction of artificially powered control of production and trade. In this period, the rate of innovation rose from 22 innovations per year to 40 innovations per year (and rising). The average annual growth rate was 1.36 percent, meaning the number of innovations doubles ever 51 years. During this era, we perfected or invented all manner of information storage, transmission, and manipulation machines, particularly the computer.

What do these five periods have in common? Two things.

First, during each of them the productivity, population, and the innovation rate grew together. The reason for this united upswing is obvious: productivity, population, and innovation are all part of what might be called the "growth cycle," a positive feedback loop in which each trend stimulated the others and they all grew together. The logic is simple: new tools often allow people to produce more food; more food permits people to produce more people; more people are more likely to produce more new tools.[20]

The second thing these five eras share is that each gave birth to a new, more powerful medium. This, of course, is no coincidence. As we've seen, each new set of economic conditions caused organized interests to search out, re-engineer, and deploy new media technologies. They did not always do so for economic reasons, but it's easy to see that the result was a mighty contribution to economic growth. The argument

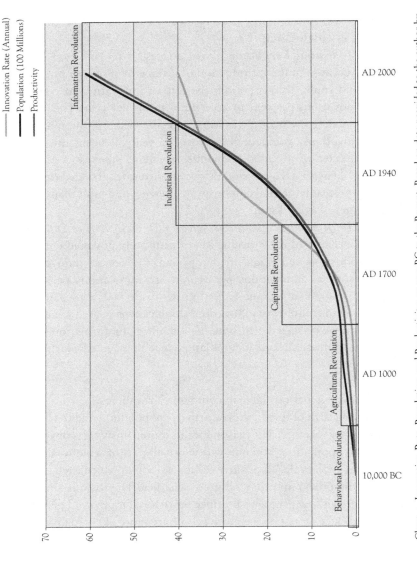

Chart 4. Innovation Rate, Population, and Productivity: 10,000 BC to the Present. Based on data provided to the author by Jonathan Huebner. On that data, see Huebner, "A Possible Declining Trend for Worldwide Innovation," 981.

here is very straightforward. As we've said, different media create differ-ent kinds of networks. Some of these are more conducive to economic activity than others. Compare, for example, a speech network and an Internet network. The speech network will be *connected* – everyone will be privy to everyone else's messages; *symbolic* – messages will be encoded; *constrained* – messages will be short; *intensive* – there will only be a relative few nodes in the network; and *substitutive* – messages will not accumulate very well. You hardly need to be a professional economist to see that literally none of these characteristics has a posi-tive impact on economic activity. New technologies and know-how can be exchanged, but only in a small circle. If they require privacy, they can-not be exchanged. If they require graphics, they cannot be exchanged. If they are too large, they cannot be exchanged. If they are compli-cated, they will be forgotten and therefore cannot be exchanged. Such a network has few of the "network externalities" – like radically increas-ing returns to network scale – and "knowledge spillover effects" – like cross-fertilization among enterprises – that specialists claim are the engines of long-term economic growth.[21] Now compare an Internet network. It is *segmented* – messages can be hidden or shared; *iconic* – messages can be pictures and words; *unconstrained* – messages can be very small or very large; *extensive* – messages can reach a few people or millions; and *additive* – messages can be saved for later reference. All of these attributes contribute to economic activity. New technologies and best practices can be widely exchanged, made public or private, rendered in any form, transmitted in any size, and archived forever. As such, an Internet network has a host of "network externalities" and "spillovers."

In truth, we did not really begin to benefit materially from better media and better networks until quite recently. This is because, as we've said, until recently we used the fruits of higher productivity to produce additional fruits from our loins. Increased productivity doesn't do you much good if it only leads to increased re-productivity. Of course, the ruling classes, as Marx would say, have always enjoyed a better standard of living than those they ruled. They could have as many children as they wanted and still enjoy more stuff. The rest of us, however, probably lived no better in AD 1800 than we had in 3000 BC. We just had more children. That changed, as we've said, in the mid-nineteenth century, when we stopped turning additional stuff into additional children and started turning additional stuff into additional stuff. The reason we did so, like any change of heart, remains something of a mystery. But it is not unconnected with the evolution of the media themselves. To understand how these two phenomena – the demographic transition and the development of the media – are connected, we need to address the role the media have played (or not played) in enhancing our sensory well-being.

MEDIA AND SENSORY WELL-BEING

Have the media made us feel, in the purely sensory sense, any better? The answer again is "yes." We know this, as we will presently explain, because (a) we know that variety – or rather safe novelty – is the spice of life; (b) we know that we produce a lot more safe novelty than ever before; (c) we know why that volume of safe novelty has increased – improved novelty productivity; and (d) we know why novelty productivity has improved – improved tools, media among them.

Measuring changes in material well-being is simple because all you need do is count materials. Measuring changes in sensory well-being is more difficult because it's not at all clear what you should count, or even if there is anything to count. Lots of different things make us feel good. Some are purely physical: sleep, drugs, and sex. Others are abstract: achievement, friendship, and beauty. And still others seem to fall between the two: music, humor, and drama. Alas, none of these things is universally enjoyed – *De gustibus non est disputandum* – and most of them can't really be counted – how much "beauty" is there in a rose? We might say that they are, or at least most of them, consumed during "leisure time" and then use leisure hours as a proxy for the amount of sensual well-being. But that won't quite work because many people derive a great deal of pleasure from their work, and work hours would be completely excluded.

One thing that all of these stimuli have in common, however, is that they are subject to diminishing returns.[22] For whatever reason, people seem to naturally enjoy novelty.[23] We have all experienced "too much of a good thing." You drink too much, and you get a hangover. You hang out with your friends too often, and you get tired of them. You watch too much TV, and you get bored. In such situations you need a "change of pace," something new and different. Of course, new and different can be dangerous. But if it's demonstrably safe, then you will, upon reaching the point of diminishing returns with your current sensual diversion, probably opt for it if it is available at low cost.[24]

This being so, the thing we want to count when measuring long-term sensory well-being is *safe* novelty. How much safe novelty is there? Is there more of it today than there was yesterday? How fast is the amount of it changing? The best way to begin answering these questions is to measure the root of all novelty, that is, variety. We might think of variety as potential novelty: the greater the variety available, the more novelty one can potentially experience. Which is simply to say that, in order to experience new things, you need new things.

There would seem to be no question that the amount of variety – or at least the kind of variety that might interest humans – has increased mightily since we evolved 180,000 years ago. Over the past 70,000 years we, *Homo sapiens sapiens*, migrated from one place (Africa) to places all over the globe. The stock of geographic variety thereby grew. Over the same period, we transformed a single culture into thousands of different cultures, each quite different from the other. Thus, the stock of cultural variety grew. Over the past 10,000 years, we transformed a simple agricultural society with a few roles into an incredibly diverse industrial society with tens of thousands of roles. The stock of social variety thereby grew. Over the past 500 years, we have employed professionals – explorers, scientists, scholars – to analyze and catalogue the natural universe. Thus, the stock of natural variety grew. Over the past 200 years we have employed another class of professionals – artists, writers, entertainers – to imagine fictive worlds. Thus, the stock of imaginary variety grew.

So we clearly have more variety than we once did. But not only that: the *rate* at which we are producing variety is increasing and has been for some time. We know this because the rate of variety-production is a function of several other kinds of production, all of whose rates are increasing. We have already reviewed three of them: the production of stuff, the production of people, and the production of innovations. Rising rates of productivity allowed us to produce more stuff with fewer resources. Given that we like novelty, more stuff also meant *different* stuff. So rising productivity created more variety. Rising rates of population growth meant more people each year. Since everyone is different, more people meant more *different* people. So rising rates of population growth created more variety. Rising rates of innovation meant more innovations each year. Because innovations are by definition new, more innovations means more *different* tools. So rising rates of innovation created more variety. We hardly need add that since productivity, population, and innovation are part of a positive feedback loop – the economic growth cycle – their upward movement drives the general rate of variety-production. If the one grew exponentially, so did the other.

The reason all of these trends grew together at roughly the same rate is, of course, improved technology. As we said, only improved tools can increase productivity – be it of stuff or variety – indefinitely.

All of this means that both the level of variety and rate of variety production have been increasing for some time. But variety is not novelty, it is only potential novelty; potential novelty doesn't contribute to our sensory well-being, only actual novelty does. There might be a lot of variety "out there," but if you can't get to it or have it brought to you, then it might as well not exist. Here is where media work their unique magic, for they can transform variety into novelty. Not, of course, by moving you to whatever difference might exist (we still haven't cracked that problem), but rather by bringing whatever variety other people might experience to you. You aren't a very good recording device, but the media are. You aren't easy to reproduce, but the media are. You aren't very mobile, but the media are. The media enable you to record, reproduce, and distribute your experiences of variety to others, thereby transforming potential novelty into actual novelty. The media, so to speak, put us all in each other's heads.

Of course they did so to different degrees, largely depending on their technical attributes and the networks that flow from them. Compare, for example, manuscript writing and the Internet. The writing network will be *concentrated* – most people won't even be fully on it because of the high cost of learning to read and write well; *symbolic* – messages will be encoded; *constrained* – messages will be short; *mono-logic* – messages will move slowly; and *unmapped* – messages will be hard to find. Clearly, a written network is not a very efficient (or fun) way to exchange experiences. If experience-bearing messages must be read, only a minority of the audience will receive them. If they require pictures or sounds, they cannot be exchanged. If they are long, they cannot be exchanged. If they need to arrive quickly, they cannot be

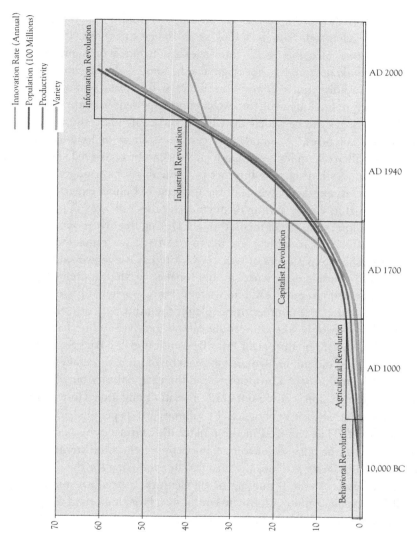

Chart 5. Innovation Rate, Population, and Variety: 10,000 BC to the Present. Based on data provided to the author by Jonathan Huebner. On that data, see Huebner, "A Possible Declining Trend for Worldwide Innovation," 981.

exchanged. If they are archived, they cannot be found and therefore cannot be exchanged. Now let's look at an Internet network. It is *diffuse* – everyone can get it; *iconic* – messages can include words, pictures, and sounds; *unconstrained* – messages can be long; *dialogic* – messages will move rapidly; and *mapped* – messages will be easy to find. The Internet is a marvelous tool for exchanging experiences. Experience-bearing messages can be widely distributed and easily understood; they can be text, pictures, or sound; they can be as short or long as you like; they will arrive quickly; and, if lost, they can be recovered simply. There is no question that the Internet is a machine for turning variety into novelty. It reveals the whole of the universe of human experiences. When we surf it, we are surfing through each other's senses.

It took a long time to get there, though. During the first 6,000 years of artificial media – roughly 3000 BC to AD 1850 – it remained very difficult to share experiences of variety. Writing, as we've just said, is a poor tool for trading experience, if only for the fact that in premodern times so few people could read and write. Print is somewhat better, but is only as good as the number of people on the print network, that is, the number of people who can produce, send, receive, and understand printed messages. The European Print Revolution may have been revolutionary, but it did not immediately bring a revolution in literacy: prior to 1800, the majority of Europeans – and the vast majority outside the Northwestern region – could not read or write. Long after Gutenberg, Europeans shared their experiences by talking, just as people had done for millennia. That changed in the nineteenth century, when governments got into the business of compelling people to become literate and the printing industry got into the business of producing for the masses of new readers. At the beginning of the century, a smallish minority of all Europeans could read; by the end of it, a large majority could.[25] At the beginning of the century, printed matter was relatively rare; by the end of it, it was in the hands of pretty much everyone who wanted it. Millions of readers and billions of texts meant the democratization of experience. The appearance of the audiovisual media and the Internet in the twentieth century accelerated and amplified this process. They allowed more experiences of different kinds to flow more rapidly through even larger networks. For the first time in human history, we began to enter each other's heads, to surf through each other's senses in very large numbers.

One can't help but notice an interesting parallel between the timing of the take-off of material well-being – the nineteenth century – and the timing of the take off of sensory well-being – the nineteenth century. This simultaneity is no accident, for they are both part of the same self-reinforcing system. We saw that the material well-being of Europeans (and, later, everyone else) began to improve when fertility began to decline. Thereafter, the economic pie continued to grow at a rapid pace while the number of pie-eaters, though still increasing, advanced at a slower pace. As a result, everybody got a bigger share of the growing pie. But what triggered the decline in fertility? This is an old question. Indeed, it finds its origins in the nineteenth century itself, when anxious upper-class intellectuals such as Francis Galton – Darwin's cousin – began to worry that "desirables" were being swamped, demographically speaking, by "undesirables."[26] We, of course, are interested in the unexpected decline of European fertility for a different reason, namely, as a condition for modern economic growth. It has not been neglected. Indeed, scholars have answered the question almost too well. In hundreds of books and thousands of papers, they have discovered dozens of factors that impelled Europeans and those who followed them down the path to modernity to have fewer children. Among the most common we find: declining mortality, increasing longevity, rising incomes, urbanization, inheritance laws, anti-child labor laws, tax laws, increasing return to education, mass education, improved contraception, the women's movement, secularism, liberalism, socialism, and – that maker of all things modern – capitalism.[27]

Another factor, and one of particular interest to us, is access to media. Since the 1990s, researchers have devoted considerable attention to the impact of exposure to mass media to the ongoing decline in fertility in the semi- and undeveloped worlds.[28] This is particularly fortunate for us, as these modern-day scholars are in fact closely observing a process quite similar to that which went on in nineteenth-century Europe during the first, pivotal fertility decline. Their conclusion is this: when access to media goes up, fertility goes down.[29] Even when other fertility-influencing factors are considered (for example, level of education, urban residence, occupation), the statistical association between media exposure and lower fertility remains significant.[30]

Of course, correlation is not causation: in order for the former to indicate the latter, we need to identify a probable mechanism or mechanisms. These are not hard to imagine. Having children takes time and money; anything that reduces the amount of time or money that can or will be devoted to child-bearing and -rearing will reduce fertility.[31] Media demand time and money, both directly and indirectly. Letter-writing, book-reading, radio-listening, television-watching, and Internet-surfing are all "time sucks," as we sometimes say. If the time sucked is right before you and your conjugal partner fall asleep, it might well have a direct impact on your fertility. Late-night television is a kind of birth control. Moreover, since the media aren't exactly given away, they are also "money sucks," though we don't say so in so many words. Money spent on media is money that you can't spend on your children, notional or actual. A big-screen TV is also a kind of birth control. The probable indirect temporal and monetary costs of media are much greater than the direct costs. The reason is simple: the media show you variety, that is, potential novelty. You are physically *here*, in this familiar space. The media take you mentally *there*, into an exotic space full of possibilities. That process of mental transportation is enjoyable enough in itself, as anyone who has read a mystery novel cover-to-cover in a single sitting, watched ten hours of a *Twilight Zone* marathon, or played "World of Warcraft" until dawn will tell you. But the media also entice you to go *physically* from your familiar space into that exotic space. In other words, they change the way you behave and how you allocate your time and money generally. You see the new shoes on the sports star, you want the new shoes on the sports star. You see the celebrity in Tahiti, you want to travel yourself to Tahiti. You see the happy sit-com couples living happy, fulfilled lives without children, you want to live a happy, fulfilled life without children.

There would seem to be no doubt that exposure to modern media is one of the forces driving down fertility in developing countries (and in developed countries, we should add). The question is whether it drove down fertility in nineteenth-century Europe, that is, during the period of transition from premodern stagnation to modern growth. It almost certainly did. The most obvious evidence of this fact is simple correlation: fertility declined where mass literacy arose and spread, that is, in Northwestern Europe and its offshoots.[32] Again, correlation is not causation; we need a mechanism. And we have one, the same that we see operating in the semi- and undeveloped worlds today: the media were making increasing demands on would-be parents' time and money. Some of these costs were direct, for example, time and money spent reading the newspaper. But far more important were the indirect costs, that is, those associated with the results of being presented with new possibilities for novelty and, by means of its consumption, personal gratification. Interestingly, Charles Darwin, who had read his share of newspapers and books, had both on his mind when he drew up a list of the pros and cons of getting married and having children in 1837 or 1838.[33] A family meant "less money for books etc," as well as less time to read them ("cannot read in the evenings"). Worse yet, a family meant he would not be free to go where he liked and associate with whom he wished. Darwin knew about the world. He'd read about it. He wanted to see it. If he "married tomorrow . . ."

. . . there would be an infinity of trouble and expense in getting and furnishing a house, – fighting about no Society – morning calls – awkwardness – loss of time every day – (without one's wife was an angel and made one keep industrious) – Then how should I manage all my business if I were obliged to go every day walking with my wife. – Eheu!! I never should know French, – or see the Continent, – or go to America, or go up in a Balloon, or take solitary trip in Wales – poor slave, you will be worse than a negro – And then horrid poverty.

Because Darwin was rich, he could have it all: he ended up marrying, having a large family, *and* seeing a good portion of the world. Those in the middle and lower classes, however, were not so fortunate. The media – print in this case – had shown them a world of possibilities much greater than anyone had ever seen in all human history. It was in newspapers, chap books, adventure stories, romance novels, pornography, picture books, and a quickly expanding universe of items designed precisely to take their time and money – advertisements. The media showed them that there was something else, something more, something better. They began to seek it outside the family. We still do, and to a degree that the Victorians could scarcely comprehend. According to the United Nations, fertility is less than the replacement rate in seventy-three countries, which together account for 43 percent of the world's population.[34] The newspaper-reading Victorians chose to have fewer children; we Internet-surfing moderns are choosing to have no children. If present trends continue, the Web will have to surf itself.

Have the media made us feel spiritually any better? The answer is "no." We know this, as we'll see, because (a) we know that our spiritual well-being arises when we believe we are "doing the right thing" in relation to some transcendental something; (b) we know that the media encourage us to do the wrong thing, and that modern media encourage us to do the wrong thing more often.

Like sensory well-being, spiritual well-being is difficult to assess. The basic problem is that it's not at all clear what "spiritual well-being" is or, whatever it may be, whether it can be measured.[35] Religious people typically say that spirituality has something to do with proximity to the divine. Faiths, however, vary tremendously, as do their notions of divinity. Others, and especially people who are "spiritual" and not "religious," would probably say spirituality has something to do with serenity, peace of mind, or enlightenment. These notions, too, come in various flavors, none of which tastes quite like any other. And still other people, especially hard-core atheists, just dismiss the notion as metaphysical mumbo-jumbo. After all, there seems to be something about the very definition of spirituality that puts it beyond the realm of the senses and therefore beyond the realm of what can be known.

As Locke might have said, spirituality seems to fall squarely into the troublesome category of "something, I know not what."[36] All, however, is not lost, for the traditional believer, the new-age spiritualist, and the tough-minded atheist can certainly agree on the following. First, that many people believe they have spirits. Whether they come from beyond (as the believer would say), are born of spiritual practice (as the spiritualists would say), or are inventions (as the atheists would say) is irrelevant. They say they have them, and that is enough to establish the existence of something, if only the claim that they have them. Second, whatever the origin of the claim, most people report the presence of a spirit as a state of mind. As such, it's subjective and can't really be shared. The only way you can make it known is by word ("I'm in good spirits") or deed ("Let me do that for you"). Neither can it be described using the vocabulary of physical sensation. A state of spiritual well-being is not bodily pleasure, nor is a state of spiritual sickness bodily pain. Rather, the one and the other are qualities of mind. Someone in good spirits will be clear, calm, and confident; someone in poor spirits will be confused, agitated, and fearful. Finally, most people explain that the spiritual state is the result of their relationship with something greater than themselves that lies beyond their comprehension. This mysterious higher power might be god, the natural world, or even society. If they "go against" it, they say, then they will be in bad spirits; if they "go with it," they say, then they will be in good spirits. Again, whether their explanation is valid is beside the point: all that matters is that this is what they believe to be the case.

To boil down all we've said, spiritual well-being is a mental quality that often results when people believe they are "doing the right thing" in relation to some transcendental something. Now to our question: have the media contributed to our spiritual well-being? Probably not.

First of all, the media have indirectly contributed to our disenchantment by helping to spur economic growth, which in turn directly allowed us to ignore spiritual questions. For almost all of human history, uncertainty and spirituality walked hand in hand. In premodern times, death was always near. Moreover, one never knew in what guise it would come or when it would arrive. It's no wonder, then, that premodern people paid a lot of attention to life's big questions: Why am I here? How should I live? What is the purpose of life? Why must I die? Neither is it any wonder that, finding no answers in this world, they sought them in another, unseen world. Nietzsche famously wrote, "If we have our own *why* of life, we shall get along with almost any *how*."[37] The unseen world gave premodern people the "why of life" and thereby enabled them to suffer their difficult "how of life." Thanks in part to the media and the economic explosion they facilitated, we live in material circumstances that no longer require constant – or even any – attention to spiritual affairs.[38] Our "how of life" is not one of suffering and a probable early grave, but rather of plenty and a probable long life. A child born in a developed country today has a very good chance of never experiencing want and of living beyond 70 years. We can put off the big "whys of life" for decades while we pursue lesser questions like whether we will get into the right college, get the right job, marry the right partner, live in the right city, have the right number of children, and pick the right place to retire. The media – that is, other people – will answer all these questions. As the end of life approaches, however, we will begin to ask questions that the media cannot answer. Even Google cannot tell you whether you have done the right thing in relation to your higher power. And since you've not paid any attention to the question for the last 70 years – years in which you doggedly pursued worldly things – you probably won't be able to answer it, either. You may die with considerable peace of mind, but probably as a result of some drug a doctor has given you.

Second, the media have directly contributed to our disenchantment by encouraging us to *think* in the wrong way. Plato knew why: uniquely among human tools, the media enable us to create synthetic worlds where the rules of men and gods somehow do not apply. The media truck in representations, and we say that representations are not realities. This being so, we believe we can do anything we like in our synthetic worlds without real penalty. Comforting though this notion might be, it really isn't true. There is a difference between representations and realities, but it does not follow that representations are harmless to those who consume them. In fact, they can be quite spiritually damaging. To achieve spiritual well-being, you need to do the right thing. But that is not enough. Years of psychological research have shown that you also need to think the right thoughts.[39] In order to do that, you need to closely monitor what goes in your mind because it will have a direct effect on what comes out in terms of your spirit. But we don't monitor what goes in at all. There was a time – actually a very long time – in which elites agreed that representations needed to be regulated. It's true that the authorities generally didn't censor representations in order to protect the spiritual well-being of the population (ecclesiastical officials being the exception), but they believed that some censorship was necessary nonetheless. As we've seen, they were fighting a losing battle against ever more powerful media and a seemingly unstoppable desire for enhanced sensory well-being. At some time in the nineteenth century, humanity chose sensuality over spirituality, and we are all living with the consequences. Disturbing images may not make you do disturbing things, but they will definitely make you think disturbing thoughts.[40] And the thing about disturbing thoughts is that they are, well, disturbing.

Finally, the media have contributed to our disenchantment by encouraging us to *act* in the wrong way. For millennia, social critics have been asking whether representations of bad things make people do bad things. Plato thought they did; modern researchers generally don't. But in fact it depends on what we understand by "bad things." Exposure to pornography does not seem to make men more likely to commit rape.[41] But exposure to pornography does seem to make men more likely to masturbate, and indeed masturbate compulsively.[42] Now, you may not think that masturbation is a "bad thing." Many people, however, do, and those among them who masturbate compulsively while looking at Internet porn are likely suffering spiritually. They are not, after all, "doing the right thing" in relation to their higher power. This sort of media-inspired self-harm is actually quite common. You know you are supposed to treat people kindly, yet you abuse others in chat rooms. You know you are supposed to study, but you watch TV instead. You know your work computer is for work, but use it to surf the web. In each of these cases, the media have led you to *do* the wrong thing in *real life*. Media-driven spiritual harm, however, does not end with the media consumer. Whether you believe porno-fueled masturbation is a "bad thing" or not, you probably think that having an active sexual bond with your spouse is a "good thing." The trouble is that the one affects the other: the more you masturbate to Internet porn, the less often you are likely to make love to your wife.[43] The former, while not a "bad thing" in and of itself, causes you to do an acknowledged "bad thing," thereby causing you spiritual harm. This sort of media knock-on effect is also quite common. Watching the reality show *Jack Ass* is not a "bad thing" until it causes you to hurt someone while acting like a jackass. Sending text messages while driving is not a "bad thing" until it causes you to injure someone in a car accident. Listening to Whitney Houston sing "I Will Always Love You" 100 times in a row is not a "bad thing" until it drives your neighbors insane.

Marx believed the future would bring an era of incredible material abundance. Using advanced new tools, people would almost effortlessly produce the stuff they needed to live comfortable lives. It would be a new world of things. He was not wrong. Using advanced new tools, some people – namely those of us in the developed world – do almost effortlessly produce all the necessities of existence. We need not work very hard to acquire all the food, clothing, shelter, and sundry accessories we could ever reasonably desire.

We do live in a new world of things. Marx, however, did not predict that we would also live in a new world of signs. For the first 170,000-odd years of our history, persistent signs were very few. The reason is shockingly simple: we talked; we did not record. Our total prehistoric output of persistent signs – carvings, statuary, ornaments, cave painting, tokens, etc. – would likely have fit into a moderately sized museum. Once we began to use artificial media, our output and stock grew. In Marx's day, the store of accumulated signs was large. It doesn't strain credulity to guess that by the mid-nineteenth century it comprised billions (10^9) and perhaps trillions (10^{12}) of signs recorded in all manner of media. They were, however, scattered around the world and unevenly distributed, so the average person had access to only the tiniest fraction of them. Marx was not an average person: he had access to the British Museum, which actually held a fair portion of them. It no longer does, for in our era the output and stock of persistent signs have both exploded. According to an estimate made in 2000, the world records between one and two exabytes of unique information on paper, film, optical, and magnetic media each year.[44] An exabyte is 10^{18} bytes, that is, a million million bytes. In other words, we produce more persistent signs *every year* than all the people who had ever lived produced between 180,000 BC and Marx's era. Moreover, we have much greater access to our sign stock than Marx did to his. He had to go to the British Museum to do his research; today the British Museum – and just about everything else – comes to us. The average person, if he or she has Internet access, can get a pretty good chunk of all the information ever recorded, a number much larger than 10^{18} bytes.

Marx foresaw none of this. Neither did he envision the way in which signs would come to dominate our lives. Marx's new world of things was about *making and consuming*; our new world of signs is about *encoding and decoding*. Marx thought people would realize themselves through unalienated labor and the unalienated product thereof. It's true that people often find meaning in their work, and that they enjoy the stuff they and others make. But work is just work, and stuff is just stuff – your appetite for both is limited. It turns out that when peoples' desires for meaningful work and fine stuff are sated, they quickly turn to encoding and decoding signs. Marx would be astonished at the amount of time we spend engaged in these activities. We wake up to the radio, read the paper over breakfast, listen to music on the commute to work, check our email once in the office, check our phone messages and make some calls, surf the web throughout the day for business and pleasure, listen to the news on the way home, put on some music while we make dinner, watch TV afterward, and wind up the day, perhaps, by reading a book as we fall asleep.

The purpose of human life, Aristotle said, was to be well. It seems hard to disagree with him. We have every right, then, to ask if the new world of signs, the world in which we live, makes us well or not. The answer we have given is mixed. The media, and particularly the modern media, contributed mightily to our material well-being. They were among the tools that produced the new world of things. The media, and particularly the modern media, improved our sensory well-being. They enabled us to break free from our own senses and experience an astounding variety of things through the senses of others. Finally, the media, and particularly the modern media, have had a rather less positive impact on our spiritual well-being. They have made us turn away from spiritual matters, and have prompted us to compulsively think and do things that plainly injure our spirits. In this regard, the new world of signs has taken control of us. As Marx might have said, we serve the signs rather than the signs serving us. Whether we will ever realize this is the case and, if so, do anything to liberate ourselves, only prophets can say.

NOTES

INTRODUCTION: MEDIA CAUSES AND MEDIA EFFECTS

1. Karl Marx and Friedrich Engels, *Werke*, 39 vols. in 41 (Berlin: Dietz Verlag, 1961–1974), vol. 3: "Die deutsche Ideologie," 20.

2. Marshall McLuhan, *Understanding Media: The Extensions of Man* (New York: McGraw Hill, 1964), 7.

3. McLuhan, *Understanding Media*, 8 and 13, respectively.

4. Though each of these men went on to write several books on orality and literacy, their seminal contributions were: Walter J. Ong, *Ramus, Method, and the Decay of Dialogue: From the Art of Discourse to the Art of Reason* (Cambridge: Harvard UP, 1958); Eric A. Havelock, *Preface to Plato* (Cambridge: Harvard UP, 1963); and Jack Goody, *The Domestication of the Savage Mind* (Cambridge: Cambridge UP, 1977).

5. For a withering critique of the Mentalist School, see John Halverson, "Olson on Literacy," *Language in Society* 20:4 (1991), 619–640; John Halverson, "Goody and the Implosion of the Literacy Thesis," *Man* (New Series), 27:2 (1992), 301–317; and John Halverson, "Havelock on Greek Orality and Literacy," *Journal of the History of Ideas* 53:1 (1992), 148–163.

6. The seminal text is a chapter in Max Horkheimer and Theodor W. Adorno's *Dialektik der Aufklärung* (Amsterdam: Querido Verlag, 1947) entitled "Kulturindustie – Aufklärung als Massenbetrug." Marcuse's contribution was the *One-Dimensional Man* (Boston: Beacon, 1964).

7. Marxist treatments of the media are somewhat out of fashion today, although they can be found. See Mike Wayne, *Marxism and Media Studies: Key Concepts and Contemporary Trends* (London: Pluto Press, 2003); Phil Graham, *Hypercapitalism: New Media, Language, and Social Perceptions of Value* (New York: Peter Lang, 2005); Matthew Fuller, *Media Ecologies: Materialist Energies in Art and Technoculture* (Cambridge: MIT Press, 2005); and Lee Artz, Steve Macek, and Dana L. Cloud, eds., *Marxism and Communication Studies: The Point Is to Change It* (New York: Peter Lang, 2006).

8. The standard-bearers – indeed, gurus – of the modern Critical Theory approach to media studies are Jürgen Habermas and Noam Chomsky. Both have written many books and have many followers. For examples of their work, see Jürgen Habermas, *Strukturwandel der Öffentlichkeit. Untersuchungen*

zu einer Kategorie der bürgerlichen Gesellschaft (Neuwied: H. Luchterhand, 1962); and Edward S. Herman and Noam Chomsky, *Manufacturing Consent: The Political Economy of the Mass Media* (New York: Pantheon Books, 1988).

9. On the shortcomings of the entire research program, see David L. Altheide, "Media Hegemony: A Failure of Perspective," *Public Opinion Quarterly* 48:2 (1984), 476–490.

10. Michael Agger, "And the Oscar for the Best Scholar...," *New York Times* (May 18, 2003), Section 2, 15.

11. See especially Jean Baudrillard, *In the Shadow of the Silent Majorities*, translated by Paul Foss et al. (New York: Semiotext(e), 1983); and Jean Baudrillard, *Simulacra and Simulation*, translated by Sheila Faria Glaser (Ann Arbor: University of Michigan Press, 1995).

12. The most thorough Poststructuralist analyses of media are those of Mark Poster. See Mark Poster, *Information Please: Cultural and Politics in the Age of Digital Machines* (Durham: Duke UP, 2006); Mark Poster, *The Information Subject* (Amsterdam: G + B International, 2001); Mark Poster, *The Second Media Age* (Cambridge: Polity Press, 1995); and Mark Poster, *The Mode of Information: Poststructuralism and Social Context* (Chicago: University of Chicago Press, 1990). For a Poststructuralist treatment of eighteenth-, nineteenth-, and early twentieth-century media, see Friedrich A. Kittler, *Discourse Networks 1800/1900* (Stanford: Stanford UP, 1990) and Friedrich A. Kittler, *Gramophone, Film, Typewriter* (Stanford: Stanford UP, 1999).

13. On Innis's life, see Donald Creighton, *Harold Adams Innis: Portrait of a Scholar* (Toronto: University of Toronto Press, 1957); Paul Heyer, *Harold Innis* (Lanham: Rowman & Littleman, 2003); and Alexander John Watson, *Marginal Man: The Dark Vision of Harold Innis* (Toronto: University of Toronto Press, 2006).

14. Harold A. Innis, *A History of the Canadian Pacific Railroad* (Toronto: McClelland and Stewart, 1923); Harold A. Innis, *Fur Trade in Canada: An Introduction to Canadian Economic History* (New Haven: Yale UP, 1930); and Harold A. Innis, *Cod Fisheries: The History of an International Economy* (New Haven: Yale UP, 1940).

15. These books include Oswald Spengler, *Der Untergang des Abendlandes: Umrisse einer Morphologie der Weltgeschichte*, 2 vols. (Munich: Beck, 1918–1923); Arnold Toynbee, *A Study of History*, 12 vols. (Oxford: Oxford UP: 1934–1961); Alfred Kroeber, *Configurations of Culture Growth* (Berkeley, Los Angeles: University of California Press, 1944); and Pitirim Sorokin, *Social and Cultural Dynamics*, 4 vols. (New York: American Book Co., 1937–1941).

16. The foundation texts are Milman Parry, "Studies in the Epic Technique of Oral Verse-Making. I: Homer and Homeric Style," *Harvard Studies in Classical Philology* 41 (1930), 73–143; Milman Parry, "Studies in the Epic Technique of Oral Verse-Making. II: The Homeric Language as the Language of an Oral Poetry," *Harvard Studies in Classical Philology* 43 (1932), 1–50; and Albert B. Lord, *The Singer of Tales* (Cambridge: Harvard UP, 1960).

17. Harold A. Innis, *Empire and Communications*, revised by Mary Q. Innis with a foreword by Marshall McLuhan (Toronto: University of Toronto Press, 1972), xiii.

18. See Harold A. Innis, *Empire and Communications* (Oxford: Clarendon Press, 1950); and Harold A. Innis, *The Bias of Communications* (Toronto: University of Toronto Press, 1951).

19. The literature on creativity, innovation (scientific and technical), and diffusion is very large. Concerning creativity, see M. A. Runco, "Creativity," *Annual Review of Psychology* 55 (2004), 657–687. On scientific innovation, see Thomas S. Kuhn, *The Structure of Scientific Revolutions* (Chicago: University of Chicago Press, 1962) and the voluminous literature that followed in its wake. For a review of theories of technical change, see Alex Roland, "Theories and Models of Technological Change: Semantics and Substance," *Technology & Human Values* 17:1 (1992), 79–100. On the diffusion of innovations, see Everett M. Rogers, *The Diffusion of Innovations* (New York: Free Press of Glencoe, 1962) and the copious literature that followed it.

20. On the myth of the "inventor" and his "discovery," see Simon Schaffer, "Making Up Discovery," in *Dimensions of Creativity*, edited by Margaret Boden (Cambridge: MIT Press, 1996), 13–53.

21. Just what causes people to be creative remains something of a mystery. For a review of the literature, see R. J. Sternberg, ed., *Handbook of Creativity* (Cambridge: Cambridge UP, 1999); and M. A. Runco, "Creativity," 657–687.

22. As a result of "network externalities" or "network effects." On these, see Michael L. Katz and Carl Shapiro, "Technology Adoption in the Presence of Network Externalities," *Journal of Political Economy* 94:4 (1986), 822–841; and, more generally, Nicholas Economides, "The Economics of Networks," *International Journal of Industrial Organizations* 14 (1996), 673–699.

23. Here I draw heavily on Michael Mann, *The Sources of Social Power. Volume 1: A History of Power from the Beginning to A.D. 1760* (Cambridge: Cambridge UP, 1986), 1–34.

24. The "network" approach to the study of society is burgeoning. For a recent review of the literature, see Duncan Watts, "The 'New' Science of Networks," *Annual Review of Sociology* 30 (2004), 243–270.

25. Karl Marx and Friedrich Engels, *Werke*, 39 vols. in 41 (Berlin: Dietz Verlag, 1961–1974), vol. 8: "Der achtzehnte Brumaire des Louis Bonaparte," 115.

26. It is remarkable how hesitant many scholars are to accept that there is such a thing as "human nature." On this tendency, see Steven Pinker, *The Blank Slate: The Modern Denial of Human Nature* (New York: Viking Press, 2002).

27. Karl Marx and Friedrich Engels, *Werke*, 39 vols. in 41 (Berlin: Dietz Verlag, 1961–1974), vol. 4: "Das Eland der Philosophie," 130.

28. See Nicholas Abercrombie, Stephen Hill, and Bryan S. Turner, *The Dominant Ideology Thesis* (London; Boston: Allen & Urwin, 1980). On the origins of values generally, see Michael Hechter, Lynn Nadel, and Richard E. Michod, eds., *The Origin of Values* (New York: A. de Gruyter, 1993); Hans Joas, *The Genesis of Values*, translated by Gregory Moore (Chicago: University

of Chicago Press, 2000); and Raymond Boudon, *The Origin of Values: Sociology and Philosophy of Beliefs* (New Brunswick: Transaction Publishers, 2001).

1. HOMO LOQUENS

1. Plato's *Phaedrus*, translated by R. Hackforth (Cambridge: Cambridge UP, 1972), 159–160.
2. "Gorgias," translated by Donald J. Zeyl in *Plato on Rhetoric and Language: Four Key Dialogues*, introduction by Jean Nienkamp (Mahwah: Hermagoras Press, 1999), 101.
3. An excellent review of recent theories on the origin of language is provided by Derek Bickerton, "Language Evolution: A Brief Guide for Linguists," *Lingua* 117:3 (2007), 510–526.
4. David Hume, *A Treatise of Human Nature*, edited by L. A. Selby-Bigge (Oxford: Oxford UP, 1888), 173.
5. Jean-Louis Dessalles, *Why We Talk: The Evolutionary Origins of Language*, translated by James Grieve (Oxford: Oxford UP, 2007).
6. This idea – "kin selection" – is ordinarily credited to W. D. Hamilton. See his "The Genetical Evolution of Social Behaviour (I and II)," *Journal of Theoretical Biology* 7 (1964), 1–16 and 17–52.
7. This theory – "reciprocal altruism" – is usually credited to Robert Trivers. See his "The Evolution of Reciprocal Altruism," *Quarterly Review of Biology* 46:1 (1971), 35–57.
8. On the formation of reputations, see Martin Nowak and Karl Sigmund, "Evolution of Indirect Reciprocity," *Nature* 437:27 (2005), 1291–1298.
9. On subgroups within primate bands, both ancient and modern, see Charlotte K. Hemelrijk and Jutta Steinhauser, "Cooperation, Coalition, and Alliances" in *Handbook of Paleoanthropology*, edited by Winifried Henke and Ian Tattersall, 3 vols. (Berlin: Springer Verlag, 2007), vol. 2: 1321–1346.
10. For what follows, see F. B. M. de Waal, *Chimpanzee Politics: Power and Sex among Apes* (New York: Harper & Row, 1982); and Richard Wrangham and Dale Peterson, *Demonic Males: Apes and the Origins of Human Violence* (New York: Mariner Books, 1996).
11. See Robin Dunbar, "Neocortex Size as a Constraint on Group Size in Primates," *Journal of Human Evolution* 20 (1992), 469–493; Robin Dunbar, "Neocortex Size and Group Size in Primates: A Test of the Hypothesis," *Journal of Human Evolution* 28 (1995), 287–296; Robin Dunbar, "The Social Brain Hypothesis," *Evolutionary Anthropology* 6 (1998), 178–190; and Robin Dunbar and H. Kudo, "Neocortex Size and Social Network Size in Primates," *Animal Behavior* 62 (2001), 711–722.
12. The idea of "relevance" was first developed by the linguists Dan Sperber and Deirdre Wilson. See their *Relevance: Communication and Cognition* (Oxford: Basil Blackwell, 1986).
13. On "costly signaling," see Amotz Zahavi and Avishag Zahavi, *The Handicap Principle: A Missing Piece of Darwin's Puzzle* (New York: Oxford UP, 1997).
14. This is true of primates generally. See Arnold H. Buss, "Evolutionary Perspectives on Personality Traits," in *The Handbook of Personality Psychology*,

edited by Robert Hogan, John A. Johnson, and Stephen R. Briggs (San Diego: Academic Press, 1997), 359.

15. This is because modern hunter-gatherers are modern. See Katherine A. Spielmann and James F. Eder, "Hunters and Farmers: Then and Now," *Annual Review of Anthropology* 23 (1994), 303–323; and Steven L. Kuhn and Mary C. Stiner, "The Antiquity of Hunter-Gatherers," in *Hunter-Gatherers: An Interdisciplinary Perspective*, edited by Catherine Panter-Brick et al. (Cambridge: Cambridge UP, 2001), 99–142.

16. For a review of the literature, see Fred Myers, "Critical Trends in the Study of Hunter-Gatherers," *Annual Review of Anthropology* 17 (1988), 261–282; and Richard B. Lee, "Art, Science, or Politics? The Crisis in Hunter-Gatherer Studies," *American Anthropologist* 94:1 (1992), 31–54. That the category "hunter-gatherers" encapsulates a remarkable amount of on-the-ground diversity is demonstrated by Robert L. Kelly, *The Foraging Spectrum: Diversity in Hunter-Gatherer Lifeways* (Washington, DC and London: Smithsonian Institution Press, 1995).

17. Roger Griffiths, "Speech Rates and Listening Comprehension: Further Evidence of the Relationship," *TESOL Quarterly* 26:2 (1992), 385–390. Griffiths says the "average speech rate" is 188 words per minute.

18. Griffiths, "Speech Rates and Listening Comprehension."

19. For a review and discussion of the research on facial memory and recognition, see Vicki Bruce and M. E. Le Voi, "Recognizing Faces," *Philosophical Transactions of the Royal Society of London. Series B, Biological Sciences*, 302:1110 ("Functional Aspects of Human Memory") (1983), 423–436. On vocal memory and recognition, see E. C. Carterette and A. Barnebey, "Recognition Memory for Voices," in *Structure and Process in Speech Perception*, edited by A. Cohen and S. G. Nooteboom (New York: Springer, 1975), 246–265; and B. R. Clifford, "Voice Recognition by Human Listeners: On Earwitness Reliability," *Law and Behavior* 4 (1980), 373–394.

20. The typology of signs presented here (icon, index, and image) is that of Charles Sanders Pierce. See his "Sundry Logical Conceptions" [based on lectures given in 1903] in *The Essential Pierce: Selected Philosophical Writings*, vol. 2: 1893–1913, edited by Nathan Houser and Christian J. W. Kloesel (Bloomington: University of Indiana Press, 1998), 273–275.

21. The distinction between motivated and unmotivated (or arbitrary) signs is Ferdinand de Saussure's. See his *Course in General Linguistics* [based on lectures given between 1906 and 1911], translated by Roy Harris (Chicago: Open Court Publishing, 1986), 130–131.

22. "Prophet's Name Growing Ever More Popular, Even in Britain," *Yemen Observer* (June 16, 2007).

23. "Wang Tops List of Surnames," *China Daily* (April 25, 2007).

24. Website: "How Many of Me?" Retrieved July 24, 2008.

25. Website: "Longest Lecture Marathon," Guinness World Records. Retrieved June 4, 2009.

26. Elaine Marieb, Jon Mallatt, and Patricia Wilhelm, *Human Anatomy*, fifth edition (San Francisco: Pearson Benjamin Cummings, 2008), chapter 11 ("Fundamentals of the Nervous System and Nervous Tissue"). The nerves in question are "Group A fibers."

27. James P. Cowan, *Handbook of Environmental Acoustics* (New York: Wiley-Interscience, 1993), 8.
28. See Frances C. Volkmann, Lorrin A. Riggs, and Robert K. Moore, "Eyeblinks and Visual Suppression," *Science* 207:4433 (1980), 900–902; and A. K. Jandziol, M. Prabhu, and R. H. S. Carpenter, and J. G. Jones, "Blink Duration as a Measure of Low-Level Anesthetic Sedation," *European Journal of Anesthesiology* 18:7 (2001), 476–484.
29. Fredrick A. Everest, *The Master Handbook of Acoustics*, fourth edition (New York: McGraw-Hill Professional, 2000), 84.
30. Everest, *The Master Handbook of Acoustics*, 55.
31. Cowan, *Handbook of Environmental Acoustics*, 37. Cowen says a "typical urban area background/busy office" is roughly 60 decibels, so we've assumed our hypothetical office is very quiet by this standard.
32. R. F. Coleman, J. H. Mabis, and J. K. Hinson, "Fundamental Frequency-Sound Pressure Level Profiles of Adult Male and Female Voices," *Journal of Speech and Hearing Research* 20 (1977), 197–204.
33. According to Norris J. Johnson, "movement is impossible and contact with others occurs all around when the occupancy rate of a space is one person per 1.6 to 1.8 feet." See "The Who Concert Stampede: An Empirical Assessment," *Society for the Study of Social Problems* 34:4 (1987), 366, note 6.
34. Herbert Jacobs created the "loose crowd" standard (10 square feet/person) while trying to estimate the size of crowds protesting the Vietnam War. See Julius Fast, *Body Language* (New York: M. Evans, 1970), 52.
35. G. A. Miller, "The Magical Number Seven, Plus or Minus Two: Some Limits on Our Capacity for Processing Information," *Psychological Review* 63 (1956), 81–97. For a revision, see N. Cowan, "The Magical Number Four in Short-Term Memory: A Reconsideration of Mental Storage Capacity," *Behavioral and Brain Sciences* 24 (2001), 97–185.
36. Thomas K. Landauer, "How Much Do People Remember? Some Estimates of the Quantity of Learned Information in Long-Term Memory," *Cognitive Science* 10 (1986), 490–491.
37. The term seems to have been coined in 1833 by Paul Tournal in French: *période ante-historique*. See Molly R. Mignon, *Dictionary of Concepts in Archeology* (Westport: Greenwood Press, 1993), 249.
38. The idea of "total institutions" is Erving Goffman's. See his *Asylums: Essays on the Social Situation of Mental Patients and Other Inmates* (New York: Doubleday, 1961).
39. See the summary statement in Richard B. Lee and Richard Daly, "Introduction: Foragers and Others," *The Cambridge Encyclopedia of Hunters and Gatherers*, edited by Richard B. Lee and Richard Daly (Cambridge: Cambridge UP, 1999), 3–5.

2. HOMO SCRIPTOR

1. *Plato's Phaedrus*, translated by R. Hackforth (Cambridge: Cambridge UP, 1972), 157. Subsequent citations in this paragraph are to this edition.
2. *Phaedrus and the Seventh and Eighth Letters*, translated by Walter Hamilton (Harmondsworth: Penguin Books, 1977), 138.

3. On literacy in the Ancient Near East, see Hans J. Nissen, Peter Damerow, and Robert K. Englund, eds., *Archaic Bookkeeping. Early Writing and Techniques of Economic Administration in the Ancient Near East* (Chicago: University of Chicago, 1994); Giuseppe Visicato, *The Power and the Writing: the Early Scribes of Mesopotamia* (Bethesda: CDL Press, 2000); John Baines, *Visual and Written Culture in Ancient Egypt* (Oxford: Oxford UP, 2007); Piotr Bienkowski, Christopher Mee, and Elizabeth Slater, eds., *Writing and Ancient Near Eastern Society: Papers in Honor of Alan R. Millard* (New York: T&T Clark, 2005); and Kathryn Lomas, Ruth D. Whitehouse, and John B. Wilkins, eds., *Literacy and the State in the Ancient Mediterranean* (London: Accordia Research Institute, University of London, 2007).

4. On literacy in Classical Antiquity, see especially Harris, *Ancient Literacy*, but also Alan K. Bowman and Greg Woolf, eds., *Literacy and Power in the Ancient World* (Cambridge: Cambridge UP, 1994); Jocelyn Penny Small, *Wax Tablets of the Mind: Cognitive Studies of Memory and Literacy in Classical Antiquity* (London: Routledge, 1997); E. Anne Mackay, *Signs of Orality: the Oral Tradition in the Greek and Roman World* (Boston: Brill, 1999); Janet Watson, ed., *Speaking Volumes: Orality and Literacy in the Greek and Roman World* (Leiden: Brill, 2001); E. Anne Mackay, ed., *Orality, Literacy, Memory in the Ancient Greek and Roman World* (Leiden, Boston: Brill, 2008). For Greece in particular, see Eric Havelock, *Preface to Plato* (Cambridge: Harvard UP, 1963). More recently see Terrence Boring, *Literacy in Ancient Sparta* (Leiden: Brill, 1979); Tony M. Lenz, *Orality and Literacy in Hellenic Greece* (Carbondale: Southern Illinois UP, 1989); Rosalind Thomas, *Oral Tradition and Written Record in Classical Athens* (Cambridge: Cambridge UP, 1992); Rosalind Thomas, *Literacy and Orality in Ancient Greece* (Cambridge: Cambridge UP, 1992); Ian Worthington, ed., *Voice into Text: Orality and Literacy in Ancient Greece* (Leiden: Brill, 1996); and Ian Worthington and John Miles Foley, eds., *Epea and Grammata: Oral and Written Communications in Ancient Greece* (Leiden: Brill, 2002). For Rome, see Mary Beard, Alan K. Bowman, and Mireille Corbier, eds., *Literacy in the Roman World* (Ann Arbor: Journal of Roman Archeology Supplementary Series, No. 3, 1991).

5. The foundational text is M. T. Clanchy, *From Memory to Written Record: England, 1066–1307* (Cambridge: Harvard UP, 1979). Also see Brian Stock, *The Implications of Literacy: Written Language and Models of Interpretation in the Eleventh and Twelfth Century* (Princeton: Princeton UP, 1983); Rosamond McKitterick, *The Carolingians and the Written World* (Cambridge: Cambridge UP, 1989); Rosamond McKitterick, ed., *The Uses of Literacy in Early Medieval Europe* (Cambridge: Cambridge UP, 1990); Karl Heidecker, ed., *Charters and the Use of the Written Word in Medieval Society* (Turnhout: Brepols, 2000); Sarah Rees Jones, ed., *Learning and Literacy in Medieval England and Abroad* (Turnhout: Brepols, 2003); Mark Chinca and Christopher Young, eds., *Orality and Literacy in the Middle Ages: Essays on a Conjunction and its Consequences in Honour of D. H. Green* (Turnout: Brepols, 2005); and Franz-Josef Arlinghaus, ed., *Transforming the Medieval World: Uses of Pragmatic Literacy in the Middle Ages* (Turnhout: Brepols, 2006).

6. Alexander Marshack, "On Paleolithic Ochre and Early Uses of Color and Symbol," *Current Anthropology* 22:2 (1981), 188–191. More generally on very early *Homo* symbolic behavior, see L. A. Schepartz, "Language and Modern Human Origins," *Yearbook of Physical Anthropology* 36 (1993), 91–126.

7. F. Bordes, "Os percé Mousterien et os gravé Acheuleén du Pech de L'Azé II, *Quaternaria* 11 (1969), 1–6. More generally on *Homo* symbolic activity in the Lower Paleolithic, see Robert G. Bednarik, "Concept-Mediated Marking in the Lower Paleolithic," *Current Anthropology* 36:4 (1995), 605–634.

8. M. Vanhaeren, et al., "Middle Paleolithic Shell Beads in Israel and Algeria," *Science* 312 (2006), 1785–1788. More generally on *Homo* symbolic activity in the Middle Paleolithic, see A. Martin Byers, "Symboling and the Middle-Upper Paleolithic Transition: A Theoretical and Methodological Critique," *Current Anthropology* 35:4 (1994), 369–399.

9. R. White, "Substantial Acts: From Materials to Meaning in Upper Paleolithic Representation," in *Beyond Art: Pleistocene Image and Symbol*, edited by M. W. Conkey (San Francisco: California Academy of Sciences, 1997), 93–121. More generally see Ofer Bar-Yosef, "The Upper Paleolithic Revolution," *Annual Review of Anthropology* 31 (2002), 363–393.

10. Gregory Curtis, *The Cave Painters: Probing the Mysteries of the World's First Artists* (New York: Knopf, 2006).

11. For a very readable account of the period following the "Last Glacial Maximum" 20,000 years ago, see Steven Mithen, *After the Ice: A Global Human History 20,000–5,000 BC* (Cambridge: Harvard UP, 2004).

12. On the Natufians and the transition to agriculture, see Ofer Bar-Yosef and Anna Belfer-Cohen, "The Origins of Sedentism and Farming Communities in the Levant," *Journal of World Prehistory* 3:4 (1989), 447–498; Ofer Bar-Yosef and V. Valla, "The Natufian Culture and the Origin of the Neolithic in the Levant," *Current Anthropology* 31:4 (1990), 433–436; Ofer Bar-Yosef and Daniel E. Lieberman, "On Sedentism and Cereal Gathering in the Natufian," *Current Anthropology* 35:4 (1994), 431–434; and Ofer Bar-Yosef, "The Natufian Culture in the Levant, Threshold to the Origins of Agriculture," *Evolutionary Anthropology* 6:5 (1998), 159–177.

13. On the Neolithic farmers, see Peter Bellwood, *First Farmers: The Origins of Agricultural Societies* (Oxford: Blackwell, 2004).

14. A.M.T. Moore and G. C. Hillman, "The Pleistocene to Holocene Transition and Human Economy in Southwest Asia: The Impact of the Younger Dryas," *American Antiquity* 57 (1992), 482–494; and O. Bar-Yosef, and A. Belfer-Cohen, "Facing Environmental Crisis. Societal and Cultural Changes at the Transition from the Younger Dryas to the Holocene in the Levant," in *The Dawn of Farming in the Near East* (Studies in Early Near Eastern Production, Subsistence and Environment 6), edited by R.T.J. Cappers and S. Bottema (Berlin: Ex oriente, 2002), 55–66. On environmental impact in the transition to agriculture more generally, see H. E. Wright, Jr., "Environmental Determinism in Near Eastern Prehistory," *Current Anthropology* 34:4 (1993), 458–469.

15. D. Zohary and M. Hopf, *Domestication of Plants in the Old World: The Origin and Spread of Cultivated Plants in West Asia, Europe, and the Nile Valley* (Oxford: Oxford UP, 2000).

16. J. Clutton-Brock, *A Natural History of Domesticated Animals* (Cambridge: Cambridge UP, 1999).

17. Brian F. Byrd, "Public and Private, Domestic and Corporate: The Emergence of the Southwest Asian Village," *American Antiquity* 59:3 (1994), 639–666.

18. On early Holocene extinctions, see P. S. Martin and R. G. Klein, eds., *Quaternary Extinctions: A Prehistoric Revolution* (Tucson: University of Arizona Press, 1989).

19. On what follows, see Kent V. Flannery, "The Origins of the Village Revisited: From Nuclear to Extended Households," *American Antiquity* 67:3 (2002), 417–433.

20. The following account is based on the work of Denise Schmandt-Besserat. See "The Envelopes that Bear the First Writing," *Technology and Culture* 21:3 (1980), 357–385; "Decipherment of the Earliest Tablets," *Science* 211:4479 (1981), 283–285; "The Emergence of Recording," *American Anthropologist* 84:4 (1982), 871–878. For a summary, see Schmandt-Besserat, *How Writing Came About* (Austin: University of Texas Press 1996). For criticism of Schmandt-Besserat's theory, see P. Michalowski, "Tokenism," *American Anthropologist* 95 (1993), 996–999; and Andrew Lawler, "Writing Gets a Rewrite," *Science* 292:5526 (2001), 2418–2420.

21. For a review of the literature on the early Near Eastern states, see Norman Yoffee, "Political Economy in Early Mesopotamian States," *Annual Review of Anthropology* 24 (1995), 281–311.

22. Margaret J. Snowling and Charles Hulme, *The Science of Reading: A Handbook* (Malden: Blackwell, 2005), 320–322.

23. On the earliest alphabetic writing known, see John Coleman Darnell et al., "Two Early Alphabetic Inscriptions from the Wadi el-ḥôl: New Evidence for the Origin of the Alphabet from the Western Desert of Egypt," *Annual of the American Schools of Oriental Research* 59 (2005), 63–124.

24. On the early spread of the alphabetic script, see André Lemaire, "The Spread of Alphabetic Scripts (c. 1700–500 BCE)," *Diogenes* 218 (2008), 45–58. More generally, see Geoffrey Sampson, *Writing Systems*, second edition (London: Hutchinson, 1987).

25. On the emergence and development of "pristine" states around the world, see Allen Johnson and Timothy Earle, *The Evolution of Human Societies: From Foraging Group to Agrarian State*, second edition (Stanford: Stanford UP, 2000); Norman Yoffee, *Myths of the Archaic State: Evolution of the Earliest Cities, States, and Civilizations* (Cambridge: Cambridge UP, 2005); and Bruce G. Trigger, *Understanding Early Civilizations: A Comparative Study* (Cambridge: Cambridge UP, 2007). For a good review of recent research on the evolution of writing in the earliest of these states (pre-3000 BC), see Stephen D. Houston, ed., *The First Writing: Script Invention as History and Process* (Cambridge: Cambridge UP, 2004).

26. On the psychology of learning to read and write and of reading and writing, see Maryanne Wolf, *Proust and the Squid: The Story and Science of Reading* (New York: Harper, 2007).

27. For a review of the literature, see S. Jay Samuels, "Success and Failure in Learning to Read: A Critique of the Research," *Reading Research Quarterly* 8:2 (1973), 200–239; Anne McGill-Franzen, "Failure to Learn to Read: Formulating a Policy Problem," *Reading Research Quarterly* 22:4 (1987), 475–490; and Philip B. Gough, "How Children Learn to Read and Why They Fail," *Annals of Dyslexia* 46:1 (1996), 1–20.

28. See David J. Silk, *How to Communicate in Business: A Handbook for Engineers* (London: Institution of Electrical Engineers, 1995), 22. The fastest longhand writers can produce 40 words per minute. See John D. Gould and Stephen J. Boies, "Writing, Dictating, and Speaking Letters," *Science* 201:4361 (1978), 1147, note 3.

29. Estimates vary depending on the measure used. For a discussion and analysis, see Ronald P. Carver, "How Good Are Some of the World's Best Readers?" *Reading Research Quarterly* 20:4 (1985), 389–419.

30. Leo Tolstoy, *How Much Land Does a Man Need? and Other Stories*, translated by Ronald Wilks (London: Penguin Books, 1993).

31. Dave Segal, "Can You Say 'War and Peace'? Great! It'll Only Take 23 Days," *Washington Post* (February 11, 2007), D01.

32. Robert Andrews, *The Routledge Dictionary of Quotations* (New York: Routledge, 1987), 220.

33. See Natalie Mears, "Counsel, Public Debate, and the Queenship: John Stubbs's *The Discoverie of a Gaping Gulf*, 1579," *Historical Journal* 44:3 (2001), 629–650.

34. See Marianna Tax Choldin, Maurice Friedberg, and Barbara Dash, eds., *The Red Pencil: Artists, Scholars and Censors in the USSR* (New York: Routledge, 1989).

35. For a recent treatment with a review of the literature, see Ann Komaromi, "The Material Existence of Soviet Samizdat," *Slavic Review* 63:3 (2004), 597–618.

36. On divine sanction in the Ancient World, see Babett Edelmann, *Religiöse Herrschaftslegitimation in der Antike: die religiöse Legitimation orientalisch-ägyptischer und griechisch-hellenistischer Herrscher im Vergleich* (Sankt Katharinen: Scripta Mercaturae, 2007); and Nicole Brisch et al., eds., *Religion and Power: Divine Kingship in the Ancient World and Beyond* (Chicago: Oriental Institute of the University of Chicago, 2008). On the Roman World, see Ittai Gradel, *Emperor Worship and Roman Religion* (Oxford; Clarendon Press, 2002). On the Medieval World, see Fritz Kern, *Kingship and Law in the Middle Ages*, translated by S. B. Chrimes (Oxford: Blackwell, 1939); and more recently, see Anne J. Duggan, *Kings and Kingship in Medieval Europe* (London: King's College London, 1993). On early modern Europe, see John Neville Figgis, *The Divine Right of Kings*, second edition (Cambridge: Cambridge UP, 1914); and more recently, Glenn Burgess, "The Divine Right of Kings Reconsidered," *English Historical Review* 107:425 (1992), 837–861.

37. James I, "A Speach to the Lords and Commons of the Parliament at White-Hall, on Wednesday the XXI. of March. Anno 1609," in *The Workes of the Most High and Mightie Prince, James . . . King of Great Britaine, France and Ireland* (London: Robert Barker and Iohn Bill, printers to the Kings Most Excellent Maiestie, 1616), 529.

38. The manifesto, "Industrial Society and its Future," was published in the *New York Times* (September 19, 1995) and the *Washington Post* (September 19, 1995). On David Kaczynski's involvement in the eventual apprehension of his brother, see Pam Belluck, "In Unabomb Case, Pain for Suspect's Family," *New York Times* (April 10, 1996).

39. Leo N. Tolstoy, *War and Peace*, 3 vols., translated by Constance Black Garnett (New York: McClure, Phillips and Co., 1904), vol. 3: 370.

40. Timothy White, "A Man Out of Time Beats the Clock," *Musician Magazine* 60 (October 1983), 52.

41. For what follows, see Wayne M. Senner, *The Origins of Writing* (Lincoln: University of Nebraska Press, 1991), 10–14.

42. Plato's *Phaedrus*, 156–157.

43. See Catherine Hezser, *Jewish Literacy in Roman Palestine* (Tübingen: Mohr Siebeck, 2001), 209–226.

44. *The Guinness Book of World Records 2004* (New York: Bantam, 2003), 320.

45. At this writing, the English Wikipedia contained approximately 1.6 billion words. See Website: "Size of Wikipedia," Wikipedia. Retrieved May 8, 2009. By comparison, the print version of the *Encyclopedia Britannica* (2002 edition) contains approximately 44 million words. See Website: "Wikipedia: Size Comparisons," Wikipedia. Retrieved May 8, 2009.

46. Website: "List of Longest Novels," Wikipedia. Retrieved May 8, 2009.

47. Website: "Patrick James, "The World's Longest Novel," *Good Magazine*, September 24, 2007. Retrieved May 7, 2009.

48. Estimates vary depending on the measure used. For a discussion and analysis, see Carver, "How Good Are Some of the World's Best Readers?" 389–419.

49. Amihud Gilead, "How Few Words Can the Shortest Story Have?" *Philosophy and Literature* 32:1 (2008), 119.

50. Wolfgang Speyer, *Büchervernichtung und Zensur des Geistes bei Heiden, Juden und Christen* (Stuttgart: A. Heirsemann, 1981).

51. For a general treatment, see Romana A. Naddaff, *Exiling the Poets: The Production of Censorship in Plato's Republic* (Chicago: University of Chicago Press, 2002).

52. Frederick H. Cramer, "Bookburning and Censorship in Ancient Rome: A Chapter from the History of Freedom of Speech," *Journal of the History of Ideas* 6:2 (1945), 157–196; and Catherine Edwards, *The Politics of Immorality in Ancient Rome* (Cambridge: Cambridge UP, 2002).

53. The French version is somewhat different, but the sense is the same. See Pascal's *Les provinciales; ou, Les lettres écrites par Louis de Montalte à un provincial de ses amis et aux RR. PP. jésuites* (Paris: Éditions Garnier frères, 1965), Letter XVI (1657).

54. Suzanna Chambers, "500,000 Letters a Week Go Astray," *Daily Telegraph* (December 8, 2002).

55. Marshall Poe, "What Did Russians Mean When They Called Themselves 'Slaves of the Tsar'?" *Slavic Review* 57:3 (1998), 585–608.

56. See Ineke Sluiter and Ralph M. Rosen, eds., *Free Speech in Classical Antiquity* (Leiden: Brill, 2004).

57. Paolo Vivante, "On Homer's Winged Words," *Classical Quarterly* 25:1 (1975), 1–12.
58. Website: "Voyager. The Interstellar Mission. Golden Record." Retrieved May 15, 2009.
59. On ethnographical writing in the Ancient World, see Edith Hall, *Inventing the Barbarian: Greek Self-Definition Through Tragedy* (Oxford: Oxford UP, 1989); Paul Cartledge, *The Greeks: A Portrait of Self and Others* (Oxford: Oxford UP, 1993); J. M. Hall, *Ethnic Identity in Greek Antiquity* (Cambridge: Cambridge UP, 1997); Tim Cornell and Katheryn Lomas, eds., *Gender and Ethnicity in Ancient Italy* (London: Accordia Research Institute, University of London, 1997); Irad Malkin, *The Returns of Odysseus: Colonization and Ethnicity* (Berkeley: University of California Press, 1998); Irad Malkin, *Ancient Perceptions of Greek Ethnicity* (Cambridge: Harvard UP, 2001); Jonathan M. Hall, *Hellenicity: Between Ethnicity and Culture* (Chicago: University of Chicago Press, 2002); and Benjamin Isaac, *The Invention of Racism in Classical Antiquity* (Princeton: Princeton UP, 2004).
60. Sandra L. Gravett, Karla G. Bohmback, F. V. Greifenhagen, and Donald C. Polaski, *An Introduction to the Hebrew Bible: A Thematic Approach* (Louisville: Westminster John Knox Press, 2008), 199–238.
61. Christopher Auffarth, "Protecting Strangers: Establishing a Fundamental Value in the Religions of the Ancient Near East and Ancient Greece," *Numen. International Review of the History of Religions* 39:2 (1992), 193–216.
62. Website: The British Museum, "Mesopotamia 1500–539BC (Room 55)." Retrieved May 19, 2009.
63. We've lost a lot, on which see James Raven, ed., *Lost Libraries: The Destruction of Great Book Collections Since Antiquity* (New York: Palgrave Macmillan, 2004).
64. The manuscript in question is "Venetus A (Marcianus Graecus 454)," currently archived in Venice. See Casey Dué, "Homer's Post-Classical Legacy," in *A Companion to Ancient Epic*, edited by John Miles Foley (Oxford: Blackwell, 2005), 399.
65. For an introduction, see David Crystal, *Language Death* (Cambridge: Cambridge UP, 2002).
66. See John Van Seters, *In Search of History: Historiography in the Ancient World and the Origins of Biblical History* (New Haven: Yale UP, 1983), 68–76.
67. On the relationship between the ancient kings lists and the Hebrew Bible, see Kenton L. Sparks, *Ancient Texts for the Study of the Hebrew Bible: A Guide to the Background Literature* (Peabody: Hendrickson Publishers, 2005), 344ff.
68. For an overview, see Ernest Breisach, *Historiography: Ancient, Medieval, and Modern*, third edition (Chicago: University of Chicago Press, 2007), 12ff.
69. One way to measure the dimensions of this explosion is by the rate of innovation. That it rose considerably after 3500 BC there can be no doubt. See Mark Kremer, "Population Growth and Technological Change: One Million B.C. to 1990," *Quarterly Journal of Economics* 108:3 (1993), 683; and Jonathan Huebner, "A Possible Declining Trend for Worldwide Innovation," *Technological Forecasting and Social Change* 72 (2005), 981.

70. Marcus Tullius Cicero, *De oratore*, translated by E. W. Sutton, 2 vols. (Cambridge: Harvard UP, 1942), 2.9.36.

71. The literature on ancient historiography is very large. A good introduction is John Van Seters, *In Search of History: Historiography in the Ancient World and the Origins of Biblical History* (New Haven: Yale UP, 1983).

72. Aristotle, *Eudemian Ethics*, 1216a 12–14 in *Aristotle: Athenian Constitution, Eudemian Ethics, Virtues and Vices* (Loeb Classical Library No. 285), translated by H. Rackham (Cambridge: Harvard UP, 1981).

73. The tale is well told by David Damrosch in *The Buried Book: The Loss and Recovery of the Great Epic of Gilgamesh* (New York: Henry Holt, 2007).

74. For an overview of the evolution of disciplinary knowledge in the Western world, see David C. Lindberg, *The Beginnings of Western Science: The European Scientific Tradition in Philosophical, Religious, and Institutional Context, 600 B.C. to A.D. 1450* (Chicago: University of Chicago Press, 1992).

75. On estates generally, see Otto Hintze, *Staat und Verfassung, gesammelte Abhandlungen zur allgemeinen Verfassungsgeschichte* (Leipzig: Koehler & Amelang, 1941); and Max Weber, *Wirtschaft und Gesellschaft*, 2 vols. (Tübingen: J.C.B. Mohr (P. Siebeck), 1925). On European estates, see Marc Bloch, *Feudal Society*, 2 vols., translated by L. A. Manyon (Chicago: University of Chicago Press), vol. 2: *Social Classes and Political Organizations*; Georges Duby, *The Three Orders: Feudal Society Imagined*, translated by Arthur Goldhammer (Chicago: University of Chicago Press, 1980). On estates in other times and places, see Rushton Coulborn, *Feudalism in History* (Princeton: Princeton UP, 1965).

76. J. L. Austin, *How to Do Things with Words: The William James Lectures Delivered at Harvard University in 1955*, edited by J. O. Urmson (Oxford: Clarendon Press, 1962).

77. The best – which is to say most historically sensitive – attempts to describe the general features of "agrarian society" are all in one way or another derivative of the work of Leslie White and, after him, Gerhard Lensky. See Leslie White, *The Evolution of Culture: The Development of Civilization to the Fall of Rome* (New York: McGraw-Hill, 1959); and Gerhard Lensky, *Human Societies: A Macrolevel Introduction to Sociology* (New York: McGraw-Hill, 1970 and many subsequent editions). Notable recent contributions include: Michael Mann, *The Sources of Social Power. Volume 1: A History of Power from the Beginning to A.D. 1760* (Cambridge: Cambridge UP, 1986); S. K. Sanderson, *Macrosociology: An Introduction to Human Societies* (New York: Harper and Row, 1988); and Jonathan Turner, *Human Institutions: A Theory of Social Evolution* (Lanham: Rowman & Littlefield, 2003).

3. HOMO LECTOR

1. *The Republic*, translated by R. E. Allen (New Haven: Yale UP, 2006), 161. Subsequent citations are to this edition.

2. On the origins of print technology, see Thomas F. Carter, *The Invention of Printing in China and its Spread Westward* (New York: Columbia UP, 1925); Constance R. Miller, *Technical and Cultural Prerequisites for Invention of*

Printing in China and the West (San Francisco: Chinese Materials Center, 1983); Tsien Tsuen-Hsuin, *Science and Civilization in China. Volume 5, Part 1: Paper and Printing* (Cambridge: Cambridge UP, 1993); and Timothy Barrett, *The Woman Who Discovered Printing* (New Haven: Yale UP, 2008).

3. On early European print, see H. J. Chalytor, *From Script to Print: An Introduction to Medieval Literature* (Cambridge: Cambridge UP, 1945); C. Bühler, *The Fifteenth Century Book: Scribes, the Printers, and the Decorators* (Philadelphia: University of Pennsylvania Press, 1960); S. Hindman, *Printing the Written Word: The Social History of Books, c. 1450–1520* (Ithaca: Cornell UP, 1991); and David McKitterick, *Print, Manuscript and the Search for Order, 1450–1830* (New York: Cambridge UP, 2003).

4. On the growth and impact of print in Europe, see Lucien Febvre and Henri Martin, *L'apparition du livre* (Paris: Éditions A. Michel, 1958); Elizabeth Eisenstein, *The Printing Press as an Agent of Change: Communications and Cultural Transformations in Early-Modern Europe* (Cambridge: Cambridge UP, 1980), 2 vols. in 1; Roger Chartier, ed., *The Culture of Print: Power and the Uses of Print in Early Modern Europe*, translated by Lydia G. Cochrane (Princeton: Princeton UP, 1989); Roger Chartier, *The Order of Books: Readers, Authors, and Libraries in Europe between the Fourteenth and Eighteenth Centuries*, translated by Lydia G. Cochrane (Cambridge: Polity Press, 1994); and Roger Chartier, *Inscription and Erasure: Literature and Written Culture from the Eleventh to the Eighteenth Century*, translated by Arthur Goldhammer (Philadelphia: University of Pennsylvania Press, 2007).

5. On orality in the Print Era, see Bruce Smith, *The Acoustic World of Early Modern England: Attending to the O-Factor* (Chicago: University of Chicago Press, 1999); Adam Fox, *Oral and Literate Culture in England, 1500–1700* (Oxford: Clarendon Press, 2000); Adam Fox and Daniel R. Woolf, eds., *The Spoken Word: Oral Culture in Britain, 1500–1850* (Manchester: Manchester UP, 2002); Alison Shell, *Oral Culture and Catholicism in Early Modern England* (Cambridge: Cambridge UP, 2007); and Mary Ellen Lamb and Karen Bamford, eds., *Oral Tradition and Gender in Early Modern Literary Texts* (Aldershot: Ashgate, 2008).

6. On manuscript-writing in the age of print, see D. F. McKenzie, "Speech-Manuscript-Print," *The Library Chronicle of the University of Texas at Austin* 20 (1990), 86–109; Harold Love, *Scribal Publication in Seventeenth-Century England* (Oxford: Clarendon Press; New York: Oxford UP, 1993); A. F. Mariotti, *Manuscript, Print and the English Renaissance Lyric* (Ithaca: Cornell UP, 1995); H. R. Woudhuysen, *Sir Philip Sidney and the Circulation of Manuscripts, 1558–1640* (Oxford: Oxford UP, 1996); P. Beal, *In Praise of Scribes: Manuscripts and their Makers in Seventeenth-Century England* (Oxford: Oxford UP, 1998); and M.J.M. Ezell, *Social Authorship and the Advent of Print* (Baltimore: Johns Hopkins UP, 1999).

7. On the business of print, see Marjorie Plant, *The English Book Trade: An Economic History of the Making and Sale of Books* (London: Allen & Unwin, 1965); Robin Myers and Michael Harris, eds., *Development of the English Book Trade, 1700–1899* (Oxford: Oxford Polytechnic Press, 1981); Peter Isaac and Barry McKay, eds., *The Reach of Print: Making, Selling, and Using*

Books (New Castle: Oak Knoll Press, 1998); Alexis Weedon, *Victorian Publishing: The Economics of Book Production for the Mass Market, 1836–1916* (Burlington: Ashgate, 2003); James K. Bracken and Joel Silver, eds., *The British Literary Book Trade, 1700–1820* (Detroit: Gale Research, 1995); Robin Myers and Michael Harris, eds., *Economics of the British Booktrade, 1605–1939* (Alexandria: Chadwyck-Healey, 1985); Barry McKay, John Hinks, and Maureen Bell, eds., *Light on the Book Trade: Essays in Honor of Peter Isaac* (London: The British Library, 2004); and James Raven, *The Business of Books: Booksellers and the English Book Trade, 1450–1850* (New Haven: Yale UP, 2007).

8. On "underground" printing, see Robert Darnton, *The Literary Underground of the Old Regime* (Cambridge: Harvard UP, 1982); Robert Darnton, *The Kiss of Lamourette: Reflections on Cultural History* (New York: Norton, 1990); and Robert Darnton, *The Forbidden Bestsellers of Pre-Revolutionary France* (New York: Norton, 1995).

9. On the censorship of print, see A. Patterson, *Censorship and Interpretation: The Conditions of Reading and Writing in Early Modern England* (Madison: University of Wisconsin Press, 1984); R. Myers and M. Harris, eds., *Censorship and the Control of Print in England and France, 1600–1910* (Winchester: St. Paul's Bibliographies, 1992); A. C. Duke and C. A. Tamse, eds., *Too Mighty to be Free: Censorship in Britain and the Netherlands* (Zutphen: De Walburg Pers, 1987); C. S. Clegg, *Press Censorship in Elizabethan England* (Cambridge: Cambridge UP, 1997); and C. S. Clegg, *Press Censorship in Jacobean England* (Cambridge: Cambridge UP, 2001).

10. On print, education, and literacy, see L. Stone, "Literacy and Education in England, 1640–1900," *Past and Present* 42 (1969), 69–139; H. J. Graff, ed., *Literacy and Social Development in the West: A Reader* (Cambridge: Cambridge UP, 1981); R. A. Houston, "Literacy and Society in the West, 1500–1850," *Social History* 8:3 (1983), 269–293; D. K. Muller, R. Ringer, and B. Simon, eds., *The Rise of the Modern Educational System: Structural Change and Social Reproduction, 1870–1920* (Cambridge: Cambridge UP, 1988); A. Benavot and P. Riddle, "The Expansion of Primary Education, 1870–1940," *Sociology of Education* 61:3 (1988), 191–210; and Yasemin Nuhoglu Soysal and David Strang, "Construction of the First Mass Education Systems in Nineteenth Century Europe," *Sociology of Education* 62:4 (1989), 277–288.

11. See the review in Carl F. Kaestle, "The History of Literacy and the History of Readers," *Review of Research in Education* 12 (1985), 26–32.

12. On the pre-Gutenberg history of print and printing technology, see Carter, *The Invention of Printing in China and its Spread Westward*; Miller, *Technical and Cultural Prerequisites for Invention of Printing in China and the West*; and Tsien Tsuen-Hsuin, *Science and Civilization in China, Volume 5, Part 1: Paper and Printing* (Cambridge: Cambridge UP, 1993).

13. For all that follows in this paragraph, see Barrett, *The Woman Who Discovered Printing*.

14. See Asa Briggs and Peter Burke, *A Social History of the Media: from Gutenberg to the Internet* (Cambridge: Polity, 2002), 15.

15. Barrett, *The Woman Who Discovered Printing*, 10–14.

16. Eltjo Buringh and Jan Luiten van Zanden, "Charting the 'Rise of the West': Manuscripts and Printed Books in Europe, A Long-Term Perspective from the Sixth through Eighteenth Centuries," *Journal of Economic History* 69:2 (2009), forthcoming; and Eltjo Buringh, *On Medieval Manuscript Production in the Latin West: Explorations with a Global Database* (Leiden: Brill, 2009). Also see R. H. Rouse and M. A. Rouse, *Manuscripts and their Makers: Commercial Book Producers in Medieval Paris, 1200–1500*, 2 vols. (Turnhout: Harvey Miller, 2000).

17. The evidence regarding book ownership is largely based on wills, thus the obvious trend – increased book ownership – may simply be a reflection of an increase in the number of surviving wills. For an attempt to collect all the data, see Susan H. Cavanaugh, "A Study of Books Privately Owned in England, 1300–1450," 2 vols. (Unpublished Ph.D. thesis, University of Pennsylvania, 1980). For an assessment of the data, see *The Cambridge History of the Book in Britain*, 6 vols. to date (Cambridge: Cambridge UP, 2007), vol. 2: 1100–1400, edited by Nigel J. Morgan and Rodney M. Thomson, 37–38.

18. Consensus is now emerging among scholars of education that the number of lay schools was increasing rapidly before the Renaissance and Reformation (contra the views of Lawrence Stone and Joan Simon). On the expansion of the number of schools (especially elementary and grammar schools) in particular English regions in the fifteenth century, see Nicholas Orme, *Education in the West of England, 1066–1548* (Exeter: University of Exeter, 1976); and Jo Ann Hoeppner Moran, *The Growth of English Schooling, 1340–1548: Learning, Literacy and Laicization in Pre-Reformation York Diocese* (Princeton: Princeton UP, 1985). For an overview, see Nicholas Orme, *Medieval Schools: From Roman Britain to Renaissance England* (New Haven: Yale UP, 2006).

19. On rising levels of literacy before print, see Hoeppner Moran,, *The Growth of English Schooling, 1340–1548*, xvi, 179, 181, 225. Also see J. Coleman, *Public Reading and the Reading Public in Late Medieval England and France* (Cambridge: Cambridge UP, 1996); and P. Saenger, *Space between Words: The Origins of Silent Reading* (Stanford: Stanford UP, 1997).

20. The literature on the rise of capitalism in Europe is very large. For a recent survey, see Richard Lachmann, "Origins of Capitalism in Western Europe: Economic and Political Aspects," *Annual Review of Sociology* 15 (1989), 47–72; and Joseph M. Bryant, "The West and the Rest Revisited: Debating Capitalist Origins, European Colonialism, and the Advent of Modernity," *Canadian Journal of Sociology/Cahiers canadiens de sociologie* 31:4 (2006), 403–444. Two recent general treatments that summarize much of the literature are Eric H. Mielants, *The Origins of Capitalism and the 'Rise of the West'* (Philadelphia: Temple UP, 2008); and Jack Goldstone, *Why Europe? The Rise of the West in World History 1500–1850* (New York: McGraw Hill, 2008).

21. Adam Smith, *An Inquiry into the Nature and Causes of the Wealth of Nations* (London: W. Strahan and T. Cadell, 1776).

22. On the rise of the bureaucratic state in Europe, see John Brewer, *The Sinews of Power: War, Money, and the English State, 1688–1783* (London: Urwin

Hyman, 1989); Charles Tilly, *Coercion, Capital, and European States, 990–1990* (Oxford: Blackwell, 1990); Brian Downing, *The Military Revolution and Political Change* (Princeton: Princeton UP, 1992); Thomas Ertman, *The Birth of the Leviathan: Building States and Regimes in Medieval and Early Modern Europe* (Cambridge: Cambridge UP, 1997); and Richard Bonney, ed., *The Rise of the Fiscal State in Europe, 1200–1815* (Oxford: Oxford UP, 1999). For a useful review of the state-building literature, see Philip S. Gorski, "Beyond Marx and Hintze? Third-Wave Theories of Early Modern State Formation," *Comparative Studies of Society and History* 43:4 (2001), 851–861.

23. William Godwin, *An Enquiry Concerning Political Justice, and its Influence on General Virtue and Happiness*, 2 vols. (London: Printed for G. G. J. and J. Robinson, 1793).

24. The connection between increases in literacy – and acknowledged fact – and the influence of Protestantism on it is subject to some dispute. But there is no doubt regarding Luther's opinion on literacy: he believed people should be able to read and understand the scripture or texts based on it. See Richard Gawthrop and Gerald Strauss, "Protestantism and Literacy in Early Modern Germany," *Past and Present* 104 (1984), 31–55; and Ruth Bottigheimer, "Bible Reading, 'Bibles' and the Bible for Children in Early Modern Germany," *Past and Present* 139 (1993), 66–89. On Protestant views concerning literacy more generally, see the discussion in R. A. Houston, *Literacy in Early Modern Europe: Culture and Education, 1500–1800* (London: Longman, 2002), 37–40.

25. S. H. Steinberg, *Five Hundred Years of Printing* (Harmondsworth: Penguin Books, 1974), 144.

26. On the history of newspapers, see Houston, *Literacy in Early Modern Europe*, 192–196.

27. Robert F. Arnove and Harvey J. Graff, eds., *National Literacy Campaigns. Historical and Comparative Perspectives* (New York: Plenum Press, 1987).

28. See William E. Ames, *A History of the Washington National Intelligencer* (Chapel Hill: University of North Carolina Press, 1972).

29. Guy Chazan and Gregory L. White, "Putin Extends Media Control to Independent Newspaper," *Wall Street Journal* (June 3, 2005), D05.

30. A. G. Dickens, *Reformation and Society in Sixteenth-Century Europe* (New York: Harcourt, Brace & World, 1966), 51.

31. "Colloquia order Tischreden," in *Dr. Martin Luther Sämmtliche Schriften*, 23 vols. in 25 (St. Louis: Concordia Publishing House, 1880–1910), vol. 22: 1658.

32. *Acta Apostolicae Sedis* 58 (1966), 445.

33. The statistics on printing in this paragraph are drawn from Houston, *Literacy in Early Modern Europe*, 173–176, 194, and 214.

34. On the population of Europe, see Jan de Vries, *European Urbanization 1500–1800* (Cambridge: Harvard UP, 1984), chapter 3.

35. The statistics on education, book ownership, and literacy in this paragraph are drawn from Houston, *Literacy in Early Modern Europe*, 52, 83–91, 166, 173, and 203.

36. On mass literacy in the nineteenth century, see David Vincent, *The Rise of Mass Literacy. Reading and Writing in Modern Europe* (Cambridge: Polity, 2000).

37. *EFA Global Monitoring Report 2006: Literacy for Life* (Paris: UNESCO Publishing, 2005).

38. *Reading at Risk: A Survey of Literary Reading in America* (Washington, DC: NEH Research Division Report 46, 2004), table 1.

39. On reading (weekdays and weekends) and television watching, see *The American Time Use Survey, 2007* (Washington, DC: Bureau of Labor Statistics, 2008), table 11.

40. The survival of orality in the early modern period is now much studied. See Smith, *The Acoustic World of Early Modern England*; Fox, *Oral and Literate Culture in England, 1500–1700*; Fox and Woolf, eds., *The Spoken Word: Oral Culture in Britain, 1500–1850*; Shell, *Oral Culture and Catholicism in Early Modern England*; and Lamb and Bamford, eds., *Oral Tradition and Gender in Early Modern Literary Texts*.

41. See David A. Kronick, "The Commerce of Letters: Networks and 'Invisible Colleges' in Seventeenth- and Eighteenth-Century Europe," *Library Quarterly* 71:1 (2001), 28–43.

42. The Correspondence of Erasmus, translated by R.A.B. Mynors and D.F.S. Thomson; annotated by Wallace K. Ferguson (Toronto: University of Toronto Press, 1974–), 12 vols. to date.

43. Website: "The Linnaean Correspondence." Retrieved May 21, 2009.

44. Website: "Darwin Correspondence Project." Retrieved May 21, 2009.

45. "Ordinance for correcting and regulating the Abuses of the Press," *Journal of the House of Lords* 6:1643 (1802), 14 June, 1643, 96.

46. Joad Raymond, *Pamphlets and Pamphleteering in Early Modern Britain* (Cambridge: Cambridge UP, 2006), 170.

47. "Slovo ne vorobei – otpustish, ne poimaiesh."

48. See Ann Komaromi, "The Material Existence of Soviet Samizdat," *Slavic Review* 63:3 (2004), 597–618.

49. Anon. (John Locke), *Two Treatises of Government: In the Former, The False Principles and Foundation of Sir Robert Filmer, And His Followers, are Detected and Overthrown. The Latter is an Essay concerning The True Original, Extent, and End of Civil-Government* (London: Printed for Awnsham Churchill, 1689).

50. The relationship between the press and the advent of democracy in the early modern period has been the subject of study and debate. See David Zaret, *Origins of Democratic Culture: Printing, Petitions, and the Public Sphere in Early-Modern England* (Princeton: Princeton UP, 1999), especially 34–35.

51. On the origins of modern "freedom of speech," see David Colough, *Freedom of Speech in Early Stuart England* (New York: Cambridge UP, 2005); Larry D. Eldridge, *A Distant Heritage: The Growth of Free Speech in Early America* (New York: NYU Press, 1994). On the origins of the modern "free press," see Leonard W. Levy, *Emergence of a Free Press* (New York: Oxford UP, 1985).

52. John Milton, *Areopagitica: A speech of Mr John Milton for the liberty of unlicensed printing to the Parliament of England*, edited by John W. Hales (Oxford: Oxford UP, 1894), 51–52.

53. Constitution of the United States of America, First Amendment: "Congress shall make no law . . . abridging the freedom of speech, or of the press" (1791); Declaration of the Rights of Man and the Citizen, Article XI: "The free communication of thoughts and of opinions is one of the most precious rights of man: any citizen thus may speak, write, print freely, save to respond to the abuse of this liberty, in the cases determined by the law" (1789). Even the Soviet Constitution of 1937 guaranteed freedom of speech and the press, though 1937 was not a good year for either. It was, however, a banner year for shooting people who tried to exercise these "freedoms" (see "Accessibility" earlier in this chapter).

54. John Stuart Mill, *On Liberty* (London: Longmans, Green, and Co., 1913), 9.

55. The idea was already common coin by 1850. See Fredrick Knight Hunt, *The Fourth Estate: Contributions Towards a History of Newspapers, and of the Liberty of the Press* (London: David Bougue, 1850).

56. Oscar Wilde, "The Soul of Man" [1895], *The Complete Works of Oscar Wilde*, 4 vols. to date, general editors Russell Jackson and Ian Small (Oxford: Oxford UP, 2000–), vol. 4, edited by Josephine M. Guy, 255.

57. See Alexis J. Anderson, "The Formative Period of First Amendment Theory, 1870–1915," *American Journal of Legal History* 24:1 (1980), 56–75.

58. See Amy M. Adler, "Post-Modern Art and the Death of Obscenity Law," *Yale Law Journal* 99:6 (1990), 1359–1378.

59. These closed libraries were called "spetskrani." See Valeria D. Stelmakh, "Reading in the Context of Censorship in the Soviet Union," *Libraries & Culture* 36:1 (2001), 143–151. Also see Andrei Rogachevskii, "Homo Sovieticus in the Library," *Europe-Asia Studies* 54:6 (2002), 975–988.

60. See Edward Kasinec, "A Soviet Research Library Remembered," *Libraries & Culture* 36:1 (2001), 21–22. Also see Marianna Tax Choldin, Maurice Friedberg, and Barbara Dash, eds., *The Red Pencil: Artists, Scholars and Censors in the USSR* (New York: Routledge, 1989), 208–209.

61. The literature on the evolution of the public sphere is enormous. The ur-text is arguably Jürgen Habermas, *Strukturwandel der Öffentlichkeit: Untersuchungen zu einer Kategorie der bürgerlichen Gesellschaft* (Neuwied: H. Luchterhand, 1962). For historical treatments, see Zaret, *Origins of Democratic Culture*; M. Warner, *The Letters of the Republic: Publication and the Public Sphere in Eighteenth-Century America* (Cambridge: Harvard UP, 1990); Peter Lake and Steven C. A. Pincus, eds., *The Politics of the Public Sphere in Early Modern England* (Manchester: Manchester UP, 2007).

62. On public and private reading, see Roger Chartier, "Leisure and Sociability: Reading Aloud in Early Modern Europe," in *Urban Life in the Renaissance*, edited by Susan Zimmerman and Ronald F. E. Weisman (Newark: University of Delaware Press, 1989), 41–61; J. Coleman, *Public Reading and the Reading Public in Late Medieval England and France* (Cambridge: Cambridge UP, 1996); James Raven, Helen Small, and Naomi Tadmor, eds., *The*

Practice and Representation of Reading in England (Cambridge: Cambridge UP, 1996); and P. Saenger, *Space between Words: The Origins of Silent Reading* (Stanford: Stanford UP, 1997).

63. See Cecile M. Jagodzinki, *Privacy and Print: Reading and Writing in Seventeenth-Century England* (Charlottesville: University of Virginia Press, 1999).

64. On the origins of print pornography, see Lynn Hunt, ed., *Inventing Pornography, 1500–1800: Obscenity and the Origins of Modernity* (New York: Zone Books, 1996); Ian Frederick Moulton, *Before Pornography: Erotic Writing in Early Modern England* (Oxford: Oxford UP, 2000); Sarah Toulalan, *Imagining Sex: Pornography and Bodies in Seventeenth-Century England* (Oxford: Oxford UP, 2007). For a lively and readable overview, see Walter Kendrick, *The Secret Museum: Pornography in Modern Culture* (Berkeley: University of California Press, 1997).

65. Samuel Pepys, *The Diary of Samuel Pepys*, edited by Robert Latham and William Matthews, 8 vols. (London: Bell & Hyman, 1970–1983), vol. 1: 59.

66. Jagodzinki, *Privacy and Print*, argues that some version of this notion can be found in the early seventeenth century. Others disagree: see Erica Longfellow, "Public, Private, and the Household in Early Seventeenth-Century England," *Journal of British Studies* 45:2 (2006), 313–334. On the emergence of "freedom of conscience," see Gary S. De Krey, "Rethinking the Restoration: Dissenting Cases for Conscience, 1667–1672," *Historical Journal* 38:1 (1995), 53–83; Andrew R. Murphy, *Conscience and Community: Revisiting Toleration and Religious Dissent in Early Modern England and America* (University Park: Pennsylvania State UP, 2001); and John Marshall, *John Locke, Toleration and Early Enlightenment Culture: Religious Intolerance and Arguments for Religious Toleration in Early Modern and 'Early Enlightenment' Europe* (Cambridge: Cambridge UP, 2006).

67. Constitution of the United States, First Amendment: "Congress shall make no law respecting an establishment of religion" (1789). On the history of the "establishment clause," see Philip Hamburger, *Separation of Church and State* (Cambridge: Harvard University Press, 2002).

68. See *Stanley v. Georgia* 394 US 557 (1969), where the United States Supreme Court held that the Constitution protected citizens' rights to read pornography in their own homes. More generally, see Susan M. Easton, *The Problem of Pornography: Regulation and the Right to Free Speech* (New York: Routledge, 1994), chapter 13.

69. That Mill himself wouldn't have liked this particular application is argued by Richard Vernon, "John Stuart Mill and Pornography: Beyond the Harm Principle," *Ethics* 106:3 (1996), 621–632.

70. For a short review of the evidence, see Cass R. Sunstein, "Pornography and the First Amendment," *Duke Law Journal* (September 1986), no. 4, 589–627.

71. See Hendrick Hertzberg, "Big Boobs: Ed Meese and His Pornography Commission," *New Republic* 21 (July 14, 1986).

72. Jeffrey G. Sherman, "Love Speech: The Social Utility of Pornography," *Stanford Law Review* 47:4 (1995), 661–705.

73. American Library Association, *Intellectual Freedom Manual* (Chicago: ALA Editions, 2006), 234.

74. Alexis de Tocqueville, *Democracy in America*, translated by Henry Reeve, 2 vols. (New York: D. Appleton and Company, 1904), vol. 2: 544.
75. Matthew Arnold, *Culture and Anarchy: An Essay in Political and Social Criticism* (London: Smith, Elder & Co., 1869).
76. On which see the entertaining Joseph Epstein, *Snobbery: The American Version* (New York: Houghton Mifflin Harcourt, 2002).
77. T. I. Polner, *Tolstoy and His Wife*, translated by Nicholas R. Wreden (New York: Norton & Co., 1945), 92. The story is attributed variously to Behr's brother (Stephen) and son (Ilya).
78. Just how few is open to dispute. Some researchers claim that early printed books were hardly identical "copies" at all. See McKitterick, *Print, Manuscript and the Search for Order, 1450–1830*, 97–138.
79. Scholars have argued about the origins of feudalism for a long time. See Donald R. Kelley, "*De Origine Feudorum*: The Beginnings of an Historical Problem," *Speculum* 39:2 (1964), 207–228. They are still arguing. See T. N. Bisson, "The 'Feudal Revolution'," *Past & Present* 142 (1994), 6–42 and the responses that followed in subsequent issues of *Past & Present*.
80. See J.G.A. Pocock, *The Ancient Constitution and the Feudal Law: A Study of English Historical Thought in the Seventeenth Century* (Cambridge: UP, 1957); and Donald R. Kelley, *Foundations of Modern Historical Scholarship: Language, Law and History in the French Renaissance* (New York: Columbia UP, 1970).
81. See Theodore M. Porter and Dorothy Ross, eds., *The Cambridge History of Science: The Modern Social Sciences* (Cambridge: Cambridge UP, 2003).
82. See J.Q.C. Mackrell, *The Attack on 'Feudalism' in Eighteenth-Century France* (Toronto: University of Toronto Press, 1973).
83. On Weber and "rationalization," see Gianfranco Poggi, *Weber: A Short Introduction* (Cambridge: Polity, 2006), 105–126.
84. On this point, see Martin Malia, *The Soviet Tragedy: A History of Socialism in Russia, 1917–1991* (New York: Simon & Schuster, 1995), 21ff.
85. See Robert Service, *Comrades!: A History of World Communism* (Cambridge: Harvard UP, 2007). Rather more polemical but still well worth reading are Joshua Muravchik, *Heaven on Earth: The Rise and Fall of Socialism* (San Francisco: Encounter Books, 2002); and Richard Pipes, *Communism: A History* (New York: Modern Library, 2003).
86. On the idea of progress through science in the Enlightenment, see Charles Frankel, *The Idea of Progress in the French Enlightenment* (New York: King's Crown Press, 1948); Leonard M. Marsak, "Bernard de Fontenelle: The Idea of Science in the French Enlightenment," *Transactions of the American Philosophical Society*, New Series 49:7 (1959), 1–64; and Thomas L. Hankins, *Science and the Enlightenment* (Cambridge: Cambridge UP, 1985).
87. Jean Lerond D'Alembert, "Discours préliminaire," in *Encyclopédie, ou, Dictionnaire raisoné des sciences, des arts et des métiers (articles choisis)*, 2 vols., edited by Alain Pons (Paris: Flammarion, 1986), vol. 1: 89, 92–93, 95, 91, and 155–156.
88. A principal exception here might be those Postmodernists – Derrida, Lyotard, Foucault – who criticize what they call the "Enlightenment Project." For a review, see Sven-Eric Liedman, ed., *The Postmodernist Critique of the*

Project of the Enlightenment (Amsterdam: Rodopi, 1997); and N. Capaldi, *The Enlightenment Project in the Analytic Conversation* (Dordrecht: Kluwer, 1998).

89. Anonymous, *Sehr grewliche erschröcklicke vor unerhörte warhafftige Newe zeyttung was für grausame Tyranney der Moscoviter an den Gefangenen hinweggefürten Christen auss Lyfland* (Nuremberg: n.p., 1561). For a reproduction, see Andrea Kappeller, *Ivan Groznyi im Spiegel der auslandischen Druckschriften seiner Zeit* (Bern and Frankfurt am Main: Peter Lang, 1972), 32.

90. See John G. Younger, *Sex in the Ancient World from A to Z* (New York: Routledge, 2005), especially 118–120.

91. But see Martha Easton, "Was it Good for You, Too? Medieval Erotic Art and Its Audiences," *Different Visions: A Journal of New Perspectives on Medieval Art* 1 (2008).

92. Gail Buckland, *Fox Talbot and the Invention of Photography* (Boston: David R. Godine, 1980).

93. See Lisa Sigel, "Filth in the Wrong People's Hands: Postcards and the Expansion of Pornography in Britain and the Atlantic World," *Journal of Social History* 33:4 (2000), 859–885.

94. Michael Ayers Trotti, "Murder Made Real: The Visual Revolution of the Halftone," *The Virginia Magazine of History and Biography* 111:4 (2003), 397–410.

95. The Germans led the way. See Chad Ross, *Naked Germany: Health, Race and Nation* (Oxford: Berg Publishers, 2005), 23ff.; and Karl Eric Toepfter, *Empire of Ecstasy: Nudity and Movement in Weimar German Body Culture, 1910–1935* (Berkeley: University of California Press, 1997).

96. See Dian Hanson, *History of Men's Magazines* (Cologne: Taschen, 2004), vols. 2–6. For a short overview, see Gail Dines, "*Playboy* Magazine and the Mainstreaming of Pornography," in *Pornography: The Production and Consumption of Inequality*, edited by Gail Dines, Robert Jensen, and Ann Russo (New York: Routledge, 1998), 37–63.

97. Arthur Lovejoy, "On the Discrimination of Romanticisms," *Publications of the Modern Language Association of America* 39:2 (1924), 229–253.

98. *The Portable Nietzsche*, translated by W. Kaufmann (New York: Viking, 1968), 84.

99. See Darrin M. McMahon, *Enemies of the Enlightenment: The French Counter-Enlightenment and the Making of Modernity* (Oxford: Oxford UP, 2001); Joseph Mali and Robert Wokler, eds., *Isaiah Berlin's Counter-Enlightenment* (Philadelphia: American Philosophical Society, 2003); and Graeme Garrard, *Counter-Enlightenments: From the Eighteenth Century to the Present* (New York: Routledge, 2006).

100. The Romantic fixation on stormy poetry and erotic images is well known, but on their enjoyment of drugs, see Alethea Hayter, *Opium and the Romantic Imagination* (Berkeley: University of California Press, 1968); Emanual Mickel, *The Artificial Paradises in French Literature* (Chapel Hill: University of North Carolina Press, 1969); and Sue Vice, Matthew Campbell, and Tim Armstrong, eds., *Beyond the Pleasure Dome: Writing and Addiction from the Romantics* (Sheffield: Sheffield Academic Press, 1994).

101. See Colin Campbell, *The Romantic Ethic and the Spirit of Modern Consumerism* (Oxford: Basil Blackwell, 1987).

102. Helmut Kipphan, *Handbook of Print Media: Technologies and Production Methods* (Berlin: Springer, 2001), 154ff.

103. "Bowker Reports U.S. Book Production Flat in 2007," Bowker Press Release (New Providence, NJ, May 28, 2008).

104. *Book Industry Trends 2008* (New York: Book Industry Study Group, 2008).

105. *Editor & Publisher's International Yearbook 2006* (New York: Editor & Publisher, 2006).

106. *The National Directory of Magazines* (New York: Oxbridge Communications, Inc., 2008).

107. *Magazine Handbook 2008–2009* (New York: Magazine Publishers of America, 2008).

108. The manuscript is found in the "Newell Codex" in the British Library (Cotton Vitellius A. xv). See Kevin Kiernan, *Beowulf and the Beowulf Manuscript*, revised edition (Ann Arbor: University of Michigan Press, 1996).

109. See James A. Winn, *John Dryden and His World* (New Haven: Yale UP, 1998).

110. Maris A. Vinovskis, "Horace Mann on the Economic Productivity of Education," *New England Quarterly* 43 (1970), 550–571.

111. Stephen White, *The Bolshevik Poster* (New Haven: Yale UP, 1990), 104–108.

112. A. Chastro-Caldas et al., "The Illiterate Brain: Learning to Read and Write During Childhood Influences the Functional Organization of the Adult Brain," *Brain: A Journal of Neurology* 121:6 (1998), 1053–1063; and Geng Li et al., "Cognitive Processing in Chinese Literate and Illiterate Subjects: An fMRI Study," *Human Brain Mapping* 27 (2006), 144–152. Mitika Brottman argues that reading may be *bad* for you. See *The Solitary Vice: Against Reading* (Berkeley: Counterpoint, 2008).

113. On the invention of stamps, see Colin G. Hey, *Roland Hill: Victorian Genius and Benefactor* (London: Quiller Press, 1989).

114. Vladimir I. Lenin, "Thesis and Report on Bourgeois Democracy and the Dictatorship of the Proletariat," *Selected Works: July 1918 to March 1919* (Moscow: International Publishers, 1967), vol. 3: 129.

115. Lenin, "Thesis and Report on Bourgeois Democracy and the Dictatorship of the Proletariat," 129.

116. Johann Huttich and Simon Grynaeus, eds., *Novus orbis regionum ac insularum veteribus incognitarum una cum tabula cosmographica* (Paris: Antoine Augerelle for Jehan Petit, 1532).

117. See Margaret T. Hodgen, *Early Anthropology in the Sixteenth and Seventeenth Centuries* (Philadelphia: University of Pennsylvania Press, 1964); and Poe, *'A People Born to Slavery': Russia in Early Modern European Ethnography*.

118. On the early history of newspapers, see Houston, *Literacy in Early Modern Europe*, 192–196. More generally, see Hannah Barker, *Newspapers, Politics and English Society, 1695–1855* (New York: Longman, 1999).

119. See Ole Peter Grellet et al., eds., *Tolerance and Intolerance in the European Reformation* (Cambridge: Cambridge UP, 2002); and Perez Zagorin, *How the Idea of Religious Toleration Came to the West* (Princeton: Princeton UP, 2003).

120. Immanuel Kant, *To Perpetual Peace: A Philosophic Sketch*, translated by Ted Humphrey (Indianapolis: Hackett Publishing, 2003).

121. Website: United Nations, "The Universal Declaration of Human Rights." Retrieved June 22, 2009.

122. Dard Hunter, *Papermaking: The History and Technique of an Ancient Craft* (New York: A. A. Knopf, 1943), especially chapter 8.

123. Hunter, *Papermaking*, chapter 12.

124. That said, a lot of books have been lost: James Raven, *Lost Libraries: The Destruction of Great Book Collections Since Antiquity* (New York: Palgrave Macmillan, 2004).

125. Houston, *Literacy in Early Modern Europe*, 175.

126. Rob Banham, "The Industrialization of the Book, 1800–1970," in *A Companion to the History of the Book*, edited by Simon Eliot and Jonathan Rose (Malden: Wiley-Blackwell, 2007), 273–290.

127. Susan B. Carter et al., eds., *Historical Statistics of the United States* (Cambridge: Cambridge UP, 2006), table Dg 225.

128. "Bowker Reports U.S. Book Production Flat in 2007," Bowker Press Release (New Providence, NJ, May 28, 2008).

129. Houston, *Literacy in Early Modern Europe*, 175.

130. *Book Industry Trends 2008* (New York: Book Industry Study Group, 2008).

131. "WorldCat Facts and Statistics" (Dublin, Ohio: Online Computer Library Center, 2008).

132. "ALA Library Fact Sheet Number 22" (Chicago: American Library Association, 2008).

133. See Ludwig Edelstein, *The Idea of Progress in Classical Antiquity* (Baltimore: Johns Hopkins UP, 1967).

134. See E. R. Dodds' review of Edelstein's *The Idea of Progress in Classical Antiquity*, in *Journal of the History of Ideas* 29:3 (1968), 453–457.

135. On the difficulties of tracing the modern idea of progress to the early Christians, see W. Warren Wagar, "Modern Views of the Origins of the Idea of Progress," *Journal of the History of Ideas* 28:1 (1967), 61ff.

136. J. B. Bury, *The Idea of Progress: An Inquiry into its Origin and Growth* (London: MacMillan & Co., 1920).

137. See especially Robert Nisbet, *History of the Idea of Progress* (New Brunswick: Transaction, 1994), part II.

138. See Peter J. Bowler, *The Invention of Progress: The Victorians and the Past* (London: B. Blackwell, 1989).

139. Cicero, *De oratore* 2.9.35.

140. George Santayana, *The Life of Reason, or The Phases of Human Progress* (New York: Charles Scribner's Sons, 1906), 284.

141. On early university faculties, see Hilde de Ridder-Symoens, ed., *Universities in the Middle Ages* (Cambridge: Cambridge UP, 1992), 307–441.

142. On the creation of modern disciplinary faculties, see Walter Rüegg, ed., *Universities in the Nineteenth and Early Twentieth Centuries (1800–1945)* (Cambridge: Cambridge UP, 2004), 393–636.

143. On professionalization more generally, see Harold Perkins, *The Third Revolution: Professional Elites in the Modern World* (London: Routledge, 1996).

144. Ryan Krieger Balot, *Greek Political Thought* (Malden: Wiley-Blackwell, 2006), 48–85.

145. Ludwig Edelstein, *The Hippocratic Oath: Text, Translation, Interpretation* (Baltimore: Johns Hopkins UP, 1943).

146. The *locus classicus* is Max Weber, "Die Protestantische Ethik und der Geist des Kapitalismus," *Archiv für Sozialwissenschaften und Sozialpolitik,* 20 and 21 (1905).

147. Emile Durkheim, *The Division of Labor in Society,* translated by W. D. Halls (New York: Simon & Schuster, 1997), 68ff.

148. Karl Marx and Friedrich Engels, *Werke,* 39 vols. in 41 (Berlin: Dietz Verlag, 1961–1974), vol. 19: "Kritik des Gothaer Programms," 20.

4. HOMO VIDENS

1. *The Republic,* translated by R. E. Allen (New Haven: Yale UP, 2006), 138–139. Subsequent citations are to this edition.

2. On telegraphy, see Lewis Coe, *Telegraph: A History of Morse's Invention and Its Predecessors in the United States* (Jefferson: McFarland & Company, 1993); and Tom Standage, *The Victorian Internet: The Remarkable Story of the Telegraph and the Nineteenth Century's On-line Pioneers* (New York: Walker & Company, 2007).

3. On photography, see Michel Frizot, Pierre Albert, and Colin Harding, eds., *A New History of Photography* (Cologne: Könemann, 1998); and Robert Hirsch, *Seizing the Light: A Social History of Photography* (New York: McGraw-Hill, 1999).

4. On telephony, see Lewis Coe, *The Telephone and its Several Inventors: A History* (Jefferson: McFarland & Company, 1995); and Claude Fischer, *America Calling: A Social History of the Telephone to 1940* (Berkeley: University of California Press, 1992).

5. On recorded sound, see Jonathan Sterne, *The Audible Past: Cultural Origins of Sound Recording* (Durham: Duke UP, 2003); and David Morton, *Sound Recording: The Life Story of a Technology* (Baltimore: Johns Hopkins UP, 2006).

6. On radio, see Tapan K. Sarkar et al., *History of Wireless* (Hoboken: John Wiley & Sons, 2006); and Alfred Balk, *The Rise of Radio, from Marconi through the Golden Age* (Jefferson: McFarland & Company, 2003).

7. On motion pictures, see Peter Kobel, *Silent Movies: The Birth of Film and the Triumph of Movie Culture* (New York: Little Brown & Co., 2007); and Geoffrey Nowell-Smith, ed., *The Oxford History of World Cinema* (New York: Oxford UP, 1999).

8. On television, see Albert Abramson, *The History of Television, 1880–1941* (Jefferson: McFarland & Company, 1987); Albert Albramson, *The History*

of Television, 1941–2000 (Jefferson: McFarland & Company, 2003); and Anthony Smith, *Television: An International History* (Oxford: Oxford UP, 1995).

9. For surveys of the history of mass (and especially audiovisual) media, see Brian Wilson, *Media Technology and Society. A History: From the Telegraph to the Internet* (New York: Routledge, 1998); Asa Briggs and Peter Burke, *A Social History of the Media: from Gutenberg to the Internet* (Cambridge: Polity, 2002); John Bray, *Innovation and the Communications Revolution: From the Victorian Pioneers to Broadband Internet* (London: Institution of Electrical Engineers, 2002); Anton A. Huudeman, *A Worldwide History of Telecommunications* (Hoboken: Wiley–IEEE, 2003); and Paul Starr, *The Creation of the Media: Political Origins of Modern Communication* (New York: Basic Books, 2004).

10. The literature on "mass media" and the rest is so large that no brief catalogue can be made. Suffice it to say that a search of JSTOR (Journal Storage) yields 39,643 articles and reviews including the phrase "mass media," 866 articles and reviews including the phrase "communications revolution," 1,479 articles and reviews including the phrase "information revolution," 2,352 articles and reviews including the phrase "information society," and 4,774 including the phrase "information age." All searches conducted on May 29, 2009.

11. See R. White, "Substantial Acts: From Materials to Meaning in Upper Paleolithic Representation," in *Beyond Art: Pleistocene Image and Symbol*, edited by M. W. Conkey et al. (San Francisco: California Academy of Sciences, 1997), 93–121. More generally see Ofer Bar-Yosef, "The Upper Paleolithic Revolution," *Annual Review of Anthropology* 31 (2002), 363–393.

12. For a recent treatment of this and other Paleolithic "Venus" statues, see O. Soffer, J. M. Adovasio, and D. C. Hyland, "The 'Venus' Figurines: Textiles, Basketry and Status in the Upper Paleolithic," *Current Anthropology* 41:4 (2000), 511–537.

13. See Michael Grant and Antonia Mulas, *Eros in Pompeii: The Erotic Art Collection of the Museum of Naples* (New York: Stewart, Tabori, and Chang, 1997); and Antonio Varone, *Eroticism in Pompeii* (Getty Trust Publications: J. Paul Getty Museum, 2001).

14. For an overview, see J. R. Green, *Theatre in Ancient Greek Society* (London: Routledge, 1997).

15. See Romana A. Naddaff, *Exiling the Poets: The Production of Censorship in Plato's Republic* (Chicago: University of Chicago Press, 2002).

16. On the capacity of the large venues in the Ancient World, see John Geraint and Rod Sheard, *Stadia: A Design and Development Guide*, third edition (Oxford: Architectural Press, 2003), 3–6.

17. For the Ancient World, see J. P. Toner, *Popular Culture in Ancient Rome* (New York: John Wiley & Sons, 2009). For medieval Europe, see Josie P. Campbell, ed., *Popular Culture in the Middle Ages* (Bowling Green: Popular Press, 1996). For early modern Europe, see Peter Burke, *Popular Culture in Early Modern Europe*, third edition (London: Ashgate, 2009).

18. For an overview of image censorship, albeit one focused on religious imagery, see Alain Besançon, *The Forbidden Image: An Intellectual History of*

Iconoclasm, translated by Jane Marie Todd (Chicago: University of Chicago Press, 2009).

19. See Arthur M. Hind, *An Introduction to a History of Woodcut* (Boston: Houghton Mifflin, 1935). For a more recent treatment, see R. W. Schribner, *For the Sake of Simple Folk: Popular Propaganda in the German Reformation* (Oxford: Clarendon Press, 1994).

20. The standard works are Beaumont Newhall, *The History of Photography from 1839 to the Present* (New York: Museum of Modern Art, 1949), and Helmut and Alison Gernsheim, *The History of Photography from the Earliest Use of the Camera Obscura in the Eleventh Century up to 1914* (New York: Oxford UP, 1955). Also see Helmut Gernsheim, *The Origin of Photography* (New York: Thames and Hudson, 1988). For a recent interpretation, see Geoffrey Batchen, *Burning with Desire: The Conception of Photography* (Cambridge: MIT Press, 1997).

21. Jean-Louis Marignier, *Nicéphore Niépce 1765–1833: l'invention de la photographie* (Paris: Belin, 1999).

22. Michael Ayers Trotti, "Murder Made Real: The Visual Revolution of the Halftone," *The Virginia Magazine of History and Biography* 111:4 (2003), 397–410.

23. See David Nasaw, *Going Out: The Rise and Fall of Public Amusements* (Cambridge: Harvard UP, 1999); and Roy Rosenzweig, *Eight Hours for What We Will: Workers and Leisure in an Industrial City, 1870–1920* (Cambridge: Cambridge UP, 1985). Also see the essays in Richard Butsch, ed., *For Fun and Profit: The Transformation of Leisure into Consumption* (Philadelphia: Temple UP, 1990); Kathryn Grover, ed., *Hard at Play: Leisure in America, 1840–1940* (Amherst: University of Massachusetts Press, 1991); and Rudy Koshar, ed., *Histories of Leisure* (Oxford: Berg Publishers, 2002).

24. On vaudeville, see Robert M. Lewis, *From Traveling Show to Vaudeville: Theatrical Spectacle in America, 1830–1910* (Baltimore: Johns Hopkins UP, 2007). On cabaret, see Lisa Appignanesi, *The Cabaret*, revised and expanded edition (New Haven: Yale UP, 2004). On burlesque, see Robert C. Allen, *Horrible Prettiness: Burlesque and American Culture* (Chapel Hill: University of North Carolina Press, 1991). On striptease, see Rachel Shteir, *Striptease: The Untold Story of the Girlie Show* (New York: Oxford UP, 2004)

25. This "lag" is deftly analyzed by Wilson, *Media Technology and Society*. Much of what follows is based on Wilson's account.

26. On the rise and expansion of the recorded music industry, see Sterne, *The Audible Past: Cultural Origins of Sound Recording*; and Morton, *Sound Recording: The Life Story of a Technology*.

27. On the rise and expansion of the movie industry, see Kobel, *Silent Movies: The Birth of Film and the Triumph of Movie Culture*; and Nowell-Smith, ed., *The Oxford History of World Cinema*.

28. Michelle Pautz, "The Decline in Average Weekly Cinema Attendance: 1930–2000," *Issues in Political Economy* 11 (2000), Appendix.

29. Susan Newman-Baudais, "Partnering Europe: Access to the European Market for Non-European Films: A Statistical Analysis," European Audiovisual Observatory (2004), table 1.

30. On radio, see Sarkar et al., *History of Wireless*; and Balk, *The Rise of Radio, from Marconi through the Golden Age*. On television, see Abramson, *The History of Television, 1880–1941*; Abramson, *The History of Television, 1941–2000*; and Smith, *Television: An International History*.

31. B. R. Mitchell, *International Historical Statistics. Europe 1750–2005*, sixth edition (Basingstoke: Palgrave Macmillan, 2007), table F10 ("Radio and Television Receiving Licenses").

32. *CIA World Factbook* 2008 (Washington, DC: CIA, 2008).

33. The literature on the Industrial Revolution is very large, but modern debate is roughly divisible into two views. The traditional Europe-centered view is represented by David Landes, *The Unbound Prometheus: Technological Change and Industrial Development from 1750 to the Present* (London: Cambridge UP, 1969). The new world-historical view is represented by Peter N. Stearns, *The Industrial Revolution in World History* (Boulder: Westview Press, 2007). On the challenge of the one by the other, see Jack A. Goldstone, "Efflorescences and Economic Growth in World History: Rethinking the 'Rise of the West' and the Industrial Revolution," *Journal of World History* 13:2 (2002), 323–389.

34. On the origins of the Welfare State, see W. J. Mommsen, ed., *The Emergence of the Welfare State in Britain and Germany, 1850–1950* (London: German Historical Institute, 1981); A. de Swaan, *In Care of the State: Health Care, Education, and Welfare in Europe and the USA in the Modern Era* (New York: Oxford UP, 1988); Susan Pedersen, *Family, Dependence, and the Origins of the Welfare State: Britain and France, 1914–1945* (New York: Cambridge UP, 1993); and Peter Baldwin, *The Politics of Social Solidarity: Class Bases of the European Welfare State, 1875–1975* (New York: Cambridge UP, 1990). For a review of the literature, see Jill Quadagno, "Theories of the Welfare State," *Annual Review of Sociology* 13 (1987), 109–128; and John Myles and Jill Quadagno, "Political Theories of the Welfare State," *Social Service Review* 76:1 (2002), 34–57.

35. Abraham Lincoln, "Address Delivered at the Dedication of the Cemetery at Gettysburg," in *The Collected Works of Abraham Lincoln*, 9 volumes, edited by Roy P. Basler (Springfield: Abraham Lincoln Association, 1953), vol. 7: 19.

36. Gerhard Ritter, *Fredrick the Great: A Historical Profile*, translated by Peter Paret (Berkeley: University of California Press, 1975), 166.

37. For recent treatments, see Herman Beck, *The Origins of the Authoritarian Welfare State in Prussia: Conservatives, Bureaucracy, and the Social Question* (Ann Arbor: University of Michigan, 1995); and E. P. Hennock, *The Origins of the Welfare State in England and Germany, 1850–1914: Social Policies Compared* (Cambridge: Cambridge UP, 2007).

38. On the role of politics in the creation of the modern media, and the origin of the split between state ownership in Europe and private ownership in America, see Paul Starr, *The Creation of the Media: Political Origins of Modern Communications* (New York: Basic Books, 2005).

39. By "cultural liberalism" we mean the idea that people should be allowed to do as they want in the cultural sphere. The notion is tightly bound up with the notions such as "freedom of religion," "freedom of the press," "freedom of

expression," the "right to privacy," and "toleration" generally. The literature on each of these ideas is sizable. For a recent summary of the liberal tradition, see Pierre Manent, *An Intellectual History of Liberalism*, translated by Rebecca Balinski (Princeton: Princeton UP, 1994). On the widening of what was permissible to write and read, say and hear, and show and watch in the United States, see Margaret Blanchard, *Freedom of Expression in Modern America* (New York: Oxford UP, 1992).

40. See Janet Clark, *'Art Made Tongue-Tied by Authority': Elizabethan and Jacobean Dramatic Censorship* (Manchester: Manchester UP, 1990); R. Dutton, *Mastering the Revels: The Regulation and Censorship of English Renaissance Drama* (London: MacMillan, 1991); and David Thomas, David Carlton, and Anne Etienne, *Theatre Censorship from Walpole to Wilson* (Oxford: Oxford UP, 2007).

41. See David Colclough, *Freedom of Speech in Early Stuart England* (Cambridge: Cambridge UP, 2005), and, more generally, Leonard W. Levy, *Emergence of the Free Press* (Oxford: Oxford UP, 1985).

42. See David M. Rabban, *Free Speech in Its Forgotten Years* (New York: Cambridge UP, 1997).

43. See Leigh Ann Wheeler, *Against Obscenity: Reform and the Politics of Womanhood in America, 1873–1935* (Baltimore: Johns Hopkins UP, 2004).

44. On what follows, see Laura Wittern-Keller, *Freedom of the Screen: Legal Challenges to State Film Censorship, 1915–1981* (Lexington: University of Kentucky Press, 2008); and Laura Wittern-Keller and Raymond J. Haberski, *The Miracle Case: Film Censorship and the Supreme Court* (Lawrence: UP of Kansas, 2008).

45. Anthony Burgess, *A Clockwork Orange* (London: Heinemann, 1962).

46. Carter et al., eds., *Historical Statistics of the United States*, table Dg 55.

47. Website: United States Postal Service, "Pieces of Mail Handled, Number of Post Offices, Income, and Expenses, 1789 to 2008." Retrieved June 4, 2009.

48. Carter et al., eds., *Historical Statistics of the United States*, table Dg 225.

49. Ellen Propper Michiewicz, *Split Signals: Television and Politics in the Soviet Union* (New York: Oxford UP, 1990), 21–22. The Soviets were hardly alone in censoring foreign broadcasts. See George H. Quester, "Coping with Transborder Penetration: The Politics of Television," *Journal of Policy Analysis and Management* 3:4 (1984), 532–543.

50. Ellen Propper Michiewicz, *Changing Channels: Television and the Struggle for Power in Russia* (New York: Oxford UP, 1997), 99.

51. Starr, *The Creation of the Media*, 315–326.

52. Starr, *The Creation of the Media*, 348–363.

53. Starr, *The Creation of the Media*, 339–346.

54. See Jerome A. Barron, "Access to the Press – A New First Amendment Right," *Harvard Law Review* 80 (1967), 1641–1678.

55. José Ortega y Gasset, *The Revolt of the Masses* (New York: W. W. Norton, 1932).

56. C. Write Mills, *The Power Elite* (New York: Oxford UP, 1956), chapter 13. One might also mention Raymond Williams, *Television: Technology and Cultural Form* (London: Fontana, 1974).

57. In most of Europe television is state-owned, which is to say completely subsidized by tax-payers. But even in the United States, the government subsidizes both radio and television production (via the Corporation for Public Broadcasting) and radio and television *consumption*. For example, the National Telecommunications and Information Administration is subsidizing the purchase of digital-to-analog converters for those 17 million Americans who do not have digital-ready televisions. See Glenn Derene, "Digital Transition Looms, but Do Americans Have a Right to TV?" *Popular Mechanics* (May 5, 2008).

58. In neither the United States nor the United Kingdom is television reception viewed as a legal "right." If someone builds a code-compliant structure that blocks your reception, you have no legal recourse. For the United States, see T. K. McQueen, "Nuisance – No Right to Interference-Free Television Reception," *DePaul Law Review* 22 (1972–1973), 870ff. For the United Kingdom, see Janet O' Sullivan, "A Poor Reception for Television Nuisance," *Cambridge Law Journal* 55:2 (1996), 184–187; and Janet O' Sullivan, "Nuisance in the House of Lords: Normal Service Resumed," *Cambridge Law Journal* 56:3 (1997), 483–485. That said, both governments have recognized that they need to take measures to ensure that all citizens have access to radio and television. More than that, for decades now legal scholars and the courts have been flirting with a positive "right to access" interpretation of the First Amendment. See Barron's seminal "Access to the Press – A New First Amendment Right" and his more recent reviews, "Rights of Access and Reply to the Media in the United States Today," *Communications and the Law* 25:1 (2003), 1–13, and "Access Reconsidered," *George Washington Law Review* 76:4 (2008), 826–844.

59. See Andrew Yoder, *Pirate Radio: The Incredible Saga of America's Underground, Illegal Broadcasters* (Salona Beach: HighText Publications, 1995); Andrew Yoder, *Pirate Radio Stations: Tuning in to Underground Broadcasts in the Air and Online*, third edition (New York: McGraw-Hill, 2002); and Sue Carpenter, *Forty Watts from Nowhere: A Journey into Pirate Radio* (New York: Simon & Schuster, 2004).

60. Website: TV Licensing. Retrieved June 30, 2009.

61. "New Generation of Television Detector Vans Hits the Streets," BBC press release, June 24, 2003.

62. Media Institute of Southern Africa, "Zimbabwe: Street Vendor Arrested for Listening to Critical Radio Program," *Africa News* (June 23, 2009).

63. See Michael Nelson, *War of the Black Heavens: The Battles of Western Broadcasting in the Cold War* (Syracuse: Syracuse UP, 1997), 63, 133, and 184.

64. Nelson, *War of the Black Heavens*, 62–66, 133–136, 163–164, 190–192.

65. Website: Carin Zissis and Preeti Bhattacharji, "Media Censorship in China," Council on Foreign Relations. Retrieved August 3, 2009.

66. Fardin Alikhah, "The Politics of Satellite Television in Iran," in *Media, Culture and Society in Iran: Living with Globalization and the Islamic State*, edited by Mehdi Semati (London: Routledge, 2008), 94–110.

67. Website: Ian Liston-Smith, "Meager Media for North Koreans" (October 10, 2006), BBC News. Retrieved June 30, 2009.

68. For what follows, see Starr, *The Creation of the Media*, 295ff.
69. Lee Hyo-won, "Living Film Legend Tells Her Story," *Korea Times* (November 23, 2007).
70. On the idea that the public "owns the airwaves," see Reed E. Hundt, "The Public's Airwaves: What Does the Public Interest Require of Television Broadcasters?" *Duke Law Journal* 45:6 (1996), 1089–1129. On the erosion of this doctrine, see Krystilyn Corbett, "The Rise of Private Property Rights in the Broadcast Spectrum," *Duke Law Journal* 46:3 (1996), 611–650.
71. On film exhibition, see Douglas Gomery, *Shared Pleasures: A History of Movie Presentation in the United States* (Madison: University of Wisconsin Press, 1992).
72. On early radio listening in public spaces, see Richard Butsch, *The Making of American Audiences: From Stage to Television, 1750–1990* (New York: Cambridge UP, 2000), 187–189. On early television watching in public spaces, see Anna McCarthy, "The Front Row Is Reserved for Scotch Drinkers: Early Television's Tavern Audience," *Cinema Journal* 34:4 (1995), 31–49; Butsch, *The Making of American Audiences*, 238–243; and Anna McCarthy, *Ambient Television: Visual Culture and Public Space* (Durham: Duke UP, 2001).
73. See Linda Williams, *Hard Core: Power, Pleasure, and the "Frenzy of the Visible"* (Berkeley: University of California Press, 1999), 58–92.
74. John Heitmann, *The Automobile in American Life* (Jefferson: McFarland, 2009), 99–100.
75. Busch, *The Making of American Audiences*, 235–236.
76. Lynn Spigel, "Television in the Family Circle: The Popular Reception of a New Medium," in *Logics of Television: Essays in Cultural Criticism*, edited by Patricia Mellencamp (Bloomington: Indiana UP, 1990), 73–97. Also see Lynn Spigel, *Make Room for TV: Television and the Family Ideal in Postwar America* (Chicago: University of Chicago Press, 1992).
77. On the Walkman, see Paul du Gay et al., *Doing Cultural Studies: The Story of the Sony Walkman* (London: Sage, 1997). On the videotape, see Julia R. Dobrow, ed., *Social and Cultural Aspects of VCR Use* (Hillsdale: Lawrence Erlbaum Associates, 1990).
78. On the video revolution and the growth of video porn, see Stephen Prince, *A New Pot of Gold: Hollywood under the Electronic Rainbow, 1980–1989* (New York: Simon & Schuster, 1999), 121–123.
79. "...wie es eigentlich gewesen ist." Leopold von Ranke, *Geschichte der romanischen und germanischen Völker von 1494 bis 1514* [1824], third edition (Leipzig: Verlag von Duncker und Humblot, 1885), Vorrede, 7.
80. The distinction between icons and symbols is drawn from the writings of Charles S. Peirce. On it, see Floyd Merrell, *Pierce, Signs and Meaning* (Toronto: University of Toronto Press, 1997).
81. On the capacity of Circus Maximus and other large venues of the Ancient World, see Hazel Dodge, "Amusing the Masses: Buildings for Entertainment and Leisure in the Roman World," *Life, Death and Entertainment in the Roman Empire*, edited by D. S. Potter and D. J. Mattingly (Ann Arbor: University of Michigan Press), 205–255.
82. For an interesting overview, see Thomas M. Fitzgerald, *The Crowd and the Mob: From Plato to Canetti* (London: Unwin Hyman, 1989).

83. On which see Michael J. Haupert, *The Entertainment Industry* (Westport: Greenwood Publishing Group, 2006).
84. See Bill Osgerby, *Playboys in Paradise: Masculinity, Youth and Leisure-style in Modern America* (Oxford: Berg Publishers, 2001).
85. For "hard-core" music, see Steven Blush, *American Hardcore: A Tribal History* (Los Angeles: Feral House, 2001). For "hard-core" porn, see Brian McNair, *Striptease Culture: Sex, Media and the Democratization of Desire* (New York: Routledge, 2002), especially 35–112. For "hard-core" drugs, see Jill Jonnes, *Hep-cats, Narcs, and Pipe Dreams: A History of America's Romance with Illegal Drugs* (Baltimore: Johns Hopkins UP, 1999), especially 205ff. A related phenomenon is "extreme sports." On them, see Robert E. Rinehart and Synthia Sydnor, eds., *To the Extreme: Alternative Sports, Inside and Out* (Albany: State University of New York Press, 2003).
86. For Mahler, see *The Guinness Book of World Records 1990* (New York: Sterling Publishing Co., 1990), 140. For Napalm Death, Martin C. Strong, *The Great Rock Discography*, seventh edition (New York: Cannongate U.S., 2004), 1061.
87. For "Heimat II," see *The Guinness Book of World Records 1996* (New York: Sterling Publishing Co., 1996), 359. For the shortest film, see website: "The 1 Second Film." Retrieved June 12, 2009.
88. For Christoph Stöckli's radio marathon, see website: Sally Mules, "Swiss DJ Sets New World Record," Swissinfo.ch. Retrieved June 12, 2009. For the one-second radio advertisement, see Eric Pfanner, "On Advertising: In the Digital Age, the Soul of Wit – Technology," *International Herald Tribune* (June 25, 2006).
89. For Kristijan Petrovic's TV marathon, see website: "Croatian Television Station Sets New World Record for Non-Stop Talk Show," wieninternational.at. Retrieved June 12, 2009. For the shortest TV commercial, see *Guinness World Records 2004* (New York: Bantam Books, 2003), 334.
90. On Suresh Joachim, see "Couch Potato, Thy Name Is Suresh," *USA Today* (September 16, 2005).
91. "Nielsen Media Research Reports Television's Popularity Is Still Growing," Nielsen press release (September 21, 2006).
92. "100 Million iPods Sold." Apple press release, April 9, 2007.
93. "U.S. Album Sales Fell 9.5% in 2007," *New York Times* (January 4, 2008).
94. *Cahiers du cinema. Hors-série "Atlas du Cinéma" 2008.*
95. *Cahiers du cinema. Hors-série "Atlas du Cinéma" 2008.*
96. *CIA World Factbook 2008* (Washington, DC: CIA, 2008), "United States of America."
97. *CIA World Factbook 2008* (Washington, DC: CIA, 2008), "United States of America."
98. "Average U.S. Home Now Receives a Record 118.6 TV Channels," Nielsen press release (June 6, 2008).
99. On what follows, see Wilson, *Media Technology and Society*, 51–146.
100. The best data available for time-use in the United States are, of course, found in the Bureau of Labor Statistics' "American Time Use Survey." According to the most recent survey (2008), the average American age 15 and older spends more than five hours every day engaging in leisure activity. Website:

"American Time Use Survey Summary," BLS news release (June 24, 2009). Retrieved August 5, 2009. Also see Linda Nazareth, *The Leisure Economy: How Changing Demographics, Economics, and Generational Attitudes Will Reshape Our Lives and Our Industries* (Mississauga: John Wiley & Sons, 2007).

101. Though there are exceptions. See Steven Johnson, *Everything Bad Is Good for You* (New York: Riverhead Books, 2005).

102. The classic and highly entertaining treatment is Paul Fussell, *Class: A Guide Through the American Status System* (New York: Summit Books, 1983). Fussell has been updated after a fashion by David Brooks, *Bobos in Paradise: The New Upper Class and How They Got There* (New York: Simon & Schuster, 2001). Also relevant are Joseph Epstein, *Snobbery: The American Version* (New York: Houghton Mifflin Harcourt, 2002); Robert Lanham, *The Hipster Handbook* (New York: Anchor Books, 2003); and Kaya Oakes, *Slanted and Enchanted: The Evolution of Indie Culture* (New York: St. Martins Press, 2009).

103. See Francis George Gosling, *Before Freud: Neurasthenia and the American Medical Community* (Urbana-Champaign: University of Illinois Press 1987). The argument is of course still with us. See Heather Menzies, *No Time: Stress and the Crisis of Modern Life* (Vancouver: Douglas & McIntyre, 2005).

104. See Robert Kubey and Mihaly Csikszentmihalyi, "Television Addiction Is No Mere Metaphor," *Scientific American* 286:2 (February 2002), 74–81.

105. For what follows, see Jerry Beck, *The Animated Movie Guide* (Chicago: Chicago Review Press, 2005), 23–24.

106. Roger Corman, J. Philip Di Franco, and Karyn G. Browne, *The Movie World of Roger Corman* (New York: Chelsea House Publishers, 1979), 20.

107. Barry Miles and Chris Charlesworth, *The Beatles: A Diary. An Intimate Day-by-Day History* (London: Omnibus Press, 1998), 63.

108. Walter S. Ciciora, James Farmer, and Michael Adams, *Modern Cable Television Technology: Video, Voice, and Data Communications* (San Francisco: Morgan Kaufmann, 2004), 258.

109. Ciciora, Farmer, and Adams, *Modern Cable Television Technology*, 258.

110. Neil F. Comins, *Discovering the Essential Universe*, fourth edition (New York: Macmillan, 2008), 386.

111. Website: Voyager Mission Operations Status Report # 2009–03–20. Week ending March 20, 2009. Retrieved July 1, 2009.

112. Patrick Humphries, *Elvis the 1 Hits: The Secret History of the Classics* (Kansas City: Andrews McMeel Publishing, 2003), 22.

113. David R. Faber and Beth L. Bailey, *The Columbia Guide to America in the 1960s* (New York: Columbia UP, 2001), 437.

114. Carle Singleton and Rowena Wildin, eds., *The Sixties in America*, 3 vols. (Pasadena: Salem Press, 1999), vol. 2: 498.

115. Dan Balz, "Sorrowful Farewell to the 'People's Princess'," *Washington Post*, September 7, 1997.

116. David Bauder, "Super Bowl Audience Second-Second Largest Ever," *Washington Post* (February 5, 2007); Stephen Brook, "World Cup TV Audiences Soar," *Guardian* (June 19, 2009).

117. Website: Nielsen's "Top TV Ratings." Retrieved July 23, 2008.

118. Daniel J. Boorstin, *The Americans: The Democratic Experience* (New York: Random House, 1973), 371.

119. The literature on multiculturalism is enormous. For a recent overview, see Anthony Simon Laden and David Owen, *Multiculturalism and Political Theory* (Cambridge: Cambridge UP, 2007).

120. There is some dispute about this claim. See Batchen, *Burning with Desire*, 124ff.

121. Jody Rosen, "Researchers Play Tune Recorded Before Edison," *New York Times* (March 27, 2008).

122. Christopher Rawlence, *The Missing Reel: The Untold Story of the Lost Inventor of Moving Pictures* (New York: Atheneum, 1990).

123. James A. Hijiya, *Lee de Forest and the Fatherhood of Radio* (Bethlehem: Lehigh UP, 1992), 101ff.

124. Thom Holmes, *The Routledge Guide to Music Technology* (New York: Routledge, 2006), 41.

125. R. W. Burns, *John Logie Baird: Television Pioneer* (London: Institution of Electrical Engineers, 2000), 122ff.

126. Frank T. Thompson, *Lost Films: Important Movies That Disappeared* (Secaucus: Carol Publishing Group, 1996).

127. Rashod D. Ollison, "Anniversary 'Thriller' CD Can't Beat Original," *Baltimore Sun*, February 12, 2008.

128. Linguists are doing their best to record many languages before they disappear. See Nicholas Evans, *Dying Words: Endangered Languages and What They Have to Tell Us* (Malden: Wiley-Blackwell, 2009).

129. Website: "Documentation," *Oxford English Dictionary*. Retrieved August 6, 2009.

130. See Ronald E. Day, *The Modern Invention of Information Science: Discourse, History, and Power* (Carbondale: Southern Illinois UP, 2001), 7–37.

131. The Moviegoer [John Grierson], *New York Sun* (February 8, 1926). For more, see Jack C. Ellis and Betsy A. McLune, *A New History of Documentary Film* (New York: Continuum International Publishing Group, 2005), 3ff.

132. Commission on Education and Cultural Films, *The Film in National Life* (London: G. Allen and Unwin, 1932), viii, 115 §174.

133. *Journal of the National Institute of Social Sciences* 15 (1931), 140: "The Project includes: (1) Research at original sources for the collection and documentation of folk dances and music." On the WPA's folk song recording projects, Nolan Porterfield, *Last Cavalier: the Life and Times of John A. Lomax, 1867–1948* (Urbana-Champaign: University of Illinois Press, 1996), 381ff.; and Richard A. Reuss with JoAnne C. Reuss, *American Folk Music and Left-Wing Politics, 1927–1957* (Lanham: Scarecrow Press, 2000), 16ff.

134. The literature on the spread of audiovisual surveillance technology is large. For an example, see Clive Norris, Gary Armstrong, and Jade Morton, eds., *Surveillance, Closed Circuit Television, and Social Control* (Aldershot: Ashgate, 1999); Clive Norris and Gary Armstrong, *The Maximum Surveillance Society: The Rise of CCTV* (Oxford: Berg, 1999); and Mike McCahill, *The Surveillance Web: The Rise of Visual Surveillance in an English City* (Cullompton: Wilan Publishing, 2002).

135. See William G. Staples, *Everyday Surveillance: Vigilance and Visibility in Postmodern Life*, second edition (Lanham: Rowman & Littlefield, 2000), 67–75.

136. See Frederick Corney, *Telling October: Memory and the Making of the Bolshevik Revolution* (Ithaca: Cornell UP, 2004), 75–82.

137. See David King, *The Commissar Vanishes: The Falsification of Photographs and Art in Stalin's Russia* (New York: Metropolitan Books, 1997).

138. Louis Liebovich, *Richard Nixon, Watergate, and the Press: A Historical Retrospective* (Westport: Greenwood Publishing Group, 2003), 73ff.

139. Howard Koch and Julius J. Epstein, *Casablanca: Script and Legend* (Woodstock: Overlook Press, 1973), 95.

140. Much effort is currently being spent developing techniques to search digital audio and video. See Stan Z. Li and Anil K. Jain, *Handbook of Face Recognition* (New York: Springer, 2005); and David C. Gibbon and Zhu Liu, *Introduction to Video Search Engines* (New York: Springer, 2008).

141. Gary R. Edgerton, *The Columbia History of American Television* (New York: Columbia UP, 2009), 113ff.

142. See Paul McDonald, *The Star System: Hollywood's Production of Popular Identities* (London: Wallflower Press, 2000).

143. For an eye-opening look at this process, see Robert Hofler, *The Man Who Invented Rock Hudson: The Pretty Boys and Dirty Deals of Henry Willson* (New York: Carroll & Graf Publishers, 2005).

144. See Clayton R. Koppes and Gregory D. Black, *Hollywood Goes to War: How Politics, Profits, and Propaganda Shaped World War II Movies* (New York: Free Press, 1987); and Tony Shaw, *Hollywood's Cold War* (Amherst: University of Massachusetts Press, 2007).

145. See Peter Kenez, *Cinema and Soviet Society from the Revolution to the Death of Stalin* (London: I. B. Tauris, 2001). For a particularly interesting look at how stars were made to serve the interests of the Soviet state, see Simon Morrison, *The People's Artist: Prokofiev's Soviet Years* (New York: Oxford UP, 2008).

146. Neil Postman, *Amusing Ourselves to Death: Public Discourse in the Age of Show Business* (New York: Viking, 1985).

5. HOMO SOMNIANS

1. *The Republic*, translated by R. E. Allen (New Haven and London: Yale UP, 2006), 227.

2. See the introduction to this book. For useful correctives, see Andrew Keen, *The Cult of the Amateur: How Today's Internet Is Killing Our Culture* (New York: Broadway Business, 2007); Lee Siegel, *Against the Machine: Being Human in the Age of the Electronic Mob* (New York: Spiegel & Grau, 2008); and Mark Helprin, *Digital Barbarism: A Writer's Manifesto* (New York: Harper, 2009).

3. The Internet has generated and is generating a stupendously large literature. JSTOR includes reviews of 208 books with the word "Internet" in the title, the vast majority of which were published between 1992 and 2004 (JSTOR has a five-year moving wall). HOLLIS, the Harvard College

Library System catalogue, lists 678 books under the subject heading "Internet – Social Aspects."

4. For a recent survey, see John Henry, *The Scientific Revolution and the Origins of Modern Science*, third edition (New York: Palgrave Macmillan, 2008).

5. There are many accounts of Brahe and Kepler. A standard version is Alexandre Koyré, *The Astronomical Revolution: Copernicus, Kepler, Borelli*, translated by R.E.W. Maddison (Ithaca: Cornell UP, 1973), 159ff. For a more recent view, see James R. Voelkel, *The Composition of Kepler's Astronomia nova* (Princeton: Princeton UP, 2001), 93ff.

6. See Paula Findlin, *Possessing Nature: Museums, Collecting, and Scientific Culture in Early Modern Italy* (Berkeley: University of California Press, 1994). For a broader view, see Arthur MacGregor, *Curiosity and Enlightenment: Collectors and Collections from the Sixteenth to Nineteenth Century* (New Haven: Yale UP, 2008).

7. Francis Bacon, *Religious Meditations. Places of perswasion and disswasion, seene and allowed* (London: Printed [by John Windet] for Humfrey Hooper, and are to be sold at the blacke Beare in Chauncery Lane, 1597).

8. On early modern European scientific societies, see Martha Ornstein, *The Role of Scientific Societies in the Seventeenth Century* (New York: Columbia UP, 1913); James E. McClellan, *Science Reorganized: Scientific Societies in the Eighteenth Century* (New York: Columbia UP, 1985); and Mordechai Feingold, "Tradition versus Novelty. Universities and Scientific Societies in the Early Modern Period," in *Revolution and Continuity: Essays in the History and Philosophy of Early Modern Science*, edited by P. Barker and R. Ariew (Washington, DC: Catholic University of America Press, 1991), 45–59.

9. On the *Encyclopédie*, see Robert Darnton, *The Business of Enlightenment: A Publishing History of the Encyclopédie, 1775–1800* (Cambridge: Harvard UP, 1979). The idea may have been Greek in origin, but there were plenty of contemporary examples at hand. See Lawrence E. Sullivan, "Circumscribing Knowledge: Encyclopedias in Historical Perspective," *Journal of Religion* 70:3 (1990), 315–339; and Richard Yeo, *Encyclopedic Visions: Scientific Dictionaries and Enlightenment Culture* (New York: Cambridge UP, 2001).

10. On Otlet, see Trudi Bellardo Hahn and Michael Keeble Buckland, eds., *Historical Studies in Information Science* (Medford: Information Today, 1998), 22–50; Ronald E. Day, *The Modern Invention of Information Science: Discourse, History, and Power* (Carbondale: Southern Illinois UP, 2001), 7–37; and Françoise Levie, *L'homme qui voulait classer le monde: Paul Otlet et le Mundaneum* (Brussels: Impressions nouvelles, 2006).

11. On the history of microfilm, see Fredric Luther, *Microfilm: A History, 1839–1900* (Annapolis: National Microfilm Association, 1959); Susan A. Cady, "Machine Tool of Management: A History of Microfilm Technology" (Ph.D. dissertation, Lehigh University, 1994); and Alistair Black, Dave Muddiman, and Helen Plant, *The Early Information Society: Information Management in Britain Before the Computer* (Aldershot: Ashgate Publishers, 2007), 14–23.

12. "Micro-Photography," *Photographic News* 1:22 (February 4, 1859), 262.

13. Willard Detering Morgan, *The Encyclopedia of Photography*, 20 vols. (New York: Graystone Press, 1970), vol. 12: 2286.

14. "Letter from Franklin D. Roosevelt to R.D.W. Conner" (February 13, 1942), *American Archivist* 5 (April, 1942), 119–120.

15. H. G. Wells, "The Idea of a Permanent World Encyclopedia," in H. G. Wells, *World Brain* (Garden City: Doubleday-Doran, 1938).

16. On Bush, see G. Pascal Zachary, *Endless Frontier: Vannevar Bush, Engineering the American Century* (New York: Free Press, 1997); and James N. Nyce and Paul Kahn, eds., *From Memex to Hypertext: Vannevar Bush and the Mind's Machine* (Boston: Academic Press, 1991).

17. Vannevar Bush, "As We May Think," *Atlantic Monthly* (July, 1945), 101–108.

18. The following is based on Janet Abbate, *Inventing the Internet* (Cambridge: MIT Press, 1999); and Katie Hafner and Andrew Lyon, *Where the Wizards Stay Up Late: The Origins of the Internet* (New York: Simon & Schuster, 1998). For a good (if now a bit dated) review of the literature, see Roy Rosenzweig, "Wizards, Bureaucrats, Warriors, and Hackers: Writing the History of the Internet," *American Historical Review* 103:5 (1998), 1530–1552. For a more recent, broader treatment of the history of the Internet and related telecommunications technologies, see Gerald W. Brooks, *The Second Information Revolution* (Cambridge: Harvard UP, 2003).

19. On SAGE, see Kent C. Redmond and Thomas M. Smith, *From Whirlwind to MITRE: The R&D Story of the SAGE Air Defense Computer* (Cambridge: MIT Press, 2000). For a short, readable account, see Robert Buderi, *The Invention that Changed the World: How a Small Group of Radar Pioneers Won the Second World War and Launched a Technological Revolution* (New York: Simon & Schuster, 1996), 380–406.

20. Herman Kahn, *On Thermonuclear War* [1960] (New Brunswick: Transaction Publishers, 2007), 278.

21. On the origins of "packet switching," see Abbate, *Inventing the Internet*, 7–42.

22. On the origins of ARPANET, see Abbate, *Inventing the Internet*, 43–82. Abbate makes clear that ARPANET was first and foremost a research network, not a "military command and control system." See her "Government, Business and the Making of the Internet," *Business History Review* 75:1 (2001), 150. For an interesting collection of documents related to the founding of ARPANET, see Peter H. Salus, ed., *The ARPANET Sourcebook: The Unpublished Foundations of the Internet* (Charlottesville: Peer-to-Peer Communications, 2008).

23. On the formation of the "network of networks," see Abbate, *Inventing the Internet*, 113–146.

24. On the origins of the World Wide Web, see Abbate, *Inventing the Internet*, 214ff. The story has been told by the very people who invented the Web. See Tim Berners-Lee, *Weaving the Web: The Original Design and Ultimate Destiny of the World Wide Web by Its Inventor* (San Francisco: HarperSanFrancisco, 1999); and James Gillies and Robert Caliliau, *How the Web Was Born: The Story of the World Wide Web* (Oxford: Oxford UP, 2000).

25. On the origins of the browser, see Abbate, *Inventing the Internet*, 217ff. Also see Jim Clark and Owen Edwards, *Netscape Time: The Making of*

the Billion-Dollar Start-Up that Took on Microsoft (New York: St. Martins Press, 1999).

26. On information capitalism, see Muddiman and Plant, *The Early Information Society: Information Management in Britain Before the Computer*; James W. Cortada, *Before the Computer: IBM, NCR, Burroughs, and Remington Rand and the Industry They Created, 1865–1956* (Princeton: Princeton UP, 1993); Thomas Haigh, "Inventing Information Systems: The Systems Men and the Computer, 1950–1968," *Business History Review* 75:1 (2001), 15–61; James W. Cortada, *The Digital Hand: How Computers Changed the Work of American Manufacturing, Transportation, and Retail Industries* (New York: Oxford UP, 2003); and James W. Cortada, *The Digital Hand*: Volume II: *How Computers Changed the Work of American Financial, Telecommunications, Media, and Entertainment Industries* (New York: Oxford UP, 2005). For critical perspectives, see David Lyon and Elia Zuriek, eds., *Computers, Surveillance, and Privacy* (Minneapolis: University of Minnesota Press, 1996); and Jim Davis, Thomas Hirschl, and Michael Stack, *Cutting Edge: Technology, Information, Capitalism and Social Revolution* (London: Verso, 1997).

27. See Arno Borst, *The Ordering of Time: From Ancient Computus to the Modern Computer* (Chicago: University of Chicago Press, 1994), especially 106ff.

28. See especially Cortada, *Before the Computer*.

29. On "Project Xanadu," see Gary Wolf, "The Curse of Xanadu," *Wired*, 3.06 (June 1995). On the "Electronic Information Exchange System," see Howard Rheingold, *The Virtual Community: Homesteading on the Electronic Frontier*, revised edition (Cambridge: MIT Press, 2000), 113ff. On "Computer Supported Cooperative Work," see Paul Wilson, *Computer Supported Cooperative Work: An Introduction* (Oxford: Kluwer Academic Publishers, 1991). On "Collaborative Networked Learning," see Peter Goodyear et al., eds., *Advances in Research on Networked Learning* (Oxford: Kluwer Academic Publishers, 2004).

30. On the surveillance state, see Christopher Dandeker, *Surveillance, Power and Modernity: Bureaucracy and Discipline from 1700 to the Present Day* (Cambridge: Polity Press, 1990); Andrew Polsky, *The Rise of the Therapeutic State* (Princeton: Princeton UP, 1991); David Lyon, *The Electronic Eye: The Rise of Surveillance Society* (Minneapolis: University of Minnesota Press, 1994); Jon Agar, *The Government Machine: A Revolutionary History of the Computer* (Cambridge: MIT Press, 2003); Helen Margetts, *Information Technology in Government: Britain and America* (New York: Routledge, 1998); John Gilliom, *Overseers of the Poor: Surveillance, Resistance, and the Limits of Privacy* (Chicago: University of Chicago Press, 2001); and Sandra Brama, *Change of State: Information, Policy and Power* (Cambridge: MIT Press, 2006). Unfortunately, much of the literature on government-sponsored efforts to gather information on citizens is reliant on Foucault and his exaggerated image of modern society as "panopticon."

31. Cortada, *Before the Computer*, 53.

32. On Defense Department subsidies of the computer industry during the Cold War, see Paul N. Edwards, *The Closed World: Computers and the Politics of*

Discourse in Cold War America (Cambridge: MIT Press, 1996); and Arthur L. Norberg and Judy E. O'Neill, *Transforming Computer Technology: Information Processing for the Pentagon, 1962–1986* (Baltimore: Johns Hopkins UP, 1996).

33. On the notion that "hedonism" or "self-fulfillment" has come to dominate postwar Western culture, see Daniel Bell, *The Cultural Contradictions of Capitalism* (New York: Basic Books, 1976); Christopher Lasch, *The Culture of Narcissism* (New York: Norton, 1979); and Robert Bellah et al., *Habits of the Heart: Privatism and Commitment in American Life* (Berkeley: University of California Press, 1984). For a revision, see Paul Lichterman, "Beyond the Seesaw Model: Public Commitment in a Culture of Self-Fulfillment," *Sociological Theory* 13:3 (1995), 275–300. On postwar permissiveness, see Arthur Marwick, *The Sixties: Cultural Transformation in Britain, France, Italy and the United States, c. 1958–c. 1974* (New York: Oxford UP, 2000). Also of interest is Ronald K. L. Collins and David M. Skover, "The Pornographic State," *Harvard Law Review* 107:6 (1994), 1374–1399.

34. J. D. Salinger, *The Catcher in the Rye* (Boston: Boston, Little, Brown, 1951).

35. Aldous Huxley, *The Doors of Perception* (New York: Harper, 1954); Jack Kerouac, *On the Road* (New York: Viking Press, 1957).

36. See Bill Osgerby, *Playboys in Paradise: Masculinity, Youth and Leisure-style in Modern America* (Oxford: Berg Publishers, 2001); Martin Torgoff, *Can't Find My Way Home: America in the Great Stoned Age, 1945–2000* (New York: Simon & Schuster, 2004); and Tom Lutz, *Doing Nothing: A History of Loafers, Loungers, Slackers and Bums in America* (New York: Macmillan, 2007), 215ff.

37. See Peter O. Whitmer with Bruce VanWyngarden, *Aquarius Revisited: Seven Who Created the Sixties Counterculture That Changed America* (New York: Macmillan, 1987). The "seven" in question are: William S. Burroughs, Allen Ginsberg, Ken Kesey, Timothy Leary, Norman Mailer, Tom Robbins, and Hunter S. Thompson.

38. On these cases, see Terry Eastland, ed., *Freedom of Expression in the Supreme Court: The Defining Cases* (Lanham: Rowman & Littlefield, 2000), 192–194 and 218–234.

39. See Howard Rheingold, *Smart Mobs: The Next Social Revolution* (New York: Basic Books, 2003); Yochai Benkler, *The Wealth of Networks: How Social Production Transforms Markets and Freedom* (New Haven: Yale UP, 2006); Cass Sunstien, *Infotopia: How Many Minds Produce Knowledge* (New York: Oxford UP, 2006); Dan Tapscott and Anthony D. Williams, *Wikinomics: How Mass Collaboration Changes Everything* (New York: Portfolio, 2008); Clay Shirky, *Here Comes Everyone: The Power of Organizing without Organization* (New York: Penguin Press, 2008). One should probably also include the many books of Lawrence Lessig.

40. "2009 Digital Future Report," Center for the Digital Future, USC Annenberg School of Communications (2009).

41. For chatting ("socializing and communicating") and TV watching, see *The American Time Use Survey, 2007* (Washington, DC: Bureau of Labor Statistics, 2008), table A-1. On reading "for pleasure," see *The American Time Use Survey, 2007*, table 11.

42. Website: "IBM Personal Computer. Model 5150," Obsolete Technology Website. Retrieved on August 10, 2009.

43. Website: "Apple Macintosh. Model M0001," Obsolete Technology Website. Retrieved on August 10, 2009.

44. For example, the 300 Baud Texas Instruments TI-99/4 modem, introduced in 1980. See Website: "Texas Instruments CC-40." Retrieved August 10, 2009.

45. Jen Aronoff, "Retailers Say Computers Hot-to-Go This Weekend," *Charlotte Observer* (August 8, 2009).

46. Stuart Kennedy, "Cheap PCs for Kids Starts a Chain Reaction," *The Australian* (July 28, 2009).

47. Simon Yates et al., "Worldwide PC Adoption Forecast, 2007 to 2015," Forrester Research (June 11, 2007).

48. Website: "Internet World Stats." Retrieved July 23, 2008.

49. Website: U.S. Census Bureau, "WorldPOPClock Projection." Retrieved July 23, 2008.

50. David Buckinham and Rebekah Willett, *Digital Generations: Children, Young People, and New Media* (London: Routledge, 2006), 255.

51. Christine Ogan, "Communications Technology and Global Change," in *Communication Technology and Social Change*, edited by Carolyn A. Lin and David J. Atkin (London: Routledge, 2007), 29. Also see Ronald Deibert et al., eds., *Access Denied. The Practice and Policy of Global Internet Filtering* (Cambridge: MIT Press, 2008).

52. See "North Korea," in *Access Denied*, 347ff. Also see Stacey Banks, "North Korean Telecommunications: On Hold," *North Korean Review* 1 (2005), 88–94; and Marcus Noland, "Telecommunications in North Korea: Has Orascom Made the Connection?" *North Korean Review* 5 (2009), 62–74.

53. According to Nolan, North Korea has about five telephone lines for each 100 inhabitants, and "most of these are installed in government offices, collective farms, and state-owned enterprises." See Noland, "Telecommunications in North Korea."

54. For the statistics that follow, see Website: "Internet World Stats." Retrieved July 23, 2008.

55. See especially James Surowiecki, *The Wisdom of Crowds: Why the Many Are Smarter than the Few and How Collective Wisdom Shapes Business, Economies, Societies, and Nations* (New York: Doubleday, 2004). A related though somewhat different idea is "crowdsourcing." See Jeff Howe, *Crowdsourcing: Why the Power of the Crowd Is Driving the Future of Business* (New York: Random House, 2008).

56. Website: Jason Lanier, "Digital Maoism," Edge.org. Retrieved August 11, 2008. Also see Keen, *The Cult of the Amateur*, 92–96; and Siegel, *Against the Machine*, 83–124. The most trenchant criticism of the "wisdom of crowds" is that the conditions that must be in place in order for crowds to be "wise" are very unusual. See Eric Klinenberg's review, "Strength in Numbers," *Washington Post* (September 7, 2004), C03.

57. Cartoon by Peter Steiner, *New Yorker* 69:20 (July 5, 1993), 61.

58. See Edward Castronova, *Synthetic Worlds: The Business and Culture of Online Games* (Chicago: University of Chicago Press, 2005); Tim Guest, *Second Lives: A Journey Through Virtual Worlds* (New York: Random House,

2008); Tom Boellstorff, *Coming of Age in Second Life: An Anthropologist Explores the Virtually Human* (Princeton: Princeton UP, 2008); Wagner James Wu, *The Making of Second Life: Notes from the New World* (New York: HarperBusiness, 2008); and Edward Castronova, *Exodus to the Virtual World: How Online Fun Is Changing Reality* (New York: Palgrave, 2008).

59. On the implications of online anonymity, see Daniel J. Solove, *The Future of Reputation: Gossip, Rumor, and Privacy on the Internet* (New Haven: Yale UP, 2007), 125–160.

60. The relationship between online anonymity and "disinhibitive" behavior is well documented. See Michael Tresca, "The Impact of Anonymity on Disinhibitive Behavior Through Computer-Mediated Communication" (Master's Thesis, Department of Communications, Michigan State University, 1998); Adam N. Joinson, "Causes and Implications of Disinhibited Behavior on the Internet," in *Psychology and the Internet: Intrapersonal, Interpersonal, and Transpersonal Implications*, edited by Jayne Gackenbach (Amsterdam: Academic Press, 1998), 43–60; John Suler, "The Online Disinhibition Effect," *CyberPsychology & Behavior* 7:3 (2004), 321–326.

61. See *Ashcroft v. Free Speech Coalition*, 535 U.S. 234 (2002). For a discussion of the legal status of virtual representations and obscenity, see Amy Adler, "The Perverse Law of Child Pornography," *Columbia Law Review*, 101:2 (March, 2001), 209–273; Amy Adler, "Inverting the First Amendment," *University of Pennsylvania Law Review* 149:4 (2001), 921–1002; Andrew Koppelman, "Does Obscenity Cause Moral Harm?" *Columbia Law Review* 105:5 (2005), 1635–1679; and Yaman Akdeniz, *Internet Child Pornography and the Law: National and International Responses* (Aldershot: Ashgate Publishers, 2008).

62. The primary exponent of this comforting, consumer-friendly view is Lawrence Lessig. See *Free Culture: How Big Media Uses Technology and the Law to Lock Down Culture and Control Creativity* (New York: Penguin Press, 2004). Also see Savi Vaidhyanathan, *Copyrights and Copywrongs: The Rise of Intellectual Property and How It Threatens Creativity* (New York: NYU Press, 2003).

63. Stephen Manes, "The Trouble with Larry," *Forbes* (March 29, 2004), 84ff.; Stephen Manes, "Let's Have Less of Lessig," *Forbes* (April 2, 2004); and Keen, *The Cult of the Amateur*; 24, 141ff.

64. Website: DomainTools, "Domain Counts & Internet Statistics." Retrieved July 23, 2008.

65. Website: Netcraft, "June 2008 Web Server Survey." Retrieved July 23, 2008.

66. Website: WorldWideWebSize, "The Size of the World Wide Web." Retrieved July 23, 2008.

67. Bin He et al., "Accessing the Deep Web," *Communications of the ACM* 50:5 (2007), 94–1001; and Alex Wright, "Exploring a 'Deep Web' That Google Can't Grasp," *New York Times* (February 22, 2009).

68. Kathryn Leger, "Stealing Time at Work on the Net; Companies Cracking Down on Cyberslacking," *The Gazette* (Montreal) (April 4, 2008); "Personal Web Use at Work Is 'Costing UK GB10.6bn a Year'," *Financial Advisor* (June 26, 2008). More generally see Patricia M. Wallace, *The Internet in*

the Workplace: How New Technology Is Transforming Work (Cambridge: Cambridge UP, 2004), 226–229.

69. Sarah Treleaven, "Goofing Off Is Good for Productivity; New Study Shows Taking a Break Boosts Efficiency," *Financial Post* (April 12, 2008), FW6; and "Workplace Internet Surfers are More Productive: Study," *The Gazette* (Montreal) (April 3, 2009), A2.

70. On the Romantics, see Charles Taylor, *Sources of the Self: The Making of Modern Identity* (Cambridge: Harvard UP, 1989), 375–392.

71. See Jane Roland Martin, "Romanticism Domesticated: Maria Montessori and the Casa Dei Bambini," in *The Educational Legacy of Romanticism*, edited by John Willinsky (Waterloo: Wilfrid Laurier UP, 1990), 159–174.

72. See especially Siegel, *Against the Machine*, 53ff.

73. A brief history of the origins of blogging software can be found in Biz Stone's *Who Let the Blogs Out: A Hyperconnected Peek at the World of Weblogs* (New York: Macmillan, 2004), 13ff.

74. There are many books on "Web 2.0." See Bradley L. Jones, *Web 2.0 Heroes: Interviews with Web 2.0 Influencers* (New York: John Wiley & Sons, 2008).

75. John Stuart Mill, *On Liberty* (London: Longmans, Green, and Co., 1913), 9ff.

76. Website: "Troll *(computing slang)*": "A person who posts deliberately erroneous or antagonistic messages to a newsgroup or similar forum with the intention of eliciting a hostile or corrective response." *Oxford English Dictionary*. Retrieved August 12, 2009.

77. This is the advice of software design guru Eric S. Raymond. See his important *The Cathedral & The Bazaar: Musings on Linux and Open Source by an Accidental Revolutionary* (Bejing: O'Reilly, 1999), 28ff. ("Release Early, Release Often").

78. On transculturalism, see Harvey Siegel, "Multiculturalism and the Possibility of Transcultural Educational and Philosophical Ideals," *Philosophy* 74:289 (1999), 387–409; Donald Cuccioletta, "Multiculturalism or Transculturalism: Towards a Cosmopolitan Citizenship," *London Journal of Canadian Studies* 17 (2001/2002), 1–11; Claude Grunitzky, *Transculturalism: How the World Is Coming Together* (New York: TRUE Agency, 2004); and Geoffrey V. Davis and Peter H. Marsden, eds., *Towards a Transcultural Future: Literature and Society in a 'Post'-Colonial World* (New York: Rodopi, 2005).

79. For an entertaining introduction, see Louis Theroux, *The Call of the Weird: Travels in American Subcultures* (Cambridge: Da Capo Press, 2007). The pull of transculturalism can be seen in the fact that academics are beginning to eschew the (slightly derisive) term "subculture." See David Muggleton and Rupert Weinzierl, eds., *The Post-Subcultures Reader* (Oxford: Berg, 2003).

80. "Two Senior Managers of Failed Bear Stearns Hedge Funds Indicted on Conspiracy and Fraud Charges," U.S. Department of Justice press release, June 19, 2008.

81. J. Scott Orr, "Trying to Preserve Today's Web for Future Generations," *Seattle Times* (April 7, 2008).

82. Website: Peter Lyman and Hal R. Varian, "How Much Information? 2003." Retrieved July 24, 2008.

83. Website: Peter Lyman and Hal R. Varian, "How Much Information? 2003." Retrieved July 24, 2008.

84. On Google Books, see Jeffery Toobin, "Google's Moon Shot: The Quest for the Universal Library," *New Yorker* (February 5, 2007), 30–35; and Matthew Rimmer, *Digital Copyright and the Consumer Revolution: Hands Off My iPod* (Northampton: Edward Elgar Publishing, 2007), 225–260.

85. For a brief introduction, see Daniel J. Solove, *The Digital Person: Technology and Privacy in the Information Age* (New York: NYU Press, 2004). Also see Daniel J. Solove, Marc Rothenberg, and Paul M. Schwartz, *Privacy, Information, and Technology* (New York: Aspen Publishers, 2006).

86. See James B. Rule, *Privacy in Peril: How We Are Sacrificing a Fundamental Right in Exchange for Security and Convenience* (New York: Oxford UP, 2007); David Holtzman, *Privacy Lost: How Technology Is Endangering Your Privacy* (San Francisco: Jossey-Bass, 2006); Christopher Slobogin, *Privacy at Risk: The New Government Surveillance and the Fourth Amendment* (Chicago: University of Chicago Press, 2007); and Jon J. Mills, *Privacy: The Lost Right* (New York: Oxford UP, 2008).

87. See John M. T. Balmer and Stephen A. Greyser, eds., *Revealing the Corporation: Perspectives on Identity, Image and Reputation, Corporate Branding, and Corporate-Level Marketing. An Anthology* (London: Routledge, 2003).

88. See Tom Peters, among many others, *The Brand You 50, Or Fifty Ways to Transform Yourself from an 'Employee' into a Brand That Shouts Distinction, Commitment, and Passion!* (New York: Knopf, 1999).

89. Plenty of people – especially politicians and corporate flacks – have been caught "managing" their Wikipedia pages. For an overview, see Solove, *The Future of Reputation*, 142–146.

90. See Toobin, "Google's Moon Shot," 30–35; and Rimmer, *Digital Copyright and the Consumer Revolution*, 225–260.

91. "Google-fu," in Andrew Peckham, *Urban Dictionary: Fularius Street Slang Defined* (Kansas City: Andrews McMeel Publishing, 2005), 59.

92. Website: "News Transcript: DoD New Briefing–Secretary Rumsfeld and Gen. Myers" (February 12, 2002), U. S. Department of Defense. Retrieved August 13, 2009.

93. On Toffler's use, see *The Third Wave* (New York: Morrow, 1980), 282ff. For early uses with reference to the Internet, see Don Tapscott, *The Digital Economy: Promise and Peril in the Age of Networked Intelligence* (New York: McGraw-Hill, 1996), 62–63; and Rick Levine, Christopher Locke, Doc Searls, and David Weinberger, *The Cluetrain Manifesto* (Cambridge: Perseus Books, 2000), xxiii.

94. On the Free Software Movement and the Open Source Initiative, see Peter Wayner, *Free for All: How LINUX and the Free Software Movement Undercut the High-Tech Titans* (New York: Harper Business, 2000). On Wikipedia, see Marshall Poe, "The Hive," *Atlantic Monthly* (August, 2006), 86–94. On user-generated content, see Shirky, *Here Comes Everybody*, 81ff.

95. Website: Larry Sanger, "Why Wikipedia Must Jettison Its Anti-Elitism," *Kuro5hin* (December 31, 2004). Retrieved August 13, 2009. Also see Keen, *The Cult of the Amateur*, 35ff.

96. Website: Clay Shirky, "K5 Article on Wikipedia Anti-elitism," Many2Many (January 3, 2005). Retrieved August 13, 2009.

CONCLUSION: THE MEDIA AND HUMAN WELL-BEING

1. Karl Marx, "Speech at the Anniversary of the *People's Paper*," in *Selected Writings*, edited by David McLellan (Oxford: Oxford UP, 1977), 338.
2. Karl Marx and Friedrich Engels, *Werke*, 39 vols. in 41 (Berlin: Dietz Verlag, 1961–1974), vol. 3: "Die deutsche Ideologie," 33.
3. Marx, "Speech at the Anniversary of the *People's Paper*," 338.
4. Karl Marx and Friedrich Engels, *Werke*, 39 vols. in 41 (Berlin: Dietz Verlag, 1961–1974), vol. 4: "Manifest der Kommunistischen Partei," 462.
5. Here we mean academic media critics, of whom there are many. For a sampler, see Alan Wells and Ernest A. Hakanen, eds., *Mass Media and Society* (Greenwich: Ablex Publishing, 1997).
6. Aristotle, *Nicomachean Ethics*, translated by Terence Irwin, second edition (Indianapolis: Hackett Publishing, 1999), 3 (1095a).
7. There is a huge and contradictory literature on the topic. For a recent review, see Daniel M. Haybron, *The Pursuit of Unhappiness: The Elusive Psychology of Well-Being* (Oxford: Oxford UP, 2008). That the notion of what "happiness" is has changed dramatically over the millennia is shown by Darrin M. McMahon, *Happiness: A History* (New York: Atlantic Monthly Press, 2006); and Nicholas P. White, *A Brief History of Happiness* (Oxford: Wiley-Blackwell, 2006).
8. John Stuart Mill, *Utilitarianism* (Boston: Willard Small, 1899), 21.
9. Website: Angus Maddison, "Statistics on World Population, GDP, and Per Capita Income, 1–2006 AD" (March, 2009). Retrieved September 15, 2009.
10. Bryan H. Bunch with Alexander Hellemans, *The History of Science and Technology* (New York: Houghton Mifflin, 2004). The exact figure is 8,583 and is drawn from Jonathan Huebner, "A Possible Declining Trend for Worldwide Innovation," *Technological Forecasting and Social Change* 72 (2005), 981.
11. For an overview of the process of transmission and accumulation, see Katherine Nelson and Richard R. Nelson, "The Cumulative Advance of Human Know-How," *Philosophical Transactions: Mathematical, Physical and Engineering Sciences* 361:1809 (2003), 1635–1653.
12. Kremer, "Population Growth and Technological Change," 683.
13. See Huebner, "A Possible Declining Trend for Worldwide Innovation," 981–982. In figuring the innovation rate, Huebner uses the formula "number of innovations per time period/world population." Both numerator and denominator have been rising, but the latter has far outpaced the former in recent times. Thus, he finds a decline in the population-adjusted innovation rate after about 1845.
14. For an overview, see Pamela R. Willoughby, *The Evolution of Modern Humans in Africa: A Comprehensive Guide* (Lanham: AltaMira Press, 2007), 20ff. For a critical view, Christopher S. Henshilwood and Curtis W. Marean, "The Origin of Modern Human Behavior: Critique of the Models and Their Test Implications," *Current Anthropology* 44:5 (2003), 627–651.

15. On the technologies of the Upper Paleolithic, see Stanley A. Ambrose, "Paleolithic Technology and Human Evolution," *Science* 291:5509 (2001), 1748–1753; and Bar-Yosef, "The Upper Paleolithic Revolution," 363–393.

16. For an overview, see Peter Bellwood, *First Farmers: The Origins of Agricultural Societies* (Oxford: Blackwell Publishing, 2004).

17. On the technologies of the Ancient and Classical Worlds, see Joel Mokyr, *Twenty-Five Centuries of Technological Change: An Historical Survey* (London: Harwood Academic Publishers, 1990), 1–16. For a more extensive treatment, see Charles J. Singer, ed., *A History of Technology*, 8 vols. (Oxford: Clarendon Press, 1954–1984), vol. 1: *From Early Times to the Fall of Ancient Empires* and vol. 2: *The Mediterranean Civilizations and the Middle Ages*.

18. For an overview, see Joseph M. Bryant, "The West and the Rest Revisited: Debating Capitalist Origins, European Colonialism, and the Advent of Modernity," *Canadian Journal of Sociology/Cahiers canadiens de sociologie* 31:4 (2006), 403–444.

19. On the technologies of medieval, early modern, and modern Europe, see Mokyr, *Twenty-Five Centuries of Technological Change*, 16ff. For a more extensive treatment, see Singer, ed., *A History of Technology*, vol. 2: *The Mediterranean Civilizations and the Middle Ages*; vol. 3: *From the Renaissance to the Industrial Revolution*; vol. 4: *The Industrial Revolution*; vol. 5: *The Late Nineteenth Century*.

20. This is the basic argument of Kremer, "Population Growth and Technological Change," 681–716.

21. On network externalities (also known as "network effects"), see, among many others, Michael Katz and Carl Shapiro, "Network Externalities, Competition, and Compatibility," *American Economic Review* 75:3 (1985), 424–440. On knowledge spillover effects, see, among many others, Zvi Griliches, "The Search for R&D Spillovers," *Scandinavian Journal of Economics* 94 (1992), S29–47.

22. The phenomenon of decreasing returns to stimulus was first theorized by Wilhelm Wundt in 1874. See his *Grundzüge der physiologischen Psychologie* (Leipzig: Engelmann, 1874). After his research was rediscovered (notably by David E. Berlyne in the 1950s), scholars began to study the dynamics of "interest," "curiosity," "sensation seeking," and their relation to satisfaction. For an overview, see Paul J. Silvia, *Exploring the Psychology of Interest* (Oxford: Oxford UP, 2006).

23. For what follows, see the discussion in Luigino Bruni and Pier Luigi Porta, ed., *Handbook on the Economics of Happiness* (Northampton: Edward Elgar, 2007), 130–134.

24. Opting for novelty doesn't *necessarily* improve well-being. See I. Simonson, "The Effect of Purchase Quantity and Timing on Variety-Seeking Behavior," *Journal of Marketing Research* 27 (1990), 150–162; and D. Read and G. F. Loewenstein, "Diversification Bias: Explaining the Discrepancy in Variety Seeking between Combined and Separated Choices," *Journal of Experimental Psychology: Applied* 1 (1995), 34–49.

25. David Vincent, *The Rise of Mass Literacy: Reading and Writing in Modern Europe* (Cambridge: Polity, 2000), 8–11.

26. See G. Jones, "The Theoretical Foundations of Eugenics" in *Essays in the History of Eugenics*, edited by R. A. Peel (London: Galton Institute, 1998), 1–20.

27. For reviews of many of the many "factors," see John C. Caldwell, "Toward a Restatement of Demographic Transition Theory," *Population and Development Review* 2:3/4 (1976), 321–366; Ronald Freedman, "Theories of Fertility Decline: A Reappraisal," *Social Forces* 58:1 (1979), 1–17; Jean-Claude Chesnais, *The Demographic Transition. Stages, Patterns, and Economic Implications* (New York: Oxford UP, 1992); Charles Hirschman, "Why Fertility Changes," *Annual Reviews of Sociology* 20 (1994), 203–233; Dudley Kirk, "Demographic Transition Theory," *Population Studies* 50 (1996), 361–387; T. Paul Schultz, "The Fertility Transition: Economic Explanations," Economic Growth Center Discussion Paper No. 833 (August, 2001); and John C. Caldwell, *Demographic Transition Theory* (Dordrecht: Springer, 2006).

28. Many studies have documented the relationship between access to media and the decline in fertility. See, for example, Robert Hornik and Emile McAnany, "Theories and Evidence: Mass Media Effects and Fertility Change," *Communications Theory* 11:4 (2001), 454–471; Robert Hornik and Emile McAnny, "Mass Media and Fertility Change," in *Diffusion Processes and Fertility Transition: Selected Perspectives*, edited by John Casterline (Washington, DC: National Academies Press, 2001), 208–239; and J. S. Barber and W. G. Axinn, "New Ideas and Fertility Limitation: The Role of Mass Media," *Journal of Marriage and the Family* 66:5 (2004), 1180–1200.

29. Hornik and McAnny, "Mass Media and Fertility Change," 208–209.

30. Hornik and McAnny, "Mass Media and Fertility Change," 209.

31. This is the basic logic of the "demand" theory of fertility. See G. S. Becker, "The Demand for Children" in *Treatises on the Family* (Chicago: University of Chicago Press), 135–154.

32. Literacy is correlated with a decline in fertility today in developing countries. See Phillip Cutright, "The Ingredients of Recent Fertility Decline in Developing Countries," *International Family Planning Perspectives* 9:4 (1983), 101–109. Also see Harvey J. Graff, "Literacy, Education, and Fertility, Past and Present: A Critical Review," *Population and Development Review* 5:1 (1979), 105–140.

33. Charles Darwin, *The Autobiography of Charles Darwin, 1809–1882*, edited by Nora Barlow (London: Collins, 1958), 231–234. Subsequent citations are to this edition.

34. United Nations, Department of Economic and Social Affairs, Population Division, "World Population Prospects: The 2006 Revision, Highlights," Working Paper No. ESA/P/WP.202 (New York: United Nations, 2007), 9. On the steep decline in fertility rates in recent decades (the "second demographic transition"), see D. J. van de Kaa, "Europe's Second Demographic Transition," *Population Bulletin* 42:1 (1987), 1–59.

35. The literature devoted to defining "spirituality" is a deep, deep ocean. The most interesting work has been done by health care professionals. See N. Cawley, "An Exploration of the Concept of Spirituality," *International Journal of Palliative Nursing* 3 (1997), 31–36; J. Dyson, M. Cobb, and D. Forman, "The Meaning of Spirituality: A Literature Review," *Journal of Advanced Nursing*

26 (1997), 1183–1188; and D. S. Martsolf and J. R. Mickley, "The Concept of Spirituality in Nursing Theories: Differing World-Views and Extent of Focus," *Journal of Advanced Nursing* 27 (1998), 294–303.

36. John Locke, *An Essay Concerning Human Understanding* [1690], edited by Roger Woolhouse (London: Penguin Classics, 1997), 268.

37. Friedrich Nietzsche, *Twilight of the Idols*, translated by Duncan Large [1889] (Oxford: Oxford UP, 1998), 6 (19).

38. On secularization due to improvements in material well-being ("development"), see Ronald Inglehart and Pippa Norris, *Sacred and Secular: Religion and Politics Worldwide* (Cambridge: Cambridge UP, 2004).

39. This is the basic finding of cognitive-behavioral therapy, or "CBT." On the history of CBT, see S. Rachman, "The Evolution of Cognitive Behavior Therapy," in *Science and Practice of Cognitive Behavior Therapy*, edited by D. Clark, C. G. Fairburn, and M. G. Gelder (Oxford: Oxford UP, 1997), 1–26.

40. Psychologists have shown that exposure to disturbing content (text, images, sound) can cause "media-induced trauma." See Joanne Cantor, "Why Horror Doesn't Die: The Enduring and Paradoxical Effects of Frightening Entertainment," in *Psychology of Entertainment*, edited by Jennings Bryant and Peter Vorderer (London: Routledge, 2006), 315–327.

41. See Milton Diamond and Ayako Uchiyama, "Pornography, Rape, and Sex Crimes in Japan," *International Journal of Law and Psychiatry* 22:1 (1999), 1–22.

42. See Dan J. Stein et al., "Hypersexual Disorder and Preoccupation with Internet Pornography," *American Journal of Psychiatry* 158 (2001), 1590–1594; M. Griffiths, "Sex on the Internet: Observations and Implications for Internet Sex Addiction," *Journal of Sex Research* 38:4 (2001), 333–342; and David J. Delmonico, "Sex on the Superhighway: Understanding and Treating Cybersex Addiction," in *Clinical Management of Sex Addiction*, edited by Patrick Carnes and Kenneth M. Adams (New York: Brunner-Routledge, 2002), 239–254.

43. For a review of the literature, see Jill C. Manning, "The Impact of Internet Pornography on Marriage and the Family: A Review of the Research," *Sexual Addiction and Compulsivity* 13 (2006), 131–165.

44. Website: Peter Lyman and Hal R. Varian, "How Much Information? 2000." Retrieved September 23, 2009.

INDEX

Made in the USA
Monee, IL
08 August 2023